Taxes and Trust

Taxes and Trust is the first book on taxes to focus on trust and the first work of social science to concentrate on how tax policy actually gets implemented on the ground in Poland, Russia and Ukraine. It highlights the nuances of the transitional Ukraine case and explains precisely how and why that 'borderland' country differs from the more ideal types of coercive Russia and compliance-oriented Poland. Through eight bespoke taxpayer surveys, an unprecedented survey of bureaucrats and more than fifteen years of qualitative research, it emphasizes the building and accumulation of trust in the transition from a coercive tax state to a compliant one. The content of the book will appeal to students and scholars of taxation worldwide and to those who study Russia and Eastern Europe.

DR MARC P. BERENSON is Senior Lecturer at King's Russia Institute, King's College, London. He has undertaken consultancy work for the World Bank in Russia and the OECD's Tax and Development Programme. After receiving his BA from Harvard University, he founded and directed the Law in Action programme for Freedom House in Ukraine before receiving his PhD in Political Science from Princeton University in 2006.

Taxes and Trust

From Coercion to Compliance in Poland, Russia and Ukraine

MARC P. BERENSON

King's College London

CAMBRIDGE
UNIVERSITY PRESS

University Printing House, Cambridge CB2 8BS, United Kingdom

One Liberty Plaza, 20th Floor, New York, NY 10006, USA

477 Williamstown Road, Port Melbourne, VIC 3207, Australia

314–321, 3rd Floor, Plot 3, Splendor Forum, Jasola District Centre,
New Delhi - 110025, India

79 Anson Road, #06-04/06, Singapore 079906

Cambridge University Press is part of the University of Cambridge.

It furthers the University's mission by disseminating knowledge in the pursuit of
education, learning and research at the highest international levels of excellence.

www.cambridge.org
Information on this title: www.cambridge.org/9781108420426
DOI: 10.1017/9781108333580

© Marc Phineas Berenson 2018

This publication is in copyright. Subject to statutory exception
and to the provisions of relevant collective licensing agreements,
no reproduction of any part may take place without the written
permission of Cambridge University Press.

First published 2018

Printed in the United Kingdom by Clays, St Ives plc

A catalogue record for this publication is available from the British Library

ISBN 978-1-108-42042-6 Hardback

Cambridge University Press has no responsibility for the persistence or accuracy
of URLs for external or third-party internet websites referred to in this publication,
and does not guarantee that any content on such websites is, or will remain,
accurate or appropriate.

To My Parents
For Their Love, Support and Wisdom

Contents

List of Figures		*page* ix
List of Tables		x
Acknowledgements		xi
1	From a Coercive to a Modern Tax State	1
2	Trust and Post-communist Policy Implementation	12
3	Reinterpreting History to Recreate the State: The Transformation of the Polish, Russian and Ukrainian State Bureaucracies in the 1990s and Today	56
4	Creating Post-communist Tax Regimes and Measuring Tax Compliance	96
5	Building Trust, Instilling Fear: Tax Administration Reform	137
6	Citizens, Subjects and Slackers and Paying Taxes	197
7	All Together? Lack of Trust in the Tax State Unifies Ukraine	229
8	Towards Greater Trust and Tax Compliance	253
	Appendix I: Poland, Russia and Ukraine Taxpayer Compliance Attitudinal Surveys 2004–2015 and the Russian Tax Officials Survey 2011	271
	Appendix II: Russian Public Officials Survey of Tax and Social Welfare Bureaucrats, 2011	292
	Appendix III: Suggested Minimal Tax Compliance Levels for 2010–2015 Surveys	303
	Appendix IV: Poland Taxpayer Compliance Attitudinal Surveys: Logit Analysis of Tax Compliance Attitudes	306

viii   Contents

Appendix V: Russia Taxpayer Compliance Attitudinal
Surveys: Logit Analysis of Tax Compliance Attitudes   309

Appendix VI: Ukraine Taxpayer Compliance Attitudinal
Surveys: Logit Analysis of Tax Compliance Attitudes   312

Appendix VII: Ukraine Taxpayer Compliance
Attitudinal Surveys – By Region: Logit Analysis of Tax
Compliance Attitudes   316

Bibliography   326
Index   353

Figures

1.1	World Bank government effectiveness global rankings for Poland, Russia and Ukraine and averages for Eastern Europe and the Baltics, the former Soviet Union and the EU-15 countries, country percentile rankings (0–100), 1996–2014	*page* 4
2.1	A model of state capacity for the post-communist states	41
2.2	Where to find bureaucratic rationalism within a state?	42
4.1	Total tax arrears as a percentage of annual total tax receipts for the corporate income tax in Poland, Russia and Ukraine	115
4.2	Total tax arrears as a percentage of annual total tax receipts for the value-added tax in Poland, Russia and Ukraine	115
4.3	Overall tax collected as a percentage of all taxes due and annual GDP growth, Poland	128
4.4	Overall tax collected as a percentage of all taxes due and annual GDP growth, Russian Federation	129
4.5	Overall tax collected as a percentage of all taxes due and annual GDP growth, Ukraine	129
8.1	State capacity in transition from coercion to trust	258

Tables

4.1 Overall tax arrears as a percentage of all taxes collected in Poland, Russia and Ukraine	*page* 112
4.2 Poland, Russia and Ukraine Taxpayer Compliance Attitudinal Surveys 2004, 2005, 2010, 2012 and 2015	119
4.3 Measurements of the unofficial economy as a percentage of GDP in selected transition countries for the early 1990s by the electricity method and for 1999–2007 by the MIMIC Method	122
5.1 Historical references in tax administration structures	160
5.2 Tax administration work philosophy	179
5.3 Structural design and oversight of tax administrations	184
5.4 Human resources in tax administrations	194
6.1 Citizens, subjects and slackers: Substantive effects that are significant in the Poland, Russia and Ukraine 2004–2005 Taxpayer Compliance Attitudinal Surveys	211
6.2 Taxpayer Compliance Attitudinal Surveys: Percentage of prior tax bureaucrat contact respondents who would follow the tax laws even if personally considered to be unfair	222
7.1 Ukraine Taxpayer Compliance Attitudinal Surveys 2005, 2010, 2012 and 2015	230
7.2 Suggestions of minimal tax non-compliance levels in Ukraine regions in 2010, 2012 and 2015	232
7.3 Ukrainian trust in the state by region	235
7.4 Nature of contact with Ukrainian tax bureaucrats by region	240
7.5 Percentage of those with good prior tax bureaucrat experience who trust the Ukrainian president	241
7.6 Tax awareness across Ukraine regions	242
7.7 Religion and the Ukraine Taxpayer Compliance Attitudinal Surveys	249
7.8 National self-identification and the Ukraine Taxpayer Compliance Attitudinal Surveys	251
7.9 Language and the Ukraine Taxpayer Compliance Attitudinal Surveys	251

Acknowledgements

This book, begun initially as a doctoral dissertation, has been a long time in the making, as all who know me can attest, and now I take great pleasure in thanking the many people who helped make it happen. I am grateful to many individuals and institutions for their support of this project and from whose advice, criticism, friendship and wisdom I have benefited. While the final responsibility for this work, shortcomings and all, is mine, this book represents the culmination of years of personal and intellectual exchanges with scores of colleagues at several institutions. Every effort has been made to thank each of them here, and my sincere apologies go to anyone I may have inadvertently omitted.

Above all, my thanks go to my wonderful PhD committee, comprising Nancy Bermeo (chair), Atul Kohli, Joshua Tucker and Chris Achen at Princeton University's Department of Politics. This project would have gone nowhere but for the unique combination of patient counsel, praise, critical insights and wise advice that they each provided.

Princeton truly is an amazing place to be a graduate student, and I feel very fortunate to have studied in such an intellectually rich community of scholars and students. For making my years there thoroughly enjoyable, I especially want also to thank Jose Aleman, Gary Bass, Mark Beissinger, Elizabeth Bloodgood, Jason M. Brownlee, Eun K. Choi, Katia P. Coleman, Wolfgang F. Danspeckgruber, Ellen Elk, Antonis A. Ellinas, Anne-Marie Gardner, Carolyn C. Guile, Eva W. Kaye, Jeffrey B. Lewis, Christopher J. Mackie, Matthew J. Fouse, Antoinette Handley, John Holzwarth, Kosuke Imai, Christopher F. Karpowitz, Stan Katz, Stephen Kotkin, Erik M. Kuhonta, Ludmila Krytynskaia, Evan S. Lieberman, Eric M. McGlinchey, Grigore Pop-Eleches, Joseph G. Prud'homme, Andrew Roberts, Robert R. Rodgers, Christa S. Scholtz, Anna Seleny, Monica Selinger, Alex Sokolowski, Ezra Suleiman, the late Robert C. Tucker, Maya Tudor, Jennifer L. Weber, Lynn T. White, Mirek Wyka and Deborah Yashar.

The number of people who assisted me in my research in the field was legendary; some of them remain close friends to this day.

xii   Acknowledgements

Having undertaken close to 400 interviews in the field, of which approximately 180 were with government officials, I am extraordinarily grateful to the many local scholars, tax experts, political experts, accountants, economists and tax administration bureaucrats in Poland, Russia and Ukraine who sat down with me and shared their experiences, insights, data, and, often, very good tea. My understanding of tax collection in these countries advanced tremendously from their generosity and openness. I have generally chosen to keep interviewees' identities confidential, especially if they worked for the government, preferred to remain anonymous or whose anonymity I wish to ensure. This commitment to confidentiality prevents me from thanking them sufficiently.

Additionally, those colleagues, scholars and experts who provided me with invaluable assistance, contacts, information and suggestions and hours of stimulating discussion while I was conducting field research that I can thank by name include, in Kyiv, Tanya and Igor Bibik, Andrii Bychenko, Vladimir Dubrovskiy, Svitlana Franchuk, Juhani Grossmann, Konstantin Kuznetsov, Craig Neal, Tim O'Connor, Inna Pidluska, Bill Remington, Bohdan Senchuk, David Snelbecker, Larisa Tatarinova, Andreas Umland, Mychailo Wynnyckyj and Tatyana Yablonskaya; in Moscow, Alexander Abashkin, Maria Belodubrovskaya, Irina Denisova, Yelena Dobrolyubova, Igor Fedyukin, Alexander Gasparishvili, Scott Gehlbach, Maria Gorban, Alexander Ionov, Larissa Kapitsa, Marina Larionova, Rory MacFarquhar, Ludmila V. Petushkova, Mikhail Pryadilnikov, Mark Rakhmangulov, Nataliya A. Yakovleva, Elena Zavyalova and Yuriy Zaytsev; and, in Warsaw, Beata Blasiak, Antoni Kamiński, Witold Kieżun, Jadwiga Koralewicz, John Kubinec, Deborah Paul, Katarzyna Piętka, Michał Wenzel, Darek Zalewda and Ryzsard Żelichowski, as well as the very helpful Małgorzata Pomianowska at the Najwyższa Izba Kontroli.

I also thank the American Councils, the Moscow School for Economic and Social Sciences, the Russian Presidential Academy of National Economy and Public Administration and the Polish Academy of Science's Institute of Political Studies for facilitating my stay and for my academic affiliation during some of my research visits to Kyiv, Moscow and Warsaw.

At the World Bank, where I joined a fascinating administrative reform project in Russia, I particularly would like to thank Oleksiy Balabushko, Ivor Beazley, Clelia Crontoyanni, Maya Gusarova, Julia Komagaeva, Tatyana Leonova, Jens Kristensen, Andrei R. Markov, Maria Ovchinnikova, Mikhail Pryadilnikov, David Shand, Khwaja Sultan and Tumun Tsydypov.

In Poland, Russia and Ukraine, I also had the wonderful pleasure of working with the PBS DDG Market Research, the CBOS Public

Opinion Centre, the Public Opinion Foundation (FOM) and the Razumkov Centre for Economic and Political Studies on the Taxpayer Compliance Attitudinal Surveys. Thanks here go to Andrii Bychenko, Aleksey V. Churikov, Ivan Klimov, Grigoriy Lvovich, Anna Petrova, Leyla Vasileva and Michał Wenzel for making the collaborative experience such a smooth and fun one.

To underscore how essential fieldwork was to this project, I need to recognise all of those who patiently helped me through the years to acquire Polish and Russian language fluency, including Anna Bobrova, the late Charles E. Townsend and Marzena James.

Having spent six delightful years as part of the Governance Team at the University of Sussex's Institute of Development Studies, I wish to thank Andres Mejia Acosta, Jennifer Constantine, Diana Conyers, Catherine Gee, Peter Houtzager, David Leonard, Edoardo Masset, Lyla Mehta, Mick Moore, Robert Nurick, Stephen Peterson, Wilson Prichard, Graeme Ramshaw, Alex Shankland, Louise Tillin, Fiona Wilson and Musab Younis for their input and feedback to this project.

At King's College London's Russia Institute, where I have been based since 2013, I want to thank my colleagues, including Sarah Birch, Alexander Clarkson, Camilla Darling, Samuel Greene, Jane Henderson, Jeremy Jennings, Natasha Kuhrt, Alexander Kupatadze, Anna Matveeva, Anthony Pereira, Gerald Schnyder, Gulnaz Sharafutdinova, Marat Shterin, Susanne Sternthal and Adnan Vatansever, for their insightful critique of my work.

I also would like to thank the organizers, participants and audience members at seminars, conferences and talks including the Social Science Research Council's 'Governance in Eurasia' workshop (2004); the University of Toronto's graduate student symposium 'New Perspectives on Contemporary Ukraine: Politics, History, and Culture' (2006); the Woodrow Wilson Center for International Scholars' Kennan Institute 'Civil Society and Democracy in Ukraine' workshop (2006); the Conference on Administrative Reform in Post-Soviet Countries Memorial University, Newfoundland (2006); the University of Ottawa's Danyliw Research Seminar in Contemporary Ukrainian Studies (2006); the 'Taxation and State-Building in Developing Countries' panel at the World Bank's Annual Bank Conference on Development Economics (2007); a presentation at Emory University's Department of Political Science (2008); the European University Institute's Max Weber Programme alumni conferences (2009, 2011 and 2016); Loughborough University's 'The Political Economy of Taxation' conference (2010); a presentation at the Centre for Economic and Financial Research (CEFIR) (2011); the University College London's 'Russia–Ukraine: Spotlight on

xiv Acknowledgements

the Regions' conference (2015); the Economic Forum in Krynica Zdrój (2015); the Europe–Ukraine Forum (2016); the Kyiv Security Forum (2016); the Chatham House roundtable 'The Role of Values and Trust in Transforming Ukraine's Public Institutions' (2016); and the 'Trust, Governance & Citizenship in Post-Euromaidan Ukraine' seminars at the International Renaissance Foundation at Ukraine House (Kyiv), King's Russia Institute and Vesalius College (Brussels) (2016), as well as several panels over the years at the American Political Science Association, the Association for Slavic, East European and Eurasian Studies, the Association for the Study of Nationalities, and the Political Science Association (UK), for their excellent questions, encouraging comments and useful feedback, including those from Hilary Appel, Dominique Arel, Andrew Barnes, Paul J. D'Anieri, Irina Denisova, Gerald M. Easter, Odd-Helge Fjeldstad, Oksana Gaman-Golutvinoj, Scott Gehlbach, Julie George, Sergei Guriev, Juliet Johnson, Svitlana Kobzar, Jeremy Leaman, Orysia Lutsevych, Jason Lyall, Eugene Mazo, James Nixey, Neema Noori, Anton Oleinik, Serguei Oushakine, Wojciech Pawlus, Natalia Pohorila, Graeme Robertson, Richard Rose, Peter Rutland, Ani Sarkissian, Roger Schoenman, Oxana Shevel, Peter Solomon, Joanna Szostek, Lucan A. Way and Sarah Whitmore.

This book project has benefited from generous awards and fellowships including those from the Open Society Foundations; the United Kingdom's Economic and Social Research Council; the John D. and Catherine T. MacArthur Foundation and the Princeton Institute for International and Regional Studies; the Social Science Research Council Eurasia Program; the Fellowship of Woodrow Wilson Scholars, Princeton University; the American Council of Learned Societies; the Institute for the Study of World Politics; the American Councils for International Education; Princeton University's Stafford Fund; Princeton University's Council on Regional Studies; and Princeton University's Center of International Relations.

My fellowship year at the Max Weber Programme at the European University Institute in Florence also proved to be most useful as I began to transform my PhD dissertation into a more focused, critical study. I am most grateful for conversations and observations from Mariano Barbato, László Bruszt, Nicola Casarini, Heather Jones, Rinku Lamba, Brigitte Le Normand, Anna Lo Prete, Ramon Marimon, Jan-Hinrik Meyer-Sahling, Ekaterina Mouliarova, Roman Petrov, Anne Rasmussen, Rubén Ruiz Rufino, Sven Steinmo, Karin Tilmans and Annarita Zacchi.

In 2014, being a Title VIII scholar at the Woodrow Wilson Center for International Scholars' Kennan Institute was tremendously useful for further research in Washington, DC, additional writing and further

Acknowledgements

feedback. I especially want to thank Mary Elizabeth Malinkin, William Pomeranz, Matthew Rojansky, Vitaliy Shpak, Yevhen Shulha and Kenneth Yalowitz, as well as Fiona Hill and Janet M. Kilian, for making the experience rewarding.

Over the years, I also have profited enormously from amazing administrative and research assistance, including that from Ida Akhtar, Emma Barr, Lyubov Belikova, Faye Bloch, Birte Bromby, Krzysztof Dynel, Michał Dobrolowicz, Aleksandra Dybkowska, Evgeny Firsov, Patrycja Gątarzewska, Radosław Jarosz, Edyta Kawka, Aleksandra Kubat, Maria Kuss, Dominika Majchrowicz, Caroline Martin, Vitaly Moroz, Oxana Nesterenko, Joanna Pauk, Paulina Sobiesiak, Pawel Sobkowiak, Marek Solon-Lipinski, Natalia Sizova, Marcin Ślarzyński, Aleksandra Topolnicka, Marta Utracka, Sinnet Weber, Marta Wenzel and Christopher Vanja.

I need to recognize and thank those who served as excellent mentors for me either before or after I began this project, namely Javier Corrales, Joel Hellman, David Leonard, Ellen Mickiewicz, Steven Solnick, Sven Steinmo, Kathryn Stoner, Charles Vincent and Carly Wade, for guiding me to and through this profession.

I wish to thank the publishers of the following articles for permission to include in this book some of the material that originally appeared there:

> Marc P. Berenson, "Less Fear, Little Trust: Deciphering the Whys of Ukrainian Tax Compliance" in Paul D'Anieri, ed., *Orange Revolution and Aftermath: Mobilization, Apathy, and the State in Ukraine* (Washington, DC: Woodrow Wilson Center Press and Johns Hopkins University Press, 2010).
>
> Marc P. Berenson, "Rationalizing or Empowering Bureaucrats? Tax Administration Reform in Post-communist Poland and Russia," Journal of Communist Studies and Transition Politics, Vol. 24, No. 1 (March 2008); in Anton Oleinik, ed., *Reforming the state without changing the model of power? On administrative reform in post-socialist countries* (Oxford: Routledge, 2008); and in Anton Oleinik and Oksana Gaman-Golutvinoj, ed., *Administrativnye reformy v contexte vlastnykh otnoshenij: opyt postsocialisticheskih transformatsij v sravnitel'noj perspektive. pod redakciej* (Moscow: ROSSPEN, 2008).

Special thanks go to those who read all or parts of drafts of this manuscript, including Nancy Bermeo, Antonis Ellinas, Samuel Greene, Peter Houtzager, David Leonard, Stephen Peterson, Gulnaz Sharafutdinova, Sven Steinmo, Adnan Vatansever, David Woodruff and two anonymous referees, who provided thorough constructive comments and

xvi   Acknowledgements

valuable suggestions, which contributed greatly to the improvements I made in the final manuscript.

At Cambridge University Press, I would like to express gratitude to Lewis Bateman for his interest in this project and to John Haslam for his superb handling of my manuscript throughout the whole publication process.

Final thanks are to my family – to my brother, Eric, and his family for all the healthy diversions and to my parents, Carole and Joel, to whom this book is dedicated. I am so fortunate to receive their ever-present moral encouragement, good humour and love.

1 From a Coercive to a Modern Tax State

The image of the state is formed in citizens' eyes by the tax inspector, the customs man, the cop. While they're on the take, people won't believe the sincerity of our anti-corruption intentions.

– Ukraine President Petro Poroshenko in his first State of the Nation Address, 4 June 2015[1]

The Puzzle

Of all the activities that a state takes up, collecting taxes is, perhaps, the most critical. Without extracting revenue from society, a state cannot function and cannot do what it sets out to do. Taxation is the sine qua non of the contemporary state and the social contract. When taxpayers pay their taxes, they enter into a financial relationship with their state, a financial reconciliation, if you will, relinquishing private information about their economic activities while trusting the state to treat them and that information fairly and confidentially.

Taxation is a prime governance function, but it is also one of the only activities where the state and society are forced to interact with one another, and it is one of the few in which citizens have an obligation to give something up to the state. Tax compliance, therefore, is both about revenue extraction for the benefit of state coffers and about an opportunity for citizens to enter into a trusting relationship with their state – one that will be repeated year after year.

At the extremes, there are, perhaps, two ways in which this process can be done. In the first, those of us who file tax declarations have become familiar with the yearly ritual of gathering up receipts and filling out tax forms or filing electronically from the comfort of our own living rooms, sometimes even seeking assistance from a local tax office, replete with help desks. We may be a bit worried about being audited, but don't have too much concern. In other places, however, groups of men, dressed

---

[1] Bershidsky.

2   Taxes and Trust

in black, donning eye masks and sporting automatic rifles, are known to burst into the offices of major local and international firms, banks, non-governmental organizations, human rights groups and even private homes, searching for financial data and records. Today's twenty-first century teched-up mafia? No, it's just the tax police.

The question that stands before many transitional and developing states across the globe and the puzzle at the heart of this book is whether such coercive methods are most effective in getting what the state wants. *And, if not, how does a state transition from a deterrent/coercive state to a legal/legitimate tax state?* A modern tax system is all about a modern economy, and the legacy of successful tax reform is a modern, legal and legitimate state capable of administering tax policy.

This book focuses on three states at three distinctly different stages of the transition from a coercive governing regime to such a state. Poland has transitioned successfully to a rule-of-law tax state, implementing client-oriented tax collection policies to ensure high levels of compliance. Russia employs a largely coercive tax system that enjoys moderate levels of tax compliance. Ukraine, meanwhile, has failed to build a tax state that is either effectively coercive or legitimate in the eyes of its citizens, resulting in lower levels of compliance. In essence, Poland has been more effective because it has a state that is more organized, embodied with more resources and more citizen-focused and a society that is more capable of being a compliant partner. Effective governance occurs when state and society interact through trust in a dualistic process.

The true test for countries taking up a fresh-start approach towards altering state–society relations lies in whether the state institutions, agencies and bureaucracies – the real heart and guts of the state apparatuses that sit below the elites and interact with citizens at street level – can be reformed and made less corrupt. This was critical for Poland in 1989, and it is vital for Ukraine today. Through a unique series of taxpayer surveys, this book, like no other, defines in the context of its neighbours the heart of Ukraine's governance crisis as lying in the extraordinarily long-term low levels of trust in their state on the part of Ukrainians. Reforming the tax administration now as part of a larger vision to overhaul the state's relationship with the public would help build a healthier state, capable of implementing its goals for the long run. Such reforms would be truly transformational.

Governance across Central and Eastern Europe and the Former Soviet Union

In many ways, the debate across Eastern Europe and the former Soviet Union over whether and how to transition to a legal, legitimate tax state

From a Coercive to a Modern Tax State 3

is part of the larger, intense debate that has erupted over the past two and a half decades regarding what tasks the state should and should not take up in economic, social and political life. Overstretching the role of the state in society ultimately led to the region's regime crises in the late 1980s and early 1990s. Yet simply shrinking the size and scope of the state's activities may not be a magic panacea, either. For if the state fails to perform well, the dual paths towards a consolidated democracy and a thriving market economy are at risk of derailment. It is clear that a state need not be as big as in Soviet times to fulfil essential tasks and to provide basic public goods. Yet, regardless of how one defines the appropriate limits of the state sector, one must question whether a state is, in fact, capable of doing what it sets out to do.

By focusing on the capacity to ensure tax compliance, this book asks why some transitional states prove more effective in administering policy than others. Specifically, why has the Polish state possessed a capacity to function in ways that the Russian and Ukrainian states have been less capable of? The truly puzzling variation in the capacity of states that once governed so extensively to ensure tax compliance demands further inquiry.

State capacity has varied widely across the post-communist region since the transitions across the two post-socialist regions began with the 1989 revolutions in the Soviet satellite states of Central and Eastern Europe (CEE) and the 1991 collapse of the Soviet Union.

In estimating the levels of governance across these regions, it is important to see how these states rank with respect to worldwide governance. The World Bank has created a statistical compilation of some 352 variables measuring perceptions of a wide range of quality of governance issues drawn from thirty-two sources and thirty different organizations.[2] One indicator, 'government effectiveness,' combines responses on the quality of public service provision, the quality of the bureaucracy, the competence of civil servants, the independence of the civil service from political pressures and the credibility of the government's commitment to policies.

To capture the variation in post-communist governance and the ability to implement state policy goals, Figure 1.1 presents the World Bank's government effectiveness indicators for Poland, Russia and Ukraine and the averages for the fifteen EU member states prior to the 2004 expansion eastward, for the Eastern Europe and Baltics region and for the

---

[2] The Governance Indicators are presented in Kaufmann, Kraay and Mastruzzi. The data are available at www.govindicators.org. A similar source for data is the Quality of Governance Institute's dataset at the University of Gothenburg, Sweden, available at http://qog.pol.gu.se/data.

4 Taxes and Trust

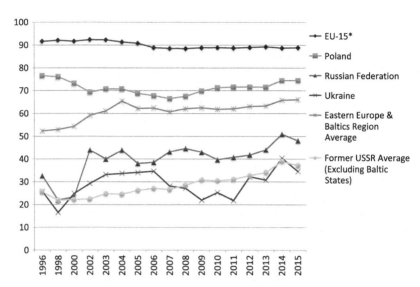

Figure 1.1 World Bank government effectiveness global rankings for Poland, Russia and Ukraine and averages for Eastern Europe and the Baltics, the former Soviet Union and the EU-15 countries, country percentile rankings (0–100), 1996–2014

former Soviet Union region. Poland ranks just above the average level of government effectiveness for the Eastern Europe and Baltics region. Meanwhile, Russia's level of effective governance ranks higher than the average of the former Soviet Union states, and is behind, since 1996, only Armenia and, since 2005, Georgia as well. At the same time, Russia has ranked lower than all the states in Eastern Europe and the Baltics in the World Bank survey, with the exception of Bosnia-Herzegovina. While it nearly always ranked lower than Russia, Ukraine did score higher than the former Soviet Union region average up until 2007, when it slipped below that average.

Other studies find similar results in terms of how Poland, Russia and Ukraine rank on governance issues. Jessica Fortin constructed a quantitative index of state capacity from the first post-communist year to 2006 based on tax capacity (measured by taxes collected as a percentage of Gross Domestic Product (GDP)), property rights enforcement, contract-intensive money (ratio of currency to bank deposits), corruption and infrastructure reform. While Chapter 4 of this book will question whether taxes collected as a percentage of GDP are the best measure for the extractive capacity of a state, Fortin does come up with a ranking quite similar to that of the World Bank – namely, one in which Poland is

From a Coercive to a Modern Tax State 5

in the top five post-communist countries, while Russia ranks both lower than all CEE states and higher than almost all other FSU states, with Ukraine leading the bottom third of post-communist states.[3]

Why Poland? Why Russia? Why Ukraine?

Selecting Poland, Russia and Ukraine as cases provides for a classic John Stuart Mill comparative design by capturing the region's variations in the capacity of the state to implement policy (here, the capacity to ensure tax compliance) and by providing for a controlled comparison in order to assess whether the culture and legacies of state–society relations or internal institutional history and design hold more causal weight.

All three states, two of which were part of the same state, the USSR, tried to govern very extensively under communism. While Russia has had the best governance in the former Soviet Union, it has had poorer levels of governance than other post-communist states and developed states. Poland, meanwhile, also has been one of the more capable states in Central and Eastern Europe and the largest post-communist state in that region, both in size and in population. Further, while it had less influence from the European Union in reforming its bureaucracies than other contemporaneous prospective entrants did, Poland did receive significant external financial and technical assistance, like Russia and Ukraine. Choosing, then, Poland, Russia and Ukraine as cases for close study allows a comparison to be made with respect to the largest country in each of the twin post-communist regions and allows a comparison to be made between the most effective post-Soviet state, an average performing post-Soviet state, and a successful former Soviet satellite state with respect to providing for good governance.

Moreover, many of the problems that have plagued Russia and Ukraine and other post-communist states have been a burden to Poland as well, posing a real puzzle to explain the variance in governance outcomes. Specifically, like those in Russia and Ukraine, the transition has not been free of poverty or corruption in Poland either. First, the transition to the market economy has meant the loss of jobs for many Poles. Unemployment in 2003, for example, was as high as about 20 per cent.[4] Inequality, while not as great as in Russia and Ukraine, has been growing in Poland, and a mid-2000s World Bank report suggested that such growing inequality has contributed to an increase in the number of those

---

[3] Fortin, p. 673.
[4] Data obtained from the Economist Intelligence Unit <www.economist.com>.

6   Taxes and Trust

below the poverty line.[5] Second, as in Russia and Ukraine, fortunes were made in the immediate aftermath of the transition from the command economy when individuals, often with ties to state officials, took advantage of ambiguity in the law. Third, those who were a part of the communist regime in Poland, even those who worked in pre-1989 security services, were not purged from participating in current state activity.[6] Finally, high levels of corruption did exist within the communist-era Polish and Soviet states.

Given the variation in state capacity between Poland and Russia, the Ukraine case becomes necessary. By including Ukraine – a state that is similarly unitary in structure and more analogous in geographical and population size to Poland, but one that has a history and a culture more like those of post-Soviet Russia – in the case selection, aspects that differentiate Poland's state capacity from that of the post-Soviet cases can be isolated while controlling for the size and federalist structure of Russia. The unique presence of a sociopolitical cleavage between Ukraine's provinces, some of whose histories trace back to Polish or Russian rule or both, allows a more focused study on how such differences, which are not as easily discernible in Poland or Russia, can make an impact on state–society relations.

Hence, choosing Poland as a case for comparison with Russia and Ukraine provides opportunities to elucidate obstacles to effective postcommunist governance and to define what approaches can realistically work within the confines of a difficult dual transition to democracy and a market economy.

The Study of the State, Post-Socialism and Tax Collection

By its very nature, this study addresses issues raised by those who have recognized that the 'state should be brought back in' to the study of political science and the pursuit of economic development. Those studying the state, such as Atul Kohli, Joel Migdal and Theda Skocpol, have underscored the importance of states possessing the capability to implement official goals.[7]

In particular, several scholars, such as Michael Mann, Peter Evans and James Rauch, have emphasized the importance of 'Weberian bureaucracies', which possess certain personnel characteristics, office structures and an autonomous relationship to the wider society, as significant

---

[5] World Bank (2005a), cited in Ash, p. 24.   [6] Michnik; Ash, p. 24.
[7] See, for example, Kohli and Shue; Migdal, 1987; Migdal, 1994; Migdal, 1997; Skocpol, 1979; and Skocpol, 1985.

From a Coercive to a Modern Tax State 7

criteria in ensuring policy outcomes.[8] International aid organizations such as the World Bank and the US Agency for International Development also have begun to recognize that good governance and effective institutional infrastructures are required in order for countries to develop. Indeed, in a macro analysis of twenty-five transitional states for the World Bank, Nauro F. Campos has found that there is a strong correlation between the quality of bureaucracy in a particular country and its level of development, as measured by life expectancy.[9] By comparing state bureaucracies in three countries, this project contributes to these literatures by identifying the ingredients for building a capable state.

In particular, this study contributes to the ongoing dialogue regarding the impact of neo-liberal economic reform programs on state institutions. Since the early 1990s, neo-liberal advisors to former communist states, such as Jeffrey Sachs and Anders Åslund, have focused on choosing the 'right' reform policies to construct a market economy in order to pre-empt a drawn-out process to create new institutions.[10] The neo-liberal advisors to the newly democratic states believed that institutions to protect property rights in the marketplace would be created through self-interest only after a propertied class was established. On the other hand, Peter Murrell and Adam Przeworski have argued that shock therapy advocates assume erroneously that new formal structures and institutions, necessary for the implementation of any comprehensive economic reforms, can be built without the inclusion of society.[11] Largely because the old institutions cannot handle the new way of doing business, these shock therapy critics argued for incorporating society – on both a democratic and an economic level – so that new institutions gradually can be supported by existing informal structures.

Part of the paradox of neo-liberal reforms was that their goal was to keep the post-communist state small in order to allow market forces to arise. 'The debate between shock therapists and gradualists that centred on the issue of the pace of liberalization overlooked the crucial importance of institutions for economic growth', economist Vladimir Popov has written.[12]

State administrations and bureaucracies, indeed, are needed to regulate a market economy. The types and natures of bureaucracies that develop in post-communist settings are important to market reforms. In particular, new, complex institutions such as a central bank and commercial bank network, a finance ministry, a system of commercial law, a

---

[8] See, for example, Evans, 1995; Evans and Rauch, 1999; Mann, 1986; and Mann, 1993.
[9] Campos. [10] Åslund, 1995; and Sachs, 1994.
[11] Murrell; and Przeworski, 1991. [12] Popov, 2000, p. 56.

8   Taxes and Trust

court system and a tax collection system must be built prior to or along with the adoption of neo-liberal reforms so that the market can work. Even the main pillar of shock therapy, privatization, requires institutions to ensure that the process goes properly. Further, social welfare institutions need to be effective in easing the burden imposed on the population throughout the changeover.

Yet, despite the need for strong state institutions to foster the development of such market forces, some post-Soviet states have had a relative weakening of the institutional capacity of the state. This study seeks to add increased clarity to the larger debate over institution-building in third-wave democracies undertaking economic consolidation by providing an analysis that explains why and to what extent state institutions have been less effective in the post-Soviet cases than in Eastern Europe.

Second, this research project bridges the gap between the East European and former Soviet Union area studies literatures. In this vein, this work follows the examples of Valerie Bunce, M. Steven Fish, Philip Roeder, Joshua A. Tucker and others who have been able to make significant contributions to the study of regime collapse, democratization, nationalism and voting behaviour precisely through the study of both regions.[13] Yet, as these scholars have examined different questions, no one, to my knowledge, has looked comparatively in a book-length work at the role of the state in the development of these two regions.

Some scholars have studied the role of the state either in Eastern Europe or in the former Soviet Union. Herbert Kitschelt, for example, has devised a theory on the new post-communist party systems in Hungary, Poland, Bulgaria and the Czech Republic that relies upon the assumption that post-communist bureaucracies vary in how they operate in each state.[14] Similarly, Steven Solnick and Kathryn Stoner have shown that Russia's federalist system has created a lack of institutional mechanisms for consolidation of the central state's power in the 1990s.[15] This book builds on the works of these scholars as it compares the roles of the state in Poland, Russia and Ukraine.

Tax collection is a great policy arena to investigate the role and function of the state. Taxation is such a wonderful and increasingly popular topic for study in the social sciences precisely because it lies at

[13] See, for example, Bunce, 1999; Fish, 1995; Fish, 1999; Roeder, 1993; Roeder, 1999; and Tucker, 2006.
[14] Kitschelt, Mansfeldova, Markowski and Tóka, 1999.
[15] See, for example, Solnick, 1996; Solnick, 1997; Stoner-Weiss, 1997; and Stoner-Weiss, 1997.

the centre of state–society interactions, at the heart of the fiscal state and at the foundation of a successful market economy. Getting citizens to pay taxes, in particular, presents a major, if not the central, problem for states pursuing greater economic development and growth. 'It is harder for states that fail to elicit high tax compliance to gain wide approval, because the quality of public goods in such states diminishes', writes Marcelo Bergman. 'Conversely, higher compliance is self-sustaining because it enables sound fiscal policies that promote improved consent.'[16]

'[T]axation is not so much a weight or a burden, imposed by one discrete entity on another', writes Yanni Kotsonis in his study on tax collection in the Russian Empire and the Soviet Union up to 1930. '[I]t is equally a nexus where basic categories meet and reshape each other, and a way to express and negotiate the tensions of a modern regime.'[17] In the Russian Empire of the nineteenth and early twentieth centuries, Kotsonis argues that taxes always were about power, not about the purse. 'In hindsight, it is clear that arrests, exiles, tortures, beatings, and wholesale reprisals avoided the point, if the point was the collection of taxes', he continues. 'Either these measures were unrelated to increasing revenue or they removed the delinquents from production and ensured that the tax would not be paid at all, or they punished the wrong people. But taxes were as much a matter of rule and spectacle. They were meant to instil in the population a fear and respect of power, and they inscribed legal distinctions in status by dividing the population into taxable and non-taxable estates.'[18] Hence, the collection of taxes, for which different regimes in different points of time have developed their own systems of rule and spectacle as they mediate the path towards modernity, merits an excellent subject for rigorous study.

Within the field of post-communism, the study of tax yields a variety of differing theoretical approaches that complement each other well. By focusing on the ability of the states to collect taxes, this study will be a valuable complement to existing texts on taxes in Russia and Eastern Europe, including Andrei Schliefer and Daniel Treisman's *Without a Map*, which focused on fiscal federalism in 1990's Russia; Scott Gehlbach's *Representation through Taxation*, which takes a large-N political economy approach to explain how and why states structure the tax base, as well as the role that collective goods provision plays in the development of certain economic sectors; Hilary Appel's *Tax Politics in Eastern Europe*, which focuses on the international and domestic influences of tax

---

[16] Bergman, p. 2.   [17] Kotsonis, p. 5.   [18] *Ibid.*, p. 51.

10   Taxes and Trust

policy development; and Gerald M. Easter's *Capital, Coercion and Post-communist States*, which takes a broader fiscal sociology approach with a focus on elites to explain how the distinct ideal-typical tax policies and regimes emerged in Poland and Russia. Through my focus on the internal Weberian aspects of the tax administrations and on the unique application of US tax compliance theory to individual-level survey data, I take a less stationary approach than some of these authors, emphasizing agency, trust and iterative action as potential sources for transition in street-level interactions between bureaucrats and taxpayers. And my approach is much more focused on the implementation of tax policy rather than on the development and adoption of tax policy.

Some twenty-five years after the collapse of communism in Europe and Eurasia, states that once exercised tight control over their populations so that state goals and policies could more or less be implemented now find that they differ greatly among themselves in their ability to do so. For all their shortcomings, communist states were able to govern for decades – roughly from 1917 to 1991 in Russia and parts of Eurasia and from 1945 to 1989 in Central and Eastern Europe. What has happened since then has been a dazzling array of variation in these states' methods and abilities to govern today. It is now time to explore why that has been the case.

To do so, this study seeks to achieve the following:

- At the meta-level, to help discern how a state transitions from a coercive state to a legal, legitimate tax state;
- At the macro-level, to determine how the Polish, Russian and Ukrainian states implement policies to ensure tax compliance; and
- At the micro-level, to establish what exactly is going on inside these countries that affects tax collection and, more broadly, governance.

This study is the first manuscript on taxation to focus on trust, and it is the first work of social science to concentrate on how tax policy actually gets implemented on the ground in Poland, Russia and Ukraine, highlighting the nuances of the transitional Ukrainian case and explaining precisely why and how that 'borderland' country differs from the more ideal types of coercive Russia and compliance-oriented Poland. The meta-level question, of course, is the very real present-day dilemma for Ukraine.

Taxes and Trust presents the culmination of more than fifteen years of original research – including nine bespoke opinion surveys – into how states go about the business of reshaping their relationships with their citizens. Focusing on two states that represent competing models of post-communist development (Poland and Russia) and on a third state caught in between (Ukraine), the book uniquely emphasizes the building and accumulation of *trust* as the main vehicle for transitioning from a coercive tax state to a modern, legal and legitimate one. For a state failing to gain the public's trust such, as today's Ukraine, reforming street-level bureaucracies like the tax administration would go a long way towards building a healthier state, capable of implementing its goals for the long run.

2 Trust and Post-communist Policy Implementation

To give the transition from communism a viable chance at success, the new countries of Central and Eastern Europe and the former Soviet Union required a state capable of governing on the ground. In order to explain why Poland, Russia and Ukraine govern the way they do, we need to explore how capable these three post-communist states are, particularly with respect to their ability to implement tax policy to raise revenue. The first step in doing so is to examine established theories in political science for variations in the capacity of states and then to construct a model of state capacity specific to post-communist states, which we can then test with respect to the ability of state administrative structures to raise tax revenue.

Defining State Capacity

State capacity is an elastic term in the literature. Despite its presence everywhere in political science, the term is not defined in a manner that entails it being easily measured and operationalized. Nevertheless, most political science definitions of state capacity include a sense of the state's ability to accomplish a task. Mary Hilderbrand and Merilee Grindle, in their study, define capacity as 'the ability to perform appropriate tasks effectively, efficiently and sustainably'.[1] Grindle, in her own work, has identified a capable state as 'one that exhibits the ability to establish and maintain effective institutional, technical, administrative and political functions'.[2] For Michael Bratton, 'Capacity is the ability to implement political decisions.' Bratton refers to Theda Skocpol's definition of capacity as the means to implement official goals.[3] Therefore, drawing upon these definitions, I define state capacity simply as *the ability to implement state goals or policy.*

Political scientists generally have had a sense that state capacity reflects the ability to achieve state goals.[4] Some have described state capacity as

---

[1] Hilderbrand and Grindle, p. 34. [2] Grindle, p. 7.
[3] Bratton, p. 235. [4] See, for example, Kohli and Shue, p. 305.

Trust and Post-communist Policy Implementation 13

the ability of state leaders to get people to do something. 'The main issues', Joel Migdal describes as the purpose of his book, *Strong Societies and Weak States*, in its introduction, 'will be state capabilities or their lack: the ability of state leaders to use the agencies of the state to get people in the society to do what they want them to do.'[5] Such a definition, then, denotes being able to identify what it means 'to define' a specific policy agenda, to distinguish who or what defines the state's goals and to discern what are the state's intentions. Moreover, related to these issues is the ability to set the rules in society (often through bureaus and state agencies) and the consistency of those rules.

Operationalizing State Capacity

The implementation of an extractive policy such as the collection of taxes is a good policy area to choose to assess state capacity, as it requires the penetration of society and utilizes a variety of resources and legitimacy on the part of the people in order to be successful.

Successful taxation through administrative structures has been viewed as an essential hallmark of a strong state. For Charles Tilly, in reflecting on how states were formed in the development of Europe, the essential ingredients for strong states are institutions (although he doesn't term them as such) that control the population. 'The singling out of the organization of armed forces, taxation, policing, the control of food supply, and the formation of technical personnel stresses activities which were difficult, costly, and often unwanted by large parts of the population', he writes. 'All were essential to the creation of strong states; all were therefore likely to tell us something important about the conditions under which strong or weak, centralized or decentralized, stable or unstable, states come into being.'[6]

Similarly, Skocpol has viewed states as 'actual organizations controlling (or attempting to control) territories and people', which is done largely through the extraction of resources and the building of administrative and coercive organizations.[7] For Skocpol, the process associated with rebuilding of state organizations 'is the place to look for the political contradictions that help launch social revolutions'.[8] While Skocpol's analysis is based on discerning the origins of social revolutions, the processes by which state structures are rebuilt and taxes are collected in the aftermath of a revolution, such as that following the overthrow, or departure, of communism in 1989 in Poland and in 1991 in Russia and

---

[5] Migdal, 1988, p. xiii.   [6] Tilly, p. 6.   [7] Skocpol, 1979, p. 31.   [8] Ibid., p. 32.

14   Taxes and Trust

Ukraine, are critically important for the construction and maintenance of social order in the post-revolutionary society.

States cannot govern effectively if they cannot collect revenue. The enormous processes of democratic and economic consolidation require states to do precisely that. Examining this policy area thus provides a clearer picture of the foremost fundamental and prior task for states.

In addition, given Eastern Europe's and the former Soviet Union's inheritance of state socialist-designed institutions, focusing on state capacity through the collection of taxes presents a unique opportunity to evaluate how country-specific variables work in altering analogous institutional designs and similar post-communist goals. Why, given the fact that the centrally planned economies in Eastern Europe imitated the tax system of the Soviet Union, did Poland's inheritance of a poorly functioning tax administration not prevent it from being able to raise adequate revenues in the 1990s? By holding some aspects of past institutional design and current state intentions constant, this book can test for how differing political, economic, geographical and cultural variables have affected state capacity across these post-socialist states.

Explaining the Variance in Governance and State Capacity of Post-communist States

As the differing degrees of state capacity to collect taxes in Poland, Russia and Ukraine are established in this study, the causal forces behind this variation are explored. Specifically, three basic theories on state capacity are reviewed to explain patterns of post-socialist state capacity: One school within political science, led by Samuel P. Huntington, views state capacity as a function of political institutions such as parties (including the different party systems as they relate to regime type).[9] A second, exemplified by the work of Migdal, sees state capacity as a function of state–society relations.[10] Finally, a third school (Chalmers Johnson, Peter Evans and Max Weber) views state capacity as a function of the structure of the state itself.[11] By examining the variables behind these theories, I evaluate the relative causal weight of three competing explanations.

Theory #1: State Capacity as a Function of Political Institutions

Bureaucratic performance may be a function of broader levels of institutionalization within the polity. In 1968, Huntington wrote in *Political*

[9] Huntington.   [10] Migdal, 1988.
[11] Evans; Evans and Rauch; Chalmers Johnson; and Gerth and Mills.

Trust and Post-communist Policy Implementation 15

Order and Changing Societies that only where the level of political institutionalization outstrips the level of political participation could there emerge stable politics working in the public interest.[12] Specifically, this theory hypothesizes that a focus on political parties – how well they are developed in relation to the state – would account for variance in state capacity.

The most important question for Huntington in his 1968 work is how states can gain the capacity to govern effectively. Huntington begins by observing that '[t]he most important political distinction among countries concerns not their form of government but their degree of government'.[13] To form capable, effective and legitimate governments, states need not hold elections, per se, but must succeed in creating organizations. What is good for the public is 'whatever strengthens governmental institutions . . . A government with a low level of institutionalization is not just a weak government; it is also a bad government. The function of government is to govern.'[14] To develop into modern polities, authority must be rationalized through specified state structures, the development of which requires increased participation by social groups throughout society.

Hence, to involve society in the development of government structures, political parties are the vehicles for the public to keep tabs on state institutions so that they can govern effectively. Political parties, states Huntington, 'broaden participation in the traditional institutions, thus adapting those institutions to the requirements of the modern polity. They help make the traditional institutions legitimate in terms of popular sovereignty . . .'[15] Furthermore, Huntington also argues that corruption – a sign that government agencies are not working as they should – 'is most prevalent in states which lack effective political parties . . .'[16] Thus, Huntington argues that those political leaders and 'promoters of modernization' who 'reject and denigrate political parties' in order to modernize their society actually will fail to make their societies politically stable.[17]

For Atul Kohli, the absence of effective parties often yields to state centralization accompanied by state powerlessness. 'Without parties or other political institutions', Kohli has written with respect to the processes by which India's leaders govern, 'the links between leaders and their supporters remain weak . . . [I]t becomes very difficult to translate election mandates into specific policies . . . Policy failure in turn paves the way for other populist challengers, thus perpetuating the cycle of

---

[12] Huntington, 1968.   [13] Ibid., p. 1.   [14] Ibid., p. 25, 28.
[15] Ibid., p. 91.   [16] Ibid., p. 71.   [17] Ibid., p. 92.

16   Taxes and Trust

centralization and powerlessness.'[18] Similarly, in *Democracy and Discontent*, Kohli associates the erosion of established authority in certain provinces in India as owing to the lack of a cohesive party structure. Kohli argues for the strengthening of party organizations and for bringing the state's capacities into line with the state's commitments.[19]

The issues raised in Kohli's work on India are quite similar to those in *Political Order and Changing Societies* insofar as 'the problem of centralization and powerlessness is an integral aspect of the imbalance between institutional development and mobilized demands'.[20] Yet, whereas the focus for Huntington is on socioeconomic change, which causes societal mobilization that needs to be structured and organized, Kohli views the spread of democratic politics as encouraging greater political activism in society, which must be channelled through parties.

Hence, regardless of whether the 1989 and 1991 revolutions were about economic modernization or democratization, the new post-communist states, according to this theory, must have developed political parties in order to capture the polities' interest in and oversight of state institutional activity. How parties are structured in relation to state structures, how they oversee such administrative institutions, whether they simply set overall agency goals or provide direction on more precise bureaucratic functions and how they incorporate society and direct public opinion to provide for oversight are deemed to be critical in accounting for variations in state performance.

Political Parties and Party Systems in Post-communist Poland, Russia and Ukraine

Poland. In *Post-communist Party Systems*, Herbert Kitschelt, Zdenka Mansfeldova, Radosław Markowski and Gábor Tóka assess how political party systems – born out of the legacy of the communist regime type and mediated through current institutions, rules and political alignment – affect pathways towards the consolidation of Central and East European democracies. In particular, the alignment of partisan divide impacts democratic governance. In the post-communist situation, the nature of a regime divide is the greatest obstacle to effective governance. 'The deeper the regime divide', the authors state, 'the more likely even small policy differences among parties undermine their capacity to collaborate in legislative and executive coalitions.'[21] The regime types of bureaucratic authoritarianism and national-accommodative communism

---

[18] Kohli, 1994, pp. 89–90.   [19] Kohli, 1991.
[20] Kohli, 1994, p. 90.   [21] Kitschelt et al., p. 89.

Trust and Post-communist Policy Implementation 17

have led to democracies that have less sharp regime divides than those party systems emerging from patrimonial communist societies.[22]

Kitschelt and his co-authors deem Hungary and Poland to have developed consensual democracy with competition around key economic issues, while the Czech Republic has produced a competitive democracy with significant divisions over economic issues coupled with incentives for collaboration.[23] The development of Poland's post-communist political party system traces its origins to the negotiated transition in the late 1980s during which the communist regime was rather tolerant in allowing opposition activity and the negotiated transfer of power in 1989. 'In terms of post-communist party system, Poland shows a rather sharp programmatic crystallization around both economic and political-cultural issues resulting in crosscutting divisions, both of which have some consequence for party competition', Kitschelt et al. remark with respect to the overall competitive nature of the Polish party system. 'In Poland, politicians' and voters' formal left–right conceptions of their own and the competing parties' positions are informed by *both* economic and socio-cultural issues.'[24]

Poland's first free post-communist parliamentary elections in 1991, which followed the first presidential elections in 1990, brought forth a mushrooming of parties, with more than 100 across the spectrum taking part. The number of parties participating in national elections thereafter decreased dramatically. Since those first elections, seven parliamentary elections and five presidential elections – all free, fair, highly competitive and accompanied by a smooth transfer of power – have taken place. Not only has the centre-right – led by those associated with the anti-communist Solidarity movement of the 1980s – and the centre-left – led by post-communists who have become Social Democrats – each controlled the parliament and the presidency, but there has been significant alternation between the two sides of the political spectrum. No governing party since the start of the transition had won re-election to parliament until Civic Platform (PO) was re-elected in 2011.

Moreover, President Aleksander Kwaśniewski, a founder of the post-communist Democratic Left Alliance (SLD) who was elected in 1995 and re-elected in 2000, was succeeded by centre-right Law and Justice (PiS) candidate Lech Kaczynski, who was elected president in October 2005 (and later died in the Smolensk plane crash of April 2010), after a much contested race with PO candidate Donald Tusk, also of the centre-right. In May 2015, PO candidate Bronisław Komorowski, who had been president since his election in 2010, was defeated by PiS

---

[22] Ibid., p. 406.   [23] Ibid., p. 403.   [24] Ibid., p. 387.

candidate Andrzej Duda. Meanwhile, after the October 2015 parliamentary elections, the nationalist-conservative PiS party returned to head the government for the first time since 2005–2007, having defeated the centre-right PO party, which had been ruling since 2007.

Hence, Poland's political party system is highly competitive between the two sides of the political spectrum, albeit especially so between the centre-right PO and the nationalist right PiS in recent years. The question, with respect to this first theory on state capacity, is whether a competitive party system is a *primary reason* for Poland's relatively greater post-communist state capacity and relatively good tax compliance.

Russia. Meanwhile, in states that succeed patrimonial communist societies such as those of the former Soviet Union, Kitschelt and his co-authors write that liberal-democratic parties tend to lack the skills, networks and resources to replace rent-seeking elites, while other parties in the system, often communist successor parties, 'exploit their control of the policy process to (re)build clientelist networks and to funnel public assets into the hands of rent-seeking groups affiliated with the party'.[25] Deep regime divides, associated most with states that succeeded patrimonial communist regimes, further complicate effective reform and institutional oversight as the party system becomes oriented to negotiating the redistribution of assets to rent-seeking groups.

When applied to Russia, this analysis of a deep regime divide, formed from a patrimonial communist past, has great saliency in explaining the first decade of the transition. Parties were, indeed, the political key to mediating poor economic reform in Russia in the 1990s. Yet, in Russia, it is not just a bad party system at work; it is also the *lack* of party politics that has yielded bad reforms, or rather, a failure to implement government policy. In Russia, the underdevelopment of political parties under both President Boris Yeltsin in the 1990s and President Vladimir Putin since 2000, for different reasons, is also another facet of the underinstitutionalization problem that is viewed as having led to poor governance.

At the beginning of the 1990s, there was great hope that the transition from one-party rule would give rise to a fully competitive political party system. 'Given Russia's thousand-year history of autocratic rule, the emergence of democracy must be recognized as a revolutionary achievement of the last decade', wrote Michael McFaul in 2002. 'Even so, Russia is not a liberal democracy. The Russian political system lacks many of the supporting institutions that make democracy robust. Russia's party system, civil society, and the rule of law are weak and underdeveloped.'[26] Moreover, in the Yeltsin era, the lack of a structured

---

[25] Ibid., p. 405.   [26] McFaul, p. 35.

Trust and Post-communist Policy Implementation 19

political party system at the national level led to a failure of Moscow politicians to link provincial politics with the national political agenda, which enabled regional elites to pursue interests in direct opposition to the centre's will.[27]

With respect to filling the seat in the highest office in Russia, Yeltsin's re-election, as well as his transfer of power to Putin, was conducted by processes that were not entirely transparent or competitive. In the 1996 re-election, the media, largely controlled by the oligarchs, gave heavily biased coverage in favour of the president, who began the race with single-digit popularity ratings, enabling him to pull ahead and beat out the Communist Party's candidate, Gennadiy Zyuganov. Near the end of his second (and constitutionally mandated final) term, Yeltsin handed power over to Putin in a manner that resembled the passing of a baton to a protégé. Putin had been appointed prime minister in 1999 by Yeltsin, who himself resigned dramatically on the last day of 1999, paving the way for Putin, the new acting president, to win the election in March 2000 handily.

Since 2000, power gradually has become much more concentrated in the president, and the Duma, Russia's lower house of parliament, largely has been perceived as voting exactly as the Kremlin wants on key decisions, rendering parties less important than they were even in the 1990s. 'The contrast between the Yeltsin and Putin presidencies is nowhere more visible than in president-parliament relations', Thomas Remington wrote in 2003, indicating that even early on in Putin's tenure party politics began to fall in line with the Kremlin. 'Whereas President Yeltsin never commanded a majority of votes in the Duma, Putin's legislative record is filled with accomplishments. Even on the most controversial issues – land reform, political parties, ratification of START – the president and government have won majorities. By comparison, Yeltsin faced a hostile Duma that came close to passing a motion of impeachment in 1999.'[28]

Meanwhile, members of the upper house of parliament, the Federation Council, are no longer elected but appointed. Similarly, regional governors were appointed by legislative bodies of the Russian Federation subjects by recommendation of the president from 2005 to 2012. Further, while Russian politics does have some aspects of pluralism and competition, as M. Steven Fish as written, 'falsification, coercion, and the arbitrary disqualification of candidates are frequent and pervasive – not merely occasional and deviant – features of elections in post-Soviet Russia'.[29] All of this has led to the virtual elimination of effective and

[27] Stoner-Weiss, 1999b, pp. 17–18.   [28] Remington, p. 39.   [29] Fish, 2005, p. 81.

20   Taxes and Trust

popular opposition political parties. Hence, as candidates for president, both Yeltsin and Putin did not need a party to be elected – or re-elected. And a unified, pro-democratic reform party never truly developed in Russia.

That said, while in office, Putin has been promoting the elevation of the United Russia party, and, in so doing, has connected himself to a political party much more than his predecessor. United Russia emerged first in 1999, according to Henry Hale, as 'a political party structure [that] could help take away votes from other parties, but also provide a significant base of support for the Kremlin in the Duma, and most importantly, could channel support from governors and corporations that might have otherwise supported an opposition party'.[30] Hence, United Russia has developed into the state's party of all sorts, enabling Russia to be governed nearly like a de facto one-party country and, most recently, in the September 2016 ballot, saw its majority control of the legislative branch grow from 238 to 343 of the Duma's 450 seats. As Brian Whitmore commented on that election, 'The Kremlin has apparently given up on even pretending to have a multiparty system.'[31]

In 2005, due in part to the lack of competitive party politics and in part to the lack of media independent from Kremlin loyalists, Russia was moved from being 'partially free' to 'unfree', according to the Freedom House classification. In January 2006, parliament passed a law, initiated by the president, that places NGOs under tighter scrutiny by the state. Hence, as Andrew Kuchins related in testimony before the US Commission on Security and Cooperation in Europe in 2006, 'President Putin has consistently and systematically eliminated competition among independent contending political forces and centralized, at least on paper, more and more political authority in the office of the Presidential administration. If Mr Putin does believe in democratic governance as he contends, he has an odd way of expressing it.'[32]

In essence, the significant absence of an effective political party system and effective political parties might account for Russia's less successful levels of governance since the fall of communism.

Ukraine. Unsurprisingly, as both emerged from the same country, Ukraine, like Russia, has a history of patrimonial communist politics and a post-communist underdevelopment of political parties. While the political process has been competitive in what is largely a

---

[30] Washington Profile.   [31] Whitmore.

[32] Kuchins, 'Russian Democracy and Civil Society: Back to the Future', Testimony for the U.S. Commission on Security and Cooperation in Europe, 8 February 2006. Available at <www.carnegieendowment.org>.

Trust and Post-communist Policy Implementation 21

presidential–parliamentary system, with parties generally having to form coalitions in order to govern once elected to the parliament, the *Verkhovna Rada*, parties by and large (with the notable exceptions of the socialists and the communists) have eschewed ideology based on economic or social–political concerns, providing for intriguing coalition governments. At the same time, party membership among the public is quite low. As Paul D'Anieri has argued, 'Ukrainian parties . . . are elite-based rather than mass-based.'[33] As such, they were not viewed early on as a necessary vehicle to political power. In Ukraine's second presidential elections in 1994, only one candidate for president was a member of a political party.

Political parties, like all things related to politics, often are viewed by the public and experts alike as being vehicles for protecting and enriching personal business, especially oligarchic, wealth. Elites have used less-than-transparent political parties and other government connections to capture the state and derive economic rents. 'However, these "opaque" and oligarchic networks were not unified, and relied on various *ad hoc* alliances; and their influence on the state did not shut out other interests altogether', writes Verena Fritz on the 1990s. 'Political parties – as a potentially balancing force – remained weak in Ukraine. To some degree, there was a self-interest in building the Ukrainian state among political leaders and the bureaucracy.'[34] As D'Anieri has remarked, '"centrist parties" remained fronts for interest politics rather than real centralist parties seeking broad electoral appeal'.[35] Further, as Steven Levitsky and Lucan A. Way have observed, both Presidents Leonid Kravchuk and Leonid Kuchma failed to be utilize parties to solidify support, as both leaders 'suffered large-scale defections and lost power to former allies' during their rule.[36]

Stephen Kotkin was a bit more direct when interviewed in March 2014 in summing up the entire post-communist political scene of corrupt networks, without nuance with respect to different parties or presidents. 'Ukraine is a wreck', he stated. 'Ukraine was destroyed by Ukrainian elites. Every regime in Ukraine since 1991 has ripped off that country. They ripped off everything that wasn't nailed down and then they ripped off everything that was nailed down. Ukraine gives corruption a bad name. The economy has shrunk . . . [T]he Ukrainian economy today is smaller than it was in 1991, by any measure. The economy in Poland is at least twice as big as it was in 1991. So Ukraine is a basket case because

---

[33] D'Anieri, 2006, p. 189.   [34] Fritz, p. 110.
[35] D'Anieri, Kravchuk and Kuzio, p. 159, quoted in Fritz, p. 142.
[36] Levitsky and Way, p. 214.

22   Taxes and Trust

of the Ukrainian political class.'[37] Hale stated, prior to the EuroMaidan Revolution of 2014, that the country has had 'little real rule of law' and can be termed 'clientelist' or 'patrimonial' because its corrupt politics is so individualist-based.[38]

In the 1990s, parliamentary politics was dominated largely by the communists, who won a surprise victory at the first post-communist parliamentary election in 1994. During Kuchma's presidency (1994–2005), parties began to be seen as vehicles for oligarchic clans, who have much greater influence to this day than their peers in Russia.

Broadly speaking, the parties that have developed over the years in post-communist Ukraine have been either pro-Western and pro-nationalist (such as President Viktor Yushchenko's Our Ukraine bloc of the mid-2000s, Vitaly Klitschko's Ukrainian Democratic Alliance for Reform (UDAR), Fatherland (formerly the Bloc Yulia Tymoshenko) and the Petro Poroshenko Bloc), supported largely by voters in western and central Ukraine, or pro-Russian and EU-sceptical (such as the reconstituted Communist Party of the 1990s and the Party of Regions from the early 2000s up until the 2014 departure of Viktor Yanukovych), drawing upon voters broadly in eastern and southern Ukraine.

There have been two main attempts to break up the patrimonial system – both of which were mass-led protest events that brought into power new pro-Western, pro-nationalist parties. Hale regards the first, the Orange Revolution of 2004, as 'dividing' but not 'eliminating' the clientelist political machine.[39] And, in part due to the falling out of the Orange duo of Tymoshenko and Yushchenko, only a year after the Orange Revolution, the Party of Regions came in first in the 2006 parliamentary elections, after which Yanukovych, whose initial election 'win' the Orange camp successfully overturned in 2004, became prime minister. Yanukovych himself was elected to the presidency in 2010. Moreover, as parliament subsequently abolished a law requiring parliamentary blocs to vote as a whole when forming a coalition, Yanukovych was able to gain control over a revived patrimonial system by appointing a government without forming a coalition with an opposition party.[40]

The second attempt, the EuroMaidan Revolution, brought the removal of Yanukovych in early 2014. The most recent parliamentary elections, which took place later that year, brought forth the most pro-Western parliament in the Rada's history, seemingly ready to consider new reform legislation to further democracy and also to get Ukraine out of its deep economic mire. Midsummer 2016, several of the

---

[37] Kotkin.   [38] Hale, p. 85.   [39] Ibid.   [40] D'Anieri, 2011, p. 40.

Trust and Post-communist Policy Implementation 23

EuroMaidan revolutionary leaders – a group of journalists and civil society activists rather than career politicians – launched a new European liberal political party, Democratic Alliance, seeking to unify the political centre and centre-right of the country by focusing on the free market, libertarian choices in private life and fierce anti-corruption endeavours that would cleave the electorate differently from previous cultural and populist approaches.[41] And, since a new law on parties was adopted, political parties in Ukraine beginning in 2016 are to be funded exclusively through the state budget in an effort to clamp down on corruption and financing, but the process, introduced in July 2016, may not be as beneficial to the reform efforts as originally intended, since the established political parties that made it into government with private funding will be awarded taxpayer money while newcomer competitors, which lack oligarch backing, will not.[42]

The question, then, is whether the degree of institutionalization of the polity through political parties actually matters with respect to the development and maintenance of effective state capacity in Poland, Russia and Ukraine – that is, whether the differences in governance levels in the three states are due to the presence of competitive parties in Poland and the lack of them in Russia and Ukraine. If the competition of the parties in Poland is the critical difference, it must be shown to be due to the focus and direction that such parties place on the bureaucracies and administration.

As a way to test this political party hypothesis in order to explain variation in governance, during my field research stage, I interviewed officials and bureaucrats in the tax administrative structures on what input they receive from parties in helping them to implement their policy priorities or tasks. In addition, I examined what impact parties have on the development of bureaucracies and the civil service and on model preferences in each country.

Theory #2: State Capacity as a Function of State–Society Relations

According to the second theory on state capacity, social explanations point to the relationships between states and societies. Migdal has argued that where states lack significant capacity, it is due to the presence of 'fragmented social controls' embedded in society that invade administrative structures. In *Strong Societies and Weak States*, Migdal argues that 'in societies with weak states a continuing environment of conflict – the vast,

---

[41] Karatnycky.   [42] Yatsenyuk; Kosmehl and Umland.

24   Taxes and Trust

but fragmented social control embedded in the non-state organizations of society – has dictated a particular, pathological set of relationships within the state organization itself, between the top state leadership and its agencies'.[43]

This enables the state, then, to become 'the grand arena of accommodation' in the polity. 'First, local and regional strongmen, politicians, and implementers accommodate one another in a web of political, economic, and social exchanges', Migdal continues. 'Second, accommodation also exists on a much grander scale... The strongmen end up with an enhanced bargaining position or with posts in the state itself that influence important decisions about the allocation of resources and the application of policy rules.'[44] Hence, 'a society fragmented in social control affects the character of the state, which, in turn, reinforces the fragmentation of the society'.[45] Indeed, across Eurasia, the rise of new post-communist forces that have not been incorporated into formal institutional frameworks might be responsible for state capture.

Joel Hellman's explanation for stalled economic reform in Eastern Europe as being the result of the rise of narrow, vested interests that benefited from rent-seeking opportunities accompanying the transition to the market also could be useful in explaining the stalled state recreation process.[46] The existence of social network ties between private sector businesses, state enterprise managers and government bureaucrats might be credited with hampering administrative reform and bureaucratic capacity. Therefore, some structural and legal constraints in the transition to a new economy imposed by the state on society are deemed to be necessary. Hence, where states lack significant state capacity, this theory suggests, it is due to the presence of 'fragmented social controls' embedded in society that invade state administrative structures.

A fragmented society also has been attributed to the nature of the political culture that reinforces such unconstructive state–society relations. John Elster, Claus Offe and Ulrich K. Preuss have argued that the conditions that favour consolidation of the transition in Central and Eastern Europe are political culture and historical legacy. The authors conclude 'that the most significant variable for the success of the transformation is the degree of compatibility of the inherited world views, patterns of behaviour and basic social and political concepts with the functional necessities of a modern, partly industrial, partly already post-industrial society.'[47] Hence, the nature of the political culture, formed in the past, carries the transition forward in different ways.

[43] Migdal, 1988, p. 207.   [44] Migdal, 1987, p. 427.   [45] Ibid., p. 429.
[46] Hellman.   [47] Elster, Offe and Preuss, pp. 307–308.

Trust and Post-communist Policy Implementation 25

In addition, while the political culture of society is seen to shape state–society relations, other cultural aspects, such as the nature of the religious background, also are seen to be important. For example, in *Making Democracy Work*, Robert Putnam argues that the nature of Catholicism, with the vertical structure of the church, has adverse effects on trusting relations between authority and society. Hence, where religious adherence to Catholicism is less intense, better governance is argued to be possible.[48] Meanwhile, with respect to Eastern Europe, there is a religious divide corresponding roughly between Catholicism, which is more ambivalent about the perception of power, in Central European states such as Poland, on one hand, and Slavic Orthodoxy, which tends to focus more on obedience, in former Soviet Union states such as Russia, on the other, and a mix of both within Ukraine. Differences, then, between the nature of state–society interaction in the two regions might be related to how the two different churches relate to their peoples.

State–Society Relations in Post-communist Poland, Russia and Ukraine

The post-communist transition began with a large disconnect between state and society. In the aftermath of the 1989 and 1991 revolutions, societies across the region shared a deep disillusionment with their bureaucratic states, which were viewed as dishonest and untrustworthy.[49] (At its nadir, the Soviet Union may very well have been, in Geoffrey Hosking's words, the 'Land of Maximum Distrust'.[50]) At a time in which much was required of both state and society to begin the transformation to a market economy and a democracy such inherited distrust of the state on the part of society made the tasks at hand more difficult.

Poland. Juan Linz and Alfred Stepan have described Poland in the 1980s as a very strong case of 'civil society against the state' – a dichotomy that emerged from centuries of struggle between the Polish nation and a foreign-imposed state authority, which became 'a politically useful concept in the opposition period because it allowed a sharp differentiation between "them" (the Moscow-dependent party-state) and "us" (Polish civil society)'.[51] (Similarly, Grzegorz Ekiert titles his book on the communist-era political crises in Poland, Hungary and the Czech

---

[48] Putnam.   [49] Rose-Ackerman, 2004a, p. 2.
[50] In his history of trust, Hosking highlights the Soviet Union during its nadir of the 1930s as the 'Land of Maximum Distrust' (Hosking, p. 9).
[51] Linz and Stepan, p. 270.

26 Taxes and Trust

Republic *The State Against Society*.[52]) In particular, the Catholic Church has been recognized by many as an institutional home for Polish national identity in opposition to the state throughout Poland's long history of foreign occupation – from the 1795–1918 partitioning of Poland by the Austrians, Prussians and Russians through to the Second World War and the post-war communist state.

After 1989, the establishment of a new state and the withdrawal of Soviet forces (and influence) allowed a complete break from this adversarial state–society relationship. However, the appearance of the new Polish state coincided with the initial shock of a severe economic recession that made society wary of state activity. Yet 1992 saw the emergence of economic growth that enabled society to begin to view the state and this new political venture of democracy much more positively. 'Economic factors were thus favourable for democracy to take root, all the more so because they had a positive influence on public opinion', Polish sociologist Lena Kolarska-Bobińska has observed. 'Over time, social acceptance of democratic procedures also increased independent of economic factors.'[53]

Nevertheless, the Polish public began to withdraw from public life as the transition progressed. Bohdan Szklarski has argued that six years after the beginning of the post-communist transition, Polish political culture and citizen perceptions appeared to carry over a 'subject-apathetic' character from the previous system. 'However, the causes of apathy, powerlessness and low efficacy lie more with the feeling of being lost in the complexity of the new reality and in the disappointment with the post-communist elites than in formal or ideological prohibitions than it used to be previously', he has written.[54] For Szklarski, then, the articulation of the general public is constrained by the fact that public policy in the economic arena 'is a product of relationship between two most powerful actors: the state and the unions'.[55]

Yet Kolarska-Bobińska has discovered that Polish society since 1989 'can be dissatisfied with elected elites, but not with the system overall, which allows it to make new choices'.[56] Hence, the inability of Polish society to articulate in a more fulfilling way to political elites regarding public policy issues has not resulted in a poor state–society relationship with respect to general support for the new system or with respect to public confidence in those more directly responsible for governing. Kolarska-Bobińska has even found that increased perception among the public has not resulted automatically in lower approval ratings for those

[52] Ekiert. [53] Kolarska-Bobińska, p. 314.
[54] Szklarski, p. 199. [55] Ibid., p. 206. [56] Kolarska-Bobińska, p. 317.

Trust and Post-communist Policy Implementation 27

in government.[57] In 1999, she observed that while local administration was listed in an opinion as the third most corrupt sector, it was listed as the most trusted level of government, aside from the president. Further, confidence in local government has remained stable and high since 1992. The perceived efficacy of these local state institutions with respect to serving local residents well might mitigate any perceptions of corruption, so that local governments can maintain their legitimacy and can enjoy the confidence of society.[58]

Russia. Throughout the 1990s, state interests in Russia were largely co-opted by societal groups. The nature of the initial economic reforms, especially the large-scale privatization by which a significant amount of property ended up in the hands of those with management or communist party ties, enabled a small minority to maintain privileged relations with the state. Indeed, the 1995 'Loans for Shares' scheme in Russia provides a powerful example of how state interests were so co-opted. That government plan, which called for the auctioning of shares in 29 large enterprises to banks that offered the largest loans, ended up benefiting only the interests behind a small group of Russian banks that oversaw the auctions.[59] Similarly, the manner in which Russian banks were able to funnel money out of the country just before the August 1998 collapse of the ruble so that bank owners benefited at the expense of small depositors also underscores the danger of government ties with concentrated private interests.[60] The irony of Russia's situation is that the application of the neo-liberal agenda with the goal of getting the state out of the marketplace in order to avoid the rent-seeking behaviour of the state actually ended up accomplishing the later.

In reaction to the neo-liberal agenda of the 1990s, Putin has initiated a number of initiatives to curb civil society since his election as president in March 2000. Several of the oligarchs who came to great wealth and influence in the Yeltsin era, some of whom even helped his election, were accused of financial fraud and tax evasion and either were placed in jail or went into self-imposed exile abroad. (According to Dmitri Trenin, about twenty-two people owned roughly 40 per cent of the Russian national economy in 2005.[61]) The state also took control of the television networks, including the only independent national station (NTV). And Putin successfully pushed forward a new law, signed in January 2006, that places significant regulations on the activity and legal status of non-profit organizations, especially those that receive foreign funding. The

---

[57] Ibid., p. 320.   [58] Ibid., pp. 321–322.
[59] Roberts and Sherlock, p. 485.   [60] See, for example, Powell et al.   [61] Trenin, p. 4.

28   Taxes and Trust

creation of a Civic Chamber, tied to the office of the president, also has largely been viewed by analysts as not being a true forum for expression of citizen views on state activity.[62] On the economic side, in 2015, approximately 55 per cent of the economy was in state hands – the largest share in 20 years, with 20 million workers directly employed by the government, equal to 28 per cent of the workforce, up from 22 per cent in 1996.[63]

Most critically, the manner in which elections are carried out throughout Putin's system of 'managed democracy' has dramatically curtailed citizen input into the governing of the state. 'As for the electoral system, it's not that bad. It's worse', Nikolay Petrov argues. 'The centre can legally exclude any candidate. A healthier Russian democracy will not emerge without decentralization and federalism. For now, the lack of meaningful elections has seriously weakened civil society.'[64] In fact, Georgy Bovt, editor of the Russian newsmagazine *Profil'*, has observed that citizens no longer participate in the electoral process at the local level, adding, 'and soon they'll stop voting in federal elections too. People boast about their lack of interest in politics. They don't read the papers. Television programs dealing with politics and social issues have been pulled because of low ratings.'[65] Hence, the lack of political choice and true public debate has led to a lack of interest in politics, evidenced most recently by the record low voter turnout of less than 48 per cent in the September 2016 parliamentary elections.[66]

In his own way, Putin appears to have a different connotation of what a 'civil society' actually is. '[W]hat is more important is a mobilization of the nation before the general threat', Putin said in his first televised address following the Beslan elementary school hostage drama, four days after it began on 1 September 2004. 'Events in other countries prove that terrorists meet the most effective rebuff where they confront not only the power of the state but also an organized and united civil society.'[67] Following the Beslan debacle, Putin did not fire the law enforcement members who were bribed by the terrorists as they passed freely from Chechnya to North Ossetia, but, according to Anders Åslund, opted for sacking the editor-in-chief of the independent newspaper *Izvestiya* 'who had committed the crime of accurate reporting'.[68] In essence, Putin seems to view a constructive 'civil society' solely as an entity to be in step with and channelled by the Kremlin.

[62] For a description of the founding of the Civic Chamber, see McAuley.
[63] Djankov, p. 3.   [64] Petrov, 2005.   [65] Bovt.
[66] Phippen.   [67] Putin.   [68] Åslund, 2005, p. 3.

With respect to political culture, three main arguments have been made in reference to the political culture of Russian society to explain its interactions with the state. First, unquestionably, the greatest applicability of this variable in explaining governance problems has been to the real lack of commitment or desire on the part of the populace to change over to a new economic system in the 1990s. In fact, Russians did not rebel en masse against their Soviet state in 1991 (at least outside of Moscow), but regretted the loss of it, especially in relation to the new one they inherited. Three years after the breakup of the USSR in 1991, 68 per cent of Russians stated in a poll that the dissolution was the wrong decision, while 76 per cent stated that the USSR's demise had affected Russian living standards for the worse.[69] 'Russians during the Soviet era', comments James R. Millar, 'indicated high levels of satisfaction (two-thirds to three-fourths reported being "very satisfied" or "satisfied") with their housing, jobs, access to medical care and higher education, and overall standard of living.'[70] The price liberalization policies initiated in 1992 encountered deep disapproval and scepticism on the part of the population towards the economic transition, which has never really gone away. In contrast, in Poland, the vast majority did not question the collapse of communism.

Second, many analysts have attributed the origins of Russia's state–society unconstructive relations to the fact that Russia is composed, for the most part, of those whose religion is Slavic Orthodoxy rather than Catholicism or Protestantism. Shock therapy architect Jeffrey Sachs has even joined in, recognizing the role that the religious divides among the different forms of Christianity played in the first decade after communism in Eastern Europe.[71]

Linz and Stepan explain that the nature of the three branches of Christianity can impact the type of support given to democratic opposition groups, while carefully recognizing that Orthodox Christianity is not inherently an anti-democratic force. They argue that 'Roman Catholicism as a transnational, hierarchical organization can potentially provide material and doctrinal support to a local Catholic church to help it resist state opposition'.[72] As such, the church could be considered as providing support to 'a more robust and autonomous civil society'. (Interestingly, Putnam's arguments on Catholicism in *Making Democracy Work* also suggest that the vertical nature of the church leads to a 'society versus the state phenomenon'.) Similar arguments could be made with regard to

---

[69] Linz and Stepan, p. 451.   [70] Millar, p. 324.
[71] Sachs, 1999.   [72] Linz and Stepan, p. 453.

30 Taxes and Trust

Protestantism, with its emphasis on individual conscience and its international networks.

'Concerning civil society and resistance to the state, Orthodox Christianity is often (not always) organizationally and doctrinally in a relatively weak position because of what Weber called its "caesaropapist" structure, in which the church is a *national* as opposed to a *transnational* organization', Linz and Stepan continue. 'In caesaropapist churches, the national state normally plays a major role in the national church's finances and appointments. Such a national church is not really a relatively autonomous part of civil society because there is a high degree, in Weber's words, of 'subordination of priestly to secular power'.'[73] Hence, according to this argument, whether the Orthodox Church supports civil society depends upon whether or not the state leaders truly are committed to democracy.

Further, how frequently individuals within a society attend religious services might also account for the nature of state–society relations, regardless of the religion. In 1993, only 16 per cent of Poles stated that they never or rarely went to church, whereas the corresponding figures for Belorussians and Ukrainians were 71 and 60 per cent, respectively.[74] (Figures were not given for Russia, but can be assumed to be similar to those for their post-Soviet Slavic Orthodox neighbours.)

Finally, there is the issue of corruption. 'The real cause [of which] lies in deeply internalized Soviet cultural practices', Vladimir Brovkin has stated. 'Defrauding the state was an accepted practice under the Soviet regime.'[75] As Thomas Graham, Jr., explained in his September 1999 testimony before the US Senate Committee on Foreign Relations, 'corruption has deep roots in the historical conflation of the private and the public in Russia. For most of Russian history, the state was for all practical purposes the property of the Tsar. There was no formal distinction between sovereignty and ownership, between the public sphere and the private sphere. Almost by definition, public positions were exploited for private gain.'[76] Communist Party rule changed little, other than that nominal ownership was transferred from the tsars to the Communist Party, so that state goods were readily available for private gain once the system began to fall apart.[77] Even US Vice President Al Gore, in defence of the US role in the reform of Russia, has attributed the prevalence of corruption in Russia to the 'legacy of communism'.[78] However, such comments do not explain the dramatic explosion of corruption in

---

[73] Ibid., p. 453.　[74] Ibid., p. 246.　[75] Brovkin, p. 24.
[76] Graham.　[77] See Solnick, 1997.　[78] See Elsner.

Trust and Post-communist Policy Implementation 31

the 1990s compared with the decade before – or even the greater growth in corruption that has accelerated under the Putin regime. The level of corruption also has increased significantly in the Putin era, beyond that of the Gorbachev and Yeltsin eras. The Putin administration's own Interior Ministry's investigation committee has stated that they saw an increase of about 13 per cent from 1999 to 2003 in corruption-related crimes. In 2003 alone, crimes of bribery rose nearly 17 per cent, and they were up again by about 28 per cent in the first half of 2004.[79] In 2004, Transparency International (TI) stated that every fifth Russian gives bribes to solve problems and that of the $1 trillion in bribes worldwide, Russia accounts for at least $38 billion.[80] In 2014, Russia ranked 136 out of 175 on TI's Corruption Perceptions Index, equal to Nigeria.[81]

The most recent comprehensive report on corruption from the INDEM Foundation, released in June 2011, found that

- the average bribe grew nearly twofold in five years from US$90 in 2005 to US$176 in 2010;
- the total volume of petty bribery in Russia grew from US$4.6 billion in 2005 to US$5.8 billion, albeit alongside inflation growth of 7–8%; and
- the average amount of a petty bribe (1,817 rubles in 2001; 2,780 rubles in 2005 and 5,285 rubles in 2010) grew faster than inflation, becoming 93 per cent of an average salary in 2010.[82]

Moreover, Russia's own Ministry of Interior relayed in August 2015 that the average bribe in the country nearly doubled, in ruble terms, from around 109,000 rubles (US$3050) in 2014 to 208,000 (US$3400) – startlingly high in any currency.[83] Hence, regardless of how high the numbers go, the general consensus of independent researchers is that despite Putin's many public statements and, most presumably, sincere wishes on curbing corruption, levels of corruption have grown since he became president.

Ukraine. As mentioned above, Ukraine has had a unique combination of oligarch-based, or rather oligarch-backed, politics with a very active civil society, willing to take to the Kyiv's Maidan (Independence) Square twice in less than a decade, demanding that their country become less

---

[79] Nemtsov and Pribylovsky.   [80] Alyakrinskaya.
[81] See, for example, Transparency International at <www.transparency.org/country/# idx99>, accessed 31 July 2015.
[82] Indem Foundation, accessed on 31 July 2015 at <www.indem.ru/en/Projects/ EverydayCorru2010.htm>.
[83] Peleschuk.

32   Taxes and Trust

corrupt and more Western and stable – in other words, in local parlance, 'normal'.

Under Kuchma's presidency, control over society was exercised through 'informal means', or what D'Anieri has labelled 'machine politics' – activities that included the bankrupting of firms owned by opposition elites, the provision of immunity for firms that support the government, and the use of tax laws and fire codes to close opposition media.[84] Such patronage-based politics was structured more through 'machine politics' than 'party politics'.

Three years after the Orange Revolution, in 2008, Freedom House labelled Ukraine as 'free' – the only Commonwealth of Independent States (CIS) country so named. In many ways, the 'free' label was related to the fact that the media in Ukraine had become freer under Yushchenko. Of course, while less controlled, the media were hardly 'independent' in the truest sense, being under the control of various large (oligarchic) business groups.

Both the Orange and EuroMaidan revolutions have been credited with enlarging and making more active Ukraine's civil society due to the prominent role that NGOs and citizens had in both protest-led movements. '[The 2014] election demonstrated', wrote D'Anieri in describing the role of civil society in the first revolution, 'not only that large numbers of Ukrainians were willing to become politically active, but also that they had considerable organizational capacity. Organizing, training and deploying, first, election monitors, and later, protestors, required considerable logistical capacity... Once organized forces got the protests started, hundreds of thousands of citizens quickly joined in.'[85]

Moreover, while participants from all around the country took part in both revolutions, greater participation has been credited to those from western Ukraine. And, indeed, there is a perception that western Ukrainians have played a large part in developing Ukraine's civil society across the whole country, drawing upon their experience from being part of the Austrian Empire. 'Imperfect as they were, the Austrian models of parliamentary democracy and communal organization', writes Serhy Yekelchyk, 'shaped western Ukrainian social life. [Western Ukraine's] experience of political participation in a multinational empire and its successors also strengthened Ukrainian national identity.'[86]

Currently, the post-EuroMaidan reform agenda, according to Olena Tregub, has been pushed from above by three distinct groups – reformers in the government; a professionalized civil society that has even drafted legislation as part of push for reforms in particular sectors; and foreign

[84] D'Anieri, 2011, p. 39.   [85] D'Anieri, 2006, p. 210.   [86] Yekelchyk, p. 20.

donor groups from the West such as the International Monetary Fund, the US Agency for International Development, the World Bank, and the Organization for Economic Co-operation and Development. 'None of them', she states, 'necessarily have the same priorities as Ukrainian society as a whole.'[87] With respect to the current post-EuroMaidan reforms, the activity of the formal civil society, largely consisting of NGOs based in Kyiv that are a product of the now decades of foreign (Western) assistance programs, has been high – evidenced by the formation of a 'Reanimation Package of Reforms' coalition of NGOs that pushes for parliamentary bills, leads protests and monitors reforms, and of a National Anti-Corruption Bureau to investigate high-level graft – but has not been matched by a groundswell of criticism and involvement in national affairs by the general public.[88]

What has been lacking – even post-EuroMaidan – has been an enlarged, spirited intellectual and political debate in society over the future of Ukraine – not just regarding its independence, but as to what type of state and what type of society should develop there. Admittedly, most of the conversation recently has been about the war in the East, whether and how the state should be decentralized and the desired return of Crimea. But, as Tymofei Mylovanov has stated, there has been little intellectual debate among prominent civil society members with regard to where Ukraine is going and how the old regime's void should be filled.[89] Ukraine needs a much more vibrant debate regarding its future direction, what type and flavour of democracy should develop and how the society should interact with the state. Further, while there has been much – and perhaps, surprising – consensus within Ukraine and the Verkhovna Rada regarding the need to push further with reforms and lively discussion as to whether the Yanukovych-era elites should be allowed to work for the state, both within the parliament and in society at large, there has been less of a discussion as to how the state institutions, agencies and bureaucracies should be reformed and made less corrupt.

In essence, most of the state–society literature suggests that governance depends on whether the society can be subordinated to the will of the state or whether society is strong enough to resist or to co-opt the state. The nature of the political culture, the historical legacy and the church in each country can contribute to the degree of independence enjoyed

---

[87] Tregub, p. 90.   [88] Economist, 16 April 2016.
[89] Tymofei Mylovanov, associate professor of Economics at the University of Pittsburgh, spoke at the London School of Economics Ideas event 'Healing Ukraine' in London on 9 March 2015.

by the society in opposition to the state. If such a relatively zero-sum relationship between state and society does account for post-communist Russia's and Ukraine's less successful levels of governance, the question becomes, then, why were the Polish people with the communist-era state, the Polish People's Republic, to a lesser extent than the Russians, and possibly the Ukrainians, were with their Soviet state while the opposite appears to have been the case since the transitions began. Presumably, the natures of the culture, history and church did not change in these societies after 1989 and 1991. Further, if state–society relations, as defined in such a zero-sum approach, account for the significant difference, it must be shown that Polish civil society is somehow more subordinated to the state than in Russia and Ukraine. And, finally, for such a theory to hold, the increased state control at the expense of society in Russia under Putin should make governance even stronger.

On the other hand, healthy state–society relations might well be necessary for good governance, but not in a manner in which an independent civil society is pitted against the state. As suggested by the levels of trust in the state (if not in politicians) in Polish society, trust in the state by society might be the foundation for a constructive (and non-zero-sum) relationship between state and society. Further, repetitive and concerted healthy interactions between state and society may well have benefits for society too, as Samuel Greene has argued. 'As iterations [between state and society] continue', he has written, 'there should ideally emerge a stable pattern of interactions, in which civic and state actors may reasonably judge the effectiveness of one or another course of action; this may be considered the consolidation of civil society.'[90]

As a way to test whether state capacity is a function of state–society relations, I conducted interviews with central and local government bureaucrats, specifically inquiring about which types of social groups, actors in society, businesses and private entrepreneurs are most useful in helping them implement their policy priorities and tasks. In addition, I organized surveys on tax compliance to examine further the nature of relations between state bureaucrats and citizens on the ground.

Theory #3: State Capacity as a Function of the Structure of the State

The third school of thought on state capacity finds its origins in Johnson's *MITI and the Japanese Miracle* and Evans' *Embedded Autonomy*.[91]

---

[90] Greene, 2014, p. 18.   [91] Evans, 1955; Johnson, 1982.

For Evans, it is the state bureaucracies that are both *coherent* and *embedded* in society, through strong ties between the state and the private sector that can make good investment decisions that will yield growth such that otherwise atomized elites will invest.

Indeed, the post-communist institutional design of the new state agencies may account for differences in state capacity. A paradox, or fatal flaw, of the *glasnost* and *perestroika* programs initiated by the last Soviet leader, Mikhail Gorbachev, concerned the fact that the problems that were inherent in the system became more acute once those institutions attempted to start their own reforms from the top down. The process of correcting problems complicated those that existed, in turn threatening the legitimacy of the regime. When a system is based on being hyper-institutionalized along vertical links, as the Soviet Union once was, that same system cannot undergo a complete overhaul of planning and management. Institutions cannot focus on their day-to-day tasks and at the same time restructure themselves by introducing new incentives for those at the bottom and reorganizing the command structure at the top. Ultimately, the Soviet system developed an economic fix requiring a clean break for new institutions to be created.

Phil Roeder, Steven Solnick and Valerie Bunce have offered three different accounts of the collapse of the Soviet Union, each of which places the cause in different aspects of the institutional design of the socialist system.[92] Roeder, in his book *Red Sunset*, has provided a neo-institutionalist approach to the collapse, stating that its cause lay with problems in the Bolshevik constitution – the fundamental rules of the Soviet system. The constitutional order was laid out in such a manner that policymakers built their power on bureaucratic constituencies, while bureaucrats in turn needed the continuing confidence of their patrons to remain in office. The institutionalization of reciprocal accountability and balanced leadership increased the stability of the polity, but it also had a perverse effect – it limited the polity's ability to innovate in policy and to adapt its institutions to social change. Instead, the Bolshevik constitution brought policy dysfunction and institutional stagnation.

Similarly, Solnick, in *Stealing the State*, offers a principal–agent model of Soviet-type bureaucracies, showing that agents were required to continue to abide by the agency contract and to manage institutional assets in the principal's interests, rather than in those of the agent. If an agent violated the contract and this went either unnoticed or unpunished (i.e., assets were not taken away from the agent by the principal), then the agent had appropriated the assets. In an analogy to a 'bank run', the

---

[92] See Bunce, 1999; Roeder, 1993; and Solnick, 1997.

36   Taxes and Trust

state's institutions began to fall apart, triggered by the *perception* that principals could no longer control their resources.

Bunce, in her book *Subversive Institutions*, also has shown how the socialist institutions, by design, divided and weakened the powerful while homogenizing and strengthening the weak interests in society. In the end, socialism deregulated itself over time – a process that became accelerated when the institutions met the international and domestic events of the 1980s. Hence, differences found in organizational charts of post-communist bureaucracies may account for variation in post-communist state capacities.

With respect to Weber's characteristics of bureaucracies, Michael Mann has stated that '*Bureaucratic offices* are organized within departments, each of which is centralized and embodies a functional division of labour; departments are integrated into a single overall administration, also embodying functional division of labour and centralized hierarchy.'[93] Mann also has explained autonomous state power as relating to enhanced territorial-centralization, a concept central to state capacity.[94] In short, for Mann and for Weber, being able to implement certain tasks requires a state structure embodied with a certain amount of autonomy such that fairly consistent rules can be applied without undue and incapacitating interference from outside groups.

Hence, according to this third theory, bureaucratic structures that are designed in a centralized, hierarchical manner to allow an autonomous relationship to the wider society are necessary in order to provide for effective policy outcomes.

The Structure of the State in Post-communist Poland, Russia and Ukraine

The communist political system in East Europe and the Soviet Union essentially blurred the distinction between state administration and the Communist Party bureaucracy. 'The almost complete subordination of economic and social life to the state', writes Jacek Kochanowicz, 'resulted in the growth of a bureaucracy tailored to manage a centrally planned, command economy through an extensive set of administrative agencies.'[95] Since the collapse of communism, states such as Poland, Russia and Ukraine have had to reconstruct their bureaucracies so that the lines between politics and policy implementation are more distinct. 'Unlike countries that must rebuild classical administrations that have collapsed or new nations that have to erect government from scratch', writes Barbara Nunberg, '[Central and East European] countries are in

[93] Mann, 1993, p. 444.   [94] Mann, 1986, p. 135.   [95] Kochanowicz, 1994, p. 213.

Trust and Post-communist Policy Implementation   37

the midst of crafting a set of "unfinished" institutions, which combine aspects of both pre-communist and communist legacies with elements borrowed from abroad and with indigenous innovations developed in response to the exigencies of the transition.'[96]

Poland. On the face of it, Poland inherited a bureaucratic history that is comparable to that of the former Soviet Union with respect to entrenched clientelism and strict hierarchical structure. Throughout Poland's complex bureaucratic history, Nunberg writes with respect to Poland's bureaucratic legacy, 'several characteristics typified the state administration: a rigid and steep bureaucratic hierarchy – that is, many layers of bureaucracy with decisional autonomy only at the top of the command structure; power derived from personal ties and seniority rather than merit; and the prevalence of inflexible rules undermined by clientelism and circumvented by the use of *załatwić* (loosely equivalent to the American slang word "pull.")'[97]

Yet there is some question to what extent such 'inflexible rules' and entrenched clientelism have continued to exist in Polish bureaucracies since 1989. On the one hand, Freedom House's *Nations in Transit 1998* report, for example, stated that corruption is less widespread in Poland than in other post-communist states.[98] On the other hand, despite Poland's advances in significant economic policy areas in the early 1990s, initial reforms such as public administration training and local government administration changes in 1989 and 1990 were not followed up with comprehensive bureaucratic reforms. State administrations held over from the communist era were required to implement the extensive economic programs required in the transition to the new economy. 'The source of most corruption', the Freedom House report does acknowledge, 'is the discretionary power of bureaucrats to issue licenses, conduct inspections, grant waivers, and award contracts.'[99] Only in 1996 was Poland's government able to push through a package of significant administrative and constitutional changes including a new Civil Service law.

More recently, as elaborated in Chapter 3, the PiS government threw out several civil service regulations right after its 2015 electoral win, furthering the notion that Polish bureaucracies are spoils for election winners.[100]

Russia. Despite the changes at the top of the system after the Soviet Collapse, the basic communist employment and administrative practices

---

[96] Nunberg, 1999, p. 3.   [97] Ibid., p. 36.
[98] Karatnycky, Motyl and Graybow, eds., 1998, p. 452.   [99] Ibid., p. 452.
[100] Shekhovtsov, 2016, p. 23; and Economist, 30 April 2016.

38 Taxes and Trust

were left intact throughout most of the 1990s. 'While only 10 per cent of the old-style nomenklatura are still in state or government posts', Freedom House reported in 1998, 'the system suffers from corruption and an acute shortage of modern managers and civil servants.'[101]

In 1995, the Russian State Duma passed the presidential version of a Law on the State Service, which divides public offices into three categories and bans civil servants from simultaneously holding any other employment, except teaching or research jobs. 'Benefiting from exposure to civil service models from abroad and discussions with foreign experts, the legislation made a good start in establishing the essential functions and public service ethos of the civil service corps', writes Nunberg. 'But, the law is not without problems, and serious consideration of amendment or clarification through subsidiary legislation or regulation may be needed to ensure that robust civil service institutions are created and maintained.'[102]

An additional unique feature of the design of Russia's institutional system is its selection of a federalist structure – a system that does not exist in any of the Central and East European states. In the 1990s, the adoption of a federalist system of government accelerated further the decentralization process that is normally associated with democratization.

Meanwhile, Putin has sought to reverse that decentralization trend and strengthen the capacity of the state with alterations in the system of fiscal federalism; the creation of seven federal districts with viceroys subordinated to the Kremlin to oversee the provinces; a reform of the Federation Council, the upper house of parliament, so that it no longer is composed of regional governors; and the appointment of officials with strong allegiance directly to the president rather than to other government institutions. Following the Beslan terrorist attack in 2004, Putin's proposal to nominate regional governors, subject to the approval of regional legislatures, was successfully passed, so that governors were no longer elected from 2005 to 2012, when direct popular gubernatorial elections resumed. Efforts were also undertaken to ensure that state agencies and bureaucracies fell in line with the strict hierarchical system of management. (And, of course, while prime minister in 1999, Putin began the second Chechen war in an effort to curb any regional secessions.) Hence, due to the 'power vertical' function of the Putin system, Russia is governed much more like a unitary state today than it was in the 1990s. And, since Putin's return to the presidency in 2012, Putin has been viewed as strengthening that 'vertical' in the executive branch even further rather than prioritizing economic reform.[103]

---

[101] Karatnycky et al., 1998, p. 496.
[102] Nunberg, 1999, p. 187. [103] Rutland, 2013.

Trust and Post-communist Policy Implementation   39

Ukraine. In many ways, the efforts being undertaken in Ukraine since 2014 are the first major attempts to reform that country's state and administrative structures. Most recently, in December 2015, Ukraine's parliament passed a new law on civil service reform that is most promising, calling for administrative and personnel reforms that are more in line with EU standards in order to root out deeply entrenched corruption.

In 2015, the first full year after the EuroMaidan, the situation with regard to corruption was viewed through Transparency International data as quite severe. Compared with the year before, the average bribe of an official rose from 30,000 to 40,000 Ukrainian hryvnia (albeit falling in US dollar terms, due to the hryvnia's depreciation). In 2015, only 19 per cent of those receiving bribes were in jail, while a tenth of all convicted of bribery were acquitted. Situations also abounded in which the fine for bribes was less than the amount of the bribe itself.[104]

Meanwhile, throughout nearly all of Ukraine's twenty-five-year history up to 2015 as an independent state, the country lacked significant legislation aimed at truly reforming its bureaucracies. As discussed in greater detail in Chapter 3, the process of administrative reform floundered under Kuchma and Yushchenko. In part, this was because the initial constitutional division of powers, drafted in the early 1990s between nationalists and older communists, was consistently up for reconsideration in Ukraine. Part of Ukraine's uniqueness, of course, lies in its hybrid presidential–parliamentary system, which has placed executive power not entirely in the presidency but in the Cabinet of Ministers as well. And Kuchma's presidency was viewed as veering towards moderate authoritarianism, with Yanukovych's presidency doing so much more. As such, amidst bureaucratic interference in the economy and amidst a truly oligarchic system in which oligarchs checked, balanced and stalemated each other as they intervened in politics, the regional governments also lacked power on their own to undertake any significant administrative reforms.

The extent to which the state is well organized and embodied with human and financial resources may well be an explanation for the state capacity outcomes in post-communist Poland, Russia and Ukraine. For this theory to hold, state structure must be shown to be primarily accountable for governance outcomes. Further, the manner in which the state is structured – in a hierarchical manner, similar to that of the former Soviet Union, or in a more Weberian one – must be shown to be of critical significance.

[104] Trebor.

40   Taxes and Trust

To test this hypothesis, I conducted interviews with bureaucrats at different levels of the Polish, Russian and Ukrainian states and examined historical and government documents in order to discern differences in the lines of authority and hierarchical patterns between the relevant policy agencies in the three states.

A Model of State Capacity for the Post-communist States

Despite the enormous contributions that each of the three theories on state capacity described above has made to the field of comparative politics, each has limitations in explaining post-socialist state capacity patterns. The first theory, with state capacity being a function of the development of political institutions such as parties, largely ignores dynamics of societal interaction with the state other than political parties. The second theory, with state capacity being a function of state–society relations, does pick up on such interaction missing in the first theory, but largely views state and society as engaged only in a zero-sum relationship. Finally, the third theory, focusing on state capacity as a function of state structure, is far too exclusively focused on the organization of the state itself. Furthermore, none of these theories highlight history and previous state–society interactions extensively. How the state has treated citizens in the past also is critically important in determining current state activity.

I revise these theories and develop a new model for state capacity. I construct a theory of state capacity for the post-communist states that incorporates some aspects of state–society interactions and relies on most of the state structural arguments. More specifically, my model focuses on the extent to which the state is organized and provided with resources in a Weberian sense and on the manner in which society becomes ready to be a compliant, willing partner in state activity. In focusing on society, the second theory on state capacity would predict that if society and social groups were powerful, one would not see effective implementation of state goals. My theory predicts, instead, that when trust is built up between state and society, society will comply. Rather than acting autonomously, I argue that the state can be effective when it penetrates civil society to complete a task by building and by drawing on trust on the part of society in the state itself.

In a broad sense, the term 'trust' and the term 'legitimacy' can be used interchangeably in this model, but I rely more on the term 'trust', as 'legitimacy' is a bit more government-specific, while 'trust' is more about the state as a whole, irrespective of government and power and focused more on the state apparatus. 'Legitimacy' also conveys notions

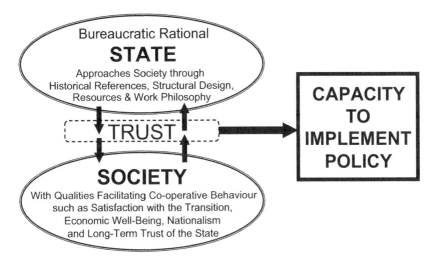

Figure 2.1 A model of state capacity for the post-communist states

related to a government being properly elected or powers being specifically allocated to rulers.

As shown in Figure 2.1, in this new model of state capacity for the post-communist states, state and society interact with each other through trust, enabling policy implementation. With respect to the state, if the question were only about building up resources and improving design, as the state structural theory would predict, then with a good police, army and military, citizens should be frightened and coerced into cooperating with the state. Instead, this new theory predicts that the state can be most effective when it involves civil society by creating citizens' trust in itself. In short, a strong, independent civil society would choose to comply with the state rather than turn away when it trusts the state. Trust is essential. When citizens trust their state, they rely on the state to fulfil its commitments to them.

To be capable of building and drawing upon trust on the part of society, the state must be bureaucratically rational in a Weberian sense. In looking within the bureaucratic rational state itself, as shown in Figure 2.2, there are four principal aspects highlighted here: the use of constructive historical references of state–societal interaction (where available), efficient and well-organized structures, human and technological resources and a productive work philosophy.[105] All of these need to

---

[105] James Q. Wilson has laid out the concept of 'Organizational Culture', similar to my term 'work philosophy' (Wilson, 1989, p. 91).

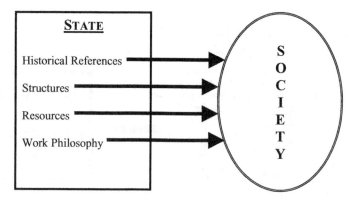

Figure 2.2 Where to find bureaucratic rationalism within a state

be oriented towards society so that trust can be built up. Hence, where attitudes of trust in the state prevail, individuals and groups in society will comply with the state regarding the given policy area, and there will be more successful policy implementation.[106]

In general, trust may be defined, as Piotr Sztompka does, as 'a bet on the future contingent actions of others'.[107] In contrast to certainty, trust, then, reflects one's confidence that others – either individuals or institutions – will act as one would expect they would and prove to be trustworthy.

Before proceeding, it is important to note that *trust in the state* is not synonymous with the other form of trust – *trust in others*, which has been referred more popularly to as *social capital* in the field of political science. Simply put, trusting the state to provide goods and to treat others fairly is not related to citizens' trust in one another. Moreover, cross-country survey research has shown that such trust in the institutions of democratic governance is not correlated with social capital. '[T]here is no strong correlation between political trust, defined as trust in democratic institutions, and social trust', Bo Rothstein has observed. 'This has led many researchers to conclude that there is no convincing

---

[106] Russell Hardin has qualified this notion of trust in the state as being necessary for state legitimacy. 'If Locke's understanding of government is that it must be grounded in trust to be legitimate, then no major government of modern times is likely to be legitimate for more than passing moments', Hardin writes. 'Evidently, however, government need not be legitimate in Locke's sense to survive and even to manage a nation through major difficulties and into prosperity. It may suffice that government not be generally distrusted.' Hardin, 1998, p. 23.

[107] Sztompka, 1998, p. 20, quoted in Rothstein, 2004, p. 18.

Trust and Post-communist Policy Implementation 43

evidence showing that trust in democratic institutions produces social trust and social capital.'[108]

In fact, with respect to post-communist Russia, Alena Ledeneva has observed that there is a lack of trust in newly built institutions, while at the same time there actually are really strong interpersonal ties within Russians' relationships with one another.[109] Hence, a citizen can trust or not trust his or her government, but that type of trust is entirely different from the type of trust he or she has in others. We simply expect different things from other individuals than we do from our state. The ability to trust others on an immediate, close basis is quite different from providing a trusting relationship with the state writ large.

Citizen trust in government falls into two different aspects. 'A trustworthy government', Margaret Levi has written, 'is one that has procedures for making and implementing policy that meet prevailing standards of fairness, and it is a government that is capable of credible commitments.'[110] Hence, first, citizens must be able to trust their government to be a credible supplier of the goods and services that governments promise to provide. Second, citizens must be able to trust their government to respond to them in a manner deemed fair (i.e., consistent with notions of procedural fairness.) Further, trust in the state on the part of citizens also is determined in large part by previous state–society interactions. How the state has treated citizens in the past and how it fulfils its implicit contract with society in the present help determine the capacity, scope and method of current state activity.

Clearly, the trust society has in the state is shaped by macro-historical development and macro-level qualities such as satisfaction with the transition, overall economic wellbeing, nationalism and long-term trust in the state. And these qualities are not static. The focus here, though, is on how government behaviour impacts societal trust – that is, how the state maximizes or minimizes the levels of trust that society has, which will then impact how well state goals are accomplished. The construction and maintenance of such trust is iterative.

Such trust is also two-way. Not only must society trust the state, but the state must also trust society to be responsible and trustworthy in fulfilling its obligations to the state without excessive coercion to do so. (Francis Fukuyama's remark 'a central lesson of tax policy, which is that extraction costs are inversely proportional to the perceived legitimacy of the authority doing the taxing' suggests an inverse relationship between the employment of trust-building, or legitimate, activities and of

---

[108] Rothstein, 2004, pp. 21–22.   [109] Ledeneva, 2004, p. 85.   [110] Levi, 2003, p. 88.

44   Taxes and Trust

coercive ones.[111]) And when citizens trust the state, they are more likely to want to earn the state's trust in them by complying with the state's rules and procedures. 'Reciprocity is the last of the factors that enhance government trustworthiness', Levi comments. 'Citizens are likely to perceive government as reciprocating their trust when they can articulate a return for their compliance and, when they feel they are being treated with respect. When government has a good track record of delivering on its promises, especially those for which its commitments are not credible, citizens are more likely to trust the government and respond with trustworthiness – even in situations where it is extremely difficult to monitor them'.[112] Citizens' trust in their government, therefore, has additional consequences for the state's ability to govern. As Levi continues, such trust of the state 'affects both the level of citizens' tolerance of the regime and their degree of compliance with governmental demands and regulations'.[113] Hence, the erosion of trust in government can lead to increased citizen noncompliance with the state's rules and regulations.

Bureaucracies particularly are critical conduits for shaping the levels of trust between citizens and their government. Agencies entrusted by the state with implementing policy are involved in all aspects of social life from the military, law enforcement and the courts; to taxation and regulation of the economy; to environmental protection and on to social welfare services and public education, to name a few. And such institutions often intervene and interact with citizens as they administer the state's business. 'In most societies, the public also has much more frequent contact with the administrative institutions of democracy than with representative institutions', Rothstein has written. 'This is especially true in the former socialist countries... The policy implementation side of democracy is thus in many ways more central to the welfare of citizens than the representative side.'[114]

Levi likewise suggests that when agents of state institutions need the compliance of citizens to implement their tasks, the government needs to be trustworthy to its citizens in order for its agents to receive such cooperation. 'The hostility of street-level bureaucrats toward clients and of regulators toward the regulated can be extremely counterproductive', Levi writes.[115] Hence, how street-level bureaucrats treat citizens – whether they treat them more like clients, for example – matters with regard to whether or not the state can build up its trust and legitimacy so that it can function properly. To strengthen that legitimacy, then, improving the quality of street-level bureaucracies is critically important.

---

[111] Fukuyama, 2011, p. 343, quoted in Hosking, p. 26.   [112] Levi, 2003, p. 93.
[113] Levi, 2003, p. 88.   [114] Rothstein, 2004, pp. 22–23.   [115] Levi, 2003, p. 93.

To make dramatic increases in the level of citizens' trust in the state generally and in street-level bureaucracies in particular, states need to overhaul their administrative structures so that they are oriented to society. To do this, the very unique character of the 1989 and 1991 transitions from communism provided a tremendous opportunity to re-create radically trust between citizens and state. A transition can allow an overhaul of state–societal trust. The unique fresh-start approach of a transition such as those in 1989 or in 1991 – or even in 2014 in Ukraine – can allow the state to enter into a new relationship with its society in order to improve trust on the part of the society. And simple items, such as the new uniforms donned by Kyiv's new police department in July 2015 (as opposed to those worn by previous law enforcement forces referred to as the city's *militia*), can symbolize a state's desire to make a fresh start with the public.

The equality afforded by communism makes exploiting such an opportunity to increase citizen trust following the transition much more possible than in the aftermath of other revolutions that have taken place across the globe. The populations across the post-communist region, especially in Central and Eastern Europe, as well as in Russia and Ukraine, are highly literate and educated. Nearly all citizens have access to television. This means that they can be clued into issues regarding the state and politics quite readily. And, most critically, there was a fairly equal distribution of income at the start of the transition. This last point means that the new governments and institutions created in the aftermath of communism did not automatically have large groups in society that could not be won over. Because there were not significantly different economic classes, large swaths of society did not have strong economic ties to the old regime. This is in marked contrast, say, to democratic revolutions in Latin America, where the outgoing dictatorship may have had allies among the upper classes, posing difficulties for the new government in trying to earn their trust. If the new post-communist state takes advantage of the revolution's aftermath by treating essentially economically equal citizens fairly and providing them with a significantly higher level of service than the communist regime, it can make giant leaps in gaining society's trust.

With respect to the nature of the transition's aftermath, the 1989 transition in Poland was perceived dramatically differently by the state and the society than the 1991 transitions in Russia and Ukraine, as mentioned above. Poles viewed the transition as allowing the creation of a new state of, by and for Poles, whereas Russians, sitting at the heart of the Soviet empire, were very uncertain as to what the transition would bring for them, both as a nation and as individuals. Meanwhile,

46 Taxes and Trust

Ukrainians were bewildered as to what independence and statehood would truly mean.

Further, Bunce has argued that the transition in Poland was a time of 'extraordinary politics', whereas in other countries such as Russia, the transition was merely a time of 'politics as usual'.[116] The transition in Poland sought to incorporate society – especially as the shock therapy program of Leszek Balcerowicz was slowed down shortly after its introduction so that those who did not benefit from the reforms could be incorporated more gradually into the new economic structures of capitalism. The abrupt nature of the 1989 transition thus allowed recreation of the state–society relationship in Poland. Meanwhile, the transition in Russia was regarded as a political opportunity for a few to benefit. Hence, Poland, which has had great consensus on the meaning of its own revolution in 1989, shows that the unique fresh-start approach of the transition itself can allow the state to enter into a new relationship with society in order to get things done. In contrast, in Russia and Ukraine, for different reasons, what the exact lessons of its 1991 revolutions actually are for state–society relations was mired in significant contention for far too long.

To aid in the recreation of a constructive state–society relationship, legacies of the past can be very beneficial in the building of trust in the present. The use of historical legacies in explaining different postsocialist outcomes has been debated in the literature. As mentioned above, Elster, Offe and Preuss argue that the conditions that appear to favour consolidation across the region are, in the end, political culture and historical legacy. The authors write, 'what matters most is the social and cultural capital and its potential for adjusting the legacies of the past to the requirements of the present'.[117] Thus, modernization – and rejection of the past in contemporary political culture – is the prerequisite to transforming communist industrialization into post-communist market capitalism.

Elster, Offe and Preuss view historical legacies in the post-communist region as bad constraints in the formation of a market economy. 'These non-institutional legacies', they write, 'have resulted in a number of constraints which have severely complicated the transition to capitalism.'[118] However, as Hellman has argued in his 'Winners Take All' essay, some societal constraints in the process of transitioning to a new economy are necessary. A legacy of constructive civil society involvement in public affairs can help provide such constraints. In short, all constraints

[116] Bunce, 2005.
[117] Elster, Offe and Preuss, 1998, pp. 307–308.   [118] Ibid., p. 158.

Trust and Post-communist Policy Implementation 47

associated with the past need not be viewed as backward and liable to stall the reform process, or the ability of the state to accomplish its goals during a time of transition. Past state–society relations can make a positive difference.

Thus, according to this new model for post-communist state capacity, it is not simply the degree to which the state is organized in a rational manner nor how powerful the forces in society are, but the trustworthy nature of the state in the view of society, which reduces any potential resistance. Whereas some maintain that successful governance depends on the extent to which the state has more power over society or on the extent to which society directs the state, I argue that state and society mutually reinforce each other's capacities. The result of their interactions is benign. The state appears to be only as strong as society.

To become a trustworthy and capable partner of society, each post-communist state utilizes historical reference points to transform partly into a version of its former self, modelled on a time when the state is perceived to have been quite capable and legitimate in the view of society. It is the creation of a bureaucratic rational state oriented towards society, the use of constructive historical legacies when available and a focus on healthy citizen–state interactions that enables trust to build up so that state activity will be accomplished more successfully. Trust is at the centre of policy implementation.[119]

Evaluating the Model with the Poland–Russia–Ukraine Tax Comparison

The new model of state capacity for the post-communist states suggests that successful implementation of government policies is an outcome of the trust that builds up as a compliant society interacts with state bureaucracies, which utilize healthy historical references (when possible), are embodied with rational structures and resources and demonstrate a constructive work philosophy among personnel. Hence, when one looks inside a capable state, peeking underneath the 'hood' or 'bonnet' of the state (depending on which side of the Atlantic one is on), the distinct components of rational administrative structures that are all oriented towards citizens should be found. And a compliant society should

---

[119] This model and this book focus on the impact of trust on governance and state capacity. I define and measure trust in the state, but I am not focused especially on explaining this trust or where it comes from. I am theorizing about the impact of trust or a lack of trust, not what causes trust, which can be overdetermined by a variety of historical issues that are too great for proper examination here.

48   Taxes and Trust

be shown to possess the attitudes and the ability necessary to partner with the state.

The rest of this book tests this model in a multi-method approach by focusing on a critical policy area in post-communist Poland, Russia and Ukraine – the bureaucracy's capacity to ensure tax compliance. All three countries are particularly important, as they had to set up new institutions at roughly the same time once the Communist Party's central role in government administration faded away, and today represent distinctly different democratic, authoritarian and transitional regime types. Poland is a case of a country that has successfully accomplished the transition to a market economy and a democratic, legitimate state. Russia, on the other hand, has remained in (or returned to) an authoritarian form of governance. Ukraine, central to the story, is a state very much in continuous transition with failed attempts towards building a rule-of-law state mixed with weak coercion. While some scholars have focused on the formation of tax policies in these countries, no one, to my knowledge, has looked comparatively in a book-length work at the role of the state primarily in implementing such policies in both an East European and a former Soviet context.

I employ both quantitative and qualitative methods to outline the implementation of these two policy areas. With respect to the use of qualitative process tracing, my evidence is based on careful field research, utilizing primary sources such as government documents and evaluations on many different aspects of tax and social welfare policy implementation. I also have undertaken interviews with local and national current and former tax officials at different levels of the state, as well as with private societal actors. While conducting field research in Poland, Russia and Ukraine, I based myself in the capital cities and visited sub-regions within each country to get a better sense of how policy flows from centre to periphery and to gain insight into the extent to which actual goals and structures vary from agency mandates and normative acts. For example, over multiple field trips from 2000 to 2015, I interviewed in each country dozens of officials or former officials who worked in the state tax administrations (STAs) in at least three provinces in each country. I focused my research in Poland particularly on the activities of the Ministry of Finance, the State Tax Revenue Chambers and the provincial tax offices; in Russia on the activities of the Federal Tax Service (formerly, the Ministry of Taxes and Dues), the Russian Academy of State Service and regional tax offices; and in Ukraine on the STA and regional tax offices. In Poland, of particular value to my work were the audit reports on the tax collection agencies going back to the mid-1980s undertaken by the *Najwyższa Izba Kontroli* (Supreme Audit Chamber), a state agency independent of the other government ministries.

Trust and Post-communist Policy Implementation 49

In addition to interviewing bureaucrats, I also interviewed other societal actors – such as law firms, accounting firms, NGOs, state statistical agencies and academics – who directly interacted with or observed the actions of the tax bureaucracies, in some cases since the start of the transition, in order to comprehend better the relationship between the state and society. In many cases, individuals working in law and accounting firms had worked until fairly recently for their country's tax administrations.

With respect to the utilization of quantitative methods, this book also is based on eight unique Taxpayer Compliance Attitudinal Surveys of more than 22,000 Poles, Russians and Ukrainians that I designed and had carried out by leading polling agencies in 2004, 2005, 2010, 2012 and 2015, as well as a Public Officials' Survey in Russia in 2011 that included over 1,000 officials across the country, over 400 of whom worked in the tax administrative structures.

This book shows that Poland governs more effectively than Russia and Ukraine and that it has done so due to a better mix of Weberian bureaucratic rationalism on the part of the state and greater compliance on the part of society. At the same time, the Russian bureaucracy is judged to have made some relatively moderate advances in Weberian terms, while society is judged to remain only partly compliant. Meanwhile, the Ukrainian tax bureaucracy has attempted to follow, albeit to a lesser extent, some of the coercive attributes of the Russian tax system, and has encountered less willingness on the part of the public to be tax compliant.

Regarding the nature of each state and tax collection, I examine specifically how structures and human and technological resources, as well as a work philosophy geared towards interacting with society, all combine to produce levels of bureaucratic rationalism. I also show that the nature of the power employed by the state depends, in part, upon how willing society is to enter into an agreement with the state and to comply with its rules. I demonstrate this in two ways: First, my findings emphasize the role of history – specifically the use by post-communist states and leaders of certain historical reference points to transform partly into a version of their former selves, modelled on an era when the state is perceived to have been quite capable. Second, with respect to more current citizen–state interactions, the provision of poor 'customer service' by bureaucrats is shown to have a negative impact on society, which may very well refuse its obligations to obey the state's laws. Finally, the research also shows, somewhat surprisingly, that political parties – how well they focus attention on state agencies and on the post-communist civil service – need not play a significant role in the building of the capacity of state bureaucracies for effective governance.

50   Taxes and Trust

In many ways, this study is a response to the call of Joseph Schumpeter, who argued for the creation of a new field of 'Fiscal Sociology' through which, in the words of Isaac William Martin, would be created various 'comparative methods to identify causal relationships between the revenue policies of particular states and the characteristics of their environing societies' including 'the relationship between effective tax administration and cultural norms that legitimate taxation'.[120] By focusing on both the tax administrative and social sides of the tax relationship, this study seeks to provide a full picture of how and why taxes are collected.

'In other words', as Venelin Ganev discerns, how tax states operate in this study of 'fiscal sociology' means recognizing that 'the capacity of modern states to tax does not just grow spontaneously as society responds to the imperatives of economic development, and neither it is simply "hardwired" into state bureaucracies by smart and dedicated local politicians or knowledgeable foreign experts. Hence interpretative accounts of the rise of particular tax states should not be reduced to analyses of tax policies, administrative reforms and fiscal measures, because such analyses implicitly presuppose that the mechanisms of taxation are already in place.'[121]

By focusing on both taxpayers and the state, and on how they engage with each other, rather than simply exploring new tax laws and administrative reforms, this study aims to focus on how such a functional infrastructure of the broader, multifaceted process of tax collection can be established. As Martin Daunton has remarked, successful taxation depends on 'institutional procedures and social norms, which sustain cooperative solutions to the problems of collective action, and provide some assurance that fellow taxpayers and the government may be trusted'.[122]

The Transformation of the Post-communist Polish, Russian and Ukrainian State Bureaucracies

In Chapter 3, I undertake a comparative study of the Polish, Russian and Ukrainian bureaucracies by reviewing how the legacies of each country's twentieth-century bureaucratic history were employed after 1989/1991, as well as each state's post-communist attempts at administrative reform to create the state. I also analyze the progress made towards creating a professional civil service in each state, review the growth and character

---

[120] Martin, 2011, p. 731.   [121] Ganev, 2011, p. 246.
[122] Daunton, 2001, pp. 10–11, quoted in Hosking, 2014, p. 98.

of the bureaucracies in the last twenty-five years, and examine general public perceptions of post-communist bureaucrats.

In particular, Poland's institutions are shown to have carried with them legacies from a more distant 'Weberian' bureaucratic past from the interwar years and from a more recent clientelist, hierarchical and patrimonial bureaucratic past from the post-war socialist state. Since 1989, Polish governing agencies have moderated between these pasts and the present without the focused attention of political parties to advance a new civil service. After a Civil Service Act was passed in 1996, its implementation was held captive by a 'spoils mentality' among political parties. Hence, theories highlighting political party institutionalization as being critical for the development of state bureaucracies are shown not to be applicable in the Polish case, as relatively strong state capacity emerged in the post-communist period without strong party development or party impact on bureaucratic reforms.

Whereas the parties have been a stumbling block to civil service reform in post-communist Poland, Russia has slowly attempted to reform the state from within. The lack of comprehensive bureaucratic reform under Yeltsin allowed new, largely economic forces to capture the attention of bureaucrats at the expense of state interests. Since that time, Putin has undertaken a series of attempts at administrative reform in order to create, or rather 'recreate', a tightly centralized Soviet-inspired state with the bureaucracies under greater control, while older bureaucrats who mostly entered government in the Soviet era seem to be replaced by former military and law enforcement personnel rather than by newly trained younger workers.

In many ways, the lack of trust in the Ukrainian government today, although it shares the same administrative history as Russia prior to 1991, has its origins in the lack of professionalism on the part of the Ukrainian state during the 1990s, as it began to undertake a triple transition to create a market-oriented, democratic and independent country without policy goals clearly defined by political leaders. After Ukraine achieved independence in 1991, it appeared as a new state with less coordination and less control than it had under the Soviet Union, largely because the main headquarters of all Soviet-era governing institutions remained in Moscow, and Ukraine thus had to build new ones in Kyiv, the design of which contributed to citizens' feeling less vulnerable to the state's deterrent efforts.[123]

---

[123] Author's interview with Vladimir Dubrovsky, leading research, Centre for Social and Economic Research, Kyiv, 20 October 2005.

52   Taxes and Trust

Thus, each post-communist state employs historical reference points where available in order to transform partly into a version of its former self, patterned after a time when the state is perceived to have functioned well in the eyes of the public.

Creating Post-communist Tax Regimes and Measuring Tax Compliance

Chapter 4 provides greater understanding, context and measurement of the object of study, tax compliance. First, the chapter provides an overview of the history and structure of the tax regimes in Poland, Russia and Ukraine, including a discussion of the foreign tax advice given to each country. At the beginning of the 1990s, Poland, Russia and Ukraine all introduced three new main taxes (the personal income tax, the corporate income tax and the value-added tax), allowing a comparative study, as all three states were required to make dramatic institutional changes in the tax arena at exactly the same time. The type of tax system constructed reflects the type of economy envisaged. For Poland, which followed Western advice more closely than the others, building a modern tax system was all about a modern economy.

At the beginning of the transition to the market economy, all post-socialist states, most of which had copied the Soviet Union's tax system during the communist era, had poorly functioning tax administrations, falling tax revenues and tax compliance problems.[124] Poland, however, was able to reform its tax system sooner than most of the other post-communist states and was able to raise adequate revenues for the state.[125] Poland is shown to be consistently able to extract revenue, though it does fall short of its goals at times and has significant (but not incapacitating) tax arrears. Meanwhile, data from Russia and Ukraine are more erratic, showing tax collection to be poor throughout most of the 1990s, with some improvement after 2000.

In recognition of the limitations of available tax data in providing accurate estimates of tax compliance in countries with a history of barter and high levels of grey sector activity, the Taxpayer Compliance Attitudinal Surveys, conducted by the author, are introduced as a unique measurement of social willingness to comply with paying taxes in the three states. In these surveys from 2004 to 2015, the Polish polity is consistently shown to be far more willing and compliant in its attitude towards

---

[124] Polomski, 1999, p. 6.
[125] See, for example, Martinez-Vazquez and McNab, 2000, p. 290.

Trust and Post-communist Policy Implementation 53

paying taxes than are the Russian and Ukrainian polities, the latter of which had the lowest level of support for obeying the tax laws. The next three chapters examine more closely how state and society interact to ensure tax compliance.

Bureaucratic Rationalism in Poland's, Russia's and Ukraine's Tax Administration

'Quasi-voluntary compliance by citizens, firms, and bureaucrats is possible only where there is a rationalized bureaucracy', Levi and Richard Sherman have written, 'In the absence of the conditions that support such a bureaucracy, the prospects for both development and democracy are reduced.'[126] In addition, human and technological resources and an esprit de corps, or work philosophy, are crucial for the development of the requisite 'rational matter-of-factness' that enables bureaucracies to accomplish their tasks.

Chapter 5 examines specifically how Polish efforts at administrative reform within the tax service have focused on rationalizing the function and duties of tax officials in a Weberian sense. In contrast, Russia's tax bureaucracies lean towards securing their own 'power' over society through their tax collection mechanisms. Meanwhile, the Ukrainian STA has built over the last decade a tax system based on coercion and bureaucratic discretion, leaving Ukrainians to develop less fear and little trust of their state with respect to tax policy administration. Comparison of the experiences of these three countries suggests that 'empowering' bureaucrats so that the state will be 'strengthened' vis-à-vis society may not provide as successful an implementation of state policy in the long run as an approach based upon 'rationalizing' the state.

Thus, the chapter partially confirms theories that argue that state capacity is a function of a well-developed bureaucracy, but also shows that bureaucracies must be greatly oriented towards society to be effective.

Social Compliance with Respect to Paying Taxes

Venelin Ganev has remarked, quoting Levi, that one of the lessons of fiscal sociology 'is that voluntary compliance is remarkably hard to cultivate, and even when cultivated, it is "always tenuous," liable to

---

[126] Levi and Sherman, 1997, p. 318.

54   Taxes and Trust

fluctuations and "extremely difficult to reconstitute."[127] Chapter 6 seeks to understand how a state can cultivate such compliance.

In 2004–2005, I designed a series of unique Taxpayer Compliance Attitudinal Surveys of 7,000 Poles, Russians and Ukrainians regarding their attitudes towards a critical obligation of citizenship. Larger follow-up surveys took place in 2010 in all three countries, and further surveys also took place in Ukraine in 2012 and 2015. The 2004–2005 surveys illustrated that the Polish polity was far more willing and compliant in its attitude towards paying taxes than the Russian and Ukrainian polities were. Unlike Poles, whose attitudes towards tax compliance are related to their trust in the state, and Russians, whose attitudes are related to their fear of the state, Ukrainians, showing the lowest levels of support for obeying the law, reacted to state efforts to increase tax compliance with less fear and little trust. Finally, in the Russian case, comparing the results of the public opinion surveys with those of my 2011 national survey of tax and social welfare officials shows that even within the state itself, attitudes towards Russia's governance model are akin to those of the general public.

Furthermore, with respect to examining the impact of 'customer service' through having had prior bureaucratic interaction in some of the surveys, for those who have contact with the tax bureaucrats, the nature of the conduct of the tax officials can make a critical difference to attitudinal support for complying with tax laws.

At the centre of current upheaval, as well as being located in between the other two cases, Ukraine merits closer attention. Chapter 7 unpacks the case of the transitional Ukraine by region, by religion, by nationality and by language. Regional analysis not only reveals, somewhat surprisingly, that the respondents from the four main regions of the country – East, West, Centre and South (not including Crimea) – do not differ greatly when it comes to overall support for obeying tax laws, but also shows that trust explains Ukrainian motivations (or lack of motivations) for complying across both far eastern and far western parts of the country, with which part of government is trusted varying according to who is in office. Meanwhile, differences based on religion, nationality and language are shown to be relatively minimal.

Taxes and Trust

Focusing on two states that embody competing post-communist models (Poland and Russia) and on a third state attempting to transition from

---

[127] Levi, 1988, pp. 69–70, in Ganev, 2011, p. 249.

one model to the other (Ukraine), this study uniquely emphasizes the building and accumulation of *trust* as the main vehicle for transitioning from a coercive tax state to a modern, legal and legitimate one. Despite the fact that all three countries adopted new tax systems at roughly the same time (1992–1994), embraced the same main tax types and had to set up new governing institutions, Poland, Russia and Ukraine are quite distinct cases. Poland governs more effectively than Russia and Ukraine. It does so because it has a state that is more organized, is embodied with higher-quality resources, and is more citizen- and outward-focused, and has a society that is more capable of being a compliant partner. Polish state and society interact to create a greater degree of trust between them enabling state activity to be accomplished.

Meanwhile, with all of its coercive capacity within its structures, Russia does not govern as much through trust or as effectively as Poland. Russians respond most strongly to a coercive state, which governs at a suboptimal level. At the same time, Ukraine's bureaucracies also seek out to empower the state 'as an end in itself' but do so in a weaker manner than their Russian counterparts, instilling less fear and less trust of their state in Ukrainians. For a state failing to gain the public's trust, reforming street-level bureaucracies such as the tax administration would go a long way towards building a healthier state, capable of implementing its goals for the long run. Trust, therefore, is an intrinsic part of revenue collection.

3 Reinterpreting History to Recreate the State
The Transformation of the Polish, Russian and
Ukrainian State Bureaucracies in the 1990s and Today

In comparison with Russia and Ukraine, Poland's moderately successful
tax bureaucracies are due in great part to a partial level of bureaucratic
rationalism, in the Weberian sense, that existed within its bureaucratic
administration structures. This chapter will show the impact of the historical development of the bureaucracy in the three states and delineate
the recent history of their administrative reforms. The use of Poland's,
Russia's and Ukraine's historical legacies will be analysed, emphasizing
in particular that the inter-war period served as a pre-existing historical template for Poland's later public institutions, whereas the historical
template for Russia's current leadership appears to be the tight hierarchy of the Soviet Union's military and law enforcement organizations.
Meanwhile, Ukraine's lack of vision at the top with respect to the nature
and mission of the transition, economic reform model, constitutional
structure and state–society relationship led to a choice by default of a
continued large and directionless bureaucratic welfare state held over,
with little reform, from the Soviet era. Hence, deciding which historical
reference points to employ for the new post-communist regimes matters
greatly for their bureaucracies today, of which, of course, the countries'
tax administrations compose a large part.

The main focus of this chapter, therefore, is not simply on analyzing
history, per se, but on introducing the notion of 'model transference',
that is, how post-communist states choose which state capacity legacies
from the past to apply in the present to demonstrate to contemporary citizens that their state is effective once again. For this reason, I employ a
mix of historical sources and post-communist media articles for showing
how past administrative legacies are employed by leaders and agencies
after 1989/1991. The origins and initial staffing of the post-communist
tax administrations are more fully developed and compared with the historical bureaucratic traditions in Chapter 5.

For Poland, since 1989, the choice has been full-fledged democratization and the creation of a true civil society. To bolster that choice,
references to the inter-war Polish Second Republic, some of which

56

Reinterpreting History to Recreate the State 57

actually began to appear in the 1980s, have been utilized in recreating state structures and state–society relations. Undoubtedly, the option of joining Europe has provided some incentive. However, Europe became the choice not primarily due to an intense love of neighbours to the West or fundamentally due to a desire to join an elite economic club; rather, the legacy of foreign domination and an authoritarian government led Poland to want democracy and to seek out support for building democratic structures. The choice of Europe was not a difficult one for Poland to make, of course, but it was still a choice.

Moreover, Poland, the largest post-communist country in Central Europe, has sought a more independent role within the European Union since it joined in May 2004 – a role strengthened by large segments of its society that are more conservative, religious and inward-looking at times, but also more oriented towards including the East and tightening up ties across the EU's eastern borders. While Poland today enjoys close economic and political ties with Germany and is well respected within the European Union, a decade ago, when the Law and Justice party was first at the helm, Poland was a bit more inward-looking. Prior to his election as president in the fall of 2005, Lech Kaczynski, then mayor of Warsaw, for example, referred to the former German leader as 'Chancellor Kohl' and declined nearly all opportunities to visit other European states.[1] He also spoke no foreign languages and was known to be suspicious of Germany, Russia and the European Union.[2] In addition, public opinion polls in late 2005 conducted by the CBOS Public Opinion Centre saw 40 per cent of respondents agree with the statement 'a strong man in power can be better than democratic governments'.[3] Hence, with such currents within Polish society, a choice for democratization and Europe was not a given. (And, of course, the return of the Law and Justice party to power in late 2015 has led many in Poland to question the depth of their country's commitment to democracy going forward.) In any case, as we shall see, after 1989, Polish society's and leaders' choice for democracy was aided by the use of historical references that positively impacted the bureaucracy and civil society's oversight of the state, even when more comprehensive civil service reform became lost amidst intense political party competition and debate. Nevertheless, by 2004, nearly half of the civil service corps in Poland was composed of fiscal administration personnel.[4]

For Russia as well, the choice of how to view the past and what aspects of the past to utilize in re-building the post-Soviet state lay in the hands of both the political leadership and society, even while political

[1] Economist, 1 October 2005.   [2] Ash, p. 24.
[3] Ibid.   [4] Ministry of Finance, 2004, p. 48.

58 Taxes and Trust

parties failed to develop successfully, as both Presidents Boris Yeltsin and Vladimir Putin have failed to advance the cause of comprehensive civil service reform, which would cover the tax administration as well. Yeltsin, of course, had a choice in the early 1990s. And he made some radical, unpopular choices, especially with respect to economic reform and shock therapy – decisions made after he and his top advisors took the advice of leading Western and, particularly, American economists. Whether or not to reform the structure of the state and create a civil service was another choice Yeltsin made, de facto, if not outright.

Ukraine and its leaders in the 1990s and early 2000s, in contrast, did not make a specific, concrete choice with respect to which historical legacy to use, especially as, in many respects, given the varied nature of the state's formation, it did not really have a historical reference point on which to model its state other than the late Soviet period. By not voicing a choice, Ukraine fostered entrenched political fighting between its *Verkhovna Rada*, president and oligarchs and declared by default a preference for continuing with a Soviet-inspired bureaucratic and patrimonial welfare state with endemic corruption at all levels.

Selected by a society and its leaders, legacies impact how a state is transformed, how it is organized and what types of work philosophy (esprit de corps) will exist within its structures. The question is not how long legacies from the past last, per se, but which legacies are chosen and when. Nor do legacies matter exclusively because countries have good or bad ones. Rather, what matters most is which legacies leaders and societies choose in constructing the basis of state–society relations.

With respect to Russia, communism is dead, but Soviet-like hierarchical government is on the rise. The popularity of the communists has diminished, but the desire to return to the Soviet era is strong within both society and its leadership. In 1996, within a matter of a couple of months, President Yeltsin saw his popularity go from the single digits to being high enough to carry him into a second term with a landslide defeat of the Communist Party candidate Gennady Zyuganov, largely out of widespread fear of returning to the communist past. On the eve of the vote, Russian state television, the most popular channel, re-broadcast the popular Oscar-award-winning film 'Burnt By the Sun', one of the first films to depict the horrors of the Stalin purges in the 1930s. A few years later, in the early 2000s, with Vladimir Putin in the Kremlin, Moscow's booming and expensive restaurant scene saw an increase in the number of popular Soviet-themed restaurants, which re-kindled warm nostalgia for the country that no longer was. Such imagery was repeated in the propaganda surrounding the 2014 annexation of Crimea.

Memories and legacies do, of course, change, but they do so as a reflection of leaders' and societies' perceptions of the present. For Russia, the Soviet era meant one thing for Yeltsin and Russian society in the early to mid-1990s, but after the turmoil of the Yeltsin era – a decade that saw a great distortion of wealth amidst an impoverishment that greatly dwarfed that of America's Great Depression, a brewing conflict in Chechnya and the loss of empire and geopolitical status, among other things – Putin and the Putin-era society began to view the Soviet era differently.

Poland's Pre-1989 Administrative Legacies

On the eve of the transition in 1989, Poland's administrative institutions carried the dual legacies of a more distant 'Weberian' bureaucratic past from the Second Republic (1918–1939) and a more recent clientelist, strictly hierarchical and patrimonial bureaucratic past from the Polish People's Republic (1946–1989). Some aspects of the Polish inter-war Weberian bureaucracy were preserved throughout the post-World War II era, or at least began to reappear in the last decade of communism, while other aspects of the past were seized upon by Polish society and its leaders at the start of the transition.

The origins of state-building in Poland did not occur under favourable conditions and were accompanied by a society that stood in opposition to the state. Even as the modern state, with a new professional bureaucracy and modern tax organs, began to be built in nineteenth-century Poland – partitioned by Austria, Prussia and Russia throughout the century – a legacy of unhealthy state–society relations, not entirely unlike those in Russia, was formed. In particular, the state bureaucracy in the part of Poland controlled by Russia was the most corrupt.[5] 'In the period of rising national sentiment during the nineteenth century, the Poles were thus socialized in three different state traditions', writes Jacek Kochanowicz. 'The Polish elite increasingly perceived the state as a foreign and alien power, because both Russia and Prussia engaged, in the second half of the nineteenth century, in intensive policies of Russification and Germanisation of the Polish population ... [T]he Poles under Russian rule developed anti-state ideologies as anti-state conspiracies.'[6] While the state, of course, was synonymous with foreign power, the challenge presented by any state following the partition of Poland lay not just in unifying the Polish people, but also in making the right choices

---

[5] Kochanowicz, 2004, p. 77.   [6] Ibid.

60   Taxes and Trust

regarding which bureaucratic aspects to retain from the nineteenth century so that an unhealthy state–society legacy could be overcome.

After 120 years of partitions by three neighbouring states, the Polish government in 1918 based its state administration on the French model. However, the new administration was constructed by those who lived in the former Austrian partition, because only in Austria were Poles given the opportunity to advance in the state service.[7] '[T]he Galician and Austro-Hungarian sector of Poland in the South and the Polish interwar government of 1918–1939 featured a highly rationalized public bureaucracy and legal code', Jarosław Piekalkiewicz and Christopher Hamilton have commented on the period. '[T]he interwar years introduced in Poland some earlier and important changes in law, social legislation, education, bureaucracy, and economic development, which survived not only the Second World War but also extended through the period of Communist-party rule up to the present day.'[8] Moreover, in a prelude to the communist era, the government's organization was characterized by centralization and 'a hierarchical subordination of the lower echelons', with civil servants responsible only to their superiors.[9]

Legislatively, much was done in the interwar period to provide a rational, Weberian bureaucracy. In 1922, Poland adopted one of the first acts in Europe that established a civil service, which was liquidated in 1939.[10] That act codified the rights and obligations of bureaucrats as well as special privileges to attract highly qualified personnel such as holidays and pensions.[11] Moreover, a resolution of the Cabinet of Ministers in September 1928 brought the appointment of a Commission for the Improvement of the Public Administration.[12] Such legislation and directives helped establish a rational, Weberian bureaucracy in the interwar period, as was described in 1992 by Zdzisław Chmielewski:

[I]t appears that on the verge of the thirties there came into existence in Poland . . . the possibility of the processing of programs on the rationalization of administrative work. From a Weberian, theoretical model of the bureaucracy, both the principle of organizational construction, and also the principle of employment and labour of people in the bureaucratic institution gradually found application. A functional continuity provided by the behaviour of impersonal forms of orderliness among other things was successfully guaranteed to the direction of Polish administrative offices. The exact separation of the organizational and authoritative positions of work was pursued. The cooperation between the supervisor and the subordinate took place according to a delineated

---

[7] Kamiński, 22 March 1999; and Hamilton and Roszkowski, pp. 136–137.
[8] Hamilton and Roszkowski, pp. 138 and 139.   [9] Rudzinski, p. 2.
[10] Office of Civil Service, 2000, p. 4.   [11] Chmielewski, p. 128.   [12] Ibid., p. 130.

Reinterpreting History to Recreate the State 61

agreement from above, which specified unambiguous salary caps and the criteria for professional promotion, as well as heralded systematic meritocratic control.

The public administration, having strong support from the side of central political factors, became all the more an efficient and active executor of the will of the state. The instructional role with respect to the citizen, however, in a way fell to the bureaucratic organization. [The bureaucracy] was convinced that only by the adaptation to the institutionalized and normalized forms of behaviour would it be possible to bring mutual advantages: to make it easier for the citizen to have contact with the bureaucratic office as well as [to make it easier] for the office to carry out adroitly their tasks. The bureaucracy tried to remain a positive, constructive instrument of informing public affairs in Poland.[13]

Undoubtedly, such efforts at rationalizing the bureaucracy in the interwar period provided post-communist Poland with a pre-existing template, a historical foundation for re-creating state structures in the 1990s. For example, the establishment of a Supreme Administrative Tribunal (*Najwyższy Trybunał Administracyjny*) in 1932 is mirrored by the 1990s' Chief Administrative Court (*Naczelny Sąd Administracyjny*, or NSA.) The Supreme Administrative Tribunal, following the Austrian example, was an independent court, to which citizen appeals regarding the infringement of legal rights by an administrative decision could be made.[14]

After the war, however, the communist era broke with these traditions to some extent, beginning with the dissolution of the civil service in 1946. While not ineffective or unprofessional, the bureaucracy under communism in Poland was politicized, with the state largely subordinate to the party. This politicized structure incapacitated bureaucrats from making decisions independently. 'The Communist Party-state was bureaucratic in nature, but this kind of bureaucracy was very remote from the Weberian model', states Kochanowicz. 'Its apparatus was not the subject of clear rules, but rather the rules were constantly redefined according to political expediency. In recruiting its staff, the party-state paid more attention to political loyalty than to professional abilities.'[15]

Despite this, the situation in Poland was not as bad as elsewhere in Eastern Europe, allowing greater autonomy of the state administration from the party and the promotion of a number of non-party specialists to posts of responsibility.[16] The formation of a Weberian-style bureaucracy prior to World War II had to have an impact to some extent on the mentality and organizational culture within the post-war administration.

[13] Ibid., p. 131. Translation from the Polish by the author. [14] Rudzinski, p. 22.
[15] Kochanowicz, 2004, p. 78. [16] Wiatr, pp. 154–155.

62   Taxes and Trust

Indeed, as Claudia Torres-Bartyzel and Grazyna Kacprowicz remark, 'Until 1989 the dominating perception of the public service in general was based on classical Weberian principles.'[17]

Within the communist system, the functional equivalent of civil servants was developed. '[Bureaucrats] were specialists with higher education and years of professional experience, often very well prepared for their jobs and motivated in a way not very different from that of their colleagues in Western democracies', writes Jerzy Wiatr. 'Within the constraints of the system, they tried their best to make the machinery of the government work.'[18] Studies on the prestige of different professions in Poland undertaken since the 1970s also confirm the high status given to mid-level bureaucrats.[19]

Moreover, Poland differs from the other post-communist countries in that it was the only state with a defined civil service system under the previous regime.[20] The State Officials Act of 16 September 1982, provided some stabilization regarding the status of bureaucrats by defining the basic regulations for bureaucrats' work and responsibilities and granting tenure to some.[21] While not allowing the development of a fully neutral civil service, the 1982 legislation, designed for a centrally planned socio-economic system, was an antecedent of the attempts at creating a true civil service in the post-communist period and is still in force in the 1990s, coexisting with more recent civil service legislation.[22] Further, many bureaucrats who were hired and trained under the State Officials Act remained in the same jobs at the start of the democratic transition. Hence, in the communist period, a certain level of bureaucratic development was achieved that was sustainable in the post-communist era.

In addition to the civil service reforms, other important administrative changes were made in the communist era that were beneficial to the start of the post-communist transition. 'Although the constitutional bases for reforms were firmly established in the early phases of the transition', Barbara Nunberg has observed with respect to Poland, 'reforms in the machinery of government were modest and, for the most part, built on institutional changes already introduced before the fall of the communist regime.'[23] Within the last decade of the socialist regime, a number of institutional structures were either amended or introduced in order 'to increase government accountability without dismantling the one-party state'.[24] Given that the 1980s began in Poland with the arrival

---

[17] Torres-Bartyzel and Kacprowicz, p. 168.   [18] Wiatr, p. 154.
[19] Torres-Bartyzel and Kacprowicz, p. 172.   [20] Ibid., p. 159.
[21] Office of Civil Service, 2000, p. 5.   [22] Torres-Bartyzel and Kacprowicz, p. 176.
[23] Nunberg, p. 47.   [24] Rose-Ackerman, 2004b, p. 13.

Reinterpreting History to Recreate the State 63

of the Solidarity movement and the establishment of martial law, as society stood ready to oppose the state, no doubt the efforts to amend or re-introduce new governing institutions were undertaken as a reaction to the public.

In 1987, for example, the office of ombudsman was established. At the same time, while audits of public finances in Poland date back to the Constitution of 1791, the Supreme Audit Chamber (*Najwyższa Izba Kontroli*, or NIK) had been established first in 1918 as a separate institution charged with the task of auditing implementation of the budget and the finances of the government and its administration. Re-established in 1949, it was dissolved in 1952 and brought back to be accountable directly to the government in 1957. Then, in 1980, NIK, which monitors the government's activity, was subordinated instead to the parliament, the Sejm, for greater independence. In 1994, a new statute strengthened and revived NIK's organization and tasks.[25]

Further, whereas interwar Poland had in force the Decree on Administrative Procedure of the President of the Republic, introduced in 1928, the communist regime only adopted an administrative code in 1960, which did not provide for separate administrative courts. In 1980, however, that code was amended to introduce Poland's first administrative court since World War II, the previously mentioned NSA.[26] It provided an avenue for citizens to have their conflicts with the public administration resolved. In 1995, a new act further codified the organization's structure, scope of jurisdiction and procedures.[27] In addition, a Constitutional Tribunal was created in 1989.[28] In pursuit of legitimacy before their society, the Polish communists in the last decade tapped into the legacies of Poland's previous experiences with democracy.

Thus, as in Mikhail Gorbachev's Russia, the leadership in 1980s Poland actually made several decisions that impacted how the state would relate to the society in their current decade and in the one following. Much more was happening in the 1980s in both countries than just a prelude to a revolution and the demise of communism. As we shall see next, despite all of the changes in the government coalitions and the lack of constructive administrative reform in the first half of the 1990s, a capable bureaucracy existed in Poland in part due to structures created and amended in the 1980s, with the aid of the inter-war legacy, and in part to the decisions after 1989 to retain those structures and build upon them, also with the aid of the same legacy.

---

[25] Galligan and Smilov, pp. 221–222.   [26] Ibid., p. 212.
[27] Ibid., pp. 214–215.   [28] Rose-Ackerman, 2004b, p. 13.

64   Taxes and Trust

Poland's Post-communist Administrative History

Polish communist-era dissident Adam Michnik, who founded the immensely successful *Gazeta Wyborcza* daily newspaper in the early 1990s and remains its editor-in-chief, argues that there were two processes of state-building after 1989. First, Poland sought to figure out how to adjust the state institutions that existed to democracy, to a state of law. And, second, Poland looked out to the legal institutions in Europe because what was practiced in Europe mattered. Once the change came – a big surprise to all Poles – the desire to get out of the Warsaw Pact and into the EU and NATO was very clear. Joining the European Union was 'not a love marriage, but a marriage of convenience'.[29]

The long legacy of foreign domination obviously impacted the choice for Polish society. In addition, the legacies from the more distant past, already utilized to some extent in the last decade of the Polish People's Republic, were called upon to help build these new democratic institutions. Yet the process of creating a civil service in the post-communist period was not as swift as that at the beginning of the Second Republic, when the need for a new public administration was broadly recognized. The highly fragmented and ideologically fluid party system of the early 1990s did not allow consensus on administrative reforms.[30]

Immediately after 1989, the transformation of the Polish economy and the Balcerowicz plan began without any changes in the Polish public sector, which was based on a uniform, centralized budget system.[31] At the beginning of the transition, if there was a recognized choice between hiring new bureaucrats and keeping the old laws, on one hand, and passing new laws to be implemented by old bureaucrats, on the other, Polish politicians chose the latter.

Despite Poland's advances in significant economic policy areas in the early 1990s, initial reforms such as public administration training and local government administration changes in 1989 and 1990 were not followed up with comprehensive reforms of the bureaucracies. State administrations, the Ministry of Finance and its tax organs included, were held over from the communist era and were required to implement the extensive economic programs that were part of the transition to the new economy. The whole process of '[d]eparting from the principle of centralized administration, complemented with the adoption of a multi-party system and the development of the local and professional

---

[29] Conversation with Adam Michnik during Professor Jan Gross' graduate seminar, 'History 563 – 20th Century European History: Totalitarian Regimes', Princeton University, Princeton, NJ, 15 March 2006.
[30] Nunberg and Barbone, p. 8.   [31] Malinowska et al., p. 34.

Reinterpreting History to Recreate the State

self-governmental structures', states the Office of the Civil Service, 'put employees of the Polish public administration in a new situation, marked by contradictions and conflicts, which in most cases they were unprepared to handle'.[32] In other words, with the exception of the entry of a number of young professionals into the system,[33] changes occurred all around the main administrative bureaucrats, who themselves saw few fundamental changes within their own structures.

Poland was slower than other post-communist states, such as Hungary and the Baltic states, in the adoption of civil service reforms.[34] In spite of this fact, successive Polish governments from the first cabinet in August 1989 onwards did demonstrate some concern and a will to reform the state administration, even if there was, as Ezra Suleiman describes, 'a lack of political consensus on the shape of the reform'. In his first speech to the Sejm as prime minister, Jan Olszewski – Poland's third post-1989 prime minister in as many years – said in 1991, 'Our state is threatened by paralysis caused by disorder in public administration and its inability to carry out its basic tasks.'[35]

From the beginning of the transition, there was a dialogue on making the administration free from political influence, evening out the political factor and making it a merit-based system in terms of function.[36] In order to meet the goals of a merit-based system, the State School of Public Administration (*Krajowa Szkola Administracji Publicznej*) was established in the early 1990s to train highly academically qualified students in a complete civil service program. Additional goals were the improvement of the efficiency of the state administration, the decentralization of the public administration, modernization of the administration through tools such as computers and a new system of allocating public funds.[37]

In October 1992, after three years of preparation, the position of the Government Plenipotentiary in Charge of Public Administration Reform finally was created in order to help lay the groundwork for a Law on Civil Service.[38] A first draft of the Civil Service Act was presented by the first government in 1991, followed by the presentation of a second draft accompanied by other administrative reform bills in 1993 by the centre-right coalition government of Hanna Suchocka with encouragement from the European Union.[39] (The EU Poland and Hungary Assistance for the Restructuring of the Economy (PHARE) program, the joint PHARE/Organisation for Economic Co-operation and Development (OECD) Support for Improvement in Governance and

---

[32] Office of Civil Service, 2000, p. 5.   [33] Torres-Bartyzel and Kacprowicz, p. 168.
[34] Goetz, p. 1035.   [35] Suleiman, p. 298.   [36] Kamiński, 22 March 1999.
[37] Wiatr, p. 156.   [38] Suleiman, p. 298.   [39] Mularczyk.

66   Taxes and Trust

Management (SIGMA) program and the British Know How Fund provided financial assistance and advice on civil service reform.[40]) However, that cabinet did not last long enough to push the bills through parliament, and there was never even a vote. By September 1994, the new team that emerged after parliamentary elections had developed yet another draft, which was in the parliament's hands for an additional two years before being passed as part of a package of administrative and constitutional reforms in 1996. In addition to a flexible Civil Service Law, 'the adopted package consisted of a reform of the central administration designed to shift governmental structures and relationships to reinforce the changes in the role of ministries and central decision-making organs that had taken place in the transition'.[41] Under the new law, the prime minister appointed 24 politicians, civil servants, and academics to a new Civil Service Council, which came into being in 1997.

While the 1996 law had established some foundations for the civil service, further issues and amendments were raised. In December 1998, a new Law of the Civil Service was voted in by the Sejm, which came into force in January 1999 and which was superseded by an even newer law in August 1999. In January 2000, the Civil Service Council began to develop a true civil service corps with a new competitive recruitment system, unified training procedures, a modified salary and promotion framework, greater transparency and constructive performance incentives.[42] 'The public employment system', Suleiman comments with respect to Poland and to the Czech Republic and Hungary, 'is considered a career system, and officials are rated on the basis of their professional performance.'[43] In particular, vacancy positions must be advertised and new recruits are given a contract for no more than three years as part of an evaluation phase.[44] More senior positions are filled through a competition and specially appointed competition teams are managed by the Head of the Civil Service.[45] Hence, the establishment of a new civil service took nearly a decade in Poland, but it was created.

The implementation of the Civil Service Act, however, has been an example of how competition within a new democracy's developing political party system can become extended to the bureaucracies. There has been a gap between legislative intent and personnel policy practice. In the late 1990s, upon assuming power, each governing coalition redrafted the Civil Service Act to ensure that bureaucrats loyal to it were appointed, subjecting the civil service to a sort of 'spoils' system. Thus,

---

[40] Torres-Bartyzel and Kacprowicz, p. 175.   [41] Nunberg and Barbone, p. 15.
[42] Suleiman, pp. 298–299; and Manning and Parison, p. 147.   [43] Suleiman, p. 302.
[44] Manning and Parison, p. 148.   [45] Ibid., p. 148.

Reinterpreting History to Recreate the State 67

the goal of allowing the new civil service to be truly independent has never been completely reached. In 1997, for example, the implementation of the Civil Service Act soon was stopped, as the outgoing left-wing Democratic Left Alliance (SLD)–Polish Peasant Party (PSL) government of the 1993–1997 period tried to fill civil service posts with many of its own supporters, terminating the implementation of the 1996 reforms.

Hence, while the public has shown little interest and has not been well informed about administrative reforms,[46] the civil service has been held captive by a spoils mentality that pervaded parties on both sides of the political spectrum. The goal has been to build up a loyal corps of civil servants, judged more on their ideological loyalty than on their professional qualifications. 'Although the Civil Service is in principle neutral, merit-based and permanent, significant hiring and firing happens at the beginning of the political term', Helen Sutch, Michał Dybula, Ryszard Jerzy Petru, Jacek Wojciechowicz and Marcin Przybyla have concluded. 'Politically motivated appointments for crucial posts usually follow the nomination of a minister. At the end of the ministerial term, political figures and senior public servants, whose nominations were mainly political, can be seen trying to find soft landings in the management of the state-controlled enterprises or in the private sector.'[47]

The ruling coalitions have not cooperated with parliamentary minorities to ensure that the system is not politicized. Upon assuming power in 1997, the right-wing Electoral Action Solidarity (AWS)–Freedom Union (UW) coalition, for example, criticized its SLD–PSL predecessors for counting work in the communist party apparatus as valuable experience for prospective civil servants.[48] The 1996 Civil Service Act had required that top officials have seven years' experience, including four years in managerial posts, which led critics to accuse the former communist SLD of preventing those who were not part of the pre-1989 communist system from matriculating to the civil service.[49] In 1998, the new government amended the civil service law to include stronger requirements and enabled more graduates from the National School of Public Administration) to get jobs, rather than public servants from the pre-1989 era.[50] At the end of the AWS–UW government in 2001, the civil service was said to have been dominated by those appointed on the basis of their political contacts rather than their qualifications.[51]

---

[46] Wiatr, p. 160.   [47] Manning and Parison, p. 146.
[48] Polish News Bulletin, 11 December 1997.   [49] Reuters, 17 July 1996.
[50] Mularczyk.   [51] Polish News Bulletin, 24 October 2002.

68 Taxes and Trust

However, in December 2001, with the SLD and PSL parties back in power, the Sejm passed an amendment enabling state institution heads to staff top administration posts with people from outside the civil service, in effect suspending the Civil Service Act.[52] Because open competitions for positions take too long, some governments also switched to directly appointing people.[53] Civic Platform (PO) deputy Jan Rokita stated at the time that the change would enable the prime minister to fill some 40,000 positions as he preferred.[54] Meanwhile, at the end of 2001, under the new SLD–PSL government, 500 of the 1,400 government administrative positions were new political appointees, while 660 of the 1,400 in the highest posts had been changed – a process, noted *Polityka* newsmagazine's Janina Paradowska, that was much faster and more radical than under the previous government.[55] Moreover, graduates of the National School of Public Administration in recent years have been unable to find jobs for which they are trained, and the school itself has become the target of political attacks.[56]

Hence, progress along the path towards an independent, professional civil service in Poland has yet to catch up to the initial legislative goals. And these setbacks have brought the displeasure of the European Commission, which in 2002 regarded the civil service as one of the weakest aspects of the new Poland.[57] While the European Union may provide some incentives, aid and advice (on a greater scale than elsewhere), how Poland orients its civil service and which direction it decides to take appear to be more directly internal matters.

Reaction to these central public administration laws within Poland has been mixed, as local academics and the public at large have commented that, while the laws were intended to reduce the number of ministries, in fact the bureaucracies have pretty much grown everywhere, that employment has not been reduced and that operations have not changed. A basic reason for the problems of the bureaucracy is, according to Antoni Kamiński, precisely the 'weakness of the political leadership, which manifests itself in the lack of clearly defined priorities and decisive will for solving key problems of the state'.[58]

A report released by the state's separate auditing body NIK in 2005 provided an especially scathing analysis of how government ministers and provincial (*voivod*) governors recruited public servants to compose

---

[52] *Polish News Bulletin*, 19 December 2001.   [53] *Polish News Bulletin*, 24 October 2002.
[54] *Polish News Bulletin*, 19 December 2001.   [55] *Polish News Bulletin*, 24 October 2002.
[56] Mularczyk; and *Polish News Bulletin*, 24 October 2002.
[57] *Polish News Bulletin*, 24 October 2002.
[58] Kamiński, 22 March 1999. Translation from the Polish by the author.

Reinterpreting History to Recreate the State 69

the civil service corps from 2000 to 2004. The report found that more than 65 per cent of high-ranking public officials were appointed to their posts without having gone through any competitive procedures and, as a result, earned even more than ministers as government office heads froze vacancies in place in order to fund pay raises or bonuses for existing staff.[59] NIK also observed that Civil Service Chief Jan Pastwa was unable to influence governing politicians to change the situation – a point on which Pastwa concurred regrettably:

Being myself responsible for the Polish Civil Service, I would prefer it if I could disagree with the NIK report. Unfortunately, its very first sentence is painfully true. NIK, basing on data gathered during an extensive audit, states conclusions that for obvious reasons the chief of the Civil Service cannot have stated ... I am particularly regretful about the efforts that have not yielded results as a result of the inertia, and sometimes blockading, that is purposefully caused within the administration and the lack of political will and responsibility. Short-sightedness and particularism in seeking short-term benefits have most frequently gained the upper hand. For many politicians and the public officials who are subservient to them, personnel manipulations still represent the simplest instrument for 'doing' politics. The NIK report shows, for the first time so well, another shortcoming of the Polish governmental administration – a system of financing salaries and training that teeters on the edge of common sense, or indeed the lack of any system.[60]

Hence, despite the relatively successful institutionalization of the political party structure within Poland, the lack of leadership on the issue of state administration appears to have been a hindrance, suggesting that what bureaucratic successes the Polish civil service has achieved may not be attributable to the top of the governmental structure. And the respect for NIK is clearly shown in the statement of the civil service head.

Into the 2000s, there still has been a lack of consensus politically on the civil service. Jolanta Itrich-Drabarek has summarized quite well how and why Polish politicians have exerted strong influence over the civil service system since 1989:

[T]he issue of civil service has always remained the subject of political bargaining. Solutions designed for the benefit of specific governments would often last no more than the government that spawned them. Even when the given piece of legislation still formally remained in force, it would be modified by way of frequent amendments by subsequent governments, losing its original shape and meaning ... [R]egardless of the particular organizational solutions, statements advocating the abolishment of the tradition of the system of spoils as well as the practices resulting with public administration becoming increasingly

---

[59] BBC Monitoring International Reports, 15 April 2005. [60] Ibid.

70   Taxes and Trust

politicized have always continued to appear in the course of the debate concerning the future of the Polish civil service.[61]

Indeed, as a fourth new Civil Service Act was adopted in November 2008 following the 2007 election win of Civic Platform over the ruling Law and Justice party, political party competition was rife. 'Polish civil service laws appear to have a proprietary nature', Angelica Ghindar has written, 'a particular civil service law is "our" civil service law, or "their" civil service law, depending on whether one takes the perspective of the current government or its political opposition.'[62] And, as Polish political parties have had differing views on whether 'open competitions' should be held for high-level positions, the 2008 Civil Service Act reinstated senior positions in the civil service and weakened the position of a reinstated Head of the Civil Service and of an already less than transparent recruitment system.[63]

More recently, in its first few days in office following its October 2015 parliamentary electoral win, the Law and Justice government threw out civil service regulations, such as those that required competitions for senior jobs and required appointees not to have belonged to a political party in the previous five years, in order to hire party members for leadership roles, including heads of state companies, which has led, along with the government's politicization of public media, to mass demonstrations across the country.[64] The latest wave of replacement and demotion of professional officials within Warsaw's ministries has contributed to the lack of an independent civil service culture and promoted the view that bureaucracies are to succumb to a system of spoils for election winners, or even to a sort of 'politics of revenge'.[65]

Moreover, since the beginning of the transition, society has viewed corruption as a greater problem. In 1991, 33 per cent labelled corruption as a 'very large' problem, with 38 per cent calling it a 'rather large' problem; ten years later, in 2001, the corresponding figures were 68 and 25 per cent, respectively.[66] Similarly, in 1995, 42 per cent surveyed believed that many high state bureaucrats derived unjustified benefits from their public functions, and 43 per cent stated that they believed there are some, but not many such bureaucrats, whereas in 2001, the corresponding figures were 70 and 22 per cent, indicating a sizeable shift.[67]

With respect to corruption within the post-communist Polish state, Timothy Garton Ash has remarked that Prime Minister Kazimierz Marcinkiewicz 'has talked darkly of a "Bermuda quadrangle" of corrupt

---

[61] Itrich-Drabarek, pp. 36–37.   [62] Ghindar, p. 13.
[63] Itrich-Drabarek, pp. 36–37.   [64] Shekhovtsov, p. 23; and Economist, 30 April 2016.
[65] Dempsey.   [66] CBOS, August 2001.   [67] Ibid.

politicians, secret police operators, businesspeople, and criminals.'[68] In the early 2000s, there were several 'money-for-influence' scandals, of which the most famous, perhaps, was 'Rywingate', in which a film producer sought a U.S.$17.5 million bribe from a business group in exchange for promising changes to be made to a mass media law.

In presenting a progress report on anti-corruption measures to the Sejm in 2003, Interior Minister Krzysztof Janik said that corruption in Poland is more the rule than an exception.[69] Indeed, in the 2010 Poland Taxpayer Compliance Attitudinal Survey (see Question #59 in Appendix I), only 27 per cent of Poles stated that their government does a good job in fighting corruption, while 46 per cent stated that the government does a poor job and 15 per cent stated that the government does not fight corruption at all.

Meanwhile, a 2012 report prepared jointly by the Institute of Public Affairs and Transparency International claimed that corruption 'is no longer a phenomenon of a systemic nature as it used to be in mid 1990s', due in some great part to the role of Poland's NIK.[70] Poland thus appears to have experienced systemic levels of corruption, like Russia and Ukraine, but has been able to move beyond them towards building a more transparent state. In 2014, the European Commission released a report on corruption in Poland, which highlighted local business concerns over corruption in obtaining access to public services and in the public procurement tender process and citizen concerns over corruption in the civil service (albeit at a lower rate than the EU average).[71] Hence, the perception of corruption is by no means unique to Poland's east.

Meanwhile, additional resources have been put into public administration, accounting for tremendous growth. The number of those who worked in the public administration grew from 161,579 in 1989 to 290,225 in 1996.[72] For 2013, the Civil Service Department stated that 636,300 work in the public administration (excluding soldiers and officers), 124,100 of whom were civil service corps members. Approximately 38.8 per cent of the civil service corps members, or about 47,135 employees, are members of the fiscal (tax) administration.[73]

Thus, Poland's legacies have interacted in different ways with the post-communist transition. The legacy of Poland's inter-war period acted as

[68] Ibid.   [69] *PAP News Agency* (Warsaw), 28 July 2003.
[70] Transparency International and Instytut Praw Publicznych, 5 March 2012.
[71] Rzeczpospolita, 4 February 2014.   [72] Office of the Civil Service (Warsaw), 2001.
[73] Office of the Civil Service (Warsaw), 'Civil Service in Numbers', accessed at <http://dsc.kprm.gov.pl/sites/default/files/pliki/civil_service_in_numbers_draft.pdf> on 30 July 2015.

72   Taxes and Trust

an ideal reference point for communist leaders in the 1980s as they decided to bring back that era's institutions in order to maintain better governance and better state–society relations. Those decisions made a positive difference in the 1990s. Rather than throwing out everything in the communist governance toolbox, the inter-war legacy was utilized by the post-communist leaders as well in deciding which institutions to retain and modify. The irony is that the institutions from the Second Polish Republic, re-built in part in the 1980s to legitimize the communist state, which was confronting an increasingly contentious society, became accepted and re-invigorated with new laws by the post-communist society in creating the new state. The year 1989, therefore, provided an opportunity for a fresh look at those existing and recently transformed state institutions such that they could be updated and re-framed to accomplish the post-communist agenda in a manner deemed acceptable by society.

Further, the legacy of foreign domination, most recently under a communist system of governance, led Polish leadership and society to look elsewhere, in particular to Europe, for models in reformatting their existing institutions along alternative underpinnings – based, not on communism, but on democracy and the rule of law. Finally, the competitive party system throughout the post-communist era has been a real hindrance to better bureaucratic governance, even if well-developed and well-intentioned civil service laws have been adopted and gradually implemented.

The Soviet Union's Legacies Bequeathed to Russia

In Russia, different perceptions on what the real legacies of communism actually are have been seized upon by the post-communist leadership and society. As the transition has progressed, Russian consensus on how things 'ought' to be done has been based less on the further pursuit of the path initiated by Gorbachev, the last Soviet leader, towards creating a true civil society that could monitor the government, and more on notions of how the pre-Gorbachev system worked to maintain continuity, stability and order.

The 1980s were used differently in post-communist Russia than in Poland as the legacy of *glasnost* and its underpinning values were re-interpreted by the end of the 1990s, largely because Yeltsin failed to seize upon them to reform the state further. The Putin era then viewed the Gorbachev era as a giant, flawed aberration in Russian history rather than as a basis for creating better governance through greater transparency, a vitalized civil society and a healthier state–society relations.

Reinterpreting History to Recreate the State 73

Hence, when President Putin told Russians in his annual state of the nation address in April 2005 that the collapse of the Soviet Union was 'a major geopolitical disaster of the century', the remark revealed how he chooses to utilize the past to shape current views of the present by invoking a belief shared by tens of millions of Russians.[74]

Thus, with such prevailing views today in Russia regarding the benefits of the Soviet model of governance (albeit separate from those of communism), it should not be entirely surprising that, despite some concerted post-1991 reform efforts, including the creation of a 'State Service' and technical assistance programs from the World Bank, the OECD and other foreign organizations, Russia still lacks a true civil service by which merit-based employment in the state is protected and by which political neutrality is guaranteed and safeguarded, de jure or de facto, in government structures.[75] Despite a new Civil Service Law signed by Putin in 2004, the OECD has remarked that in Russia today, '[t]he interface between the political and administrative appointments is blurred, as state civil servants in executive positions are largely appointed by discretionary means (although minimum qualifications for such positions are established by law). The president has influence over the appointment/dismissal of top and middle management, with the minister and others in [the] ministry having influence over that of lower grades. All top management turns over with a change in government, as well as many middle managers.'[76] The bureaucracy, as in Poland, is treated as a 'spoils system' of sorts, but unlike Poland, there has been no change in the direction of government by and large since Putin came to power in 1999.

A poor view of Russian bureaucrats dates back to the Soviet period, when bribes were in widespread use, just as they had been in Tsarist Russia. Corruption – and crackdowns on corruption – do have a long history in Russia. Beginning in the ninth and tenth centuries, Russian princes would send their representatives to the provinces without paying them, so that the local population would provide for them, in a

---

[74] This phrase's exact meaning in English has been discussed greatly in the media. The Kremlin archived translation of the 2005 speech, accessed at <http://archive.kremlin.ru/eng/speeches/2005/04/25/2031_type70029type82912_87086.shtml>, states that Putin called the collapse 'a major geopolitical disaster of the century', while the Associated Press and the BBC, among others, translated the phrase as 'the greatest geopolitical catastrophe of the century', as found at <www.utsandiego.com/uniontrib/20050426/news_1n26russia.html> and <http://news.bbc.co.uk/1/hi/4480745.stm>. All were accessed on 31 July 2015. Meanwhile, Russian speakers recognise, of course, that the Russian language does not distinguish between the indefinite article 'a' and the definite article 'the'.

[75] Manning and Parison, p. 45.   [76] OECD, 6 December 2012.

74   Taxes and Trust

practice known as 'feeding'. Later, in 1497, Ivan III introduced legislation restricting corruption, while, in 1550, Ivan IV (a.k.a. 'Ivan the Terrible') codified a death sentence for bribery. Peter I (a.k.a. 'Peter the Great') and, a couple of centuries later, the Romanov dynasty waged unsuccessful battles to curb corruption.[77] In spite of these attempts to halt corruption in Tsarist Russia, service to the state was viewed as a way to gain material wealth and a position of respect within society. Meanwhile, as Karl Ryavec has observed, 'Russia lacked both a civil society and an independent legal system to limit bureaucrats, while the bureaucrats lacked a "public service" culture that might have formed a system of self-limitation.'[78]

After 1917, in terms of bureaucratic habits, little changed. Instead of monetary compensation, bribes in the Soviet days were often given in the form of *blat*, an exchange of favours using government resources. Being a bureaucrat meant having power over other citizens. A report prepared by the administrative department of the Communist Party's Central Committee as part of an effort in clamp down on bribery in the five-year period of 1975 to 1980 found that in one year there were more than 6,000 cases.[79]

In a study of bureaucrats' biographies just prior to the Soviet collapse, David Lane and Cameron Ross discovered, somewhat surprisingly, that the Communist Party had very little control over the personnel in the government bureaucracy. They found that 'the recruitment of personnel to many of the key sectors of the government bureaucracy appeared to be determined by the applicants previous experience and tenure in the bureaucracy . . . [and] . . . that the attempts by party leaders to control the bureaucracy failed, and that the relative autonomy of the government apparatus was an important contributing factor in the collapse of the communist state'.[80] Hence, such research indicates that the 1980s actually yielded some success in de-politicizing the bureaucracy and making it more independent from the party.

In many ways, the *glasnost* and *perestroika* programs were the result of both a personality-based 'Gorbachev factor', the view taken by Archie Brown, and a society-based 'Gorbachev phenomenon', Moshe Lewin's perspective.[81] In June 1986, a few months after becoming general secretary, Gorbachev stated in a closed meeting with a group of Soviet writers, 'The society is ripe for change. If we step away, the society will not agree for a return. The process must be made irreversible. If not us, then who? If not now, then when?'[82] Hence, the impetus for reform, Gorbachev

---

[77] Alyakrinskaya.   [78] Ryavec, p. 15.   [79] Alyakrinskaya.
[80] Lane and Ross, p. 19.   [81] Brown; Lewin.   [82] Quoted in Tucker, p. 140.

Reinterpreting History to Recreate the State 75

saw at the time, was emerging from society, which in turn required him as its leader to act.

For Lewin, the 'Gorbachev phenomenon', was the re-politicizing of the political system as a consequence of the social environment's effects upon the political arena. In particular, Lewin believed that urbanization, initiated under Stalin but consolidated under Brezhnev, created an 'emerging civil society'. Yet Lewin did not speak of the same view on civil society that Robert Putnam and Alexis de Tocqueville had, in the sense that citizens form autonomous, non-governmental organizations to resolve problems with the state in an open manner. Rather, he referred to 'the aggregate of networks and institutions that either exist and act independently of the state or are official organizations capable of developing their own, spontaneous views on national or local issues and then impressing these view on their members, on small groups and, finally, on the authorities.'[83] Most significantly, urbanization had created independent and autonomous modes of thought, which the party through some of its leaders and cadres understood. The leadership, thus, took up the challenge and sought to take such an independent, burgeoning 'civil society' and place it back in the political arena.

For Archie Brown, however, Gorbachev, the man, was at the centre of the process of change. The reform program was Gorbachev-led, rather than society-led. John Dunlap concurs that Gorbachev mattered, but largely because he 'unwittingly' destroyed the Soviet Union. Dunlap sees Gorbachev as embarking on a second *perestroika* period, a campaign of 'democratization' in mid-1986 to replace powerful competitors with allies in the Politburo.[84] The goal was not to destroy or transform the system, but to reject Stalinism and return to the 1920s-era ideals of Marxism-Leninism through a cleansing and strengthening of the party. (This was exemplified, among many works and events, by the 1988 play *Onward... Onward... Onward!* by Mikhail Shatrov, which exposed on the Moscow stage the Stalinist crimes, but called for a return to the Leninist ideals.)

Furthermore, while Brown explains the fact that repression was not used to hold the USSR together as due to a personal choice of Gorbachev,[85] Gorbachev probably knew that the status quo ante could never be restored. As Dunlap states, 'Events moved with such blinding speed between 1987 and 1989 that it must soon have become evident to Gorbachev that only a crackdown of Stalinist dimensions could halt the changes that he had unwittingly unleashed.'[86] (And, in fact, Gorbachev tried unsuccessfully to use what repression he could to hold the Soviet

[83] Lewin, p. 80.   [84] Dunlap, p. 10.   [85] Brown, p. 309.   [86] Dunlap, p. 10.

76   Taxes and Trust

Union together, for example, in Tbilisi in 1989, in Azerbaijan in 1990 and in Vilnius in 1991.) Society by the late 1980s truly had changed; Soviet-style repression would no longer be successful in keeping down the popular movements and was accompanied by backlash.

In fact, there were two intrinsic paradoxes, or fatal flaws, of the *glasnost* and *perestroika* programs, which by their nature could not be implemented successfully and leave the system intact. The first is concerned more with the *glasnost* campaign, the second more with *perestroika*. First, in embarking on the necessary reforms, the government had to maintain its legitimacy throughout the reform process. Yet to embark on a more open path, the lies of the Soviet system had to be exposed. The starting point for *glasnost* proponents was an open rejection of official truth; as a result, the destruction of one-party rule was only a matter of time. If one could question whether the Stalin era, which constructed the Soviet system, was built upon lies, corruption and unjust repression, one could begin to question whether the system itself was the problem – and whether the problems in the system began not with Stalin's rise to power but with Lenin.

Second, the problems that were inherent in the system became more acute when those institutions attempted, through *perestroika*, to start their own reforms from the top down by giving more independence to those at the bottom, as Steven Solnick has shown.[87] The process of correcting problems complicated and worsened the existing problems, in turn threatening the legitimacy of the regime. Once the system was hyper-institutionalized along vertical links, it could not undergo a complete overhaul and still continue to function throughout the transition.

The existence of these dual Gorbachev-era flaws is known well by post-Soviet society and leadership. However, rather than seeing these flaws as providing lessons to authoritarian states, many Russians have interpreted them as providing the paradigm rationale for curtailing further opening up of a state that actually began the transition in the early 1990s with democracy in greater reach than ever before.

Russia's Post-communist Administrative History

Similarly to the course set in Poland, reforming state structures in Russia took a backseat to economic reforms at the beginning of the transition. Nevertheless, just as in Poland, the early 1990s saw a recognized need for administrative reforms as several proposals began to circulate within the presidential administration. Reform-minded experts and politicians

---

[87] Solnick, 1997.

who surrounded Yeltsin pushed for a new body, the Chief Department of Personnel Training (*Roskadry*), which was established in 1992 to oversee civil service reform, the training of government officials and other administrative reforms, but was abolished in early 1994.[88] Prime Minister Yegor Gaidar's government in 1992 also made public the first draft Law on Civil Service and sought to reorganize administrative structures – the first of such reform attempts.[89] These efforts suggest that the failure to implement comprehensive civil service reform was not inevitable for Russia.

In stark contrast to Poland, though, there were no regulations for a civil service up until 1995. In 1995, the Law on the State Service appeared. However, that document did little to reform the bureaucracy, but rather laid out the 'privileges, prerequisites and protections afforded [to] civil servants and to an intricate hierarchy of titles and posts that recalled the Table of Ranks of imperial Russia'.[90] Many of its provisions were said to remain only on paper.[91] Similarly, a Civil Service Code was drafted in 1997, but it was not adopted, let alone published.[92] Meanwhile, the Bill on Countermeasures against Corruption was passed by the Federation Council twice in the 1990s, but Yeltsin vetoed it, and the Duma failed to pass it in 2001.[93]

While Soviet era personnel largely remained in place, the Yeltsin decade did see a very diverse group of bureaucrats, including 'people from the 1960s', 'deputy directors of laboratories', politicized intelligentsia, Yeltsin's 'fellow countrymen' and military to whom Yeltsin was catering because of the fear of losing power.[94] As the transition progressed, with the rise of oligarchs, however, a 'feeding' of bureaucrats ensued by which administrative resources were used for profit.[95] 'The system worked', write Sergei Viktorov and Vadim Bardin. 'The bureaucrats received a small salary; one and all took bribes (especially from the oligarchs) and looted budgetary finances. The Russian statehood in this very way was strengthened (in the Peter [the Great] meaning of this word. Boris Yeltsin held on to power.'[96] In the absence of leadership at the top to democratize the bureaucracies further, the old Soviet system gradually was revived with new, post-communist forces, which were not incorporated into formal institutional frameworks, much to the detriment of long-term state goals.[97]

Meanwhile, just as the communist era bequeathed to post-communist Poland several administrative law institutional structures, the Soviet

---

[88] Kotchegura, pp. 21, 22.   [89] Ibid.   [90] Huskey and Obolonsky, pp. 24–25.
[91] Kotchegura, pp. 21–22.   [92] Ibid., p. 25.   [93] Alyakrinskaya.   [94] Kostikov.
[95] Ibid.   [96] Viktorov and Bardin.   [97] See, for example, Hellman.

78 Taxes and Trust

period also laid an administrative legal foundation through a 1968 Supreme Soviet Presidium degree, 'On the Procedures for Consideration of the Proposals, Submissions, and Complaints of the Citizens', which continued after 1991 to regulate internal appeals regarding citizen–state disputes.[98]

As the design of the reform agenda developed gradually over nearly a decade prior to Putin's 2005 address on administrative reform, those within the upper levels of the Russian government were the main actors. From September 1996 to May 1997, 12 versions of a Concept on Administrative Reform were produced within the Presidential Administration. On May 27–30, 1997, a meeting held under the provisional name 'Round Table' resulted in the establishment of five expert working groups tasked with preparing a new Concept note. In May 1998, the text of the Concept was awarded to the new Chairman of the RF Government, Sergey Kiriyenko, with the purpose of publication, but it was not published.

In the fall of 1999, the text of the Concept note was transferred from Putin, then, as prime minister, the Chairman of the RF Government, to an outside, non-governmental think tank that had direct ties to the Government – the Centre for Strategic Research, led by German Gref, which served as the Campaign Headquarters of then-Prime Minister Putin. Gref's think tank introduced the concept of nation-building, absorbed the basic ideas of the concept of administrative reform in the 1998 proposed structures and emphasized the need to revive citizens' trust in the institutions of representative and direct democracy. In the spring of 2000, Gref's project lay dormant with the presidential election, but as T.Ya. Khabrieva, A.F. Nozdrachev and Yu.A. Tikhomirov describe, 'By the autumn of that year, the real reason for inhibition became clearer, as the priorities of government had been shifted to other tasks: strengthening the vertical of power, federal relations, changes in the upper chamber of the Russian Federal Assembly, etc. Administrative reform was once again postponed.'[99]

Under President Putin, a revived attempt at administrative reform was launched in 2001. The outward goal of the reforms was to reduce the number of ministries. However, the entire project appears actually to have been part of Putin's plan for creating a tightly centralized state with the bureaucracies under greater control. Indeed, in March 2003, Putin placed a few government agencies under the Federal Security Service (FSB), the successor organization to the Soviet-era KGB, for

---

[98] Galligan and Smilov, p. 277.
[99] Naryshkin and Khabrievoĭ, p. 9. Translation from the Russian by the author.

Reinterpreting History to Recreate the State 79

which Putin once worked and which he later headed, and the Defence Ministry, ostensibly to streamline the government, but also to centralize control.[100] Throughout the spring and summer of 2003, additional plans were announced to initiate administrative reform, but little progress was made beyond forming commissions. Despite the fact that Putin declared in 2002 that he wanted the reforms to be completed by the end of 2003,[101] the reform plans were declared by *Vedomosti* at the time to be practically broken, as some 231.7 billion rubles allocated by the 2003 budget for the administrative reform projects had not been appropriated.[102]

Administrative reform efforts were re-started the following year with the arrival of Mikhail Fradkov as the new prime minister in March 2004 and Putin's re-election that same month. In a series of decrees, Putin eliminated thirteen ministries (including the Ministry of Taxes and Dues, which was absorbed by the Finance Ministry), two state committees, one federal commission, four federal services and four federal agencies, while he created five new ministries, five new federal services and one new federal agency on the basis of the old entities.[103] In commenting on the reforms, Olga Khryshtanovskaya, head of the Elite Studies Centre at the Russian Academy of Sciences' Sociology Institute, stated that the total number of government departments actually had increased and that the system had become more complex.[104] Former State Duma Deputy Aleksandr Shokhin also argued that the reforms were flawed, as oversight bodies were subordinated to the very ministries that they had been intended to oversee.[105]

Putin also significantly reduced the number of deputy ministers, but Moscow's *Kommersant-Daily* soon reported that many of them continued to oversee the same areas as they previously did, but with new job titles.[106] Meanwhile, a month after his re-election, Putin also decreed a pay raise of up to five times for top-level bureaucrats, ministers as well as himself.[107] Government privileges and in-kind benefits for bureaucrats and their families, however, were not touched at all (even while the government began to monetize non-cash benefits in 2005 – which were widely perceived as welfare benefits cuts and led to the largest and most wide-scale protests yet in the Putin era, forcing the government to do a U-turn on the measure and cementing in the government's thinking regarding the critical need to secure the public's approval with respect

[100] Wines.   [101] Saradzhyan.   [102] Bekker.
[103] RFE/RL Newsline, 10 March 2004.   [104] RFE/RL Newsline, 2 March 2004.
[105] RFE/RL Newsline, 19 March 2004.
[106] McGregor; and RFE/RL Newsline, 26 March 2004.
[107] RIA Novosti, 1 April 2004; and McGregor.

80   Taxes and Trust

to service delivery).[108] In November 2005, Fradkov introduced another administrative reform blueprint, a three-year action plan that sought to update the bureaucracy with standardization and regulation reforms and to abolish or privatize one-third of some 25,000 state enterprises and organizations.[109]

The 2003-to-2005 period saw much headway made with regard to the optimization of functions of executive bodies and structures, public service reform and the improvement of management procedures due to leadership from the Presidential Administration and a new Commission for Administrative Reform.[110] In 2003, President Putin noted, 'We need to radically reduce the functions of state organs. Of course, it should be calculated very accurately.'[111] And, in that year, Putin issued several decrees, which became known immediately in the media as the Administrative Reform Decrees, by which he called for a radical reduction in the functions of government agencies.[112]

Yet there was an increase in the number of state workers in the middle of the decade. 'The stated goal', according to I.A. Baranov and N.N. Fedoseeva, was 'reducing staff, reducing corruption, improving the efficiency of the device. The result: an increase in the number of federal agencies, more expensive units, and an increase in bribes.'[113] Further, according to the Higher School of Economics, the number of federal civil servants steadily increased from 2001 to 2010, regardless of reform and the number of agencies.[114]

In 2004, the draft federal target program 'Administrative Reform' was developed, which gave rise to a new Commission for Administrative Reform that was envisioned to have greater authority than it eventually did. RF Presidential Decree 910 'On Measures to Good Governance' of 16 July 2004 created a Commission that comprised three interagency working groups on major issues of administrative reform, one of which focused on providing for openness and accessibility for citizens.[115] Those who took part in this Commission worked from the framework of foreign

---

[108] Paton Walsh; RFE/RL Newsline, 28 July 2004; and Nemtsov and Pribylovsky.
[109] Frunkin.   [110] Naryshkin and Khabrievoĭ, p. 9.
[111] Address of President Putin to the Federal Assembly of Russian Federation, 16 May 2003, Moscow.
[112] See, for example, RF Government Resolution 451 of 31 July 2003, 'On the Government Commission for Administrative Reform' and RF Presidential Decree 824 of 23 July 2003, 'On measures for administrative reform in 2003–2004 Government of the Russian Federation.'
[113] Baranov and Fedoseeva, pp. 3–5.
[114] The official site of the RF State Statistics Service accessed at <www.gks.ru/free_doc/new_site/gosudar/grafl.htm>.
[115] Naryshkin and Khabrievoĭ, p. 10.

Reinterpreting History to Recreate the State 81

reform models. 'None of the reforms undertaken in Russia in the past fifteen years was so tightly developed within a context of international practice as reform', A.B. Logunov has written. 'Russia has chosen ideology of administrative reform in the countries in which the public administration is being visibly transformed into "New Public Management" and where state institutions are actively being introduced principles and technology of a standard business management.'[116] The project proposed to create a special agency to manage the reform – the so-called Directorate – that was to be given wide powers. However, the Ministry of Finance did not approve the additional costs of implementing the program. Instead, the Centre for Strategic Research and the Ministry of Economic Development and Trade, together with technical and financial support of the World Bank and the UK's Department for International Development, developed another Concept of Administrative Reform.[117] At the same time, the primary responsibility for implementing the administrative reform still lay with the Government Commission on Administrative Reform.

From 2006 to 2010, the main activities of administrative reform were carried out in five phases:

- Late 2005 – The development and adoption of the framework of administrative reform activities.
- 2006 – The development of a regulatory framework for administrative reform, including public service standards, standards for public services provided by the federal executive bodies and their implementation at the federal and regional levels.
- 2007 – The elimination of redundant government functions, development and implementation of most of the administrative regulations of the federal and regional executive authorities, implementation of management procedures based on priority public service standards and the establishment of pilot multipurpose centres for state and municipal services (MFSCs).
- 2008 – The development and adoption of anti-corruption programs, the development of a regulatory framework of public service delivery in electronic form and the provision of public services via telecommunication technologies.

---

[116] Logunov, p. 5. Translation from the Russian by the author.
[117] This concept laid the foundation made in accordance with the Protocol of the RF Government meeting of 21 October 2004, on the Concept of Administrative Reform in the Russian Federation in 2006–2008 and the action plan for conducting administrative reform in the Russian Federation in 2006–2008, formally approved by RF Government Decree № 1789-p of 25 October 2005 (Lazarev).

82   Taxes and Trust

- 2009–2010 – The creation of MFSCs to provide state and municipal services across Russia and the transition of federal executive bodies to the provision of public services in electronic form through the national state data centre.

Meanwhile, the Concept note did not provide additional funding from the federal budget for the activities of administrative reform, which were to be undertaken by federal authorities with funds provided in the existing federal budget for relevant federal executive authorities.[118] Beginning in 2006, while not involved in the distribution of funds between federal agencies and stakeholders, the Ministry of Economic Development began to hold grant competitions in which federal executive and regional bodies competed for funding to implement provisions of the Administrative Reform Concept.[119] A similar competition was held again in March 2007.[120]

Administrative reform was the least funded of all the ongoing institutional reforms in public administration. For example, in 2009, M.A. Gintova stated that the average size of the support allocated per region or the federal executive authority was 190 million rubles for a pilot health care reform project; 150 million for an integrated education reform project; 100–120 million for a regional finance reform program; and at least 100 million for an experiment to introduce performance-based budgeting result, but only 25 million rubles for an administrative reform project in a RF subject and 7.8 million rubles for an administrative reform project in a Federal executive body.[121] The differences in the amount of financial support to potential participants indicate a low priority and low political importance of administrative reform in comparison with other institutional reform. Consequently, according to some experts, the theme of improved governance has been divided artificially into several blocks in a piecemeal haphazard manner that is controlled and managed inconsistently by various federal agencies.

Perceptions of how satisfied the Russian public is with state public services as a whole do vary, but, overall, more Russians found government services to be working better over the previous two to three years in 2011 than they did in 2008.[122]

---

[118] The results and study methodology of federal bodies regarding administrative reform can be found in Zhulin et al.

[119] Lazarev.   [120] Sharov.   [121] Gintova.

[122] Fond Obshchestvennoe Mnenie, pp. 12, 13, 16–23. This is a report based on a nationwide public opinion survey of 6,032 Russians carried out in 64 RF Subjects in March 2011 for the World Bank/Department for International Development of the UK 'Public Administration Reform in the Russian Federation' project, for which the author was a consultant.

Reinterpreting History to Recreate the State 83

Nevertheless, administrative reform of public service delivery in Russia has been bogged down by the simple fact that it is not an easy task to introduce any reform that affects a wide spectrum of existing government organizations that already have their own laws and regulations governing their activity and to try to do so amid changing reform objectives and without a large-scale investment of large sums of funding at ready disposal. As such, where administrative reform in the area of public service delivery has been slow to progress, it has been due to the difficulty of applying a single methodology, a single template, a single oversight body to the process and a single path towards legislative adoption of new laws while competing with other Kremlin policies and objectives seeking greater control over structures.

The administrative reform plan goes hand-in-hand with Putin's introduction of seven federal districts (*okrugi*) as a layer of government between the regions and the central government. 'Federal reform as it was being implemented was only partially about relations between the centre and the regions', writes Nikolai Petrov. 'It was primarily about power. And more about power at the national level than at the regional level. And it is no coincidence that Putin's presidency began precisely with this. By creating federal districts that he fully controlled, Putin set the stage for taking control over the military, security and law enforcement bodies – first in the regions, then in Moscow.'[123] Furthermore, in establishing the seven federal districts, Putin's reforms also brought under presidential control the Monitoring Administration and the Cadres Administration, which were based in the provinces.[124]

Putin sought to create a 'power vertical', a term which, according to Aleksandr Belousov at the Law of the Urals Division of the Russian Academy of Sciences, does not exist in the RF Constitution and cannot be found in Russian laws written before the Putin era. Belousov has argued that 'the term "power vertical" is neither a juridical term nor a scientific concept', but rather is a powerful 'political metaphor' to describe an array of things. Further, while Putin, a lawyer, has been extremely precise when using legal terms, he has been remarkably 'ambiguous' when using the words 'federal' or 'federation'.[125]

In many respects, Putin's efforts to centralize control over Russia's provinces (89 in number at the start of Putin's presidency, but, according to the RF Constitution, 85 provinces now, after some consolidations and after the 18 March 2014 annexation of Crimea) were a process of reversing the efforts of both Yeltsin and Gorbachev to decentralize the state. A personal example illustrates the point: In July 2000, three months after

---

[123] Petrov, 22 May 2003.   [124] Huskey, pp. 124–125.   [125] Goble.

84   Taxes and Trust

Putin was elected president, I travelled to Yakutsk, the capital city of the Sakha-Yakutia province, to interview federal officials based in the region. Coinciding with my visit, a planeload of bureaucrats came from Moscow to review the activities of the federal state in the province. When I met with the assistant director in charge of the RF Employment Fund for the region, he told me that in the six years he had worked there, this was the first time someone from Moscow had come out to check on their work.[126] Clearly, from the beginning of his term, Putin sought to waste little time in putting a strict hierarchical system of control back in place.

Since the formation of the Soviet Union in 1922, true federalism, in fact, never really existed in either the USSR or the Russian Socialist Federated Soviet Republic (RFSFR.) 'Quite unlike classical Western notions of federalism, which strike a balance of power and responsibilities between centre and periphery, the Soviet version of federalism denie[d] the Union's constituent republics the crucial element of sovereignty in handling their own political, social and economic affairs', Peter Pavilonis has written. 'The republics' constitutions [were] carbon copies of the USSR Constitution and there [was] little difference in republican versions of all-Union legislation drafted in Moscow.'[127]

Gorbachev meanwhile allowed republican leaders to adapt the USSR's legislation to their own republics.[128] 'Whereas Gorbachev employed *glasnost* in the mid-1980s as a means of collecting reliable information on political and economic conditions in the country', Eugene Huskey has written, 'Putin opted for a new bureaucracy of *kontrol'* that could at once offer the president a more accurate picture of developments in the periphery and incriminating evidence (*kompromat*) on provincial leaders.'[129] Hence, Putin did have a choice as to which legacy to follow when interacting with the provinces – either to push forward with Gorbachev–Yeltsin *glasnost*-like federalizing measures or to opt for trend-reversing 'Back in the RFSFR' measures.

While Putin has been trying to place the bureaucracies under more direct control, the ranks of the state agencies in the 1990s and 2000s have been filled with older bureaucrats who mostly entered government in the Soviet era and who were replaced by former military and law enforcement personnel rather than by newly trained younger workers. According to Vladimir Gimpelson, every other bureaucrat in the organs at the federal level in the early 2000s worked in the Brezhnev era, and

---

[126] Interview with the Assistant Director, RF State Employment Service, The Department of Employment of the Population of the Republic of Sakha-Yakutia, 3 July 2000, in Yakutsk.
[127] Pavilionis.   [128] Ibid.   [129] Huskey, p. 119.

Reinterpreting History to Recreate the State

with workers from the Gorbachev period, such bureaucrats compose 60 per cent of the current workforce. Three-quarters of higher-level bureaucrats were hired before 1990. '[D]espite all of the numerous reorganisations of the ministries and institutions', writes Gimpelson, 'the "new" cadre more often is extracted from the same multiply re-shuffled deck of cards.'[130]

Moreover, with a 2002 presidential decree and the 2003 passage of Putin-sponsored legislation, the Kremlin sought to establish a ranking system for state and military employees akin to the 'Table of Ranks' that Peter the Great introduced in 1722, with promotions tied to length of time in service rather than to job performance.[131] The move would make it easier for retired army and police officers to find jobs as bureaucrats (rather than providing for newly trained younger bureaucrats.)

Instead of promoting those with party ties, per se, Putin's regime has brought an influx of people with military, law enforcement or security service backgrounds, commonly referred to as the *siloviki*, especially into the tax administration, as will be shown in Chapter 5. A study by the Institute of Sociology in Moscow found that up to 70 per cent of the presidential envoys' staff in the seven federal *okrugi* are from the military, while the number of people with military or security backgrounds more than doubled from 2000 to 2003.[132] Khryshtanovskaya has estimated that up to 75 per cent of Putin's top government appointees in his first term also had such backgrounds, while such people composed only five per cent of Gorbachev's Politburo.[133] Meanwhile, 35 per cent of the deputy ministers appointed to the economic ministries in the first term have military or security backgrounds, most of whom are still 'active reserve officers' of the FSB, which requires them to report to the FSB as well as to their own ministers.[134]

Khryshtanovskaya and Stephen White explain that Putin's choice of armed forces and state security personnel is based upon the reputation of these organizations as being more honest, apolitical, professional and conscientious in fulfilling their duties than other societal groups. They also state that Putin opted for the *siloviki* because the armed forces and state security agencies retained their vertical organizational structures across the country, penetrating society, even while other institutions collapsed and disappeared when the Soviet Union fell.[135]

---

[130] Gimpelson, p. 26. Translation from the Russian by the author.
[131] Yablokova; RFE/RL Russian Political Weekly, 15 July 2004; Prime-TASS News, 21 November 2002; and IPR Strategic Information Database.
[132] Khryshtanovskaya. [133] Russkii Fokus. [134] Khryshtanovskaya.
[135] Khryshtanovskaya and White, p. 291.

86   Taxes and Trust

Yevgenia Albats, meanwhile, found in 2004 that over 50 per cent of some 706 federal officials surveyed were opposed to transparency.[136] In the 2011 survey of Russian tax officials, only four out of five (80 per cent) bureaucrats believe that there are few dishonest tax employees, with 14 per cent stating that there were many and 5 per cent declining to answer (see Question #3 in Appendix I). And that 2011 survey also shows that just less than half of the tax officials believe that the state fights corruption well, with 34 per cent stating that the state does a poor job, 10 per cent stating that the state does no job and 9 per cent refusing to provide an answer (see Question #59, also in Appendix I.) Finally, only 53 per cent of these officials trust other bureaucrats (see Question #51.)

In 1990, there were 663,000 Russian bureaucrats.[137] Statistics vary somewhat with respect to the size of the Russian bureaucracy today. According to the presidential office's figures in 2002, the number of state officials was 1.53 million, not including army, law enforcement or emergency services personnel.[138] In 2004, the RF State Statistics Service stated that the number was 1,300,500.[139] In 2005, Khryshtanovskaya estimated in 2005 that the figure was two million.[140] Meanwhile, in 2013, the number of officials was deemed to be 1.45 million.[141]

Since 1991, corruption has escalated dramatically in Russia. Elena Panfilova, director of Transparency International's office in Russia, has argued that the corruption of government officials further enhances greater control within the system as bureaucrats are promoted, because the presence of corruption means greater pliability. 'A corrupt official is a more loyal official', she states, adding that punishment occurs only when spoils aren't shared or when an official steps on somebody else's turf.[142]

Meanwhile, Georgy Satarov, head of the InDem Foundation, adds that the State Duma often grants general amnesties that include those convicted on charges of corruption. 'In other words', he states, 'if you have taken a bribe, there is an extremely small chance that you will be caught red-handed. The chance that you will be convicted is even less. And even if you happen to be found guilty, it is highly probable that you will get a suspended sentence or an amnesty.'[143]

As mentioned in Chapter 2, corruption has grown significantly under Putin, and unsurprisingly, Russians share similar views on corruption

[136] Albats.   [137] Paton Walsh; and Simankin and Blinova.
[138] Prime-TASS News, 21 November 2002.   [139] RFE/RL Newsline, 14 May 2004.
[140] Abdullaev.   [141] *Moscow Times*, 15 October 2014.
[142] Economist, 20 October 2005.   [143] Alyakrinskaya.

Reinterpreting History to Recreate the State 87

and on bureaucrats. Of Russians polled in 1999, 61 per cent believed that it is impossible to eradicate corruption in Russia.[144] In the same poll, 70 per cent of Russians surveyed said that corruption on the part of government servants had increased within the last year or two.[145] In addition, 81 per cent the same year also considered local bureaucrats to be corrupt and to be abusing their positions for private goals.[146] Further, in the 2010 Russia Taxpayer Compliance Attitudinal Survey (see Question #59 in Appendix I), only 17 per cent of Russians stated that their government does a good job in fighting corruption, while 51 per cent stated that the government does a poor job and 23 per cent stated that the government does not fight corruption at all.

In spite of widespread distrust for the state, a turnaround has been made with regards to Russians' trust of institutions held over from the past and the new post-Soviet institutions. 'It is a reversal of the situation in the early 1990s when Russians tended to be warmer toward the new institutions than the old ones', Vladimir Shlapentokh has written. 'Russians have more confidence in the old institutions than the new ones. An important point should be made about the country's historical processes: the new institutions, with their low status in the Russian mind, could not compensate for the decline of the old institutions, including the government, security forces and the police.'[147] In this respect, Putin's focus on revitalizing institutions through the military and law enforcement are a reflection of how both he and his society view the more recent past, especially as confusion exists with respect to what benefits there actually are in opening up the state's structures to society.

Ukraine's Default Choice to Maintain a Large, Bureaucratic Soviet-Like State

On 24 August 1991, two days after the putsch had ended in Moscow and roughly four months before the end of the USSR, Ukraine's parliament began procedures to vote for independence, during which one speaker got up and expressed a great fear shared by many in the room as to what life outside the Soviet Union would be by declaring, 'I don't see why we should be independent. We've done nothing wrong.'[148]

While failing to stave off independence, those remarks may as well have summed up the political leadership's approach in the 1990s and early 2000s to the Ukrainian state and governance – namely, that there is

---

[144] Fond Obshchestvennoe Mnenie, Moscow, 13–14 March 1999.   [145] Ibid.
[146] Fond Obshchestvennoe Mnenie, Moscow, 12–13 June 1999.
[147] Shlapentokh.   [148] Cowley, p. 3.

88   Taxes and Trust

nothing wrong with continuing forward with a large, Soviet-style bureaucratic social welfare state. And, indeed, throughout Ukraine's twenty-five years as an independent state – amidst struggles between presidents and parliaments, oligarchs and outsiders – the country never truly has reformed its bureaucracies. '[E]ven today, the methods of governing have been left almost unchanged since the Soviet era', Ihor Koliushko and Viktor Tymoshchuk observed in 2000. 'No one carries real responsibility for the state of affairs in the country, while the non-transparency of the state structure for the public and its totally corrupt nature have ultimately undermined the trust of the citizens in their Government and the state as a whole.'[149] Similarly, as Anders Åslund wrote in 2015, 'While it has depoliticized state administration, Ukraine has yet to rejuvenate and professionalize it. The main problem is corruption, which is linked with the continuity of the Soviet state administration. The Ukrainian state administration has changed less than in any other post-Soviet country.'[150]

Under President Leonid Kuchma (1994–2005), the executive branch was characterized as having 'poor co-ordination of actions on the part of different executive structures, inconsistency and the contradictory nature of decisions; low executive discipline; duplication of similar functions performed by different bodies; excessive concentration of administrative functions at the highest levels of the executive branch; unbalanced regional policy; inaccessibility of the executive power bodies to public control; corruption and economic crime within the state structures, and the low prestige of public service in Ukraine'.[151] The situation was little better during President Viktor Yushchenko's term in office (2005–2010), which was characterized by a lack of coordination, inefficiencies, shortage of personnel resources and a lack of highly professional civil servants.[152]

The process of administrative reform, which began with a state commission drafting the Concept in 1997, was supposed to ameliorate these issues with the bureaucracy, but was prolonged, drawn out and criticized for reorganizing and liquidating ministries prior to an evaluation of their functions in a process that was not always transparent to the general public.[153] Meanwhile, throughout the 1990s, the World Bank appeared to be the only client for administrative reforms. In other words, no one really wanted administrative reform to take place in Ukraine except for

---

[149] Koliushko and Tymoshchuk, p. 59.   [150] Åslund, 2015, pp. 146–147.
[151] Razumkov Ukrainian Centre for Economic and Political Studies (UCEPS), 2000, p. 10.
[152] Razumkov UCEPS, 2007, p. 66.   [153] Razumkov UCEPS, 2000, pp. 19, 25 and 30.

Reinterpreting History to Recreate the State 89

the Bank, which, Koliushko and Tymoshchuk remarked, 'shared the main ideas behind the Concept of Administrative Reform in Ukraine, and stepped forward as virtually the only client "placing orders" for changes in the system of state administration in our country (as unpleasant as this is to admit). It was under their pressure (and as a rule, prior to a scheduled visit for loans), at least cosmetic attempts were made to take some steps towards administrative reform.'[154]

The process of administrative reform continued initially with renewed intensity after the 2004 Orange Revolution, but it also lacked any coordinator or official in charge, a situation aggravated by the fact that the task was a secondary duty for those in the Government charged to work on such reforms while other critical policy tasks associated with running the government took precedent.[155] Administrative reform during Yushchenko's term brought surprisingly little reform and more floundering. 'There was no qualitative breakthrough', the Kyiv-based Razumkov Centre's journal *National Security & Defence* concluded. 'The key laws necessary for administrative reform in the institutional, procedural, human, and territorial domains were not passed. The lack of a strategic vision of the process of reform and realization of individual steps is striking. Due to the lack of a clear idea of changes in the new authorities, a lot of time was wasted.'[156]

Under Yushchenko, little success was attained as well in adopting a civil service bill in 2005 as upon its 'finalization, involving representatives of many state bodies, educational establishments, and trade unions showed that the personal interests of civil servants prevail over the interests of the people', according to the *National Security & Defence*. 'The reformist potential of the bill [was] impaired, while the social aspect [was] boosted. The attention to the draft "Code of Ethics" weakened after the Minister of Justice was replaced.'[157]

Meanwhile, the post-Orange parliament also exhibited a complete lack of understanding regarding what the civil service was all about by amending regulations for a civil service personnel reserve to extend benefits to former MPs and for replacing nearly a hundred civil servants who left supposedly 'on their own will' with newly hired personnel from a single region. Such a 'decision illustrates misunderstanding of the elementary principles of good governance by the authorities', commented the journal in 2007. 'Widespread resignations of civil servants of the highest level "at their own discretion" and dominance from one region taking

---

[154] Koliushko and Tymoshchuk, p. 60.
[155] Razumkov UCEPS, 2006, pp. 19–20; and Razumkov UCEPS, 2007, p. 23.
[156] Razumkov UCEPS, 2005, p. 35.   [157] Ibid.

90 Taxes and Trust

executive positions is testimony to systemic problems of the institution of the civil service, as well as a compromise of citizens' rights to equal access to the civil service, its stability and political neutrality.'[158] Hence, outside experts in Ukraine clearly saw expectations raised several times, but little reform of the bureaucracy in the end.

More recently, the *Verkhovna Rada*'s 10 December 2015 passage of a civil service reform law showed promise. The law calls for all civil service appointments to be made through open and competitive appointments; the creation of a special selection committee that will independently decide all top appointees across all of Ukraine's government bodies, half of whose members will come from civil society; a ban on senior bureaucrats' holding membership in any political party; the creation of a new position of state secretary in all of Ukraine's ministries – chosen through a new competitive process – that will manage the ministry in alignment with the European Union, where administrative and political functions are separated; limiting senior bureaucrats' tenures to a maximum of two five-year terms; and a change in the salary structure for personnel. If implemented properly – and a summer 2016 attempt to pass a new bill threatened to eliminate the special selection committee's ability to choose the heads of local administrations and pass that responsibility back to the president – the law truly would bring a sea-change in corruption within Ukraine's administrative structures.[159]

The reasons for the decades-long inertia in re-creating the post-communist Ukrainian state are multifold and, perhaps, over-determined. First, as Taras Kuzio has remarked, Ukraine had a limited pre-Soviet legacy upon which to draw.[160] The piecemeal nature of the process by which the Ukrainian Soviet Socialist Republic was constructed, with parts composed of lands ruled by the Russian Empire for centuries and other parts never having experienced Russian rule until after World War II, meant that there was no clearly identifiable governance model for the bureaucracy, as there was for Poland or Russia.

Second, as Åslund reminds us, Ukraine's independence was achieved by a compromise between the nationalists and the older communist elites, who viewed a large state apparatus for them to rule as indicative of a strong state. 'They favoured a big state apparatus', he wrote, 'ignoring its quality.'[161] Indeed, as the number of social welfare benefits, pensions and subsidies shows, the basic policy goal was a large state role. And maintaining such a large state led to an unorganized monolith

---

[158] Razumkov UCEPS, 2006, pp. 18–19.
[159] Cohen, 22 December 2015; Cohen, 5 July 2016; and Herbst.
[160] Kuzio, p. 1017.   [161] Åslund, 2015, p. 147.

Reinterpreting History to Recreate the State 91

of bureaucracy. '[W]hile maintaining its claim to a wide scope, the state had become porous', commented Verena Fritz. 'Financially, a considerable share of programs formulated by decision-makers went unfunded. Moreover, the horizontal and hierarchical integration of the state was frayed. Thus, several sources of rulemaking competed with each other, both in the issuing of legal rules and in bringing crucial institutions (such as the [State Property Fund], [National Bank of Ukraine]) under their control. Faced with contradictory rules, lower levels of the administration failed to implement orders from above.'[162]

Third, there was a lack of vision on almost everything economic at the top of the political system, muddling the imperative for administrative reform and not allowing a larger debate in society as to what the role of the state should be. 'The Ukrainian leadership lacked a clear vision of what socio-economic model to strive for', wrote Fritz. 'On the one hand, leading politicians sought reforms, on the other hand, they rejected "shock therapy" initiated by the liberal elite in Russia.'[163] By seeking out, but not yet coalescing around, an economic reform program in the 1990s, the need for a reform of the bureaucracy – and how it could assist in economic reform – was put off as well. Externally, the impetus for economic reform was mooted also, since the European Union did not provide as significant support to Ukraine, despite Ukraine's support for greater integration with the West, as it did to other East European states, who were offered the 'carrot' of membership and were separated off from Ukraine by the European Union in their aid programs. (The 1980s' Poland did not become the Poland of today without significant help from the West, foreign aid programs and the cancelling out of all Polish historical debts in the 1990s. Moreover, Europe always divided off the former Soviet Union (FSU) states like Ukraine, keeping the twinned aid programs for Central Europe and the former Soviet Union, PHARE and TACIS, separate from each other so that there was little interaction programmatically across Central and Eastern Europe, including the Baltic states, on the one hand, and the FSU on the other.)

Fourth, while power became concentrated within the presidency from the late 1990s up until the 2004 Orange Revolution, the parliament and the president vied over the constitutional distribution of power throughout this period.[164] Even though Poland's political parties certainly fought over the power to influence the bureaucracies on a 'spoils' basis, the constitutional distribution of powers in Poland was not considered as being up for revision to the extent that it was continually so in Ukraine. The long delay of the Constitution, finally adopted in 1996 – and, to a lesser

[162] Fritz, p. 133.   [163] Ibid., pp. 113–114.   [164] Ibid., p. 109.

92   Taxes and Trust

extent, the prolonged absence of a fundamental law 'On the Cabinet of Ministers', adopted in 2008 – meant that all branches and powers of government were open to 'ad hoc tests of strength' and that even the president and the prime ministers would contest domination over policy making.'[165] And, when the Constitution did arrive, it did not resolve who was in control, as it stated that the government was '"responsible to the President of Ukraine and [...] under the control of and accountable to the *Verkhovna Rada*" (Art. 113)'.[166] The government thus had two masters seeking to control it.

In the late 1990s and early 2000s, administrative bodies were subordinated de facto to the president when they should have been subordinated to the government – which muddled the laws and rules of the state as Kuchma tried to create a presidential state.[167] In many ways, Kuchma's regime focused on centralizing the government in order to maintain strength, *National Security & Defence*'s editors concluded, 'rather than to attain democratic standards in the delimitation of powers of the bodies of state governance, lay down a solid legal basis for their activity, and bring the practice of governance into compliance with the Constitution'.[168] Remarking on the conflicts at the top over administrative reform during the period 1997–2000, the Razumkov Centre's Analytical Report stated, 'Co-operation among working groups of the *Verkhovna Rada*, the Government, and the President of Ukraine at the stage of draft law (draft presidential decree) preparation was virtually absent. As a result of this, almost every law approved by the *Verkhovna Rada* was vetoed by the President several times; likewise, the *Verkhovna Rada* blocked draft laws introduced at the initiative of either the Government or the President of Ukraine.'[169]

After the Orange Revolution, a similar lack of legislative support for Yushchenko's attempts at administrative reform meant that many promised fundamental laws on the running of the government were not adopted, while efforts to strengthen the executive branch over local self-government bodies led to increased tension between the centre and the regions.[170] A hasty dismissal of nearly 20,000 state employees in the executive branch in 2005 was viewed as 'political persecution' of those who worked under the Kuchma regime.[171]

Fifth, as the economy collapsed in the first half decade after the Soviet Union collapsed (and even today Ukraine remains one of the very, very few countries in the world that have not yet reached their own 1989 levels

---

[165] Ibid., p. 116.; and Razumkov UCEPS, 2000, p. 13.   [166] Fritz, p. 139.
[167] Koliushko, p. 62.   [168] Razumkov UCEPS, 2005, p. 31.
[169] Razumkov UCEPS, 2000, p. 22.
[170] Razumkov UCEPS, 2005, p. 35.   [171] Ibid.

Reinterpreting History to Recreate the State

in growth per capita), the structure of the Communist Party of Ukraine was dissolved, and few strong political parties came forth (although a re-emerged Communist Party commanded the largest parliamentary factions from 1994 to 2002), the state was held together by 'networks' of former Communists. Hence, absent political structures that were prevalent in other countries, the networks of former communists from the Soviet days ensured the continuity of the Soviet bureaucratic structures.

Sixth, Ukraine retained very little fiscal experience from the Soviet days. Unlike Poland or Russia, Ukraine did not inherit a full set of financial and fiscal institutions or any state organizations involved in planning and budgeting, as those tasks had been carried out in Moscow prior to 1991 – which was not helpful, as the Soviet collapse brought economic breakdown for the newly independent state.

Finally, unlike Poland's NIK, Ukraine's Accounting Chamber was very weak. After parliament overturned a May 1996 presidential veto of a parliamentary law giving the Accounting Chamber significant powers, Kuchma submitted the law to the Constitutional Court, which greatly reduced the Accounting Chamber's role so that it could not monitor budget revenues, only budget expenditures.[172]

After February 2014, the world began to see what many Ukrainians and Ukrainian analysts had known all too well – that the government of President Viktor Yanukovych (2010–2014) brought unheard of levels of corruption to the country. In 2012, Ernst & Young placed the country among the three most corrupt in the world, along with Colombia and Brazil.[173] Both Yushchenko's and Yanukovych's terms in office also saw a slide in Transparency International's Corruption Perception Index, with Ukraine falling from 107th place in 2005 to 118th place in 2007, to 134th place in 2010 and to 142nd place in 2014.[174]

Indeed, the level of corruption has been perceived by Ukrainians as being worse than their Polish and Russian counterparts. In the Ukraine Taxpayer Compliance Attitudinal Surveys (see Question #59 in Appendix I), for example, only 10 per cent of Ukrainians in 2010 and 5 per cent of Ukrainians in 2015 stated that their government does a good job in fighting corruption – figures that are almost half and one-third of those in Russia, respectively, and almost one-third and one-fifth of those in Poland, respectively. Meanwhile, 54 per cent of Ukrainians in 2010 and 51 per cent in 2015 stated that the government does a poor job, and 28 per cent in 2010 and 34 per cent in 2015 stated that the government does not fight corruption at all.

---

[172] Ibid., p. 166.   [173] Tkachuk.
[174] See www.transparency.org, accessed on 5 August 2015.

94 Taxes and Trust

The EuroMaidan revolution, from which Yanukovych fled on 21 February 2014, led to a reform-minded government being installed under the leadership of President Petro Poroshenko and Prime Minister Arseniy Yatsenyuk, who have declared that they will fight corruption head on. Indeed, the task is quite hefty, given the size of the public sector and the lack of an overall plan for reducing it.[175] Ukraine has one of the largest government workforces, with 4.42 million employed by the state in 2012, amounting to 26.7 per cent of the country's workforce. In 2014, that figure included to 433,269 public employees in the state administration, comprising 335,270 state-level civil servants and 97,999 local government officials.[176]

After the EuroMaidan revolution, the most prominent debate in Kyiv regarding state employees focused on the issue of lustration of those who served in top government positions during the Yanukovych era. A law passed in September 2014 barred ranks of officials from holding public office, and more than 700 former officials had been lustrated by July 2015. In November 2015, those lustrated were said by Yatsenyuk to include 'first deputy ministers, deputy ministers, 42 per cent of the higher officials of the State Fiscal Service [Ukraine's tax administration] that were closer to the status of millionaires than to the status of real civil servants, and 15 per cent of the leadership of the State Fiscal Service in the regions'.[177] However, the reality of lustration may be quite limited in its success. A top prosecutor in Kyiv, who should have been barred from office, managed, through both connections and knowledge of the legal system, to avoid the ban by obtaining in advance from a court a preventive ban on his dismissal that was kept secret from the public for months.[178]

For post-communist Poland, Russia and Ukraine, the use of legacies to build trust and improve state–society connections has mattered greatly. And such use has mattered more than just cultural and historical predispositions. Political leaders, societies and bureaucracies alike all view their relations with one another based on current interactions as well as on how they perceive similar past interactions to impact on the present. The selection, interpretation and application of past legacies by intent or by default are particularly important in times of transition, when choices on which institutions need abolishing, updating or retaining are made.

For Poland, the irony is that bringing back some of the inter-war institutions in the 1980s – a decade that began with the strikes at the Lenin

[175] Lough and Solonenko, p. 9. [176] Åslund, 2015, p. 134. [177] Yatsenyuk.
[178] Gorchinskaya, 18 July 2015.

Shipyard in Gdańsk, the formation of Solidarity and the establishment of martial law – was done in order to legitimize the communist state in the eyes of its society, but ended up legitimizing the transitional state in the 1990s. The legacy from the past that was used in the 1980s as part of an effort to re-build communist governance actually benefited the communists' successors, as these institutions were in place when other reform efforts were initiated. (This becomes particularly clear in the discussion of bureaucrats' implementation of the new tax policies in the 1990s, to follow in Chapter 5.) Further, as the Polish case illustrates, political parties need not play a guiding role in using legacies from the past in order to update and re-build the new post-transition states.

In some ways, the leadership in both Poland and the Soviet Union in the 1980s began to tap into solutions to governance dilemmas that could have been beneficial in the long run – if only, of course, their governments had not been toppled first. The regime collapses that did end the 1980s came about because the bold and necessary prescriptions for better governance – greater transparency, better citizen–state interactions and societal oversight of the bureaucracy – were antithetical to the essence of authoritarianism, whether it was practiced benignly or not. How to interpret that decade – and the legacy it left behind, replete with still-standing state institutions and bureaucracies – became the choice of new leaders and new societies. Poland chose which institutions to keep and update, using the more distant inter-war legacy to further legitimize the state as it did so. Russia, on the other hand, saw the *glasnost* efforts to build a civil society founder under Yeltsin and that legacy be reversed in the Putin era. Meanwhile, Ukraine did not engage in much soul-searching regarding its historical legacies bequeathed to the state, but opted by default for a continued Soviet-like monolithic bureaucracy that led to disarray by avoiding serious reform in any direction.

In the chapters ahead, we will explore the different approaches that the Polish, Russian and Ukrainian systems took in the first twenty-five years of the transition in utilizing existing state structures to collect the newly established taxes. We'll start in Chapter 4 with an examination of the tax regime and different economic and tax policy explanations for tax collection, which will be followed, in Chapter 5, with an analytical view of the inner workings of the tax bureaucracy and, in Chapters 6 and 7, with a focused look at how different types of state-society relationships contribute to tax compliance.

4 Creating Post-communist Tax Regimes and Measuring Tax Compliance

Most centrally planned socialist economies in Eastern Europe imitated the tax system of the Soviet Union. Thus, all post-socialist states at the beginning of the transformation to market economies had poorly functioning tax administrations and falling ratios of tax revenues to Gross Domestic Product (GDP), as well as tax compliance problems.[1] Yet Poland, like a few other Central European states, moved sooner than the other post-communist states to reform its tax system and was able to raise adequate revenues throughout this period.[2] Poland was more effective than Russia and Ukraine in collecting taxes during the past quarter century.

Before discerning why that was the case, it is necessary to present how it was the case. Namely, it is necessary to begin by specifying as precisely as possible how well each country collects taxes. That is the main goal of this chapter. Before that, the chapter provides an overview of the structure of the tax regimes in Poland, Russia and Ukraine. At the beginning of the 1990s, Poland, Russia and Ukraine all introduced three new main taxes (the personal income tax (PIT), the corporate income tax (CIT) and the value-added tax (VAT)), allowing a great comparative study, as the three states were required to make dramatic institutional changes in the tax arena at exactly the same time. Finally, a further goal for this chapter is to analyze the use and limitations of economic explanations and tax rates to account for the diversity of tax revenue outcomes. In short, this chapter provides better understanding, context and measurement of the object of study, tax compliance.

Tax Regimes in Poland, Russia and Ukraine

The primary focus throughout this study is on the two direct income taxes, the PIT and the CIT, and the indirect VAT. These three taxes, non-existent in the communist era, are the main source of fiscal

---

[1] Polomski, p. 6.   [2] See Martinez-Vazquez and McNab, p. 290.

96

Creating Post-communist Tax Regimes and Tax Compliance 97

revenues for Central and Eastern Europe (CEE) and are the basis for taxation in the EU countries. Poland introduced the PIT and CIT on 1 January 1992 and the VAT on 5 July 1993. Meanwhile, Russia inherited a profits tax for enterprises from the Soviet era and introduced the PIT and VAT on 1 January 1992. (A 13 per cent flat rate for the PIT was introduced in Russia in January 2001.) And, in 1992, Ukraine introduced an enterprise income tax – which in the early years shifted back and forth between being a tax on profits and a tax on income and was later called the corporate income tax – and the value-added tax, which functioned as a sort of turnover tax until 1997. A PIT with progressive tax rates was introduced in Ukraine in 1992, while a flat PIT rate of 13 per cent was introduced in 2004, which was increased to 15 per cent in 2007, before a second higher rate of 17 per cent was introduced in 2011. The second rate for Ukraine's PIT increased to 20 per cent in 2015, and the rate changed to a flat 18 per cent in 2016.

In his analysis of key conceptual and measurement issues raised by cross-national taxation studies in political science, Evan Lieberman finds that taxes on income and profits (and on capital gains), often grouped together under the label of 'direct taxes', are well suited for comparing state capacity because they 'reflect levels of state–society and intra-society coordination and cooperation'[3]:

Most analysts would probably agree that the 'purest' form of taxation includes those taxes levied on income, profits and capital gains. Such taxes are paid over to the state directly by individuals and firms, often with graduated rates for different levels of income. Political scientists studying taxation have tended to develop indicators based on the standard assumption that these taxes have the qualities of being among the most progressive, most difficult to administer, most transparent, and least requited of any government revenue streams. As a result . . . higher levels of income tax collections are generally associated with greater levels of capacity . . . [4]

Hence, if two different states are found to extract similar amounts of income and profits from similar-sized and similarly wealthy tax groups, then the states can be said to be similar in their capacities to extract revenue, provided that the two tax groups behave and respond similarly to their respective states' tax authorities.

CIT, often referred in Russia and Ukraine as the profits tax, and PIT require significant administrative work, as they affect many more taxpayers and hence involve greater 'penetration of society' than other, more 'indirect' consumption taxes, such as the VAT and other sales and excise

---

[3] Lieberman, 2002, p. 100.   [4] Ibid., p. 99.

98   Taxes and Trust

taxes. In Poland, the PIT affects all individuals who are employed or earn income (except for some farmers), whereas in Russia and Ukraine, after the adoption of the flat rate for the PIT in 2001 and in 2004, respectively, most individuals let their employers pay their taxes for them. Out of a population of 39 million, the number of Poles who paid taxes was around 23 or 24 million throughout most of the 1990s, whereas 17.25 million taxpayers paid PIT in 2014.[5] In Russia, out of a population of approximately 145 million, 105 million individuals were on the tax administration's lists in 2003.[6] In Ukraine, about 20 million individuals, out of a population of roughly 47 million, were deemed to be taxpayers in 2006 and 13.87 million were deemed to be PIT taxpayers in 2014.[7]

Domestic consumption taxes, which include the VAT and other sales and excise taxes, are generally paid by a limited group of retailers and manufacturers that are fewer in number than the individuals on a state's income tax rolls. However, the burden of such consumption taxes is usually carried by consumers in the form of higher prices for goods and services. With respect to analytical constructs such as state capacity, Lieberman states that such 'indirect' taxes are considered to be less complex for bureaucracies than the first group of taxes, but still require functioning and capable tax administrations. 'Taxes on consumption', he writes, '... tend to be easier to collect than taxes on income because they are collected indirectly, incrementally, and generally at the point of purchase.'[8]

Nevertheless, within the post-communist environment, the VAT tax is a particularly tricky tax to implement and administer due to the rise in the number of fictitious firms, which try to claim a VAT refund for non-existent sales. Hence, by choosing to focus on the PIT, the CIT and the VAT consumption tax when undertaking field research on how tax laws are implemented by bureaucrats in Poland, Russia and Ukraine (as will be shown in Chapter 5), a somewhat easier tax to collect can be compared with the more difficult income taxes so that a more complete range of administrative capabilities can be analyzed in these three states.

---

[5] Najwyższa Izba Kontroli (NIK), 8 June 1998, p. 62; and NIK, June 2001, p. 63; and Ministry of Finance, 2015, p. 10.
[6] RIA Oreanda.
[7] Alm, Saavedra and Sennoga, p. 9; International Monetary Fund (IMF), January 2016, p. 36.
[8] Lieberman, 2002, p. 103.

Creating Post-communist Tax Regimes and Tax Compliance 99

Taxation in the Command Economy

In the early 1990s, unlike Poland, both Russia and Ukraine adapted and adjusted Soviet-era tax laws, seeking to operate within – rather than to replace – the existing legal framework.[9] Under state socialism, the economy in both Poland and the Soviet Union was based on a narrow revenue stream, emanating from a relatively small number of large, state-run enterprises.[10] Taxes in the command economy were, basically, transfers from the public enterprise sector to the state itself. 'The planning office set wages and prices at levels that would generate surpluses in the public enterprises', writes Vito Tanzi, who attended the first International Monetary Fund (IMF) mission to Russia in 1991. 'Since there were no "parametric" or objective tax rates stated in tax laws, most of the transfers were the result of negotiations between the managers of the enterprises and officials from what was called the tax administration. Thus, these taxes were largely arbitrary. They often reflected administrative or bureaucratic decisions, not legislation.'[11]

The nature of these taxes, then, did not require that the communists develop a large tax administration. 'In the pre-reform system most revenues were simply transferred to the budget through the debiting of enterprise accounts at the state bank', Barry W. Ickes and Joel Slemrod comment. 'Hence there was little need for tax administration. Indeed, by the 1960's the Soviet tax administration system was dismantled and its functions carried out by the Ministry of Finance. A separate tax inspectorate was set up in the Ministry of Finance only in July of 1990. Hence tax administration in the Soviet Union (and by extension other reforming socialist economies) is rather undeveloped.'[12] For Poland as well as for Russia and Ukraine, then, implementing, adopting and adjusting to new forms of taxes in the early 1990s required the building of a new tax administration system, nearly from scratch.

Poland's Tax Regime

In Poland, the most important taxes are administered at the national level and include, as mentioned above, the CIT, the PIT and the

---

[9] Alexeev and Conrad, pp. 247–248.
[10] Easter, 2002, p. 604.   [11] Tanzi, pp. 10–11.
[12] Ickes and Slemrod, pp. 387–388. In Tsarist Russia, Tsar Nicholas II approved a much-delayed general income tax law that was to have come into effect in early 1917, but the Russian Revolution rendered the personal income tax and Russian citizens' experience with it moot. (Franklin, p. 141.)

100 Taxes and Trust

VAT – listed in order of increasing importance to the Polish state budget. Social security contributions, shared by employers and employees, also compose an important revenue stream. The PIT is subject to a progressive income tax, and from 2014, two different tax rates on income apply – 18 and 32 per cent with a threshold of 85,528 Polish złoty (PLN) for the higher rate. Rates have varied over the years, with the top PIT rate as high as 45 per cent in 1995–1996.[13] Also, in 2014, the CIT was reduced from 40 per cent (its highest since the mid-1990s) to 19 per cent.[14] The VAT has had a top rate of either 22 or 23 per cent since its introduction in 1993. Other taxes include the tonnage tax, inheritance and donation tax, tax on civil law transactions, agricultural tax, forest tax, real property tax, transport vehicles tax, taxes on the extraction of certain minerals, excise duties and gambling tax.[15]

Political Origins of Poland's Tax Regime

Given the narrow tax base inherited from the command economy, Poland, according to Gerald M. Easter, sought a social pact with labour in order to shift the tax burden from state-run industrial enterprises that were dependent on the state for financing to worker households through the introduction of a new PIT.[16]

In many ways, the public battle over the *popiwek* – the Polish tax on excess wages established in order to enforce wage ceilings on public sector workers – laid the groundwork for the introduction of the PIT. 'The implementation of the new tax was facilitated by certain compromises entailed in this social pact', continues Easter. 'First, with the establishment of the Tripartite Commission [composed of the government, management, and the trade unions], labour was accorded a formal means for participation in the wage policy process. Second, as part of the bargain, workers' wages would keep pace with inflation. As the personal income tax went into effect, wages were raised to offset an immediate adverse impact on worker households. Finally, in March 1994, the *popiwek* was abandoned by the government.'[17] In short, due to a combination of unproductive state firms, an unpopular tax on wage ceilings and political negotiations that included both firm managers and workers, the

[13] Trading Economics website, accessed 29 August 2016 at <http://www.tradingeconomics.com/poland>.
[14] Ibid.
[15] Ministry of Finance of Poland, accessed 29 August 2016 at <http://www.finanse.mf.gov.pl/documents/766655/936176/20111026_tax_system_of_Poland.pdf>.
[16] Easter, 2002, p. 609.   [17] Ibid., p. 612.

Creating Post-communist Tax Regimes and Tax Compliance 101

PIT emerged in Poland as a major revenue source for the state, second only to the VAT.

Russia's Tax Regime

During the Yeltsin years, when regions sought greater autonomy, the number of taxes across Russia began to mushroom. By 1999, there were 'about 30 separate federal taxes and over 170 local and regional taxes'.[18] Nevertheless, the most important taxes in Russia have been administered at the national level and include the PIT, the CIT, the VAT and the Natural Resource Extractment Tax (NDPI), or the Mineral Extraction Tax (MET), with the largest source of federal tax revenue varying by year between the CIT, the VAT and the NDPI. Until 2001, the PIT was a progressive income tax, with the top marginal rate from 1993–1998 being 35 per cent even as most Russians paid the lower 12 per cent marginal rate. Since 2001, Russia has had a flat personal income tax rate of 13 per cent. The CIT has had different rates over the years, with a high rate of 43 per cent in 2001. Since 2009, the rate for the CIT has been 20 per cent.[19] While the VAT's standard rate was cut in January 1993 from 28 to 20 per cent, the top rate has been 18 per cent since 2004.[20] Together with excise taxes, the VAT, the CIT and the PIT composed roughly three-quarters of total tax collections in the consolidated budget in the 1990s.[21] Excise taxes, tariffs and mineral taxes, which function like royalties, also have been strong sources of revenue.[22]

As for how these laws are perceived by the tax collectors themselves, even a good number of Russian tax officials think that their country's tax laws are unfair. According to the 2011 Russian Public Officials' Survey, 18 per cent stated that the tax laws are not fair, with a further 10 per cent refusing to say (Appendix I, Question #26.)

According to Michael Alexeev and Robert F. Conrad, the tax system in Russia has been deemed to work well largely because the tax administration makes it difficult for exporters to obtain VAT refunds and because of overtaxation of the oil and gas sector, estimates of the revenue share of which range from 35 to 60 per cent once CIT, VAT, mineral extraction charges and export taxes, among others, are added up.[23]

---

[18] Himes and Milliet-Einbinder.
[19] Trading Economics website, accessed 17 September 2016 at <http://www.tradingeconomics.com/russia/>.
[20] World Bank, 1996, p. 18; and Trading Economics website.
[21] Alm, Martinez-Vazquez and Wallace, p. 2.   [22] Alexeev and Conrad, p. 250.
[23] Ibid., pp. 246, 253.

102   Taxes and Trust

Political Origins of Russia's Tax Regime

In the early 1990s, Russia needed to construct a new tax system that would obtain revenue from the newly privatized sectors of the economy. To do so, it relied on elite bargaining with the owners of a very narrow, but quite profitable and identifiable revenue base of the new economy – the large-scale extractive industries involved in exporting commodities, including the oil and gas firms and companies involved in minerals and metals, which had recently broken off from the state itself, had benefited from Russia's concentrated economy and profited from the loans-for-shares program, and were well known to the tax authorities. 'Elite bargaining was a hybrid system of revenue extraction that combined the new conditions of the transition economy with practices familiar to the command economy', writes Easter. 'It rested on a complex web of informal elite ties stretching across political and economic spheres and from centre to regions.'[24] Similarly, Pauline Jones Luong and Erika Weinthal argue that after the 1998 financial crisis, the interests of government and the large oil firms coincided, making reforms on oil-sector-specific taxes and profits taxes possible.[25]

Such elite bargaining with respect to this small, but profitable and unique-to-Russia sector of the economy led to a heavy burden for the selected few companies. This has led Scott Gehlbach to conclude that the structure of Russia's taxation helps to explain the form of capitalism that has developed. 'With the focus in the former Soviet Union on a number of key revenue sources, tax authorities never learned to extract revenues from other sorts of enterprises or from individuals', writes Gehlbach. 'As a consequence, politicians . . . were led to promote those sectors that they knew would produce tax revenue, at the expense of those that would not. In contrast, in Eastern Europe – where tax systems had been structured to cast the revenue net more widely – there were fewer such perverse incentives.'[26] Unsurprisingly, with the state invested in such a focused sector of the economy, tax arrears from the energy sector were more accepted by the state. '[T]he state would tolerate tax arrears so long as the energy sector continued to supply even delinquent customers, thus preventing too rapid a collapse of key employment-providing enterprises and service-providing public-sector organizations', write Andrei Shleifer and Daniel Treisman. 'Of the growth in budget arrears in [the mid-1990s], more than 90 per cent reportedly resulted from state-sanctioned exemptions.'[27]

---

[24] Easter, 2002, p. 614.   [25] Jones Luong and Weinthal.
[26] Gehlbach, p. 13.   [27] Shleifer and Treisman, p. 73.

Creating Post-communist Tax Regimes and Tax Compliance   103

In addition to the firms involved in exported extracted commodities, the regional governments, which gained powers in the 1990s from Russia's dysfunctional federalism, also were involved in the elite bargaining process, which influenced Russia's tax structure for decades to come. Regional governments united with the large-scale extractive industries 'to undermine reformers' attempts to restructure the tax system in ways that would have improved incentives for growth and tax collection', continue Shleifer and Treisman. '. . . Large enterprises and regional governments also colluded to weaken the collection of federal taxes and thus keep more resources in the regions. Their strategies involved diverting a growing share of economic activity into the unofficial economy and increasingly turning to nonmonetary means of payment.'[28] As a result, just as the state had tolerated arrears by some large firms, the federal government in the 1990s tolerated tax withholding (or allocated larger transfers) to the regions that threatened to declare sovereignty, stage strikes or vote for the opposition.[29]

The 1998 financial crisis, however, brought unity to the large-scale extractive industries and the government, setting the stage for the major tax reforms of 2000 and 2001, which, under President Vladimir Putin, brought forth the 13 per cent flat PIT and the unified social tax (UST), replacing various social contributions; reform of the VAT; and a decrease in the CIT rate and in the dividend tax rate. Assisting in these reforms was former Prime Minister Yegor Gaidar's Institute for the Economy in Transition.[30]

Ukraine's Tax Regime

As in its neighbours, the most important taxes administered in Ukraine are the PIT, the CIT and the VAT, in reverse order of significance to the state budget. The PIT rate has been less stable than in Russia. Since January 2016, the PIT rate has been set at a flat 18 per cent for all salaries regardless of amount. Just prior to this, the PIT rate was tied to the amount of personal income, with a rate of 15 per cent applied if income did not exceed ten times a minimum monthly salary or 20 per cent for income in excess of that amount.[31] Up until 2003, the PIT was a progressive tax, but, from 2004 to 2010, a flat rate of 13 per cent (as in Russia) and, from 2007 to 2010, a flat rate of 15 per cent applied. Since August 2014, as a response to the war against Russia in the Donbas region, a temporary military tax of 1.5 per cent of taxable

---

[28] Ibid., p. 90.   [29] Ibid., p. 110.
[30] Alexeev and Conrad, pp. 248–249.   [31] Baker & McKenzie, Kyiv Office.

104   Taxes and Trust

income has been introduced for all those who pay a tax on their personal income.[32] Social security contributions have been shared by employers and employees, but since January 2016, employers are deemed fully responsible for paying a 22 per cent tax on salaries – significantly down from rates that had earlier ranged from 36.76 to 49.70 per cent.[33]

Since the late 1990s, the CIT rate in Ukraine has been slowly dropping from a high of 30 per cent to a current level of 18 per cent, and the VAT has had a top rate of 20 per cent.[34] Other taxes include excise taxes, vehicle ownership tax, real estate tax, rent tax, fixed agriculture tax and the simplified small business tax.[35] The last, which since its introduction in 1998 has played an important role in Ukraine due to its low rate and due to the ease with which individuals have been able to switch their employment status from employee to 'independent' consultant while still working for the same firm, applies to individual entrepreneurs and legal entities whose annual income does not exceed 5 million Ukrainian hryvnia (approximately U.S.$200,000 in mid-2016) – down significantly in 2016 from a previous income of 20 million Ukrainian hryvnia. From 2016, the rate for this simplified system has increased to 3 per cent for VAT payers and to 5 per cent for non-VAT payers.[36]

Political Origins of Ukraine's Tax Regime

Whereas the 1990s debate over the tax regime in Russia was resolved in the early 2000s, just as Putin ascended to office, the process for Ukraine took even longer and occurred in an even more fragmented manner. Not until late 2010 was a tax code adopted in Ukraine. Much of the delay likely is due to the 'unholy alliance between an executive interested in possibilities for selective enforcement, oligarchs interested in a system with privileges rather than a level playing field, and a Communist Party opposed to a market economy' that emerged in the 1990s and continued, more or less, up to the EuroMaidan Revolution.[37]

Emblematic of the uncertainty and discord among policy makers in the 1990s was perhaps the VAT tax, which constantly changed in that decade with respect to rates, tax base and exemptions. 'In 1999, Serhyi Teriokhin, head of the tax and customs subcommittee of the *Verkhovna*

---

[32] Contact Ukraine website accessed 18 September 2016 at <http://www.contactukraine .com/taxation/individual-tax-in-ukraine>.

[33] Baker & McKenzie, Kyiv Office.

[34] Trading Economics website, accessed 18 September 2016 at <http://www .tradingeconomics.com/ukraine/>.

[35] Vasil Kisil & Partners.   [36] Ibid.   [37] Fritz, p. 150.

Rada [Ukraine's parliament]', writes Verena Fritz, 'estimated that "since independence, Ukraine [...] has revised its value-added tax rules more than 200 times."'[38] Similarly, the Razumkov Centre tracked the number of regulatory acts that define all tax payment procedures as adopted each year in the 1990s[39]:

1991	1992	1993	1994	1995	1996	1997	1998	1999
21	31	103	142	291	329	436	664	500

The dramatic increases in regulations by the end of the decade surely must have bewildered accountants and state tax employees alike!

Ukraine's adoption in March 2003 of the flat personal income tax, two years after Russia's, came under a 'For a United Ukraine' coalition government with few right-wing members, veering from an East European pattern in which right-wing governments sought the adoption of the flat tax. Hilary Appel has argued that the passage of the flat tax largely was due to 'economically liberal politicians' who held powerful positions in the Rada, including Teriokhin, who claimed that the new flat tax rate would bring in more taxpayers and reduce the shadow economy.'[40]

Under President Viktor Yanukovych, in December 2010, Ukraine at last adopted a tax code, which sought to define the status, rights and responsibilities of the taxpayers and of the tax administration structures. Coming into force in January 2011, the tax code since has seen multiple changes incorporated into it. Among other things, the code abolished the simplified tax for small business entrepreneurs, forcing at least one million to close shop in the first year, while enabling easier transfer pricing, which benefited larger businesses by enabling them to transfer their profits abroad without paying any tax.[41] In subsequent amendments, after significant protests by thousands of small entrepreneurs in Kyiv,[42] the popular simplified taxation was brought back into the code.

Since the EuroMaidan Revolution, Ukraine's new wave of Rada deputies and politicians have been trying to reform the country's tax legislation, largely in order to broaden the tax base and to simplify

---

[38] *Ibid.*, p. 151.
[39] 'Graph: The number of regulatory acts that define tax payment procedures', in Razumkov UCEPS, 2000, p. 9.
[40] Appel, 2011, p. 105.
[41] Åslund, 20 October 2011; Åslund, 26 November 2013.
[42] RFE/RL, 16 November 2010.

106   Taxes and Trust

the administration of tax collection, as well as to lower rates in order
to appeal for public support for the post-Yanukovych reform process
and bring more income out of the shadow economy.[43] (Broadly speaking, though, these long-unfulfilled objectives have remained the same in
Ukraine since the debate over tax reform began in the mid-1990s.)

At the same time, policy-making with respect to taxation is a multi-
institutional process in Ukraine, usually forcing the Rada deputies to
depend upon other state agencies that serve as the primary authors of
draft tax legislation. In February 2015, Andrei V. Zhurzhiy, first deputy
chair of the tax committee within the Rada and a new MP since 2014,
remarked that he did not consider the package of tax reforms passed in
late December 2014 to be true reforms, as they had been prepared by
the Ministry of Finance and the tax administration and did not reach
MPs in sufficient time to review, let along make changes. New tax laws
needed to be passed before a new year began so that businesses could
begin to operate under them. Such a late arrival of the draft legislation
on deputies' desks was quite a revelation for the former businessman.[44]
A year later, on the eve of 2016, a compromise was found between the
Ministry of Finance's first draft and one prepared by the Rada Committee on Taxation and Customs Policy, headed by Nina Iuzhanina.[45]

International Tax Assistance for Poland, Russia and Ukraine

In creating their tax systems, Poland, Russia and Ukraine each had
different reactions to the tax system reform advice they received from
abroad. The type of tax system constructed reflected the type of economy envisaged.

From the very start of the transition, Poland, Russia and Ukraine all
faced international pressures to get their fiscal houses in order, but also
received technical and financial aid from abroad. In addition to the foreign aid programs of the United States, the European Union and other
foreign governments, coupled with the advice of academics and global
think tanks, particular key roles in the tax reform process were played by
the International Monetary Fund (IMF) and World Bank.[46] In the early
1990s, Poland, for one, had a tremendous foreign debt inherited from
the Polish People's Republic (PRL) and needed the Bank and the IMF,
which provided loans that came with conditions for all three states. 'Over

[43] Åslund, 9 November 2015.
[44] Author's interview with Andrei V. Zhurzhiy, Kyiv, Ukraine, 9 February 2015.
[45] Petrukhina.
[46] For a full list of PHARE (EU) projects with respect to the Polish tax administration and
tax system from 1997 to 2003, see Ministry of Finance, 2004, pp. 88–89.

the following years, the IMF's Fiscal Affairs Department would play an important role in tax policy and tax administration in Russia', writes Vito Tanzi in his biography. 'During the decade of transition, the department would help Russia establish a new tax system and a true tax administration. But it would take several years and a lot of hard work on the part of many staff missions.'[47] The World Bank also sponsored Tax Administration Modernisation Projects (TAMPs) in Russia and Ukraine, described in greater detail in the next chapter.

The Organisation for Economic Co-operation and Development (OECD) was active from the beginning of the transition as well, with training of tax officials.[48] The OECD also worked with Russia during the enactment of its tax code in the late 1990s and early 2000s to ensure that the legislation would coordinate with international standards.[49] (Similarly, by 1999, with the work on the code, Tanzi remarked, 'things were finally going much better than in previous years and . . . for the first time, the Russians were listening to the advice received [from the IMF] and there were concrete signs of progress'.[50])

In terms of following the advice offered from abroad, most of the transition countries closely followed guidance on changing tax policy – and most followed suit with legislation, but many ignored changing their tax administrations and incorporating more established western accounting practices.[51] Poland (along with the Czech Republic, Hungary, Slovenia, and the Baltics) acted quickly on foreign advice and introduced comprehensive reform almost immediately, while there was less broad consensual support for tax reform in countries such as Russia and Ukraine, enabling vested interests to block reforms.[52]

Easter describes three waves of tax reform in Central and Eastern Europe: A first wave of capitalist-style tax reforms that accompanied the macro structural reforms of the early 1990s that was assisted by Western economic advisors was followed, for those EU accession countries like Poland, by a second wave in which indirect sales taxes (the VAT) were aligned with those in the rest of the European marketplace. (VAT, of course, became the indirect tax of choice not just for those states aspiring to join the European Union but also for the other transition states as well.) A third wave, caused by the transition economies' low tax morale, weak tax administration and poor economic capitalization, followed in the 2000s with the arrival of the flat-tax and other rate-cutting reforms of personal and corporate direct income taxes.[53] (While Poland

---

[47] Tanzi, p. 11.   [48] Appel, 2011, p. 32.   [49] Ibid., p. 32.   [50] Tanzi, p. 50.
[51] Martinez-Vazquez and McNab, p. 277.   [52] Ibid., pp. 277–278.
[53] Easter, 2013, pp. 1148–1149.

108   Taxes and Trust

did not adopt the flat PIT tax as did its neighbours Russia and Ukraine, it did lower its direct tax rates during this period.) In short, the first wave involved Western advisors, especially from the IMF; the second involved the European Union; and the third originated from learning and copying other Central and Eastern European states in the region – as flat taxes became an Eastern European rather than a Western European phenomenon.

The IMF's influence, especially in the first wave, was greater with respect to tax policy, macroeconomic and technical issues than it was with respect to providing practical advice on structural and institutional reforms. Getting advice accepted in 1990s Russia, though, was difficult, in part due to the fact that many Russians felt it to be 'humiliating' to ask the IMF for loans.[54] The IMF's activities in the 1990s – such as technical assistance, posting a senior tax administration expert at the State Tax Service, and setting targets for revenue collection as conditions for loan disbursements – failed to have much of an impact on revenues in Russia.[55] However, with the drafting and adoption of the new tax code, the IMF's influence grew. 'In the case of tax policy reform', writes John Odling-Smee, 'major changes did not come until 2001 under President Putin. The seeds of some components of this reform had been sown earlier, partly by the IMF and other technical assistance advisors. The IMF staff had opposed other components, however, notably the move to a flat rate personal income tax, which, although desirable on structural grounds, had seemed to the staff to carry the risk of a temporary loss of revenue.'[56]

With respect to the influence of the European Union, particularly with regard to Easter's second wave, the evidence is mixed. To start with, Poland was not the only CEE state to join the European Union in 2004. Seven other states did as well, all with varying levels of tax arrears and fiscal imbalances. Revelations that the prime minister had lied about fiscal imbalances led Hungarians to protest in 2006, while Bulgaria and Slovakia – states that held high enthusiasm for EU accession – had difficult tax problems. In some ways, what entrant states can do is narrowed by the process of EU integration, and states cannot do what citizens want them to do. On the other hand, getting into the European Union does not provide states with any more incentives to collect more taxes in and of itself, especially if the European Union is to provide subsidies.

Appel argues, with respect to the second wave of indirect sales tax reforms, that the European Union maintained a strong influence on Poland and the other EU accession countries through the exertion of

---

[54] Odling-Smee, p. 156.   [55] Ibid., p. 175.   [56] Ibid., p. 177.

Creating Post-communist Tax Regimes and Tax Compliance   109

international leverage supporting once-stalled tax reforms. 'Their tax laws had to be harmonized with existing EU law, and all areas of indirect taxes had to follow the *acquis communautaire*, the body of EU law whose adoption was required for membership', writes Appel. '... In practice this meant that the East Europeans imported their consumption tax regime from abroad with virtually no concessions to domestic groups. Since consumption taxes generate the largest portion of tax revenue, the loss of control over taxation was enormous.'[57]

Easter, on the other hand, maintains that the EU-directed reforms were delayed, incomplete and partially successful and that domestic political and structural constraints were just as determinative in the formation of the post-communist tax regimes. 'Even in the case when international leverage was at its highest (EU accession reform)', states Easter, 'domestic political considerations (rooted in revenue bargains) prompted post-communist governments to resist, delay and renegotiate particular features of the tax policy reform. In the end, the European Commission acquiesced to an incomplete tax harmonization at the point when membership was conferred on the post-communist candidates.'[58] Appel, for her part, does agree that domestic politics was decisive with respect to the development of and approach to taxing personal income in Central and Eastern Europe.[59]

In short, throughout the transition, all of the transition states benefited from advice and assistance from abroad in constructing their tax systems, but the extent to which such foreign input mattered is mixed, piecemeal and contested. For the most part, foreign assistance offered to all three of these states was greatest in the 1990s and into the early 2000s. Ukraine, though, received assistance for a more prolonged period of time, and as will be explored in Chapter 8, some of that advice has been forthcoming more recently, with the re-launch of reforms after the 2014 EuroMaidan Revolution.

Measuring Tax Compliance in Poland, Russia and Ukraine

Throughout the transition to a market economy, Poland was shown to be consistently able to extract revenue, though it did fall short of its goals at times and had significant (but not incapacitating) tax arrears. Meanwhile, data from Russia and Ukraine are more erratic, but show tax collection to be poor throughout most of the 1990s with some improvement after 2000.

[57] Appel, 2011, pp. 2–3.   [58] Easter, 2009, pp. 49–50.   [59] Appel, 2011, p. 5.

110   Taxes and Trust

Extractive capacity, measured in terms of tax extraction, is the most commonly used measure of a state's capacity.[60] However, obtaining measures for the ability to collect taxes – especially in a series over time that is comparable across countries – is not easy. One of the most frequent methods of reporting tax revenue statistics is to present the amount of revenue collected as a percentage of national income, usually the country's GDP.[61] In his review of different methodologies for analysing states' tax income, Lieberman explains that tax collection data are often presented in this manner 'because analysts implicitly agree that the problem or challenge for states is to collect a portion of the total economy in tax revenues, and that opportunities and constraints on taxation for policy-makers and the bureaucracy are ultimately determined by the size of the economy'.[62]

However, presenting tax collection data as a percentage of GDP does have some limitations – especially if the focus of concern is assessment of a state's capacity to tax. First, as Lieberman has observed, displaying data in this way assumes that no matter what the size of the economy actually is, the collection of a certain percentage of a country's national income would imply that the effort was just as difficult as if a similar percentage in GDP terms was collected from a country with markedly different national income. 'By looking at income tax collections as a share of GDP', Lieberman writes, 'the measure controls for the relative size of the economy, but assumes that the challenge of collecting direct taxes from any economy is basically the same problem.'[63] In other words, the task of collecting taxes may be far more challenging for a new nation embarking on the task of state-building than for a more established state with a much larger economy. The size of the wealth and how it is distributed in society might be significant as well.

---

[60] Fukuyama, 2013, p. 353.

[61] As a comparison from 1990 to 2011, the OECD member states collected an average of 12.0 per cent of GDP per year in direct tax revenue (measured as income, profits and capital gains taxes) and an average per year of 11.0 per cent of indirect tax revenue (measured as taxes on goods and services.) Meanwhile, Poland fared better in indirect than direct taxes over the 1992–2013 period, averaging 8.1 per cent of GDP per year collected in similarly measured direct taxes and 12.2 per cent of GDP per year collected in indirect taxes. Russia over the 1992–2013 period fared relatively poorly in comparison, collecting 8.7 per cent of GDP per year in direct taxes (profits tax (CIT) and PIT) and 8.2 per cent of GDP per year in indirect taxes (VAT, excise taxes). Meanwhile, Ukraine from 1994 to 2013 collected an average of 9.7 per cent of GDP each year in direct taxes and 12.0 per cent of GDP per year in indirect taxes. (Poland and OECD data from the OECD; Russia and Ukraine data from the IMF.)

[62] Lieberman, 2003, p. 106.   [63] Ibid., p. 62.

Creating Post-communist Tax Regimes and Tax Compliance   111

In addition, while readily available for cross-national purposes, such 'taxes collected as a percentage of GDP' data do not account for the actual tax rates and expected tax levels. Some states do, in fact, have significantly lower tax rates than others, but this may not imply that such states are less capable of raising revenue that they want or need. 'There is a difference between extractive potential and actual extraction rates', writes Francis Fukuyama. 'Actual tax rates are set not just by extractive potential, but by policy choices regarding the optimal rate and types of taxation.'[64] The fact that the United States collected more tax revenue during the two World Wars than before or after reflects differences in policy preferences as to what the size of government should be during times of war and peace. Moreover, some governments have better or worse perceptions of their own societies, including how they envision wealth and income to be distributed. As Alexeev and Conrad also remark, 'the fact that a country collecting significant tax revenue is not necessarily evidence of the tax system efficiency or even effectiveness of tax administration. This is because tax effort [taxes as a share of GDP] regressions do not include either a measure of statutory tax burden or a measure of welfare loss associated with tax collections. That is, a country with a very efficient tax system and tax administration might be characterized by low tax effort simply because its population prefers to have a small public sector. Conversely, a country that exhibits high tax effort might be collecting taxes in an inefficient way.'[65]

Hence, what may be needed is a measure of tax collection that incorporates states' perceptions of themselves and their societies, one that includes, from the earlier definition of *state capacity* presented in Chapter 2, the concept of *state goals* and *objectives*.

A perfect measure of tax collection, then, would be the amount collected as a percentage of what the state believes should ideally be collected in order for it to accomplish the tasks it would like to carry out. Examining tax arrears as determined by a country's Ministry of Finance or Tax Administration – the amount of taxes not collected but what the state thinks it should have collected – can help to approximate the state's view of those data at an aggregate level. Further, it is critically important to assess, if possible, the willingness of citizens to comply with the state and pay their dues. Therefore, this chapter will present data on tax arrears and data from a bespoke series of surveys on citizen attitudes. With this two-pronged approach, tax capacity will be assessed at the aggregate and individual levels.

---

[64] Fukuyama, 2013, p. 353.   [65] Alexeev and Conrad, p. 250.

112   Taxes and Trust

Table 4.1 *Overall tax arrears as percentage of all taxes collected in Poland,[a] Russia[b] and Ukraine[c]*

	1994	1995	1996	1997	1998	1999	2000	2001	2002	2003	2004
Poland	na	6.0	5.7	5.0	4.7	6.1	7.7	9.7	11.4	10.7	10.3
Russia	11.2	16.1	27.6	31.1	49.4	41.7	31.2	25.5	22.4	19.5	15.8
Ukraine	na	6.0	6.5	9.5	44.0	45.2	31.7	17.4	53.3	42.0	22.3

	2005	2006	2007	2008	2009	2010	2011	2012	2013	2014	2015
Poland	9.3	8.9	7.7	7.7	8.3	8.8	9.1	10.4	12.8	15.2	na
Russia	19.3	13.9	10.9	7.2	8.9	8.8	7.2	6.2	6.4	6.1	6.0
Ukraine	8.7	5.7	3.6	3.7	5.3	6.0	3.9	2.6	3.1	6.7	4.7

Poland average (1995–2014)	8.8
Russia average (1994–2015)	17.8
Ukraine average (1995–2015)	15.8

[a] For Poland, Ministry of Finance, 2000, p. 15; 2001, pp. 4, 14; 2002, pp. 4, 29; 2003, pp. 4, 16; 2004, pp. 5, 19; Ministry of Finance websites (<www.archbip.mf.gov.pl/bip/7786.html>) accessed 8 July 2014 and (<www.finanse.mf.gov.pl/budzet-panstwa/>) accessed 18 July 2016. The Overall Tax figure was compiled using data for corporate income tax, personal income tax, taxes on goods and services, excise tax, games tax and abolished taxes. Also, note that in 2002 overall taxes do not include arrears from excise taxes.

[b] Data compiled by author with statistics from Rosstat, 1998, pp. 22–24, 59; 2000, pp. 68, 72; 2002, pp. 58, 62; 2004, pp. 72, 76; 2006, pp. 73, 77; 2008, pp. 77, 83; 2010, pp. 82, 87; and 2012, pp. 81, 86. On 18 July 2016, 2012–2014 data were accessed from Finansy Rossii 2014 at www.gks.ru/wps/wcm/connect/rosstat_main/rosstat/ru/statistics/publications/catalog/doc_1138717651859, while 2015 data were accessed at: <http://www.gks.ru/wps/wcm/connect/rosstat_main/rosstat/ru/statistics/finance/#> and at <www.gks.ru/free_doc/new_site/finans/fin210g.htm>. The Overall Tax figure was compiled using aggregate data for all taxes received, which include corporate income tax, personal income tax (although arrears data are not provided separately for this tax as in Poland and Ukraine), taxes on goods and services, excise taxes, payments for the use of mineral wealth and natural resources, and property taxes. In 1994, a special tax also was included in the taxes collected figure, and from 2000 to 2003, Rosstat also includes a separate sales tax and a taxes on gross revenue.

[c] Unlike the Polish and Russian tax arrears data, the Ukraine data do not come from a single source, as no institution or organization, including the Ukrainian Ministry of Finance, has time series data from the mid-1990s until the present. Obtaining financial and tax data in Ukraine is not just a problem for independent researchers, but also has been regarded as a problem for government policy makers trying to make policy projections. The 1995 data are from the IMF, 1999, pp. 100, 102. 1996–2001 data are from a World Bank Ukraine office document entitled 'Descriptive and Diagnostic Analyses,' pp. 2 and 3. 2002–2004 data are from World Bank, 2007, p. 23, but the CIT and VAT tax arrears data for 2002–2003 are from the IMF, 2005, pp. 28, 31. The 2005–2014 data were obtained from the State Fiscal Service of Ukraine by a direct request from a Ukrainian parliamentary deputy's office. The 2015 figure was provided in a personal e-mail from the World Bank's Washington, DC office on 2 June 2016.

Creating Post-communist Tax Regimes and Tax Compliance 113

Comparing Levels of Aggregate Tax Arrears with What Is Collected

Presenting data on aggregate tax arrears – that is, presenting information on the size and collection of each year's unpaid taxes – provides a view as to how good a state is at collecting tax revenue in light of what it believes is owed to it. Table 4.1 displays overall tax arrears as a percentage of all taxes collected, derived by the author utilizing data from the Ministry of Finance in Poland, from the RF State Statistics Service, and from the IMF, World Bank and the State Fiscal Service in Ukraine.

Overall, the Polish tax system has been remarkable in its ability to raise tax revenue for the state without any major obstacles. With respect to unpaid taxes, the total amount of year-end arrears averaged just 8.8 per cent of all taxes received by the state for the years 1995 to 2014. This places Poland's performance close to the 4–6 per cent range typical for Canada, the United States and Australia.[66] By further comparison, from 2000 to 2002, the average amount of tax arrears in the United States as a percentage of all taxes collected was 3.8 per cent.[67]

As Table 4.1 shows, for all arrears in Poland from 1995 to 2014, the amount of tax arrears for the most part can be described as significant, but not overwhelming. Throughout the 1990s, Poland had a moderate level of tax arrears. Indeed, the total stock by the end of 1999 was nearly 6 per cent of all taxes collected.[68] Yet Poland fell out of that range after 1999, when tax arrears increased to an average of 9.1 per cent of tax receipts for the years 2000–2010, and the overall level of tax arrears in relation to annual total tax receipts appears to have doubled from the 1990s figures in the more recent years 2013–2014.

The relatively low rate of Poland's tax arrears in the 1990s does not suggest, however, that Poland was as efficient as some of the better Western countries in collecting arrears. Poland's Ministry of Finance's own figure of only 28.8 per cent of all tax arrears having been realized as of 31 December 1999 suggests that overall, in more than 7 out of 10 cases, tax arrears continued to go unpaid.[69] Comparing Poland with Sweden, for example, one finds that in 1998, while Poland had an overall 4.7 per cent ratio of net tax arrears to tax receipts, Sweden had a 1.2 per cent ratio of new arrears to total taxes. Moreover, of these new arrears for that year in Sweden, 33.6 per cent were paid.[70] Matching that figure up with

---

[66] IMF, April 2002, p. 61.   [67] OECD, October 2004, p. 68.
[68] Ministry of Finance, March 2000, p. 36.
[69] Ibid., p. 33. This is a figure of realized arrears from past years, calculated as a percentage of income on these arrears in proportion to a general sum of all arrears from past years.
[70] Swedish National Tax Board, p. 152.

114   Taxes and Trust

the 28.8 per cent figure suggests that Poland performs somewhat well with respect to tracking down tax arrears. Poland's main problem (and Russia's and Ukraine's, as we shall see) is that it had more arrears to start with than a Nordic country like Sweden, posing a greater administrative challenge from the beginning.

Meanwhile, in Russia, the total amount of year-end arrears averaged just 17.8 per cent of all taxes received by the state for the years 1995–2015. Further, in Ukraine, from 1995 to 2015, the total amount of arrears averaged 15.8 per cent of all taxes received by the State Tax Administration (STA), placing Ukraine much closer to Russia than Poland and other OECD states.

In general, tax arrears have been far more significant in Russia and Ukraine than in Poland. Whereas the overall stock of total tax arrears amounted to just under 6 per cent of all tax receipts in Poland by the end of 1999 and the total amount of tax arrears as a percentage of a year's tax revenue climbed gradually to 15.2 per cent in 2014, the total amount of tax arrears never dipped below 15 per cent of total tax income in Russia from 1995 until 2005 or in Ukraine from 1998 to 2004. Moreover, in both Russia and Ukraine, in the late 1990s (1997–2000), the total stock of arrears averaged from a third to half of all tax income. Indeed, around 28 per cent of all registered legal entities in Russia had tax arrears in 1998.[71] As the IMF observed, even though the stock of arrears in the mid- to late 1990s was reduced by high levels of inflation, arrears have continued to remain high in comparison with those in OECD countries.[72] (The IMF in 1999 did place Russia's voluntary tax compliance rate at less than 70 per cent, in contrast to compliance rates of about 80 per cent in the United States, 85 per cent in the European Union and 95 per cent in the Nordic countries.[73])

Figures 4.1 and 4.2 present the annual tax arrears for the CIT and the VAT for the three countries. (Separate data for PIT arrears were not available at all for Russia or for many years for Ukraine.) For all three states, the VAT tax has proven to be the most difficult of the taxes to collect in full. However, in Russia and Ukraine, the VAT arrears have been gigantic, averaging 36.1 per cent from 1994 to 2015 for Russia

---

[71] ITAR-TASS News Wire, 19 February 1998.   [72] IMF, April 2002, p. 61.

[73] The IMF, however, does provide a caveat to making a direct comparison of the Russian voluntary compliance statistics, suggesting that Russian tax compliance may be even worse than such a comparison illustrates. 'However', it writes, 'in Russia compliance rates relate only to payments of assessed taxes, and *not* to whether or to what extent such assessments cover the real taxes that are legally owed under the statutes. Thus, the 70 per cent is not directly comparable to the 80–85 per cent figure for developed countries, which covers a much higher proportion of truly owed tax' (Ibid., p. 63).

Creating Post-communist Tax Regimes and Tax Compliance 115

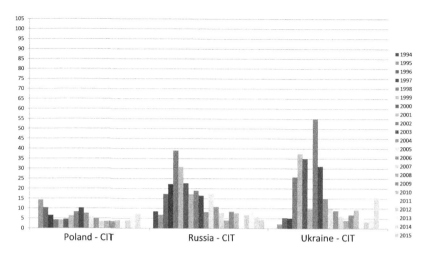

Figure 4.1 Total tax arrears as a percentage of annual total tax receipts for the corporate income tax in Poland, Russia and Ukraine

and 23.9 per cent from 1995 to 2014 for Ukraine. Yet, noticeably, the flow of total tax arrears began to lessen somewhat gradually after the early 2000s for all three states, suggesting either that there were fewer additional arrears each year or that the tax administration was, perhaps, becoming more effective in collecting old arrears.

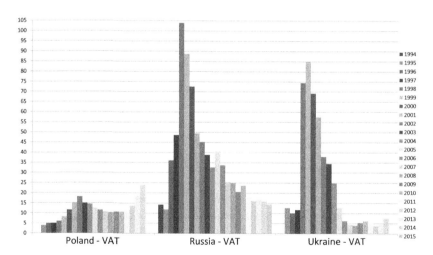

Figure 4.2 Total tax arrears as a percentage of annual total tax receipts for the value-added tax in Poland, Russia and Ukraine

116   Taxes and Trust

Moreover, despite these tax arrears statistics, outside experts differ with regard to what are, in fact, the actual tax collection rates in Russia. According to the Moscow-based Economic Expert Group, an independent group which was founded by the Ministry of Finance and which works closely with it and the Ministry of Economic Development and Trade, the collection of VAT in the early 2000s did not exceed 62 per cent, while outside experts at the Centre for Economic and Financial Research and the Russian Union of Industrialists and Entrepreneurs (RSPP) thought in 2003 that the VAT tax was not being collected at more than 50 per cent.[74] Moreover, Russian Prime Minister Mikhail Kasyanov was quoted in April 2002 as stating that the current overall tax collection rate was 92–93 per cent, compared with 55–60 per cent in 1998.[75] A year earlier, Kasyanov stated that tax collection in 2000 was 60 per cent.[76] Hence, the true rate of tax collection might actually be far lower than in the data provided by the Ministry of Finance, which shows that levels have approached Poland's only since 2001.

The reliability of the tax arrears data presented here for Ukraine also could be of some concern. Unlike those for Poland and Russia, the data for Ukraine are from three distinct sources rather than from one source throughout the time series, and the different sources – when they do have overlapping data – are not consistent. For example, the World Bank provides a much higher figure for 2006 when it states that the overall tax arrears as a share of tax revenues were 18 per cent, whereas the State Fiscal Service provides data that yield a figure of 5.7 per cent.[77] Similarly, using World Bank data to derive overall tax arrears yields a figure of 6.5 per cent of all taxes collected in 1996, but using IMF data yields 10.4 per cent. As the lower figures are used to assess Ukraine's tax arrears in Table 4.1, it is difficult to distinguish greatly between Russia and Ukraine with respect to the annual tax arrears averages over the entire period, but it can be firmly concluded that both countries performed significantly worse than Poland and the OECD states.

Tax Offsets in Russia and Ukraine

Accompanying the rise of tax arrears, especially in Russia and Ukraine, was the phenomenon of tax offsets – that is, the cancellation of debts between the taxpayer and the government in which negligent taxpayers exchanged their tax debts for government arrears or payables, which created significant damage to the administration of tax collection. The tax

---

[74] Ivanova and Onegina.   [75] Prime-TASS News, 24 April 2002.
[76] Associated Press Newswires, 5 April 2001.   [77] World Bank, 2011, p. 69.

Creating Post-communist Tax Regimes and Tax Compliance   117

offsets, as well as the swapping of promissory notes among firms and governments (national and local), enabled some tax officials overseeing the arrears to overestimate the value owed, opening the door to graft and corruption and creating an incentive for firms not to pay taxes.[78] In 1997, Jennifer L. Franklin wrote that the Russian Finance Ministry had estimated that an approximate U.S.$28.6 billion worth of tax breaks was offered to the wealthy and politically connected in Russia each year.[79]

Jorge Martinez-Vazquez and Robert M. McNab have estimated that in the transition countries, revenues collected through offsets peaked at around half of what was actually due from tax revenues in 1996–1998.[80] Hence, the decline in Russia's revenue in the 1990s may have been even greater, if one were only examining cash revenues and excluding non-cash revenues, or what are referred to as 'cash offsets'. 'The decline in cash revenues at the federal level has been dramatic', write Liam Ebrill and Oleh Havrylyshyn at the IMF. 'Revenues for regional governments, including tax offsets, during the period 1993 to 1997 remained at about 22 per cent of GDP, while federal government cash revenues declined from about 14 per cent to just over 9 per cent of GDP. This difference has less to do with fiscal-federal relations than it does with the extensive and growing use of tax offsets by regional governments. The precise extent to which tax offsets are used by regional governments is not known, but they are believed to account for the bulk of revenue at present. At the federal level, the use of such offsets, on the order of 3 per cent of GDP in 1997, is reflected in the revenue data during the years prior to 1997.'[81] Moreover, the Russian state had to accept such tax offsets, weakening its control over spending priorities and taxpayers' dues.[82] Such regular granting of tax offsets created further expectations that their employment would be repeated, impacting tax payment discipline negatively.[83]

An additional problem of the 1990s was the continued use of tax amnesties, which led to increases in tax arrears as taxpayers began to expect that such amnesties would be offered in the future.[84]

Hence, from the data presented here, one can judge Poland's tax collection to be 'moderately successful', with some decreased success in 2012–2014, while Russia's and Ukraine's performance can be judged as varying from 'quite poor' to 'improving'. Throughout the transition as a

---

[78] Alm, Martinez-Vazquez and Wallace, p. 5. See also Martinez-Vazquez and McNab, pp. 288–289; and Gaddy and Ickes, 1998.
[79] Franklin, p. 159.   [80] Martinez-Vazquez and McNab, p. 289.
[81] Ebrill and Havrylyshyn, pp. 4, 6.   [82] Appel, 2011, pp. 28–29.
[83] Highfield and Baer, p. 5.   [84] Martinez-Vazquez and McNab, p. 288.

118   Taxes and Trust

whole, the Polish tax system has been able to raise tax revenue for the state without any major obstacles and, at times, close to or above its target levels. It consistently is able to extract revenue from society year by year, but it does fall short of its goals at times and has significant, though not incapacitating arrears. Meanwhile, data from Russia and Ukraine are more erratic. Tax collection was poor and tax arrears high throughout the late 1990s for these countries. After 2000, tax arrears are not as great and, by measures of the state's intentions, tax collection rates are up.

What accounts for Poland's moderate success and for Russia and Ukraine's moderately poor results? In the rest of this chapter, after presenting individual-level data on tax compliance, we will examine how the economy can affect the changes in tax collection from year to year. Then, in Chapters 5 and 6, we will proceed to examine how the ability to raise revenue on the part of the Polish and Russian states depends upon a mix of bureaucratic rationalism and social compliance.

Obtaining Individual-Level Data on Tax Compliance

'The empirical study of tax compliance is cumbersome because individual-level data is very difficult to collect', Marcelo Bergman has written. 'Most government agencies are reluctant or legally unable to allow research on individual tax returns. Even when such information becomes available, it is usually impossible to create data sets that also include individual preferences and attitudes, which are needed to explain tax behaviour.'[85]

While Bergman was writing about studying tax compliance in Latin America, nowhere more, perhaps, are his words more appropriate than with respect to trying to obtain data from tax administrations in Eastern Europe and the former Soviet Union – especially with respect to today's geopolitical climate and Russia. Yet, in gauging specifically how well residents in new states such as Poland, Russia and Ukraine become true citizens, it is necessary to measure how compliant the populace is with respect to taxes. So is it possible to delineate exactly how willing post-Soviet and post-socialist societies are to pay taxes?

While there is a lack of data on taxpayer compliance rates in these three countries, results from a series of unique Taxpayer Compliance Attitudinal Surveys designed by this author and carried out by the *Centrum Badania Opinii Społecznej* (CBOS Public Opinion Research Centre) and the PBS DDG Market Research firm in Poland, the Public Opinion

---

[85] Bergman, p. 22.

Creating Post-communist Tax Regimes and Tax Compliance 119

Table 4.2 *Poland, Russia and Ukraine Taxpayer Compliance Attitudinal Surveys 2004, 2005, 2010, 2012 and 2015*

	Poland 2004	Poland 2010	Russia 2004	Russia 2010	Ukraine 2005	Ukraine 2010	Ukraine 2012	Ukraine 2015
Question: Would you follow the tax laws even if you do not consider them to be fair? (Appendix II: Question #22, Percentage of Responses)								
Yes	83	77	53	52	36	44	39	45
No	6	15	28	30	37	37	36	34
Hard to say	10	8	19	18	27	20	25	22

Sources: Surveys conducted by Marc P. Berenson; PBS DDG Market Research, Sopot; CBOS Public Opinion Centre, Warsaw; Public Opinion Foundation, Moscow; Razumkov Centre for Economic and Political Studies, Kyiv.

Foundation (FOM) in Russia, and the Razumkov Centre for Economic and Political Studies in Ukraine in 2004, 2005, 2010, 2012 and 2015 do further illustrate how Poles, Russians and Ukrainians view paying their dues. Questions for some of the survey questions were based on earlier studies of tax compliance in the United States.[86]

Recognizing the limitations of the available tax data in providing accurate estimations of tax compliance in countries with a history of barter, high levels of black market activity and less than transparent finance ministries and tax administrations, one of the survey questions that asks respondents whether they 'would follow the tax laws even if you do not consider them to be fair' is highlighted (see Table 4.2.)

The surveys constitute an effort to obtain a direct measure, assessed at the individual level, of tax compliance[87] in light of the fact that these countries' tax administrations have yet to release any direct self-reports of individual taxpayers, such as anonymized tax returns. Indeed, it would be very difficult to gauge whether or not respondents paid their taxes in full and on time, short of receiving such individual-level data from the STAs in each country. (The IRS in the United States, for example, has periodically shared such data with academic researchers, after omitting personally identifiable data.[88])

---

[86] See, for example, Slemrod; Roth, Scholz and Witte; and Roth and Scholz.
[87] The Taxpayer Compliance Attitudinal Surveys are considered a 'direct' measures rather than 'indirect' measures with respect to tax compliance in the language of Webley et al., pp. 29–30.
[88] Ibid., p. 31.

120   Taxes and Trust

Obviously, obtaining such measurements through surveys is a bit tricky, complicated especially by the fact that this survey of a sensitive topic, laid out more fully in the first Appendix, is the first set of survey questions designed to test tax compliance theories in these states, all of which have a history and tradition of authoritarian rule. Moreover, the surveys are taken at just two points in time in Poland and Russia and four points in time in Ukraine. Further, any reforms or improvements with respect to tax law or tax procedures undertaken by the state in recent years may not have caught up in the minds of respondents as they form their current overall attitudes towards paying taxes. In addition, while attitudinal decisions are important components of behaviour, surveying attitudes towards compliance is not precisely the same as measuring tax compliance itself.[89] As no one has undertaken such a comprehensive survey on attitudes in these transitional countries to test tax compliance theories, the data from the surveys are suggestive, not definitive.

Nevertheless, asking individuals directly whether or not they pay their taxes on time and in full is not likely to yield accurate and honest responses in most parts of the globe. But the Taxpayer Compliance Attitudinal Survey Question #22 does seek to replicate as much of a 'real world' scenario as possible, one in which individuals every day do choose to follow or not the tax laws even when they disagree with them. It is a measure of individual attitudes towards tax compliance, and the research to come in Chapters 6 and 7 is an examination of the links between those attitudes that are an inherent and essential part of behavioural decisions to comply or not to comply. Hence, because it presents as much of a realistic situation as possible, one in which individuals decide for themselves what makes for fairness in taxation or not, Question #22 is chosen as the main dependent variable for analysis in the upcoming chapters, where the focus is on why variation exists among these three countries.

And, indeed, the three countries do have distinctly different responses to this question on an individual level. Whereas 83 per cent of Poles in

---

[89] The limitations of such survey data should be underscored here: Survey data reflect what respondents tell interviewers rather than actual compliance; hence, further research such as individual-level data over time constructed from tax returns or audit results would be required to make the link even more conclusively. For example, as Roth, Scholz and Witte observe, 'survey research has consistently found that taxpayers who report high moral commitment to obey tax laws are unlikely to report cheating on their taxes. However, it is not clear whether this pattern reflects actual behaviour or merely a desire to report behaviour that is consistent with one's proclaimed attitudes.' Roth, Scholz and Witte, p. 8.

Creating Post-communist Tax Regimes and Tax Compliance 121

2004 (and a similar 77 per cent in 2010) would follow the tax laws even if they regarded them as unfair, only 53 per cent of Russians in 2004 (and a nearly identical 52 per cent of Russians in 2010) and 36 per cent of Ukrainians in 2005 (and a somewhat similar 44 per cent of Ukrainians in 2010, 39 per cent of Ukrainians in 2012 and 45 per cent of Ukrainians in 2015) would do the same (Question #22). (Expressed another way, and as shown in Appendix III, when compared with the answers to Question #26 regarding whether or not the respondent viewed his or her country's tax laws as fair, in 2010, a minimum of 12 per cent of Poles, a minimum of 21 per cent of Russians and a minimum of 37 of Ukrainians did not have any intention of complying with their countries' tax laws.)

By design, the Taxpayer Compliance Attitudinal Surveys focus on individuals rather than directly on businesses. This is in part because it is difficult to assess the intentions of businesses with respect to tax matters without examining their tax returns – largely because it is not clear whether one should survey accountants, employees, or executives, but due as well to access. Nevertheless, the surveys, as general surveys of the Polish, Russian and Ukrainian publics, presented here of course include individuals who work in businesses. Moreover, additional questions are included in the survey (such as Question #2 in Appendix I), which inquire as to how respondents paid their taxes – by themselves directly, through their employers or by other means. Individuals who pay their own taxes are likely to have higher incomes and/or work at two or more jobs, as opposed to those who have their employers file their taxes for them – especially in Russia and Ukraine, which had flat personal income taxes during the time of the surveys. In addition, one of the sociodemographic questions employed in the surveys asked about occupation, with an option for those who are managers and/or entrepreneurs. Both of these factors were considered in the analysis undertaken in Chapters 6 and 7, and as will be detailed in greater detail there, both factors were found to have little or no impact, especially compared with the critical variables under analysis, suggesting that those who work in business have attitudes towards the state similar to those of the populations as a whole. Nevertheless, assessing attitudes towards tax compliance in businesses through targeted surveys aimed at firms of all sizes would yield important and interesting data, especially as the popular Business Environment and Enterprise Performance Survey (BEEPS), a joint project of the European Bank for Reconstruction and Development (EBRD) and the World Bank, only asks a few questions regarding tax issues, and none on tax compliance.

Table 4.3 *Measurements of the unofficial economy as a percentage of GDP in selected transition countries for the early 1990s by the electricity method and for 1999–2007 by the MIMIC method*

	1989	1990	1991	1992	1993	1994	1995	1999	2000	2001	2002	2003	2004	2005	2006	2007	Avg
Czech Rep.	6	7	13	17	17	18	11	19	19	19	19	19	18	18	17	17	16
Georgia	12	25	36	52	61	64	63	68	67	67	66	66	65	64	62	66	56
Hungary	27	28	33	31	29	28	29	25	25	25	25	24	24	24	24	24	27
Lithuania	12	11	22	39	32	29	22	34	34	33	33	32	32	31	30	30	28
Poland	16	20	24	20	19	15	13	28	28	28	28	28	27	27	26	26	23
Russia	12	15	24	33	37	40	42	47	46	45	45	44	43	42	42	41	37
Ukraine	12	16	26	34	38	46	49	53	52	51	51	50	49	48	47	47	42

Source: Kaufmann and Kaliberda, p. A-4. Also cited in Johnson and Kaufmann, p. 183. The measurements of the unofficial economy were calculated from differences between reported GDP and electricity power consumption figures. Kaufmann and Kaliberda produce estimates for 1994, but not exact percentages for that year. Johnson and Kaufmann use the same methodology and baseline estimates to provide the exact percentages for 1994 and 1995. Data for the average of 1999–2007 were derived using a Multiple Indicator Multiple Cause model approach by Schneider and Williams, pp. 149–154.

Creating Post-communist Tax Regimes and Tax Compliance   123

The Influence of Economic Factors

The Black Market

In the first four years of Poland's transition (1990–1993), the share of the unofficial economy, according to an electricity consumption estimate, averaged about 20 per cent of the country's GDP.[90] In contrast, in Russia, the average was about 38 per cent of the country's GDP in the first four years after the collapse of the Soviet Union (1992–1995). Ukraine's average was about 42 per cent over the same period. In other words, at the very beginning of the transition, Russia and Ukraine's black market economies were about twice as big as Poland's relative to the total economies. For 1999 to 2007, utilizing Daniel Kaufman and Aleksander Kaliberda's MIMIC method, the share of the unofficial economy was found to be about 27 per cent for Poland, 44 per cent for Russia and 50 per cent in Ukraine.[91] These figures could suggest that on the average about this much of GDP is hidden from taxation each year in each country.[92] (As a means of comparison, the underground economy is deemed to be about 2 to 10 per cent of GNP in Western economies, with perhaps 7 to 10 per cent being a reasonable estimate for the United States.)[93]

In addition, as shown in Table 4.3, Poland had less of its economy hidden than many other transition states. In short, the black market economy and the non-cash (or barter) economy were much larger in Russia and Ukraine than in Poland, massively cheating state treasuries of needed revenue.

In addition to such cross-national data, the Gdańsk Institute for Market Reforms found in 1994 that 29.6 per cent of those Poles surveyed reportedly had worked on the black market. The survey also found that about 13.8 per cent of all personal income in Poland is not registered.[94] Similarly, in January 2005, CBOS reported that 13 per cent of Poles surveyed stated that taxes on their salaries were not paid in full or in part to

---

[90] Such a figure is also in line with the 20 per cent estimate for 1992 calculated by the Research Centre for Economic and Statistical Studies of the Central Statistical Office (GUS) and the Polish Academy of Sciences (PAN) as described by Szolno-Koguc, p. 159.

[91] In November 2001, former Russian Prime Minister Mikhail Fradkov, who was then head of the Tax Police, told the Russian newspaper *Nezavisimaya Gazeta* that up to 40 per cent of Russia's economy was 'in the shadow sector', with about U.S.$20 billion leaving the country annually. RFE/RL Russian Political Weekly. 3 March 2004.

[92] Economist Vladimir Popov, among others, has made a direct link between the increase in the size of the black market economy during the 1990s and the decline in tax revenues over the same period of time. See, for example, Popov, November 2004.

[93] Cowell, in Webley et al., p. 4.   [94] Szolno-Koguc, p. 159.

124   Taxes and Trust

the social security system (ZUS), whereas 87 per cent stated that their social security taxes were paid in full.[95] Hence, taking these figures as a proxy for social compliance with respect to taxation, Poles would appear to have complied with registering their incomes from 70 to 87 per cent of the time after the transition began.

In contrast, in Russia, in 1994, a survey of businesses carried out by the Working Centre for Economic Reforms under the Russian government found that only 1.5 per cent of respondents said that they registered all business transactions on their books, 33.1 per cent acknowledged that they hid up to 25 per cent of transactions, 28.9 per cent stated that they hid up to 50 per cent, and 18.4 per cent admitted to not registering up to 100 per cent of transactions.[96] Assuming equal weight on the size of the transactions reported and unreported, up to 59 per cent of all economic activity was not reported by businesses in Russia that year.

In addition, a survey conducted by the Sociology Institute of the Russian Academy of Sciences four months after the introduction of the flat rate for the PIT in 2001 found that only 48 per cent of Russians polled in Moscow and St. Petersburg received a salary paid in full compliance with the tax laws. Of those polled, 39 per cent were considered 'grave' tax evaders, receiving their salaries in cash in agreement with their employers.[97] In 2005, Deputy Finance Minister Sergei Shatalov reported that 'under-the-table salaries' make up 30 per cent of the country's total payrolls.[98]

Moreover, whereas 4,700,000 individual businesspeople and 3,300,000 organizations were on the tax lists as of 1 January 2003,[99] as of that date 2.2 million companies and self-employed individuals did not submit reports to tax authorities and about 920,000 companies and self-employed individuals submitted zero reports – figures that suggest that 38.5 per cent of all companies and self-employed individuals do not pay taxes.[100] In 2006, despite a decrease of 1 per cent a year in the number of 'grey salaries' immediately after the flat PIT was adopted, the figure for 'grey salaries' rose again to more than 32 per cent.[101] Similarly, even two years after the corporate tax rates were lowered, many firms were said still to be maintaining double account books out of

---

[95] Wenzel, p. 7.   [96] Morozov, p. 8.   [97] Kuzmenka.
[98] *ITAR-TASS*, 23 November 2005.   [99] RIA Oreanda.
[100] RIA Novosti, 4 April 2003. Meanwhile, the RF State Statistics Service found in 2003 that the number of Russians engaged in the unofficial economy is approximately 8.6 million, or 13 per cent of the total employed population. See Andreyev.
[101] RIA Novosti, 7 March 2007.

Creating Post-communist Tax Regimes and Tax Compliance   125

a fear that the new tax policies and tax rates would change yet again.[102] Hence, the size of the black market economy during the transition in Russia may well range from 32 per cent to 59 per cent in the early 2000s. If that much of the economy is out of the domain of what is taxed, only 41 to 68 per cent of economic activity may well be reported to the tax authorities.

In the first half of 2015, Ukraine's Economy Ministry estimated that 42 per cent of the nation's economy, or about US$18 billion, went unaccounted for, and according to economist Friedrich Schnieder, since 2008, an average of 44.5 per cent of Ukraine's GDP has not been on the books.[103] And, as shown in Table 4.3, Ukraine's share of the black market ranges from 34 to 53 per cent in the first decade after the collapse of the Soviet Union, suggesting that only 49 to 66 per cent of economic activity in the country might have been reported to the tax administration. Iuzhanina, chair of the Rada's Tax and Customs Policy Committee, has written that around 80 per cent of PIT is collected from government employees' salaries, simply because 'it is nearly impossible to dodge the tax on government wages', while the private sector 'chooses to pay its workers under the table to avoid the tax altogether'.[104]

If, indeed, the unofficial economies are this large and the tax declaration rates were 70 to 87 per cent for Poland, 41 to 63 per cent for Russia and 49 to 66 per cent for Ukraine, it would appear that the tax arrears figures reported by the three state's tax administrations should have been much larger. The fact that they are not suggests that these post-communist governments are neither able nor willing to reach out and uncover all of the income derived from unreported economic activity, and they are not considering such income when deriving estimates for real amounts of tax due. And, because the size of the black market economy is greater in Russia and Ukraine than in Poland, the ability or willingness of the Russian and Ukrainian state tax organs to capture all economic activity taking place within state borders is less.

---

[102] Interview with lawyer at Moscow office of international legal firm, Moscow, 7 August 2003. Moreover, in Russia, there are many different ingenious schemes employers use in order to pay little or no tax on their employees' salaries. In one scheme, invented by local banks, money is put on deposit in a bank and earns extraordinary high rates of interest, which is used as salary, and is therefore taxed at a lower rate. In another scheme, employees receive life insurance payments as salary. (Head Law Partner, Moscow office of one of the Big Four international accounting firms, Moscow, 28 July 2003.)

[103] Rachkevych.   [104] Iuzhanina.

126   Taxes and Trust

The Barter Economy

A main underlying factor fuelling the unofficial economy is, of course, the use of barter between firms in the post-communist economies. Barter, especially as a form of payment in Russia's and Ukraine's regions, in many ways was a holdover from the Soviet system, in which commands and orders, rather than money, were what was needed to get things done. From the beginning of the transition, there was a relative scarcity of money in the Russian economy due 'to both the lack of the very concept itself in the socialist planning system and to the consequence of the drastic devaluation of the working capital of enterprises after the price liberalization of 1992'.[105] David Woodruff's *Money Unmade* and Clifford G. Gaddy and Barry W. Ickes's *Russia's Virtual Economy* detail precisely how the Russian state struggled as it sought to root out barter and make money supreme again in the 1990s. The authors also lay out precisely how political conflicts ensued between, on the one hand, bank-led industrial groups and large firms, like Gazprom, which stood to benefit from a monetary-based economy and for which evading taxes had greater risks, and, on the other hand, local coalitions in the regions, which benefited from barter and which included newly created firms that had unaccounted cash sales and that resorted to tax evasion.[106]

For those that engaged in the barter economy, there were multiple reasons. Barter, or transactions by regional governments, banks or enterprises through the use of promissory notes (or *veksels*), write Shleifer and Treisman, 'was a way of avoiding holding cash in bank accounts that could be confiscated by tax collectors if taxes went unpaid. It was also a way of getting around a law that prohibited selling below cost – prices could be artificially manipulated in a barter deal. In addition, paying taxes in kind rather than in cash was a way to favour the regional and local over the federal budgets, since accepting tax payments in concrete or cucumbers was easier for a city government than for the State Tax Service in Moscow.'[107] In Ukraine, the share of the barter economy was said to be over 35 per cent of GDP in 1994 and more than 40 per cent of GDP in 1997–1998.[108]

Without a doubt, the barter economy has played a strong role in the story of post-communist tax collection – not just because part of the economy was hidden through barter activity, but also because the tax

---

[105] Iakovlev, p. 82.
[106] Woodruff; Gaddy and Ickes, 2002; see also Gaddy and Ickes, 1998, and Iakovlev, p. 82.
[107] Shleifer and Treisman, p. 97.   [108] Luzik, p. 7.

Creating Post-communist Tax Regimes and Tax Compliance   127

authorities also engaged in barter by collecting tax debts partly in the form of nonmonetary, in-kind transactions. The rise of barter made collecting taxes complicated, especially at the federal level in contrast to the local level, where fiscal responsibilities could be conceived in less monetary terms. 'The builders of the Soviet economy', writes Woodruff, 'had "hardwired" the ability to tax *particular* economic actors in kind into the very social infrastructure of Russia.'[109] As a result, local governments and later the federal government began to accept in-kind taxation. Woodruff calculates that by 1996 approximately 60 per cent of local tax receipts were in kind, and at the federal level, the share of tax income that was nonmonetary was about 19 per cent in 1995, 33 per cent in 1996 and 40 per cent in 1997.[110]

While the phenomenon of in-kind taxation appears to have been in decline after 2000 – certainly after Russia's 2001 tax reform – and while this author did not encounter any reports of nonmonetary taxation after his research began in the early 2000s, the fact that the size of the unofficial economies still has remained substantial in subsequent years implies that in-kind taxation could well continue in some form to this day. '[I]t is important to note that Russia widely uses nonmonetary taxation where federal, regional or local authorities invite a company to participate or invest in some sort of project where it is implicitly understood that the company will not show a profit', writes Mikhail Glazunov. 'Using nonmonetary taxation gives authorities additional opportunities for realization of important projects without dipping into the official budget, as well as developing opportunities for the personal enrichment of members of the authorities.'[111] Hence, as the post-transition period marches on, the forms in-kind taxation takes may well be more discreet and hidden than they were in the 1990s.

The Economic Explanation

Unexpected declines in economic growth are important factors in analyzing why certain tax collection goals, placed in the budget law in August or the early fall of the previous year, may not be met. For Poland, the tax revenues, which were higher than forecast in the budget laws for the years up to 1998, could be viewed, for example, as being largely due to the higher-than-expected inflation in those years,[112] suggesting that the above-perfect or near-perfect tax performance compared with the

---

[109] Woodruff, p. 114.   [110] Ibid., pp. 2, 166–167.   [111] Glazunov, pp. 158–159.
[112] Author's interview with Marek Trosiński, Vice-Director, Department of the State Budget, NIK, Warsaw, 8 November 2001.

128   Taxes and Trust

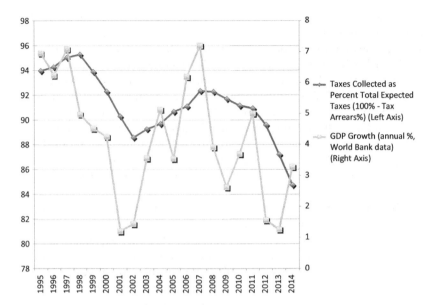

Figure 4.3 Overall tax collected as a percentage of all taxes due and annual GDP growth, Poland

budget was based on a devaluation of money over the course of the year. Meanwhile, in Russia, the improvement in tax collection in the 2000s could be due to a rebound in the overall economy and to higher-than-expected world oil prices.

To understand better the relationship between the economy and tax collection, Figures 4.3, 4.4 and 4.5 depict comparisons of the annual rate of GDP growth with taxes collected by the Polish, Russian and Ukrainian states, respectively, as a percentage of all taxes due[113]. Overall, in comparing macroeconomic statistics with aggregate tax data, there are times when there is a general direct correlation between the rise and fall of tax income and the rise and fall of the overall general economy over the course of the post-transition period in all three states. The amount of tax arrears appears to rise and fall with GDP growth but not approaching a direct correlation. For Poland, in Figure 4.3, the percentage of taxes collected decreases as the GDP falls, roughly from 1997 to 2002, but after that, the rise and fall of taxes and the GDP do not seem to be in a clear,

[113] This is calculated by taking 100 per cent minus the percentage of tax arrears collected, which is shown in Table 4.1. Utilizing tax data formulated from tax arrears information as a comparison to economic growth statistics is preferable to comparing a country's GDP with the amount of taxes collected as a percentage of GDP to discern more clearly the tax–economy relationship.

Creating Post-communist Tax Regimes and Tax Compliance 129

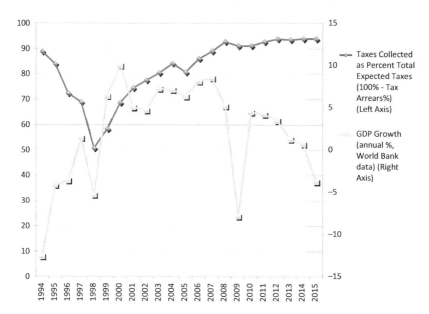

Figure 4.4 Overall tax collected as a percentage of all taxes due and annual GDP growth, Russian Federation

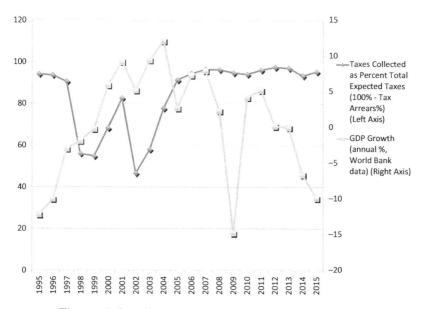

Figure 4.5 Overall tax collected as a percentage of all taxes due and annual GDP growth, Ukraine

130   Taxes and Trust

direct relationship. Similarly, for Russia, in Figure 4.4 the percentage of taxes collected rises with economic growth from 1998 to 2000, but also continues to rise since then even though the economy sees declines. And, for Ukraine, in Figure 4.5, there appears to be a correlation from 1997 to 2003, but the percentage of taxes collected continues to rise after 2007 despite economic declines. Hence, there are years in each graph where the tax measures rise but the macroeconomic measures fall and vice versa. Further, the rates at which the tax revenue rises or falls from year to year do not seem to correlate exactly with those of the economy. Nevertheless, the trend is there, suggesting that the general state of the economy is a major factor in tax revenue outcomes.

In Poland, such a correlation between the health of the economy and tax collection was noted by both the Ministry of Finance and the Supreme Audit Chamber (*Najwyższa Izba Kontroli*, or NIK.) With respect to tax arrears in the 1995–1999 period, the Ministry of Finance lists a few critical reasons, including the difficult transformation of state sector enterprises at the beginning of the 1990s and the lack of restructuring of certain branches of industry.[114] In particular, the Ministry of Finance attributes the growth in arrears from 1998 to 1999 to four sectors of the economy that have yet to be restructured, namely the hard coal industry, the defence industry, the steel industry and light industry.[115]

NIK in its annual reports on the budget tends to concur with the Ministry of Finance on the rationale for such large arrears. Back in 1992, NIK mentioned that a sizeable portion of tax arrears were from many large state-owned firms,[116] and its 1993 report on the budget even goes as far as listing the top 20 firms in Poland with the most tax arrears and the amounts owed.[117] Its 1999 budget report also cites the growth in VAT arrears as being due to the coal and mining industries.[118]

As the Russian economist Vladimir Popov (and several others) has pointed out, from 1990 to 1998, the Russian government's share of revenues and expenditures, in real terms, decreased dramatically by two-thirds in comparison with the Soviet days, and, as a percentage of GDP, was cut in half, even while the GDP itself fell by nearly 50 per cent.[119] While a great deal of this can be attributed to the financial crisis of August 1998, as the collection of income and profits taxes hit the lowest levels in 1998 and 1999, the decline, again at least for direct taxes, began much earlier in the 1990s.

---

[114] Ministry of Finance, March 2000, p. 8.   [115] Ibid., p. 16.
[116] NIK, July 1993, p. 32.   [117] NIK, July 1994, pp. 29–30.
[118] NIK, June 2000, p. 57.   [119] Popov, November 2004.

Creating Post-communist Tax Regimes and Tax Compliance   131

While budget projections, which are adopted by the Sejm in Poland, by the State Duma in Russia and by the Rada in Ukraine at the beginning of each year, are based on analysis of expected inflation and expected economic conditions, a change in inflation, economic growth or, in the case of Russia, oil prices from that which is expected can impact the amount of tax revenue actually collected. For example, in Poland, 2001 data show a decline in taxation from expected amounts, reflecting the downward change in the Polish economy during that year. In its report on the fulfilment of the 2001 budget, NIK states that 'a significant part of the difference (about 50 per cent), between the planned and factually realized income of the budget of the state, can be explained by the non-performance of macroeconomic indicators adopted for the budget, that is a low pace of economic growth and a faster than expected growth of unemployment.'[120] But NIK comments that part of the blame for the poor 2001 budget figures was due to a failure in drawing up those projections to begin with. 'However', NIK writes, 'it's necessary to attribute the remaining amount of unrealized income ... to an overassessment of the results of systemic changes as well as to the infeasibility of the assumed tax collection indicators.' In short, NIK concludes that 'during the drafting of the 2001 Budget Law, a serious planning error was committed'.[121]

Measurements of the overall health of the economy do help to explain the variation from year to year of the collection of taxes. It is clear that the fluctuations in the economy, often unexpected, have affected the rise and fall of tax revenue in Poland, Russia and Ukraine, as they would in any state. Moreover, for example, when the economic conditions worsened comparatively for Poland in the late 1990s (as Poland's remarkably high growth rate eased off), higher-than-actual rates of growth were still utilized in the forecasting of the planned tax revenue, which was conducted annually in the early fall of the previous year, leading to lower-than-expected levels of tax returns. In short, because economic forecast data were used in the planning of tax revenue each year, one should not be surprised to see such a correlation, especially in comparison with the forecasts made in each year's original budget law.

However, even if we grant that a lot of the impact is economic, the relationship is not as straightforward, since receiving more income creates more opportunities to hide it and opportunities to choose not to comply, causing tax arrears to go up. And, even if Figures 4.3, 4.4 and 4.5 were to show direct relationships between taxes collected and GDP (which they do not), the correlation between the overall health of the

---

[120] NIK, June 2002, p. 38. Translation from the Polish by the author.
[121] Ibid., p. 38.

132   Taxes and Trust

economy and the tax revenue levels does not undermine the role of other factors that enable the bureaucracy to extract revenue from society. In fact, the ability of a country's tax administration to oversee the collection of revenue depends on more than pure economic factors. As will be argued in the next three chapters, the moderate success of tax collection in Poland and the relatively poorer performance in collecting revenue in Russia and Ukraine in the first decades after communism depend upon institutional factors within the state and within society, namely a mix of bureaucratic rationalism on the part of the state and social compliance on the part of the society. Moreover, with respect to the Taxpayer Compliance Attitudinal Surveys, the responses to Question #22 were quite similar for each country across the different years of the surveys, even though there was significant variation in the level of economic growth across the survey years in the three countries. This further suggests that while economic growth matters, other factors are at play – especially in explaining individual-level attitudes towards paying taxes.

The Impact of Tax Rates

Similarly to economic factors, tax collection also relates to changes in tax rates and in tax structure design. One of the most discussed tax policy changes in Central and Eastern Europe since 2000 has been the adoption of the flat tax – especially the adoption of a flat, or single-rate, personal income tax for all taxpayers in at least a dozen countries, including Russia in 2001 and Ukraine in 2003, but not Poland. The impact of the flat tax, especially in Russia, on tax collection especially has been questioned within the literature, although Ukraine changed to the same flat rate two years later as well. As part of a package of tax reforms passed in 2000, Russia introduced a flat 13 per cent personal income tax (PIT) rate, which replaced the earlier 12, 20 and 30 per cent tiered rates. The following year, the revenues from PIT increased 46 per cent in nominal and 26 per cent in real terms, from 2.4 per cent to 2.9 per cent of GDP. PIT revenues increased another 3.3 per cent in the following year.[122] Of the over a dozen countries that adopted the flat tax in the region, Appel has stated that IMF calculations in 2006 showed only Latvia, Lithuania and Russia to have seen an increase in revenue in the year following adoption.[123]

While some have claimed that the increases in tax collection in 2001 and 2002 were due to the lowering of tax rates, particularly with the

---

[122] Papp and Takáts, p. 3.   [123] Appel, 2011, p. 86.

Creating Post-communist Tax Regimes and Tax Compliance 133

introduction of a flat personal income tax rate,[124] it is very unclear whether the increases in income tax collection in Russia were mainly due to tax rate reduction. The IMF has stated that the increase was caused by the expansion of the tax base, tightening control over tax minimization schemes, primarily insurance schemes, high global oil prices and real growth in incomes.[125] In addition, the IMF also has observed that in 2001 tax performance 'exceeded expectations across the board, even more so for taxes other than the PIT'.[126]

Vahram Stepanyan at the IMF, moreover, has written that 'there seems to be little evidence of a substantial improvement in personal income tax revenues that resulted simply from a reduction in the top marginal tax rates'.[127] He points out that PIT revenues did in fact increase from the year 2000 to the year 2001, but only from 2.5 to 2.6 per cent of GDP. Moreover, he also points to changes in revenue sharing agreements between the federal and local governments that might have given the local governments more of an incentive to enforce PIT administration better.[128]

Mikhail Pryadilnikov and Elena Danilova write that the increase in tax revenue in the immediate years after the 2000 tax reforms was due to a combination of reforms and factors, and not to the rate changes alone. Accompanying changes to the Tax Code, rates and tax administration structure, they write that 'the Tax Service began a rapid effort to expand the registration of individual taxpayers. It rolled out its plans in a massive advertising campaign filling every Russian town with billboards explaining the importance of paying taxes on time. The agency also offered amnesty to individual taxpayers and expanded its staff to cover the anticipated increase in individual declarations. These initial efforts worked.'[129] Appel also concurs that the flat tax was part of a broader series of reforms. 'At the same time as the flat tax took effect, the Russian government issued taxpayer identification numbers, eliminated ceilings for overdue taxes, increased significantly the legal authority of the tax administration, and bolstered the state apparatus', she writes. 'Social insurance taxes were lowered, and there were changes to corporate taxes and later energy taxes ... Given the simultaneity of reforms, scholars have found it nearly impossible to calculate the effect of the flat tax on revenue or growth.'[130] Moreover, Alexeev and Conrad

---

[124] The Wall Street Journal, 11 July 2003; The Wall Street Journal, 26 November 2002; and Katzeff.
[125] Novecon, 6 March 2003; and What the Paper Say (WPS): The Russian Business Monitor, 10 February 2003.
[126] IMF, April 2002, p. 72.   [127] Stepanyan, pp. 22–23.   [128] Ibid., p. 17.
[129] Pryadilnikov and Danilova, p. 34.   [130] Appel, 2011, pp. 85–86.

134   Taxes and Trust

conclude that after the initial improvements in the immediate years following 2000–2001, 'the situation has deteriorated considerably a few years later, particularly in terms of tax administration'[131] and that the 2000 tax reforms 'had only marginal effects on tax effort and perceptions'.[132]

To sort through the impact of the flat tax rate, particularly in light of the overall 2000 package of tax reforms, Anna Ivanova, Michael Keen and Alexander Klemm undertake several statistical analyses to determine whether the increased tax revenue was a consequence of the tax rate changes themselves, only to find that it is unclear whether the increased compliance came from the reforms themselves or the methods of enforcement.[133] Gorodnichenko, Martinez-Vazquez and Peter (2009), however, find that lowering tax rates can, in some situations, reduce the level of tax evasion, using indirect methods to measure tax evasion, but that the Russian flat tax did not lead to much of an increase in economic productivity on the supply side.[134] Appel has argued that 'Certainly a large portion of growth in GDP and income tax revenues can be traced to the surge in gas and oil prices. For example, speaking to the efficacy of the Russian tax reform, the IMF's representative in Moscow attributed 80 per cent of the increase in Russian revenues in 2001 to the strength of the oil and gas sector.'[135] Hence, the data and findings on whether the flat tax rate led to increased tax compliance are mixed and still up for debate, largely because of other factors and reforms that took place simultaneously.

Yet, if changing marginal rates were to have an effect on compliance, one would expect at the individual level that attitudes towards compliance would be responsive to the lowering of rates. Yew, Milanov and Gee find in their study over a three-year period that the major changes in Russia's tax structure in 2001 did not impact individual tax morale.[136]

But, how sensitive are attitudes on tax compliance to tax rates? The 2010 and 2015 Taxpayer Compliance Attitudinal Surveys help provide an answer by asking questions regarding how Poles, Russians and Ukrainians perceive tax rates. First, being reactive to low or high rates requires that one know exactly what the rate is. In 2010, in Poland, of those who knew the personal income tax rate (see Question #36 in Appendix I), only 6 respondents stated that they would not obey a tax law even if they thought it was unfair (Question #22), while 72 stated that they would – that is, 92 per cent of those who knew the tax rate

---

[131] Alexeev and Conrad, p. 246.   [132] Ibid., p. 1.   [133] Ivanova, Keen and Klemm.
[134] Alexeev and Conrad, p. 247.   [135] Appel, 2011, p. 86.
[136] Yew, Milanov and McGee, p. 72.

stated that they would comply with tax laws, much higher than for the general population as a whole (77 per cent). That same year in Russia, 46 per cent (or 1160 respondents) knew their personal income tax rates, and 750 (or 65 per cent) of them stated that they would obey a tax law even if it were considered personally unfair – a figure higher than the 52 per cent who stated in Question #22 that they would obey. Further, in Ukraine, in 2010, of those who knew the correct personal income tax rate, 220, or 62 per cent, stated that they would obey tax laws even if they found them to be unfair; and in 2015, 249, or 57 per cent, stated the same. Hence, if being sensitive to the tax rates requires individuals to know what those tax rates currently are, then the data from these surveys suggest that those who do know are quite supportive of complying with the law, regardless of the rate.

In addition, the Taxpayer Compliance Attitudinal Surveys also inquire whether respondents are supportive of lowering the tax rates (see Question #38 in Appendix I). If lowering tax rates is to have an impact on tax compliance, then, presumably, those who supported lowering the rates for the personal income tax (as opposed to increasing, modifying or cancelling outright the PIT) would be less likely to support obeying tax laws even if they disagreed with them. In 2010, in Poland, of those who supported lowering the PIT, 777 respondents, or 85 per cent, said they would obey – a bit higher than the 77 per cent who answered Question #22 directly. In Russia the same year, 553 respondents, or 58 per cent of those who called for lowering the PIT rate, stated that they would obey – higher as well. And, in Ukraine, of those who wanted to lower the PIT rate, 851 respondents, or 56 per cent, in 2010, and 987 respondents, or 57 per cent, in 2015, stated that they would obey tax laws regardless as to whether they perceived them as unfair – again, figures that are higher than when survey respondents were asked about their attitudes towards compliance outright. Hence, from these surveys, there is no evidence to suggest that those who either knew their tax rates or wanted them lowered were more supportive of being non-compliant then the general population as a whole; in fact, the opposite appears to be true.

Finally, even if lowering tax rates makes taxpayers comply more because they recognize that their obligations are cheaper and that the state recognizes a need for them to retain more of their income, no state can, of course, continuously decrease rates to bring in more taxpayers and revenue. At some point, there is a limit to how low taxes can go, and to improve tax collection, other factors – including especially those focused on the tax administration and its procedures and behaviours – matter greatly.

136   Taxes and Trust

In spite all of the variation in tax rates, tax policies, tax laws and economies over the past two and a half decades, or perhaps in part because of all of the rapid changes taking place in transition societies, an environment of instability was created for both taxpayers and the tax administration, producing uncertainty and inefficacy in fulfilling their respective tasks. Reforming the tax regimes and adopting new laws may have been easier than building and reforming the new tax administrations. Yet, for some transition states, such as Russia and Ukraine, an insufficient amount of the latter may be causing greater problems for the tax system. '[T]he way tax inspectors interact with taxpayers needs to be reformed far more than taxes per se or tax rates', reported *Ukrainian Week*. 'This, in fact, is the most complicated aspect of reforms and the most challenging task facing Ukraine's reformers. In order to attain a balance that would prevent individual tax officials from interpreting legislation as they please, to demand a bribe or to power trip, while taxpayers get to pay a fair rate, the system needs to be changed from within.'[137]

Moving forward, the next chapter will begin to unpack the understudied tax administrations, while Chapters 6 and 7 will look more carefully at the impact of different approaches by the tax state to taxpayers at the individual level.

[137] Shavalyuk.

5 Building Trust, Instilling Fear
Tax Administration Reform

'The tax administration must be constructed practically from the ground up, yet there is a legacy of distrust of the state that will hamper the creation of any tax system.'[1]

– Barry W. Ickes and Joel Slemrod, 1991

Why has Poland been able to perform much better at ensuring tax compliance than Russia and Ukraine since the early 1990s? The answer is due in great part to a partial level of bureaucratic rationalism that exists within Poland's tax organs. Polish efforts at administrative reform within the tax service have focused on rationalizing the function and duties of tax officials in a Weberian sense. In contrast, Russia has designed a tax administration that is consistent with Anton Oleinik's concept of 'power in a pure form', or, more generally, 'power over'.[2] That is, Russia's tax bureaucracies lean towards securing their own power 'over' society through their tax collection mechanisms. The tax agencies thus seek 'power as an end in itself' rather than focusing on rationalizing their function and roles in order to build a more constructive state–society relationship, built on trust and fairness, that will better serve the state in the long run. Meanwhile, Ukraine's tax bureaucracies also seek to empower the state 'as an end in itself', but do so in a weaker manner than their Russian counterparts, instilling less fear and less trust of their state in Ukrainian taxpayers.

Efforts to reform the tax administrative system in Poland and Russia, therefore, have different goals in mind – one Weberian rationalism and the other empowerment of the state over society. Polish reforms have sought to rationalize the tax bureaucracy by focusing on institutional design and by reducing the ability of bureaucrats to function with undue discretion. Meanwhile, in Russia, the implementation of reforms designed to make the tax administration more 'rational' in a Weberian sense often fails to shift the course of the state's goal of seeking power for

---

[1] Ickes and Slemrod, p. 396.   [2] Oleinik.

137

138   Taxes and Trust

itself, especially at the expense of society at large. Fewer comprehensive reforms also have occurred in Ukraine's tax structures.

Poland's moderately successful level of taxation is due in great part to a partial level of bureaucratic rationalism in the Weberian sense that exists within the tax administration structures. In Chapter 3, Poland's, Russia's and Ukraine's administrative histories were analyzed, emphasizing in particular that the interwar period served as a pre-existing historical template for Poland's later public institutions, whereas the historical template for Russia's current leadership appears to be the tight hierarchy of the Soviet Union's military and law enforcement organizations. Lacking a unified vision of the past, Ukraine's leaders, meanwhile, opted instead for continuing with a Soviet-inspired bureaucratic and patrimonial welfare state (*Historical References*).

This chapter will show that structures and human and technological resources, together with historical reference points, all combine to produce mixed bureaucratic rationalism on the part of the tax administration in Poland and moderately low, but improving bureaucratic rationalism on the part of Russia's and Ukraine's tax administrations. First, the tax administrative structures are examined to show that the structural design in Poland provides a significant number of checks and balances, while the imperfect coordination between two branches of the tax administration in Poland, the partial adoption of major administrative reforms in Russia and the lack of such administrative reforms in Ukraine means that all three systems probably have not been designed in their most efficient configuration (*Structures*).

Second, the training and planning on the part of the tax administration in introducing the new taxes in Poland show that its system is more consumer-oriented, more compliance-driven, and less target-driven than Russia's and Ukraine's. By building a more compliance-driven system, tax collectors in Poland are less focused on reaching a *monetary target* than their Russian and Ukrainian counterparts – a philosophy that treats taxpayers more like clients. By contrast, a more collection target (*plan*)-driven system, such as in Russia and Ukraine, makes the focus for tax inspectors not ensuring compliance with tax laws, but merely trying to fulfil quarterly or yearly targets (often to get financial bonuses), by going after those taxpayers who have already paid, as more revenue can be obtained from those known to have it. Such a system, by design, does not require tax bureaucrats to seek out those who have failed to comply altogether (*Human Resources* and *Work Philosophy*).

Third, the reforms in the hiring practices are shown to have been more helpful in Poland than in Russia and Ukraine, but not sufficient

Building Trust, Instilling Fear: Tax Administration Reform   139

for improving the quality of the tax administration personnel in any country (*human resources*). Finally, the existence of certain structural constraints in Poland is examined as being more beneficial than those in Russia and Ukraine in the prevention of corruption (*structures*).

Rationalizing or Empowering Bureaucrats?

Rationalizing the State Bureaucracy: The Weberian Option

With respect to Max Weber's characteristics of bureaucracies, Michael Mann has stated that 'Bureaucratic offices are organized within departments, each of which is centralized and embodies a functional division of labour; departments are integrated into a single overall administration, also embodying functional division of labour and centralized hierarchy.'[3] Mann also has identified autonomous state power as relating to enhanced territorial centralization, a concept central to state capacity.[4] In short, for Mann and for Weber, being able to implement certain tasks requires a state structure imbued with a certain amount of autonomy, so that fairly consistent rules can be applied without undue and incapacitating interference from outside groups.

The administrative reforms in the Polish tax system have sought to 'rationalize' the role of state bureaucrats and to limit the degree of discretion afforded to tax officials in order to constrain corruption. The structures and the human resources provided, together with the use of historical reference points, combine to produce mixed bureaucratic rationalism on the part of the tax administration in Poland. It is the appropriate choice and application of past institutional models – a structural design infused with flexibility and constraints and the availability of personnel trained and capable – that enables the Polish tax system to function well in implementing its policy goals. That being so, the tax bureaucracy is more capable of building a healthy relationship with the public, enabling long-term goals to be accomplished.

Empowering the State Bureaucracy: The 'Power in a Pure Form' Option

In applying Oleinik's concept of 'power in a pure form' to Russia today, the descriptions of Valeri G. Ledyaev, who argues that President

---

[3] Mann, 1993, p. 444.   [4] Mann, 1986, p. 135.

140   Taxes and Trust

Vladimir Putin's regime is one of 'bureaucratic authoritarianism', and of Oxana V. Gaman-Golutvina, who finds that the bureaucracy today is even farther from the Weberian ideals than it was under the Soviet Union, are quite apt.[5] For Ledyaev, the application of the concept of the 'power vertical' through administrative and bureaucratic mechanisms enables the state to expand its control over society. Similarly, Gaman-Golutvina argues that widespread patronage, lack of transparency and low levels of public sector discipline, alongside extremely high levels of corruption, have enabled Russia's administrative apparatus to operate as its own business group at the expense of society, particularly outside business sectors. The significant lack of 'Weberianness' in the bureaucracy, which has led to the rise of a bureaucratic authoritarian state, can be seen both in the state administrative organs as a whole and specifically in the tax agencies.

With respect to the tax administration, not only have the reforms in this sector not led to substantial improvements on the Weberian scale, but also the tax administration itself has become a primary tool of the bureaucratic authoritarian state – through its day-to-day contact with the public as well as more specific and targeted political use of the tax bureaucracy. As will be shown below, in contrast to the processes in Poland, the administrative reforms in the Russian tax system have brought about the 'empowerment' of the state, by increasing the state's ability to impose its control over society, while failing to limit the degree of discretion afforded to tax officials. The task of building a healthier relationship with the public simply does not exist for the Russian tax administration.

Indeed, in the 2011 Russian Public Officials Survey, 22 per cent of tax officials stated that if an enterprise were to fulfil all the demands of the tax organs, it would be ruined – that is, nearly one in four tax bureaucrats recognized that their system is excessive (see Appendix II, Question #2). (A similarly asked question found in 2001 that 58 per cent of Moscow tax inspectors and 52 per cent of Nizhniy Novgorod tax inspectors agreed that if enterprises paid all taxes they would have gone bankrupt a long time ago.[6])

An analogous tax administration design, accompanied by fewer administrative reforms, for the Ukrainian tax system has brought less control over society than in Russia while failing to eliminate tax bureaucrat discretion.

---

[5] Ledyaev; Gaman-Golutvina.   [6] Pryadilnikov and Danilova, p. 27.

Administrative Reform in the Context of the Tax Service: Towards Rationalization or Empowerment of the State

Poland's Tax Administration Structure

The history of how Poland's tax administration was constructed mirrors the history of Poland itself – with alternating organizational structures that reach back to the inter-war period. The origins of some of today's tax agencies trace back to the beginning of the Second Republic, when the Ministry of the Treasury was formed in 1919 with an internal structure similar to the Austrian example and was staffed by bureaucrats from the former Austrian territory. Similarly to today, tax chambers (*izby skarbowe*) and tax offices (*urzędy skarbowe*) were placed in charge of the collection of taxes, which included a personal income tax (PIT). After the Second World War, the tax offices and tax chambers returned until 1950, when they were liquidated,[7] and then, in 1983, they reappeared as subordinates to the Ministry of Finance.[8] That structure remained in place from the beginning of the transition until 1992, when the Sejm (the lower house of the Polish parliament) created the tax audit offices (*urzędy kontroli skarbowe*) and divided up the audit function.

In contrast to countries such as Russia and Ukraine in the late 1990s and the early part of the 2000s, the tax administration is not a separate entity, but is headed by the Ministry of Finance, an institution that has achieved a 'comparable level of autonomy' with respect to the parliament and government and whose powers in the budgeting process gives it 'far-reaching control over government policy'.[9] Throughout the 1990s, there were 355 tax offices across Poland, collecting more than 85 per cent of the income of the state's budget.[10] The tax offices in each province (*wojewódstwo*) are subordinate to a tax chamber. Tax chambers and tax audit offices both number one per province and are subordinated directly to the Ministry of Finance. Unlike the case in other parts of the former communist bloc, the tax offices in Poland do not depend upon the local government, by law or in practice, which provides the system with a degree of consolidation.

After the territorial reform of January 1999, the numbers of tax chambers and tax audit offices were reduced from 49 to 16 each, reflecting the reduction in the number of provinces. In 2000, the 16 tax audit offices

---

[7] Author's interview with Tax Office Head, Warsaw, 20 November 2001.
[8] Author's interview with Tax Chamber Director, Warsaw, 15 November 2001.
[9] Kamiński, 1997, p. 110; and Goetz and Wollmann, pp. 874–875.
[10] NIK, October 1994, p. 3.

142   Taxes and Trust

(also referred to as 'fiscal control offices') employed 8,501 people, the 16 tax chambers employed 4,147 employees, and the 355 tax offices was staffed by 37,475 people.[11] The last figure is almost double that of the 19,310 workers employed in 1991 by the then 320 tax offices.[12] The growth in staff can be attributed in part to the introduction of the new taxes.

In 2015, in addition to the 16 tax audit offices, there were 16 tax chambers, 380 tax offices, 20 large (specialized) taxpayer offices, six National Information Offices that issue individual rulings and tax law advice via call centres, and a Tax Information Exchange Office that specializes in exchanging tax information with EU member states and other countries.[13] In 2013, over 39,000 were employed in the tax offices and over 3,780 were employed in the tax chambers; tax administration employees compose 35.3 per cent of all civil servants in the country.[14]

The actual collection of taxes appears to be a very routine procedure. Most taxpayers file a declaration and pay taxes such as the PIT by themselves. (The social security office known as the *Zakład Ubezpieczeń Społecznych*, or ZUS, also provides some assistance to the collection process by automatically deducting taxes from pensions. Approximately 20 per cent of those surveyed in 2000, 2001 and 2002 had their tax returns filed for them by their place of employment or by ZUS.[15]) If a taxpayer does not pay on time, he or she is given seven days to pay, after which a 'title of seizure' is issued. (In the mid-1990s, the Supreme Audit Chamber (*Najwyższa Izba Kontroli*, or NIK), however, found significant delays in issuing such 'titles of seizure' among the tax offices it surveyed.[16]) Perhaps thanks to the ease of processing one's tax return, the tax office in one 1999 public opinion poll was viewed favourably by half of the respondents – the highest among public institutions in that survey.[17] (In contrast, in 2001, businessmen in Russia were asked to rate their attitude toward a variety of characters with whom they have to deal. Tax inspectors and tax policemen were given the least positive appraisals on the list, with the exception of a 'bandit'.[18])

In addition to registering and collecting taxes from all taxpayers, tax offices usually conduct audits of taxpayers with little tax due. Tax audit offices audit taxpayers (usually large firms) with significant liabilities. Appeals from the initial audits of both the tax offices and the tax control offices are made to the tax chambers. From there, a second appeal can be

---

[11] Ministry of Finance, September 2000, p. 12.   [12] NIK, April 1993, p. 3.
[13] Ministry of Finance, 2014, p. 8.   [14] Ibid., p. 12.   [15] CBOS, May 2002.
[16] NIK, May 1997, p. 4.   [17] Wrobel.
[18] INDEM Foundation, Part 4, pp. 23–24.

made to the Chief Administrative Court (NSA), which judges whether the tax chamber has infringed a law or ordinance. Hence, the tax offices and tax audit offices are known as offices of 'first instance', while the tax chambers are referred to as offices of 'second instance', a concept of Polish administrative law that dates back to the inter-war regime.[19]

Informal cooperation does exist between the heads of the tax chambers and the tax audit offices, but owing to the unique structural arrangement between the two organizations, some incongruence, lack of coordination, and lack of sharing of information on audited economic entities does arise – a phenomenon that Poland's NIK has noted on several occasions.[20] While the tax chambers supervise the tax offices, they do not supervise the tax audit offices, from which they receive cases. This situation was characterized by a vice-director at a tax chamber as 'a strange formation, [by which] the tax chamber does not possess control over the tax audit office and can not issue to it a decision whereas the tax chamber can give its records directly to a tax office for review'.[21] The tax audit offices, which act as a form of tax police, are distinguished in that, unlike a regular tax office, the inspector functions as an organizational unit himself, empowered to make decisions on his own. Hence, employees of the tax chamber can have direct contact with individual tax audit office inspectors on cases, but they do not have direct contact with the entire tax audit office.

In addition, the tax audit offices also have a different timeline for the appeals process. At the tax office, a taxpayer has twenty-one days to make an appeal, whereas this period is only three days at the tax audit office. 'Whether a taxpayer has three or twenty-one days for appeal is at times in general not important', commented the vice-director, 'but at times it is very important – as it depends on what the audit affirms.'[22]

Moreover, a tax chamber may regard the tax offices directly subordinate to it as being better qualified than the tax inspectors at the tax audit office. For example, within one province in 2000, while the tax chamber repealed 38.5 per cent of cases originating in the tax offices, it repealed 63.3 per cent of decisions from the tax audit office.[23] Also telling is the fact that NIK in 2000 regarded the level of cooperation between the tax audit offices and the tax chambers and offices in the sharing of information in the cases conducted by tax audit office inspectors as insufficient and ineffective.[24]

---

[19] Borkowski, p. 40.   [20] NIK, December 1994, p. 4; and NIK, May 2000, p. 3.
[21] Interview with a Tax Chamber Vice Director, Gdańsk, November 26, 2001.
[22] Ibid.   [23] Ibid.   [24] NIK, May 2000, p. 4.

144   Taxes and Trust

While the initial goal of separating out the tax audit offices was to draw more attention to large cases, at the end of 2001 plans appeared within the Ministry of Finance for dissolving the tax audit offices, placing the inspectors in the tax chambers and tax offices in such a fashion that the line of command is more direct and competition between the different bodies is eliminated.[25] Thus, with the exception of the relationship between the tax audit office and the tax office, the tax administration does appear to have a clear, disciplined structure subordinate ultimately to the Ministry of Finance, as well as some consistent practices for collecting tax revenue.

Russia's Tax Administration Structure

In March 1991, the State Tax Service of Russia (STS) was formed on the basis of the USSR's State Tax Service, then part of the Ministry of Finance.[26] (In the Soviet Union, taxes existed in a narrow sense, with turnover tax and enterprise payments tax the most common.) The STS, which became responsible for collecting all revenue for federal and regional budgets (except for customs duties), was separated from the Ministry of Finance later in 1991 as an independent agency. In December 1998, the STS was upgraded in status as the Ministry of Taxes and Dues. In 2004, the Ministry was eliminated, and the Federal Tax Service put in its place under the Ministry of Finance.[27]

The STS grew from 50,000 to 60,000 employees at the beginning of the transition to 161,790 in 1995 to around 180,000 in 2003 (with around 1,100 in the central apparatus and territorial organs.)[28] In July 1995, the STS had 710 employees in the central apparatus and 161,790 bureaucrats in its offices across the country; despite the mid-1990s target goals of a staff of 200,000, Tax Minister Gennadiy Bukayev (2000–2004) stated in 2001 that the tax agencies' staff just numbered above 160,000, suggesting that there had not been that much growth in recent years.[29] IMF representatives found there to be less than 1,000 employees in the STS's headquarters in Moscow in 1999, regarding the number as far short of what was needed.[30] In 2003, there were 82 directorates for

---

[25] Zasuń.

[26] Morozov, p. 1; and interview with former head of the department of civil service and personnel, Ministry of Taxes and Dues, Moscow, 8 August 2003.

[27] Samoylenko, March/April 2004; and Samoylenko, November/December 2004.

[28] Morozov, p. 2; and Interview with former head of the Department of Civil Service and Personnel, Ministry of Taxes and Dues, Moscow, 8 August 2003.

[29] Morozov, p. 2; and BBC Monitoring Former Soviet Union – Economic, 26 November 2001.

[30] Highfield and Baer, p. 4.

Building Trust, Instilling Fear: Tax Administration Reform   145

the then 89 regions of Russia, plus inter-regional inspection offices in the seven new federal districts (*okrugi*), which control and supervise the directorates.[31]

Traditionally, Soviet institutions that were spread out across the vast country were accompanied by a strict hierarchical system of control, usually led by the Communist Party. However, in the 1990s, relaxed relations between the regions and Moscow and the rise of locally elected leaders weakened intra-institutional control. Such was also the case with the tax administration. At a minimum, as a US Treasury official who had worked with the State Tax Administration (STA) for several years in the late 1990s observed, there existed very little communication across the immense bureaucratic organization, in which only one-third of one per cent of the employees worked in the centre.[32]

At worst, especially in the 1990s, dual subordination existed, whereby local tax officers served two masters, Moscow and the regional governments, which often supplied infrastructure facilities (such as housing and health-care services), as well as, in some cases, trying to finance local tax offices through regional budgets.[33] 'As a result', the IMF has written, '[local tax offices] exerted more effort in collecting taxes for local governments than for the national government, e.g., collecting first those taxes where the local take was highest; did not remit to the federal government all that it was owed; and provided more favourable tax treatment to locally based enterprises.'[34] 'With a tax inspectorate located in just about every local political unit across Russia', Richard Highfield and Katherine Baer found, 'the existing organizational setup appears to largely reflect local tax considerations, notwithstanding that local taxes constitute a minute proportion of the overall taxes collected ... This has led to the emergence in practice of a ... variable system of revenue sharing in place, [with tax officials] often competing for tax revenue from the same pool of taxes. This problem is compounded by a headquarters' administration that emphasizes the optimal collection of federal budget revenues, rather than the collection of all federal and regional taxes.'[35]

After Mikhail Fradkov became prime minister in March 2004, a consolidation plan for all the Russian Federation's ministries began to be implemented, and the Ministry of Taxes and Dues was eliminated and its functions transferred to a newly created Federal Committee for Tax

---

[31] Author's interview with division head, department of international co-operation and information exchange, Ministry of Taxes and Dues, 22 July 2003.
[32] Author's interview with U.S. Treasury official, Moscow, 3 June 2003.
[33] Morozov, p. 4.   [34] IMF, 2002, p. 60.   [35] Highfield and Baer, pp. 3–4.

146   Taxes and Trust

Control (later named the Federal Tax Service), placed under the Ministry of Finance. Indeed, the transfer of the tax functions to the Ministry of Finance was part of a revived attempt at administrative reform, which began under Putin back in 2001 and which proceeded at a relatively slow pace. The outward goal of the reforms is to reduce the number of ministries. However, the entire project actually appears to be part of Putin's plan for creating a tightly centralized state with the bureaucracies under greater control, as described in Chapter 3.

Hence, while being part of the government's overall administrative reform plans to reduce the number of ministries, the March 2004 elimination of the Ministry of Taxes and Dues was thought to be part of a move to consolidate tax policy within the Ministry of Finance so that there is a single voice on the issue.[36] Nevertheless, the transition has been said not to be smooth, as the International Tax and Investment Centre (ITIC), an independent non-profit foundation that provides tax and investment policy information to businesses and also trains key policy makers in the former Soviet Union, remarked repeatedly in its monthly bulletins that the process was fraught with disorganization, slow integration, and 'continued uncertainty among many key staff positions'.[37] The process also was delayed because a new law was required to abolish the Ministry of Taxes and Dues and to integrate it into the Ministry of Finance.[38] Even the World Bank has cited in its own reports that the slow reorganization was a reason for the delays and lack of progress in the second phase of the transition.[39] However, while the process has been slow and somewhat chaotic (and late in comparison to the subordination of tax administrations to the finance ministries much earlier in other countries such as Poland), the effort may be beneficial down the road, leading to better supervision of tax collection activities.

In recent years, at least seven to nine specialized inter-regional tax inspections have been established that focus on particular types of large-scale business activity (such as oil and banking).[40] Moreover, such specialization has taken place within Moscow, where the 45 or so tax inspection offices, each of which once concentrated on a particular geographical area of the city, now focus each on a particular type of business or personal income activity.[41] (In Poland, a smaller country, by 2011,

---

[36] Samoylenko, March/April, 2004, pp. 1–2.   [37] Ibid., p. 1.
[38] Ibid., p. 2.   [39] World Bank, 2005b, p. 913.
[40] Author's interview with division head, department of international co-operation and information exchange, Ministry of Taxes and Dues, 22 July 2003; Bureau of Economic Analysis, p. 5; and Samoylenko, June/July 2004, pp. 1–2.
[41] Interview with former head of a Moscow tax inspectorate, 5 August 2003.

there were some 20 such national specialized large taxpayer offices.[42] Meanwhile, Ukraine opened a central office for large taxpayers in Kyiv in May 2012.[43]) It appears that Russia's recent reform efforts have been the result of available technical assistance and of redoubled efforts by ministerial leadership to improve the efficiency of tax collection. Nevertheless, the greatest problem in Russia remains the fact that the tax system is target-level driven rather than compliance-driven (in contrast to Poland), which provides different incentives for tax inspectors.

The Tax Administration Modernization Project in Russia In the midst of the somewhat disorganized nature of governing institutions in Russia, a reform program, the Tax Administration Modernization Project (TAMP), attempted to make at least part of the tax system more bureaucratically rational. The TAMP program, which was essentially geared towards the introduction of US-style audit-free filing of taxes in a country where all firms generally are audited at least once every two years, was initiated in 1994 with World Bank, IMF and US Treasury support in two regions of Russia, Nizhniy Novgorod and Volgograd, in addition to the capital. Prior to the reforms, neither customer service, education or compliance activities had been carried out nor was personnel training organized systematically in either region.

One of the key tasks of the program was to set up special units for information services, customer service and taxpayer education and for tax compliance promotion and minimal contact with taxpayers as they deliver their tax returns and accounting statements. In Volgograd Oblast, a Training and Information Centre at the regional level tax office was established. Taxpayer consultation offices capable of providing taxpayer consultations, handling complaints and communicating on tax questions with society and the media through television, radio, newspapers, discussion groups and clubs also were founded in every local-level inspection office. As a result of these reforms, taxpayers in the oblast were served approximately nine times faster, requests were processed ten times faster, the need to approach only the same tax inspector each time was removed so that corruption opportunities were reduced, and an increase in taxpayer responsibility and a reduction of errors in tax declarations by 2.2 times were observed.[44]

Among the many other outcomes achieved were a reduction in processing time, a reduced number of tax procedures performed by each

---

[42] Polish Information and Foreign Investment Agency S.A., p. 5.
[43] Ukrinform News, 28 May 2012.
[44] Ministry of Taxes and Dues, Volgograd, 2000, pp. 3–4, 26–27.

148   Taxes and Trust

inspector, a doubling of settled tax arrears in Volgograd oblast in 1999 in comparison with 1998, an increase in regional tax collection that outpaced the national average, an increase in the proportion of tax returns filed on time from 50 to 75 per cent between 1998 and 2000, and a fall in the arrears rate by 90 per cent in Nizhny Novgorod and by 170 per cent in Volgograd between 1998 and 2000.[45]

The project itself took five and one-half years to implement, instead of the originally planned three and one-half years, because from 1996 to 1999 project supervision was suspended, as the government wanted to cancel it. Indeed, a former deputy head of one of the program's regions suggested that the government would have succeeded in nixing the project just after the World Bank loan had provided new equipment and computers were it not for the fact that the project region had already begun implementing several of the new reform proposals ahead of Moscow's expectations and lobbied for the project to continue.[46] Furthermore, as evidence of Moscow's uncertainty about the reform project, the Volgograd project regional directorate head was dismissed even after a few years of dramatic increases in tax collection within his region because newer, much higher target levels set by the centre could not be met.[47] Such was the emphasis from above on target levels rather than on improving compliance through a more rational bureaucracy.

Fast forward a decade, with the TAMP project completed and new management in charge, and the story is a bit different in Volgograd Oblast. In the 2012 Business Environment and Enterprise Performance Survey (BEEPS), which included representative samples for 37 Russian regions conducted by the EBRD and the World Bank and in collaboration with the Centre for Economic and Financial Research (CEFIR) and Russia's Ministry of Economic Development, the tax administration was regarded as the second biggest obstacle for firms in Volgograd Oblast, constraining their business, second only to general 'corruption'.[48] Hence, a decade later, the benefits obtained in the early 2000s in terms of tax administration reform in Volgograd have dissipated.

[45] World Bank News Release, 'Outcomes of the Russia Tax Modernization Project Supported by the World Bank and International Monetary Fund', 17 November 2000; and World Bank, 2003, p. 6. As a comparison, in looking at data published by the RF State Statistics Service of in the 2000, 2002 and 2004 editions of *Finansy Rossii*, the amount of tax arrears as a percentage of total tax income to the RF Consolidated Budget as a whole fell from 49.40 to 31.20 per cent from 1998 to 2000, a level of decline of approximately 37 per cent.
[46] Author's interview with former deputy head of regional tax directorate, 18 August 2003.
[47] Author's interview with US Treasury official, Moscow, 3 June 2003.
[48] European Bank for Reconstruction and Development, pp. 43–44.

Nevertheless, despite some earlier reluctance on the part of the government, some of the principles of the pilot reform project (but not the audit-free filing aspects) began to be implemented across Russia in 2002 and a second phase of the TAMP was launched in 2003 aimed at modernizing data-processing centres in five federal *okrugi* and 12 to 16 regional tax administrations with World Bank (but no longer US Treasury) support.[49] For example, one of the successful reform tasks involved in the first phase of the project was to re-design the structure of the local tax offices so that employees were not divided into units based upon tax types or taxpayer categories (as is done throughout Russia and was done in Poland up until 2010[50]) but were organized according to the more efficient and more transparent 'functionality principle', by which each tax worker performs the same task regardless of the type of tax.[51] In 2002, some tax organs in other regions began to be re-organized according to the 'functionality principle' as part of the first stage of a federal targeted program, 'The Development of the Tax Organs (2002–2004)', confirmed by the government in late 2001.[52] Up until then, the design structure of the tax offices had varied across Russia because there were no regulations.[53]

In short, at the time, the success of the TAMP program in Volgograd and Nizhniy Novgorod illustrates that, given alternative training, a different structure and new incentives to allow a work philosophy oriented towards 'customer service', Russian tax collectors can work much more effectively and efficiently. Hence, even in a country with a different history and culture, a change from a target-driven method to an audit-free, compliance-driven method yields much higher tax compliance. Thus, the degree of policy implementation need not vary by country because of cultural differences: Policies to improve effectiveness can be applied across different states.

The Tax Police in Russia In 1992, within the State Tax Service was formed the Main Division of Tax Investigations, which in 1993 was transformed into an independent governmental body, the Department

---

[49] World Bank, 2002.
[50] Author's interview with Kierownik Działu Obsługi Bezpośredniej, Urząd Skarbowy Warszawa Wola, Warsaw, 27 April 2012.
[51] 'Tax Administration Modernization Project of the Russian Federation, Volgograd Oblast, 1995 (January)–2000 (June), Report, Executive Summary, Volgograd Oblast Tax Administration.
[52] Bureau of Economic Analysis, p. 4. Translation from the Russian by the author.
[53] Author's interview with former head of the Department of Civil Service and Personnel, Ministry of Taxes and Dues, Moscow, 8 August 2003.

150 Taxes and Trust

of Tax Police, and in 1995 became the Russian Federal Tax Police Service. The tax police was created in response to the fact that tax inspectors were not allowed into some firms that were not paying taxes in 1992.[54] Also, in one year, Russian citizens were said to have burned down the homes of 40 tax collectors.[55] In 1996, 26 tax collectors were murdered, 74 injured and 6 kidnapped, while 18 tax offices were 'shot up'.[56] Hence, the initial 'need' for masks and guns when approaching taxpayers – accessories that were used less as time wore on. The main duties of the tax police became the 'exposure, prevention and suppression of tax law violations and crimes'.[57] In 2003, Putin signed a decree disbanding the 40,000-strong force of tax police officers.[58] However, the tasks were merely transferred to the interior ministry and later to a new body named the Investigative Committee, so that the federal tax police activities continued to live on even after the official 'demise' of the organization.[59]

The personnel for the federal tax police came from those who were sacked from the KGB, the Soviet army and other military organizations at the beginning of the 1990s.[60] The tax police had regional and subregional offices throughout Russia. While the tax police had close contacts with the State Tax Service's regional directorates and local offices, they (and the interior ministry divisions that took over their activities in 2003) differed from the tax audit office structure in Poland in that they were an entirely separate government organization. The tax police were not accountable to the other tax administration bodies and did not have their cases reviewed by them.

As Highfield and Baer of the IMF found in 2000, the regular audit staff of the Ministry of Taxation were prevented from independently pursuing cases of tax fraud relating to legal and illegal economic activities, as those cases were in the tax police's domain.[61] Cases were either located by the tax police officers themselves or were referred to them by local tax offices, which would provide information on an individual basis rather than through open access to their files.[62] The ITIC has remarked that

[54] Author's interview with former assistant to deputy head of Moscow city tax police, Moscow, 28 July 2003.
[55] Reynolds, Neil.   [56] Franklin, p. 136.
[57] Author's interview with former assistant to deputy head of Moscow city tax police, Moscow, 28 July 2003.
[58] Nicholson.   [59] Samoylenko, March/April, 2004, p. 2.
[60] Author's interview with manager, Moscow office of one of the 'Big Four' international accounting firms, Moscow, 13 August 2003.
[61] Highfield and Baer, p. 4.
[62] Author's interview with former assistant to deputy head of Moscow city tax police, Moscow, 28 July 2003.

Building Trust, Instilling Fear: Tax Administration Reform   151

as tax auditors 'seem increasingly under pressure to find "problems" to report to their superiors', criminal investigations are automatically triggered as a result of the Russian tax code, thus providing continuous work for the 'tax police'.[63]

Given the lack of transparency in the activities of both the Federal Tax Police and the Ministry of the Interior, it is unclear to what extent co-operation between the two bodies and the STA has been better or worse in Russia compared with the corresponding organizations in Poland. However, there may have been some disagreement as to exactly how much extra revenue the tax police brought in on its own. For example, from 1992 to 1994, according to one senior tax police officer, the tax police collected as much as the tax authorities collected when taxpayers willingly paid.[64] Meanwhile, a former deputy head of a regional tax directorate stated that the tax police tended to write down that they worked on cases that actually were carried out by the regular tax offices.[65]

The methods used by the tax police have been deemed questionable. A lot of what they have done was political or paid persecution, according to one Moscow-based international lawyer.[66] The tax police are viewed by private businesses as using scare tactics. For example, according to another managing tax partner at one of the Big Four international accounting firms, immediately after a company receives a visit from the tax police, outside 'security firms' often approach the company offering 'help' in dealing with the tax police for a fee; such incidents were said not to happen with the regular tax authorities.[67] The tax police also have appeared to work on a quota system. An inspector could open up a case against a company at the end of one year, which he would then close at the beginning of the New Year in order to meet his quota.[68]

Andrew Bowen noted that the 'Tax Police became extremely aggressive and received a portion of the money that it collected (the only limitation on their equipment was that they were not allowed to use police dogs, armoured vehicles or water cannons) ... The Tax Police was known to simply show up at a business and threaten the owner with investigation unless they paid a percentage of their assumed tax bill ... '[69] Meanwhile, Jorge Martinez-Vazquez and Robert McNab wrote in 2000 that 'The prejudgement that all taxpayers are potentially criminals predisposes tax

---

[63] Witt, p. 2.   [64] Morozov, p. 2.

[65] Author's interview with former deputy head of regional tax directorate, 18 August 2003.

[66] Lawyer, Moscow office of a leading international law firm, Moscow, 11 August 2003.

[67] Head law partner, Moscow office of one of the 'Big Four' international accounting firms, Moscow, 28 July 2003.

[68] Ibid.   [69] Bowen.

152   Taxes and Trust

administrations in [transition states] to call in the 'tax police' to solve issues of compliance and erodes voluntary compliance.'[70]

Just before the Federal Tax Police Service was officially disbanded, the Tax Police gained in February 2003 the right to use lie detectors on those suspected of committing tax crimes or deemed likely to do so.[71] Within the legislation of the Tax Police, according to one tax lawyer, informers on those who did not pay taxes were eligible to receive a 10 per cent cut.[72] Moreover, the Tax Police also had the right to place people undercover in companies, although this was not heard of in practice.[73] Finally, Tax Police officers have been regarded as a breed apart. After the difficulties in deciphering the tax legislation, one senior Tax Police officer named the 'presumption of innocence' on the part of accused taxpayers as *the* greatest obstacle to the work of the Tax Police.[74]

In 2003, to approach Russian government officials and to seek out the assistance of the Organisation for Economic Co-operation and Development (OECD), the United States and the United Kingdom, the ITIC formed a working group to help promote changes in the regulations governing the criminal tax enforcement activities of the Tax Police (Ministry of Interior), including the automatic 'triggering' of criminal investigations whenever disputes are over the ruble equivalent of U.S.$50,000, which had resulted in such investigations being a regular routine for most firms.[75]

As large companies began to comply more with paying taxes under Putin, such tactics have been deemed excessive for use in pursuing small and medium-sized firms. However, the tax police were judged to have been used successfully as a political weapon of sorts, as Vladimir Gusinsky and Boris Berezovsky's businesses, among others, were targets of their investigation in 2000. In addition, the fact that Putin might have wanted to bring more control and a more accountable structural design to the organization may have been his reason for disbanding it in 2003 and centralizing the activities in another ministry.

In September 2007, a new, powerful agency named the Investigative Committee of the Russian Federation was created with Aleksandr

---

[70] Martinez-Vazquez and McNab, p. 288.   [71] *Moscow Times*, 17 February 2003.
[72] Partner, Moscow office of one of the Big Four international accounting firms, Moscow, 28 July 2003.
[73] Ibid.
[74] Author's interview with former assistant to deputy head of Moscow City Tax Police.
[75] Samoylenko, March/April 2004, p. 2; Samoylenko, September/October 2004, p. 2; and Samoylenko, November/December, 2004, p. 2.

Bastrykin, a former law school classmate of Putin's, as its chair.[76] It was later given the right to investigate tax-related cases based on information given to it by tax inspectors – something that had previously been vested in the Ministry of the Interior and other law enforcement bodies.[77]

In late 2013, the Russian Duma passed a bill that gave the Investigative Committee the authority to initiate at their discretion criminal prosecutions in the tax arena based on information submitted by other law enforcement agencies, and not necessarily by tax inspectors of the Federal Tax Service. Back in 2011, then President Dmitry Medvedev had abolished such practices, but this new bill, introduced to the Duma by President Putin over the heads of the government, revived the approach.[78] When, for the first time since he became prime minister, Medvedev spoke out publicly against the bill on 12 November 2013, which had caused consternation among the business community, stating, 'Anything can be initiated, especially on order and for money, which often happens when one structure fights against another one', Putin responded by suggesting that Medvedev could leave the government if he disagreed.[79] As political analyst Tatiana Stanovaya relayed of the incident, 'Putin chose the path of boosting the repressive machine. At the same time, he made it clear that all those displeased, including the Russian prime minister, can resign.'[80]

Ukraine's Tax Administration Structure

The Ukrainian STA, like other state institutions, can trace its origins as a weak tool of the state back to the early 1990s, when the main headquarters of all Soviet-era governing ministries remained in Moscow, and Ukraine thus had to build new ones in Kyiv, essentially from scratch.[81]

As in Poland, the tax administration in Ukraine was founded on the basis of the Soviet Ministry of Finance's financial and revenue offices,

---

[76] Brian Whitmore, 'Russia: Powerful New Investigative Body Begins Work', *RFE/RL*, accessed 8 March 2015 at <http://www.rferl.org/content/article/1078611.html>.
[77] Tatiana Stanovaya, 'A Warning to Medvedev', Institute of Modern Russia website, accessed 25 August 2015 at <http://www.imrussia.org/en/politics/608-a-warning-to-medvedev>.
[78] Bowen; Ernst & Young, *Russia Tax Brief*, p. 2, accessed 25 August 2015 at <http://www.ey.com/Publication/vwLUAssets/EY-RTB-July-2014-Eng/$FILE/EY-RTB-July-2014-Eng.pdf>.
[79] Bowen; Stanovaya, 'A Warning to Medvedev'.
[80] Stanovaya, 'A Warning to Medvedev'.
[81] Author's interview with Vladimir Dubrovsky, Centre for Social and Economic Research, Kyiv, 20 October 2005.

154   Taxes and Trust

which existed in every district throughout the country.[82] While the law 'On the Taxation System' was adopted on 25 June 1991, former Soviet Union regulations existed from the very beginning until the tax and financial system of the new country was fully formed. Initially, until 1992, Ukraine's tax service was a division of the Ministry of Finance, although most revenue agents were said to come from internal security.[83] In the early days of the 1990s, the few firms that did exist were likely to have been more cooperative with the state. One regional tax official in an oblast commented that at the beginning of the 1990s, 'the work was a lot, but such words as "arrears" we almost never heard as enterprises and organizations transferred adequate funds to the budget in a timely manner.'[84] Nevertheless, a few years into the decade saw economic instability, hyperinflation of the country's currency up to September 1996 (the Ukrainian *karbovanets*) and chronic state budget deficits, which did affect the tax administration's activities as well as its internal resources.

Already in the 1990s, criminal groups were alleged to have close ties to the tax administration in Ukraine that they used to extort money from businesses, which found it cheaper to pay the groups than the tax authorities.[85] The weakness of the STA as it interacted with society contributed to a feeling of less fear of the state and the tax authorities than in Russia. This was the case even as President Leonid Kuchma and STA chief (and more recently finance minister and then prime minister under President Viktor Yanukovych) Mykola Azarov began to turn the STA into a stronger tool in the second half of the 1990s by establishing a strict hierarchical structure, which has been widely referred to as *zhorstkoyu kontrol'* (cruel or strict control), putting political pressure on larger firms while letting smaller and medium-sized firms fall under the discretion of local tax officers. Anders Åslund regarded the STA as having been the 'main repressive organ of the state' under Azarov.[86] Such changes coincided with the formation of the STA, replacing the Ukrainian tax service, in 1996. In short, Ukraine built a tax system based on a mixture of coercion and bureaucratic discretion.

In the years that followed, Azarov's successors, who led the STA under Kuchma before the Orange Revolution, varied in the degree to which

---

[82] Fritz, p. 117; and Interview with State Tax Inspector in a Ukrainian Oblast, Ukraine, 20 May 2011.

[83] Emil Sunley, Formerly of the IMF, Interview with the author, Washington, DC, 20 August 2014.

[84] '[Regional Oblast]'s Tax Service Past and Present', Unpublished manuscript, 2009. Translation from the Russian by the author.

[85] Shelley, p. 655.

[86] Anders Åslund, Interview with the author, Washington, DC, 22 August 2014.

Building Trust, Instilling Fear: Tax Administration Reform   155

they created a more 'Weberian' tax bureaucracy in order to strengthen the state. A former STA official stated that STA head Yuri Kravchenko gave more autonomy to his subordinates, whereas his successor, Fyodor Yereshenko, a protégé of Azarov who earlier had served as his first deputy, was said to have taken away any personal initiatives on the part of the STA staff in a manner more like a 'Beria' – a reference to Lavrenty Beria, the notorious Soviet secret police boss who carried out purges under Stalin in the 1930s and 1940s.[87] (In March 2005, Kravchenko was found shot twice in the head, with a suicide note, on the day that he was to be questioned by the prosecutor regarding the murder of the Internet journalist Georgi Gongadze.) Meanwhile, the corruption of the Kuchma years most likely did not help raise public support for the STA. Before the 2004 election, for example, corrupt VAT refund schemes were rumoured to have been employed in the nation's regions for political campaigns by both sides.[88]

After the Orange Revolution, the STA continued to have an ambiguous status because it reported only to the president, giving the government little authority to change its behaviour and practices and enabling it to continue to be a political tool of sorts.[89] In early 2006, a constitutional amendment addressed the subordination issue, making the STA accountable directly to the central government. Yet even after this amendment (but before the August 2006 selection as prime minister of Yanukovych, who quickly named Azarov's protégé, Anatoliy Brezvin, as the new STA chief), the STA was subordinated in practice to President Viktor Yushchenko, who once in office appointed a friend, Oleksandr Kireev, as its head.[90] Kireev was seen by local analysts as wanting to see the STA become a partner with society rather than a mere tax collector, but politics did become a factor, because his position enabled him to 'punish' some more than others.[91]

While, at times, the STA formally has been subordinated to the Ministry of Finance, problems of coordination existed in practice, even when the STA was underneath the Ministry. By the end of the Kuchma era, the tax administration was subordinated directly to the Cabinet of Ministers, but with the arrival of the Yushchenko government in 2005, the

---

[87] Author's interview with former senior official, State Tax Administration, Kyiv, 29 July 2006.
[88] Author's interview with U.S. government official, Kyiv, 10 August 2006.
[89] Author's interview with senior associate, Kyiv office of one of the Big Four international accounting firms, Kyiv, 26 October 2005.
[90] Author's interview with Igor Lavrinenko, expert, Centre for Political and Legal Reforms, Kyiv, 24 July 2006.
[91] Author's interview with Bohdan Senchuk, Blue Ribbon Analytical and Advisory Centre, United Nations Development Program, Kyiv, 17 October 2005.

STA was brought under Ministry of Finance control.[92] Nevertheless, in that year, the Razumkov Centre noted that the Ministry of Finance's powers with respect to human resources management at the State Customs Service and the STA were limited.[93] By 2006, when such subordination of the STA to the Ministry did exist, the Ministry of Finance and the STA already had a long-standing disagreement as to whether the Ministry could gain certain information from the STA – something that Yushchenko had yet to make a decision on whether to permit.[94] And, in 2015, when the STA was no longer formally under Ministry of Finance control (as it is in Western countries), Åslund commented that the Ministry of Finance had control and information only on the STA's expenditures but not on revenues.[95]

Despite a significant lack of external structural restraints on the STA's activities, one of the improvements since the Orange Revolution has been the transfer in September 2005 of the authority to resolve disputes between the STA and taxpayers from the commercial courts to the administrative courts, which has provided greater protection of the rights of taxpayers.[96] Hence, some alternation of the administrative design can affect the type and nature of citizens' interaction with the tax system, providing a strengthening of trust in the state. Meanwhile, a 'Charter of Tax Relations' was drafted in 2005 by the National Commission on Fiscal Reform, consisting of deputies and representatives of the Presidential Secretariat, the Cabinet of Ministers, other state agencies and non-governmental organizations, calling for a number of bold new initiatives, including reduction in public spending on the tax service, improvement in the culture of service to taxpayers, elimination of the tax police, decentralization of tax revenues, expansion of the role of local budgets, merger of the tax and customs services and implementation of further activities under the control of the Ministry of Finance, which ultimately was unfulfilled.

Under Yanukovych, the signing of presidential decree 1085, 'On the Systems Optimization of Central Executive Organs', on 9 December 2010, did not bring any immediate changes to the tax administration, despite the fact that that administrative reform decree was expected to bring a reduction in the numbers of tax personnel. In fact, in 2011, one Ministry of Finance official complained that there was a lack of strategic policy documents at the Ukrainian government level on the main directions of the tax administration's development, and what few

---

[92] Fritz, p. 200.   [93] Razumkov UCEPS, 2005, p. 32.
[94] Ibid.   [95] Åslund, 2015, pp. 135, 147.
[96] Author's interview with senior partner, leading local tax and legal firm, Kyiv, 3 August 2006.

Building Trust, Instilling Fear: Tax Administration Reform   157

had been adopted seemed to be annulled by new, succeeding govern-ments. In February 2007, the Cabinet of Ministers approved a Con-cept of reform that was cancelled in 2009, when the new government in December 2009 adopted a different tax system reform strategy, which in turn was cancelled by the new prime minister in June 2010, leaving the tax administration without a strategic document in 2011.[97]

During Yanukovych's presidency, an alternative 'tax system' also was created by which the country was divided up into a system of so-called '*ploshchadki*' (or 'playing fields') – groups of enterprises that minimized their taxes through fictitious VAT refunds offered by the 'optimiza-tion services' of tax bureaucrats, who received a set percentage of ficti-tious transactions.[98] Åslund has described something on a similar scale. 'Billions of dollars have disappeared from the Ukrainian government each year, equivalent to an amount sufficient to cover the US$30 bil-lion budget deficit run up during Yanukovych's term', he has written. '...Billions of dollars are extracted each year out of the State Tax Administration and the State Customs Committee. Some appears to be sheer embezzlement, some is in the form of bribes passed on to the top, and some comes from commissions demanded on VAT refunds for exporters. A reasonable assessment of this embezzlement would be $3 billion to $5 billion a year.'[99] Meanwhile, Ukrainian economist Vladimir Dubrovsky has said of the Yanukovych years that 'The offi-cial public servants were stimulated to collect as much fines as possible and actually destroy business... This is a kind of institutional memory that cannot fade away quickly. It's selective enforcement of impractica-ble laws. At least some of the tax departments are corrupted 100 per cent.'[100]

After the EuroMaidan revolution, Tax Agency Head Oleksandr Kly-menko, a close ally of Yanukovych, was suspected of large-scale cor-ruption and became wanted on criminal charges. His successor, Igor Bilous, meanwhile, was suspended amid concerns of financial corruption in February 2015. After a probe indicated that the performance of tax and customs offices worsened under his watch, Bilous was permitted to continue, but resigned and was replaced through a competitive process by Roman Nasirov, who himself was accused of corruption for leaving off a London apartment from his list of properties.[101] Meanwhile, in 2014,

---

[97] Fritz, pp. 164, 176, and 193.
[98] Author's email correspondence with an anonymous expert who is a tax consultant and professor at the Ukrainian State Trade and Economic University, 1 June 2016.
[99] Åslund, 19 December 2013.   [100] Kovensky.
[101] Gorchinskaya, 19 May 2015; Vertsyuk; *Kyiv Post*, 16 September 2015; and *Kyiv Post*, 23 March 2015.

158   Taxes and Trust

the Ministry of Revenues and Dues was replaced, or renamed, as the State Fiscal Service of Ukraine, which was headed by Nasirov and which has begun a process of decentralization that will see more revenue going to local budgets. In August 2016, Ukraine's Prosecutor General Yuriy Lutsenko announced that U.S. $120 million was stolen by the tax service during Yanukovych's presidency under the leadership of Klymenko as the post-EuroMaidan leadership tried to recover funds lost during the previous regime.[102]

The Tax Administration Modernization Project in Ukraine Beginning in 2003, a much-delayed project, titled the 'Modernization Program of the State Tax Service of Ukraine', funded by the World Bank and the Ukrainian government and with outside advice from the Netherlands, the European Commission, and others, finally began and ran until 2012, aimed at reorganizing and modernizing the tax authorities, especially with respect to the registration of taxpayers' payment records, processing tax statements and payments, document management and tax employee training with benchmarks for the voluntary payment of taxes, taxpayer costs for paying taxes, the likelihood of tax evasion and the quality of the functioning of the tax authorities. The project resulted in the establishment of an automatic Call Centre enabling taxpayers to obtain information by phone or e-mail and the introduction of risk-based audit selection for planned audits, reducing the on-site inspection burden for firms, as well as implementation of electronic filing of VAT and Enterprise Profit Tax returns.[103]

Despite the ambitious plans and the laudable results, the project's implementation has been assessed fairly critically. First, the end-date of the project, initially set for June 30, 2008, was delayed twice. Second, according to the published results of several audits conducted by the Accounting Chamber of Ukraine, the project disbursed only U.S.$19 million of its U.S.$40 million budget (or 47.5 per cent) over the first seven years, while part of the World Bank funds helped finance other tax authorities' needs.[104] Other criticisms of the project included weak performance monitoring and remarks that the project's Supervisory Board's observations were left without proper evaluation and without reaction from the leadership of the STA and the Ukrainian government.

The Tax Police in Ukraine In Ukraine, the Tax Police, which exists as part of the tax administration, was formed in February 1998

---

[102] *UT* Ukraine Today, 10 August 2016.   [103] World Bank, 2012.
[104] Accounting Chamber of Ukraine, March 2011.

Building Trust, Instilling Fear: Tax Administration Reform 159

on the basis of staff from the Ministry of Interior who had worked on economic crimes, so that the cases could be conducted 'in house' rather than be transferred to the Ministry of Interior. The organization consists of special subdivisions for combating tax offenses, and it monitors compliance with the tax laws and carries out operational-search, criminal-procedural and protective functions. Yushchenko, when he was running for president in 2004, promised the liquidation of the Tax Police, which he called a 'repressive body used to exert pressure on businessmen', but the status of the Tax Police did not change once he was in office, and, unlike in Russia, the Tax Police still exist at the end of 2016, both formally and in practice.[105] The Tax Police are tasked with preventing crimes and other offenses in the area of taxation; tracing taxpayers who evade taxes and other payments; and security and prevention of corruption in the tax administration itself.[106]

After the Orange Revolution, the Tax Police occupied an uncertain position, formally existing but seen as less of a threat due to the reduction of raids on private offices.[107] Nevertheless, even before 2005, the Tax Police were never seen as a strong, coercive threat in Ukraine as they were in Russia.[108] After the EuroMaidan Revolution, it was uncertain in early 2016 whether the Tax Police would be abolished. Pavlo Kukhta, an expert at the Reanimation Package of Reforms, said that cuts already had succeeded in trimming half of the Tax Police, which was once 40,000 to 50,000 at its peak and which might be reduced to 5,000 or 6,000, mostly to personnel sitting in Kyiv and the oblast centres.[109] At the same time, the IMF was said to support the idea of liquidating the Tax Police, while the State Fiscal Service head, Roman Nasirov, was less than keen on the idea.[110]

Table 5.1 summarizes how historical references *have* been used in the formation of the tax administration structures in the three states.

Reducing or Broadening the Scope of Tax Bureaucrats' Discretion

How the Polish, Russian and Ukrainian states view their 'power' relationship with the public is best illustrated, perhaps, by the degree of discretion afforded to their tax bureaucrats. And, despite some recent

---

[105] Razumkov UCEPS, 2005, p. 41.
[106] Author's interview with State Tax Inspector in a Ukrainian Oblast, Ukraine, 20 May 2011.
[107] Author's interview with senior partner, leading local tax and legal firm, Kyiv, 3 August 2006.
[108] Author's interview with partner, tax and legal services, leading international accounting firm, Kyiv, 1 August 2006.
[109] Kovensky. [110] *Kyiv Post*, 12 July 2016; and UNIAN News Service, 1 June 2016.

160   Taxes and Trust

Table 5.1 *Historical references in tax administration structures*

	Poland	Russia	Ukraine

Findings	• Inter-war Weberian structures and legislation carry through to 1990s:
	  • Civil service
	  • Supreme audit chamber
	  • Chief administrative court
	  • Tax chambers
	  • Tax offices
		• Rejection of '80s *Glasnost* model
		• Lack of civil service in USSR
		• Soviet-inspired administration
		  • Military and law enforcement personnel
		  • Strong hierarchical control
			• Emulated Russia, but weaker tool
			• Lack of civil service in USSR
			• STA chief Azarov created system with both political and fiscal purposes through *zhorstkoyu kontrol'* with strong and weak outcomes.

Societal Approach	More citizen-based	More coercive	Weakly coercive

reforms in Russia, the basis for the differences in the degree of discretion given to the tax officials in the three states is accounted for largely by the fact that the Polish tax system focuses to a greater extent on compliance, while Russia's system is more target-level driven. Compliance- and target-driven systems provide different incentives for tax inspectors, which are illustrated best by explaining how the tax collection process operates in practice and by examining additional corruption constraints placed (or not placed) on the tax inspectors.

Collecting the New Taxes in Poland

Just as NIK and the tax offices harken back to designs from before 1989, the taxes collected in the 1990s are based on earlier taxes as well, even though the goals of taxation under state socialism and capitalism are entirely different. The commonalities of the taxes enabled the function and workload of those employed in the tax offices to share some similarities as they were being implemented. For the tax administration workers, many of whom still held the same jobs they had in the communist era, this made the task of collecting the new taxes less daunting. For example, the PIT replaced the payroll tax, the tax on pay collected from employers; the equalization tax, a rural tax that covers the income from certain types of farming; and the income tax for those who worked at their own expense.[111] The CIT replaced a previous enterprise tax that

[111] Szolno-Koguc, p. 122.

Building Trust, Instilling Fear: Tax Administration Reform 161

dated back to 1989. Meanwhile, the VAT tax replaced the turnover tax. For some, VAT was viewed as being much easier to implement because the tax offices already had information about the firms and knew how many there were, and concretely who they were, due to past tax data on hand.[112]

In the early 1990s, several administrative reforms designed to have the bureaucrats interact more constructively with the public were introduced by the Polish tax administration in order to ensure that the newly adopted taxes would be implemented appropriately. First, training of heads and managers of selected divisions of the tax offices was conducted by the tax chambers in 1991, with tax office workers being trained in the first two months of 1992 prior to the rollout of the PIT that year.[113] Similar training was conducted in 1992 and 1993 for the introduction of the VAT.[114]

Second, a tax information campaign coordination unit was formed in the Ministry of Finance, which oversaw activities that disseminated knowledge about the new taxes to the public.[115] In advance of the introduction of the new taxes, the tax chambers published brochures and conducted a mass media program, including special tax broadcasts on radio and television. As part of their work, tax administration employees were interviewed. 'On the one side, society was interested', commented one tax chamber vice-director, who took part in such interviews. 'On the other side, we were interested that the tax laws were understood and worked.'[116] In this regard, Poland truly was unique among the three countries in that tax bureaucrats really went out into the public to educate people as to what this newly founded thing called taxes was. That type of public interaction simply did not take place farther east.

Third, inside the tax offices and tax chambers, 'information points' were established and staffed by employees who knew the laws. Already, in 2001, many tax offices and tax chambers had their own websites, which enabled taxpayers to write to their own tax offices.[117] This ties into the fact that many employees within the tax administration, when interviewed, described taxpayers as 'clients' whom they assisted. At the beginning of the 2000s, one large tax office even was sending out a survey asking its 'clients' how the tax office treated them and how they could be better served.[118]

---

[112] Author's interview with Tax Office Manager, Gdańsk, 27 November 2001.
[113] NIK, April 1993, p. 34.   [114] NIK, October 1997, p. 28.   [115] Ibid., p. 27.
[116] Author's interview with a tax chamber vice director, Gdańsk, 26 November 2001.
[117] Author's interview with tax chamber director, Warsaw, 15 November 2001.
[118] Author's interview with tax office head, Białystok, 7 December 2001.

162   Taxes and Trust

Fourth, the tax offices were instructed by the Ministry of Finance not to penalize taxpayers too harshly when these taxes were first being introduced.[119]

Finally, the numbers of those working in the tax offices increased with the introduction of the new taxes. Hence, all of these Weberian reform programs were geared towards ensuring that tax bureaucrats would help the taxpayer comply with the new tax legislation and making the transition smoother for bureaucrat and taxpayer alike.

However, despite such preparation, an audit by NIK of selected tax offices revealed that 90 per cent of them had increased delays in book-keeping regarding PIT information, which negatively influenced the reliability of budget reports.[120] In defence of the tax office workers, many of the regulations, especially with respect to the VAT, were seen as being adopted too quickly and without preparation.[121] (In fact, nearly all of the bureaucrats within three tax chambers, six tax offices and three tax audit offices interviewed by this author in the fall of 2001 mentioned that the constantly changing and poorly worded new laws and regulations on taxes were the greatest problems in completing their work.)

Some of these problems aside, the tax administration's numerous efforts to make the transition to the new tax system smooth appear to have been successful. A year after the PIT came into existence, about half of taxpayers chose to file directly with their local tax offices, while the others chose to file through their employers, forgoing the opportunity to claim any deductions, but during the second year, queues would form at banks in mid-December as the state offered citizens the opportunity to buy government bonds in exchange for tax reductions.[122] 'Today, in the seventh year since the introduction of the new tax requirements', wrote Joanna Szczesna in 1998, 'the average citizen has become a true expert in tax law ... [O]ne thing is certain: the past six years have seen a period of fundamental legal education for the average citizen who, if more than 40 years old, could sense for the first time the workings of the law in a state living under the rule of law.'[123]

Collecting the New Taxes in Russia

In contrast to Poland, the work of the tax authorities in Russia has been more target-driven and less consumer-oriented – an emphasis that provides the tax bureaucrats with greater discretion, to the extent that

[119] Author's interview with tax chamber department head, Bialystok, 3 December 2001.
[120] NIK, April 1993, p. 34.   [121] Szolno-Koguc, p. 101.
[122] Szczesna, pp. 76, 77.   [123] Ibid.

Building Trust, Instilling Fear: Tax Administration Reform   163

the state can 'impose' its will over the public as the state's coffers are filled. This is noticeable especially in the manner in which the tax inspectors have been conducting audits. In 2005, the federal tax service deputy head, Tatyana Shevtsova, remarked, 'Every tax audit visit must be 100 per cent effective. Otherwise the inspector has merely wasted his or her time.' The comment provides a concise overview of how the tax service sees its own function, and Russian tax experts interpreted it as an explicit instruction for tax inspectors to increase the tax bill with each audit rather than to seek and verify taxpayer compliance.[124] Moreover, it also implies that the tax administration views every firm as a tax violator and therefore expects that every company should be inspected.

Indeed, according to the Russian Public Officials Survey (2011), 48 per cent of tax officials – or nearly every other tax bureaucrat – stated that the job of tax inspectors was 'to replenish the budget at any cost' (see Question #4 in Appendix II), and 44 per cent of tax officials stated that their work was assessed by the 'amount of taxes collected' (see Question #7 in Appendix II.) Further, 47 per cent of these tax bureaucrats stated that the overwhelming reason for which penalties or sanctions have been given out to someone in their organization was 'non-fulfilment or violation of duties' (Question #13.)

The biggest issue with respect to audits is who is selected. Tax inspectors, pressed to reach target (*plan*) goals, mostly pursue legitimate taxpayers who have all their paperwork together, rather than locating companies that are paying no taxes at all.[125] This was especially the case during the late 1990s, when more than half of local companies were bankrupt, many of which simply did not report income. 'This nonreporting of income is facilitated by the Russian tax police's tendency only to scrutinize those taxpayers with the "cleanest financial records and transparent investments,"' commented Jennifer L. Franklin in 1997. 'Therefore, generating no paper trail with the State Tax Service almost guarantees that the tax police will not come knocking.'[126] Further, the system even allowed unlimited time to return and do audits; multiple audits also could be conducted simultaneously.[127] (Even in 2015, a firm could still be subjected to multiple audits, with the authorities able, if certain criteria were met, such as a higher tax authority reviewing the

---

[124] Vremya Novostei, 10 October 2005.
[125] Author's interviews with head law partner, Moscow office of one of the 'Big Four' international accounting firms, Moscow, 28 July 2003; and with lawyer, Moscow office of a leading international law firm, Moscow, 11 August 2003.
[126] Franklin, p. 150.
[127] Interview with partner, Moscow office of one of the 'Big Four' international accounting firms, Moscow, 28 July 2003.

164   Taxes and Trust

audit of a lower authority, to undertake more than one field tax audit with respect to the same taxes and the same tax period.[128]) By 2009, the Federal Tax Service was said to have introduced 'a system of risk assessment which quickly became the guiding principle for selection of firms for additional auditing.'[129]

In the 2011 Russian Public Officials Survey, approximately one-third (32 per cent) of tax bureaucrats stated that inspectors are unable to 'catch out' those who fail to comply with the requirements of the tax organs – suggesting that it is far easier to demand payment, pre-payment or extra payment from firms known to exist and have funds than to seek out those that have interacted very little with the tax authorities (Question #3 in Appendix II). (In a similarly worded question asked in 2001, 52 per cent of Moscow tax inspectors and 66 per cent of Nizhniy Novgorod inspectors concurred that tax inspectors are unable to catch those who avoid paying taxes.[130]) Also, in the 2011 survey, over 30 per cent of tax officials thought that anyone could easily hide income from the authorities (Question #5 in Appendix II).

Moreover, when looking at deductions during audits, the tax authorities lacked the ability to look through the substance and merit of a deduction, but instead often focused on paperwork – whether it was in order, completed, signed and stamped appropriately, in an attempt to throw out as many deductions as possible (and, most likely, try to reach the tax collection quota).[131] Before the tax code of 1999, there were many gaps in the legislation that were subject to interpretation, which enabled the tax authorities to interpret the legislation as they wanted it to be – sometimes in a very inconsistent manner within and between regions.[132] Similarly, today, the tax officers are viewed as intentionally creating problems in order to compensate for solving them. 'Generally, [a] tax officer tries to create as many problems as possible, to be remunerated for a solution of the problem', a former tax inspection officer has stated. 'Creating obstacles is a cheap activity (in fact it is pronounced as protection of state interests) and remuneration is high, so it never ends.'[133]

Following the Kremlin's 2003 assault on the Yukos oil company and its 'oligarch' chief executive officer and owner, Mikhail Khodorkovsky, who was charged with fraud and tax evasion in a move deemed to be political, businessmen have viewed the affair as giving tax bureaucrats

---

[128] Deloitte, pp. 81–82, 85.   [129] Pryadilnikov and Danilova, p. 27.   [130] Ibid.
[131] Author's interview with head law partner, Moscow office of one of the 'Big Four' international accounting firms, Moscow, 28 July 2003.
[132] Author's interview with partner, Moscow office of one of the 'Big Four' international accounting firms, Moscow, 28 July 2003.
[133] E-mail correspondence with Moscow-based lawyer on 26 January 2016.

Building Trust, Instilling Fear: Tax Administration Reform   165

the go-ahead to interpret tax laws as they like. The tax service also has seen a so-called beneficial 'Yukos effect' on tax collection. Federal Tax Service Deputy Head Tatiana Shevtsova stated in 2005 that tax receipts had more than doubled within the previous year and a half, due to the fear generated in the business community by the Yukos case.[134]

Such arbitrary power, combined with a lack of detailed knowledge on the part of tax inspectors regarding the firms and industries they audit, has even allowed the prosecution of taxpayers for 'bad faith'. Such a 'rationale' for prosecution has been seen as a creative necessity for the tax service officials, given the fact that Yukos' efforts to reduce its tax liabilities before 2003 were deemed by the business community to be within the law.[135] A further shock to the business community was the 2007 raid on Price Waterhouse Coopers' Moscow office, which led to the international audit firm facing allegations of concealing evasion by Yukos in its 2002–2004 audit of the oil company; Deloitte & Touche, another leading international accounting firm, also had been brought up on tax evasion charges in 2004.[136] Ernst & Young, a third of the 'Big Four' accounting firms, also received a U.S.$16 million back tax claim in 2008.[137]

In the late 1990s, when audits were not adequate in raising extra revenue to meet a quota, some tax inspectors were said to have contacted good companies requesting payment in advance because of the regional budget crisis or because the tax collector had a target plan that needed to be reached for him to receive his bonus.[138] Furthermore, when a taxpayer went before a tax office with a view to paying arrears, some even have said that the tax inspector received 10 per cent of the extra revenue received.[139] Historically, tax authorities have had an informal relation with taxpayers whereby each taxpayer was assigned to one person in the tax inspection office during '*kameralny*' audits (audits at the tax agency office), which led to lots of issues being dependent upon personal relations. However, since the adoption of the 1999 tax code, which specified taxpayer rights, the relationship has been more formal than it used to be.[140]

---

[134] Vremya Novostei, 10 October 2005. Similarly, Hilary Appel also noted that the rise of the *siloviki* under Putin at this time brought forth an 'atmosphere of fear, which spurred greater compliance with tax laws.' (Appel, 2008, p. 312.)

[135] Bush.   [136] Medetsky and van der Schriek.   [137] RIA Novosti, 9 April 2008.

[138] Author's interview with partner, Moscow office of one of the 'Big Four' international accounting firms, Moscow, 28 July 2003.

[139] Author's interview with Aleksei A. Mukhin, director of the Centre for Political Information, Moscow, 23 May 2003.

[140] Author's interview with lawyer at Moscow office of international legal firm, Moscow, 7 August 2003.

166   Taxes and Trust

In fact, by 2003, in Moscow (one of the sites of a reform program), there often was no direct interaction with the taxpayer, who dropped off his tax documents in a drop box. (Taxpayers would drop off two copies, one of which was stamped and returned.[141]) Back in the mid-1990s, the situation was a bit different, as taxpayers were required in practice to appear before tax inspectors with their tax documents, and would be liable if the mail lost the documents or if the tax inspectors had any questions; this resulted in long queues on the two or three days a week in which Moscow tax offices received taxpayers (and in fines for delayed tax reports.)[142]

In 2005, the ITIC took note of the recent high-profile tax disputes involving Russian firms, stating, 'Perhaps the greatest cause for concern is subjecting employees of companies to criminal liability that automatically arises from tax disputes that can themselves be the result of honest mistakes and disagreements with tax auditors... The tax auditors seem increasingly under pressure to find "problems" to report to their superiors. While many of these audit findings are overturned by administrative or judicial appeal, Russian legislation (Part I of the Tax Code) automatically triggers a 'tax police' (Ministry of Interior) criminal investigation. This poses a criminal liability for key company employees (both Russian and foreign.)'[143]

In a 2005 survey of large Russian and international firms published by Ernst & Young, some 80 per cent stated that they had had some type of dispute with the tax administration within the previous three years. Interestingly, though, some 92 per cent of those disputes were taken to court by the taxpayers, and 90 per cent of such cases were resolved to the satisfaction of the firms.[144] Hence, for all of the coercive measures practiced by the tax service, the courts have become, at times, a remedial tool for private enterprises. That said, Russian firms and the tax service have different perceptions as to who wins in tax litigation. While firms claim victory if the court reduces even slightly the total amount of taxes due, the tax service will claim that it has won a case if not all of the taxpayers' demands are accepted, enabling the vast majority of cases to be claimed as 'won' by both sides simultaneously.[145] Further, the tax administration also initiates cases with the courts regarding tax offences, with fines ranging from 10 to 40 per cent of the amount unpaid usually collected through the courts. Almost 91 per cent of cases filed by the tax

---

[141] Author's interview with Manager, Moscow office of one of the Big Four international accounting firms, Moscow, 13 August 2003.
[142] Morozov, p. 8.
[143] International Tax and Investment Centre, p. 2.   [144] Dranitsyna.
[145] E-mail correspondence from a Moscow-based lawyer, 26 January 2016.

Building Trust, Instilling Fear: Tax Administration Reform 167

agencies at the Higher Arbitrazh Court from 1999 to 2004 were won by the plaintiffs, with most cases regarding defendants who refuse to pay taking no more than ten minutes of the court's consideration.[146]

After the 2014 judicial reform that unified the Supreme Court and the Higher Arbitration Court, when most Higher Arbitrazh Court judges were fired, firms were not finding the court system to be so favourable to them, as many judges, some of whom were said to be Federal Security Service (FSB) members also, appeared to rule in favour of a state that was urgently seeking revenue.[147]

As the new taxes were introduced throughout the 1990s, the tax authorities in Russia did not engage as much in public education campaigns as in Poland. According to some, the tax administration placed a low priority on educating taxpayers.[148] For example, there were few or no seminars between tax officials and taxpayers. While the 1999 tax code allowed taxpayers to ask the tax authorities for explanations, the tax authorities were reluctant to provide them, and the responses were found by some taxpayers to be usually not very helpful, although courts at times have provided more stable answers.[149]

Nevertheless, beginning in the late 1990s, the tax authorities began to try to persuade the population of the necessity of paying taxes. Eighty-seven per cent of Russians surveyed in 1999, for example, had seen television advertisements urging them to pay taxes.[150] In one very memorable television advertisement, a man clutches his head in frustration in a darkly lit bedroom with an attractive, frustrated woman awake in bed beside him when a caption displays the words: 'Lost your drive? Pay your taxes and sleep peacefully!'[151] Other television adverts consisted of frightening cartoons aimed not so much at children as adults.[152] The encouragement in Soviet times to denounce one's neighbours still existed in 1998 when 10 per cent of the tax amount recovered was written into the Tax Code for those individuals who informed on others for evading taxes.[153]

And yet a significant portion of society did not know how to pay taxes. While admittedly most taxpayers do not pay their own PIT (because, especially since 2001, taxes usually are withheld from salaries by

---

[146] RosBusinessConsulting.
[147] Telephone conversation with Moscow-based lawyer, 17 August 2015.
[148] IMF, 2002, p. 63.
[149] Author's interview with lawyer at Moscow office of international legal firm, Moscow, 7 August 2003.
[150] Fond Obshchestvennoe Mnenie, Moscow, 6–7 March 1999.
[151] Butler.   [152] Stanley.   [153] Ibid.

168   Taxes and Trust

employers), the percentage of those who did not know the procedures for paying taxes increased, not decreased, throughout the late 1990s:

Q: Do you know in what way citizens of Russia ought to pay taxes on their income?[154]

	September 1997	April 1998	March 1999	March 2000
I know (as a percentage)	55	65	43	42
I don't know (as a percentage)	36	33	48	52

A lack of basic procedural knowledge on taxes also is evident from the fact that the vast majority do not even realize that they are entitled to tax deductions. While 41 per cent of Russians surveyed in February 2002 had expenses the previous year for medical treatment or education, only 15 per cent knew that they had a right to receive a tax refund for such expenses and only 4 per cent had applied for such a refund.[155] (By comparison, the numbers of Poles who utilized a tax exemption or tax allowance on their tax return grew from 10 per cent in 1993 to 65 per cent in 1997 – a relatively short time after the introduction of taxes there.[156]) Hence, even though the tax authorities have been engaging in active propaganda on the importance of paying taxes, sufficient education of the population on the mechanisms for doing so appeared to be lacking.

Proposed reforms during 2005–2006 further illustrate ambiguity within the government as to how coercive and client-oriented the tax collection system should be. In 2005, Finance Minister Alexei Kudrin, whose ministry took control of the STA in the previous year, proposed that each tax inspectorate should have a separate complaints department, an internal review for tax claims above a certain amount and further restrictions on the types of tax investigations and methods used.[157] An additional measure suggested later was the imposition of a limit on the number of tax audits performed on a taxpayer within a year.[158] Businesses were able to agree with the tax administration that there should be no more than two tax inspections per year, but the business community in mid-2005 was said to be unable 'to identify which official body will sanction additional inspections of large companies.'[159]

[154] Yadova.
[155] All-Russian Centre for the Study of Social Opinion (VTsIOM), February 2002.
[156] CBOS, May 2002.   [157] Faulconbridge.
[158] Grigorieva and Frumkin.   [159] Yurova.

Building Trust, Instilling Fear: Tax Administration Reform   169

Other proposals, however, would not restrict the 'power' of the tax bureaucrats or require them to be particularly 'consumer-oriented'. In 2005, the government suggested giving the tax agencies the power to fine companies without a court decision, and in January 2006 such a law went into force, allowing fines to be levied, provided that the penalty for each tax was no more than 5,000 rubles for entrepreneurs and 50,000 rubles for firms.[160] Furthermore, the tax authorities were said in 2005 to be turning to individual taxpayers and to be intentionally failing to inform citizens regarding property and car taxes so that fines for unpaid taxes were 'accumulating like an avalanche'.[161] Back in 1995, tax collectors' salaries also were said to be tied to the amount of fines they brought in.[162]

In 2005, there was some ambiguity with respect to whether the tax administration would still use tax collection 'targets' as a way of managing the activities of its tax inspectors rather than requiring tax inspectors to focus on seeking to ensure citizen compliance with the tax laws. Following President Putin's annual address to the nation on 25 April 2005, in which he renounced the use of such 'targets' in favour of broad 'budget directives', the Federal State Tax Service stated four months later that it was now giving its inspectorates 'indicative indices'.[163] 'The change did not immediately benefit the tax agency', Mikhail Pryadilnikov and Elena Danilova found, 'as a number of inspectors complained that their bonuses were still tied to the plan fulfilment (renamed general budget directives).'[164] To muddle the issue of targets further, the finance ministry's draft budget for 2006 was said in August 2005 to assume that an extra U.S.$1 billion would be collected through additional inspections of businesses by the end of 2005, and that more than double that amount would be collected through additional corporate audits in 2006.[165] Meanwhile, a former tax inspector confirmed that targets were still in place after 2005 and that they still existed in 2016.[166] Today, a collection 'target' is presented by the analytical department within a tax inspection that is the result of preliminary tax analysis of a firm to be audited, which is given to tax inspectors prior to making a field tax audit at the site of the firm. Meanwhile, the notion of a 'target' (or 'plan') refers to the general target plans for the entire tax inspection office and is based on the average sums of taxes levied from an average inspection.[167] Hence, it appears that targets never really went away.

---

[160] RosBusinessConsulting; Dranitsyna.   [161] Yurova.   [162] Kaminski.
[163] Vedomosti.   [164] Pryadilnikov and Danilova, p. 35.
[165] *Moscow Times*, 24 August 2005.
[166] E-mail correspondence with Moscow-based lawyer, 26 January 2016.
[167] Ibid.

170   Taxes and Trust

In any case, the frequency of audits has become a real issue for businesses in Russia in recent years. In 2010, Ernst & Young found that 6 per cent of firms were audited more than once a year, 23 per cent were audited once a year and 37 per cent were audited once every two years.[168] In other words, two-thirds of all firms were audited at least once every two years. Further, nearly two-thirds (63 per cent) of firms surveyed in 2010 stated that they were charged with additional tax liabilities as a result of tax audits performed in 2009.[169] Of these, 97 per cent were charged with additional profit tax (CIT) liabilities and 77 per cent were charged with additional VAT liabilities.[170] Only 29 per cent agreed with the additional tax liabilities charged by the tax authorities as a result of on-site tax audits performed in 2009.[171] Such is Russia's approach to collecting revenue through labour-intensive audits.

And what the tax service has been unable to uncover during audits, it has tried to obtain through tax amnesties. One such amnesty, which took place in 2007 as a result of tax collections having decreased since the 2001 introduction of the PIT flat tax reform, left many taxpayers confused as to what safeguards or protections would be provided if they decided to participate.[172]

Thus, it perhaps should not be surprising that when asked which issues should be considered for reform by the Russian state, 76 per cent of firms in 2010 declared improving tax administration, which also was the second most cited issue three years in a row after requests to simplify tax legislation, and 44 per cent also cited the need to enhance control over the tax authorities.[173]

Political Use of Tax Collection in Russia In 2003, the Kremlin began its assault on Yukos and Khodorkovsky by charging both with fraud and tax evasion. Khodorkovsky was immediately jailed and later given an eight-year sentence in a Siberian labour camp. It has been assumed that he became a target once Putin saw him as a political obstacle.

In recent years, although perhaps not due to politics in every case, other large firms and oligarchs have been sent hefty tax bills, including oil giant Sibneft, which was owned by Roman Abramovich, was planning to merge with Yukos in 2003 and was taken over by the state-controlled gas monopoly Gazprom in 2005; the Tyumen Oil Company (TNK-BP), a Russian–British concern formed in 2003 with British Petroleum; the head of Hermitage Capital Management, Bill Browder, who had had a

---

[168] Ernst & Young, p. 5.   [169] Ibid.   [170] Ibid.
[171] Ibid., p. 7.   [172] Stickgold.   [173] Ernst & Young, pp. 24–25.

Building Trust, Instilling Fear: Tax Administration Reform   171

multi-billion US dollar investment fund in Russia since the 1990s; and the mobile phone operator VimpelCom. In September 2007, the Federal Tax Service announced plans to create a special inspections unit to carry out audits of 'major taxpayers', a move that was considered to be aimed at ensuring that the oligarchs kept in line during the upcoming election cycle.[174]

Other cases, however, appear to be linked to the preservation of the current authoritarian regime in Russia. In many ways, though, the tax systems in Russia and Ukraine were probably not designed chiefly just for extracting revenue from society. They are also about control, in the way an internal affairs organization such as the KGB was in different era. In September 2005, the United States-funded Russian–Chechen Friendship Society – a small, non-profit human-rights organization that was one of the few entities to provide independent information about the war in Chechnya – was accused by the Federal Tax Service of evading taxes.[175] In 2006, tax authorities demanded 5 million rubles from the Centre for the Promotion of International Defence, which had helped Russian citizens prepare appeals to the European Court of Human Rights in Strasbourg.[176] Tax authorities also conducted raids against Hermitage Capital (which led to the ouster of Bill Browder from Russia, led to the death in Butryka prison of Sergei Magnitsky and led the company to accuse Moscow tax bureaucrats of tax refund fraud) and Alexander Lebedev (the owner of the United Kingdom's *Independent* and *Evening Standard* newspapers).[177]

Moreover, since returning to the presidency in 2012, Putin has gone after Amnesty International, Transparency International and Human Rights Watch, and domestic human rights NGOs such as Memorial, Ksenia Sobchak (the daughter of the late former St. Petersburg Mayor Anatoly Sobchak under whom Putin once served), election watchdog group Golos, the Moscow offices of the German Friedrich Ebert Foundation and Konrad Adenauer Foundation and even a chocolate factory owned by Ukrainian President Petro Poroshenko, among others, with accusations of tax violations, and the tax system was the institutional mechanism of deliberate choice for this.[178] Clearly, opening tax investigations is the repressive mode of choice as a cover for silencing or jailing dissidents, as such cases cause less public outcry at home and abroad. Using the tax authorities as a method of curbing opposition both in

---

[174] RFE/RL Newsline, 26 September 2007.   [175] Myers.
[176] Interfax (Moscow); Tishinsky and Shmelev, 24 July 2006.   [177] Pan; Parfitt.
[178] Walker; Bierman; BBC News, 22 March 2013; BBC News, 27 March 2013; Tétrault-Farber; Associated Press, 25 March 2014; and Tass, 9 September 2014.

172   Taxes and Trust

politics and in civil society is viewed as effective by the Kremlin, at least in the short term.

With the uncertainty surrounding what the Kremlin's preoccupation with political control will lead to next, businesses in Russia have been given more reason to be wary in recent years, adding to an increased lack of trust in the state on the part of a vital sector of society. Coercive measures, therefore, are viewed at all levels of the tax system as being effective both financially and politically.

Collecting the New Taxes in Ukraine

Despite the fact that laws were being enacted in Ukraine in the first half of the 1990s, few tax inspectors actually were familiar with these laws, which enabled them to use 'bureaucratic discretion' in applying the rules to the process of tax collection.[179] Hence, the nation's bureaucrats could define the rules by which they played rather than have the rules defined for them, as is typical in a Weberian bureaucracy. The newly appointed bureaucrats found an opportunity to behave as they had formerly done by selectively applying the law, enabling the public not to perceive that there was a 'rule of law' but rather to experience the rule of the *nachal'nyk* (the government official who acts as a boss rather than as a *chynovnyk*, or bureaucrat).[180] Thus, this discretionary process focused less on ensuring actual compliance on the part of taxpayers and failed in the construction of healthier bureaucrat–citizen relations.

As STA head and creator of the existing tax administration, Azarov instituted a coercion-based approach to tax collection in Ukraine, which included setting tax collection targets by region and by tax type.[181] The number of fines and sanctions was even said to have targets.[182] Up until 1998, a provision was said to allocate 30 per cent of fines for STA development purposes, providing a further financial incentive to collect fines.[183] In 2016, inspectors were still said to receive bonuses based on the fines they collected.[184] Moreover, because a target-based approach to tax collection provides an incentive to return to those taxpayers who have paid their taxes, as they are known to have money, rather than to seek out those individuals and firms that have yet to pay their taxes

---

[179] Author's interview with Dubrovsky.   [180] Ibid.

[181] Author's interview with World Bank official, Kyiv, 21 October 2005.

[182] Author's interview with senior associate, Kyiv office of one of the Big Four international accounting firms, Kyiv, 26 October 2005.

[183] Author's interviews with senior associate, Kyiv office of one of the Big Four international accounting firms, Kyiv, 26 October 2005; and with former senior official, State Tax Administration, Kyiv, 29 July 2006.

[184] Kovensky.

Building Trust, Instilling Fear: Tax Administration Reform   173

altogether, Ukrainian firms have recognized that they can enter a Catch-22 of sorts because the more often one is audited, the more one needs to show a profit, and the more profit one has, the more one is audited so that the state can extract extra revenue.[185]

One common practice among Ukrainian tax inspectors as part of the 'tough fiscal measures' has been to request over-payment of income taxes (also known as 'payment in advance') to ensure that the state budget goals were achieved. Under the leadership of both Azarov and Kravchenko, tax inspectors collected taxes in advance from firms and individuals in order to fulfil targets (most likely based on plans for districts rather than for specific firms) – a practice that can place firms in the trap of being compelled to do so again and again after they once have paid ahead of schedule. So, in 2004, one finance ministry employee revealed that the implementation of the state budget was achieved through the overpayment of income tax, with tax overpayments amounting to 4.1 billion Ukrainian hryvnia in the first ten months of 2004 and to 7.2 billion for the first 11 months.[186]

Under the Yushchenko presidency, it is believed that collection of taxes in advance also occurred, but to a more limited extent from 2004 to 2006.[187] The aftermath of the 2004 presidential election brought forth a need for the state to focus first and foremost on raising revenue to cover its debts from the previous regime, which may have provided a reason for maintaining a target-based collection approach. Indeed, because the STA had a need to fulfil this plan, several companies paid their taxes early, in August 2005 rather than in September.[188] Some Ukrainian firms in 2006 maintained that such targets still existed, even though the STA had stated that they did not, suggesting perhaps that the targets might have been internal.[189]

Once the financial crisis hit in 2008–2009, similar practices continued, with the amount of overpayments of tax payments being 4.2 billion hryvnia in 2007, 8.6 billion hryvnia in 2008, 11.7 billion hryvnia in 2009 and 14.5 billion hryvnia for the first 9 months of 2010. Of course, making additional tax payments or payments deprives firms of their

---

[185] Author's interview with Yurij Kuz'myn, research analyst, International Finance Corporation (IFC), Kyiv, 20 October 2005.

[186] Ministry of Finance official, 14 November 2011.

[187] Author's interviews with tax manager, leading international auditing firm, Kyiv, 26 July 2006; with former senior official, State Tax Administration, Kyiv, 29 July 2006; and with partner, tax and legal services, leading international accounting firm, Kyiv, 1 August 2006.

[188] Author's interview with Senchuk.

[189] Author's interviews with Kuz'myn; and with senior associate, Kyiv office of one of the Big Four international accounting firms, Kyiv, 26 October 2005.

174   Taxes and Trust

working capital and can lead to depressed economic growth and wage arrears.[190]

Such practices also are said to have continued into the post-EuroMaidan era. Dubrovsky in 2015 remarked that 'Burdensome administration and other "implementation problems" hide the fact that the whole system is essentially grounded on blackmailing, which is the main tool for "mobilization of taxes" according to planned targets and to large extent regardless of the law. For example, Ukrainian firms were forced to pay "in advance" UAH 26 billion [Ukrainian hryvnia, or about USD $2 billion] by September 2014 allegedly as their CIT for some future times.'[191]

Because Azarov was primarily concerned with focusing on big firms for political and economic reasons, he largely gave local STA offices more autonomy in how to handle small and medium-sized businesses.[192] Furthermore, one tax lawyer has speculated that Azarov's desire to utilize the tax system as both a political weapon and a method of dispensing political favours for the Kuchma regime gave him an incentive not to build a truly modern, efficient and transparent system.[193] Hence, from its creation under Azarov in 1996, the system was not designed to create trust or focus on compliance on the part of the public; instead, it was constructed with both political and fiscal purposes in mind, leaving great discretion to local tax inspectors as they fulfilled their tasks. Moreover, because family prosperity is seen as a more important goal by Ukrainians than being caught evading taxes, given that the chances of being caught are deemed to be low, Ukrainians believe that even if one is caught, the practice of 'bureaucratic discretion' will enable them to negotiate (or bribe) local tax officials to escape full punishment.[194]

Some of this discretionary practice was said not to have changed after the Orange Revolution.[195] In 2005, there was still a lack of proper monitoring, systems control, ability to audit electronically and general oversight.[196] However, a new modernization project was aimed at reducing direct contact between tax bureaucrats and taxpayers by enabling

---

[190] Ministry of Finance official, 14 November 2011.   [191] Dubrovsky.
[192] Author's interview with senior partner, leading local tax and legal firm, Kyiv, 3 August 2006.
[193] Author's interview with partner, tax and legal services, leading international accounting firm, Kyiv, 1 August 2006.
[194] Author's interview with senior associate, Kyiv office of one of the Big Four international accounting firms, Kyiv, 26 October 2005.
[195] Author's interview with Dubrovsky.
[196] Author's interview with World Bank official.

Building Trust, Instilling Fear: Tax Administration Reform 175

more taxpayers to file their taxes electronically.[197] And part of the reforms introduced in early 2015 was to make the VAT process electronic. This should have decreased the ability of tax bureaucrats to practice personal 'discretion' as to which firms were able to receive a VAT refund, reduced corruption and led to an end for the haphazard administration of VAT refunds that had plagued Ukrainian businesses for years.

As in Russia, full inspection audits of taxpayers were done much more frequently than in Western countries. Back in the mid-1990s, large firms were to be inspected once every six months, if there were enough tax personnel.[198] Since then, the frequency of scheduled audits of taxpayers has been determined by the degree of risk associated with taxpayers' activities. Taxpayers with low risk are included in the audit schedule, which is formed and approved by the STA in Kyiv, no more frequently than once every three years; with average risk, not more often than once every two years; and with high risk, no more than once per year.[199] In 2008, research prepared by the GfK market research group illustrates the high frequency of audits, as their survey found that 81.9 per cent of some large firms, 68.2 per cent of medium-sized firms and 51.1 per cent of small firms stated that they had been audited by the STA within the previous year.[200] Meanwhile, during the financial crisis of 2008–2009, some taxpayers were given the option of paying their dues to the state in instalments.[201]

Even with all the political changes in recent years, there is still some question as to whether patterns of corruption have been altered significantly in the collecting of taxes. Corruption in Ukraine in general was said to have decreased in the first nine months of 2005, perhaps due to a psychological holdover from the Orange Revolution, but it began to increase in the fall of that year, after Yulia Tymoshenko was fired from the post of prime minister, and was said to have continued through the summer of 2006, when there was great uncertainty as to whether there would be a new government and what form it would take.[202] While Tymoshenko was prime minister in the first half of 2005, she tried to

---

[197] Author's interview with head of State Tax Administration of Chernihivskiy Oblast, Chernihiv, 11 August 2006.
[198] Sluchinsky.
[199] Author's interview with State Tax Inspector, in a Ukrainian Oblast, Ukraine, 20 May 2011.
[200] GfK Ukraine, 25 May 2009. The N for the study was roughly 500 large firms, 500 medium-sized firms, and 500 small firms.
[201] Author's interview with State Tax Inspector in a Ukrainian oblast, Ukraine, 20 May 2011.
[202] Author's interview with Lavrinenko; and interview with executive director, leading foreign business association, Kyiv, 8 August 2006.

176   Taxes and Trust

fight corruption by increasing salaries, especially of those who headed tax offices and were responsible for making decisions.[203] Even so, in the opinion of one tax inspector, when internal anti-corruption campaigns seeking to 'uncover' bad inspectors do occur, with a 'plan' with respect to how many, there is a risk that attempts by the tax authorities to catch corrupt tax officials can sweep up good inspectors as well.[204]

In any case, the level of tax collection was deemed in 2010 to have 'low profitability'. That is, the costs of collecting 100 units in the domestic currency were judged to be higher in Ukraine by 3 to 4 times than in other EU member states, indicating that the tax service collects at a poor rate of efficiency.[205]

Political Use of Tax Collection in Ukraine In contrast to Russia, political attempts in Ukraine to use the tax system to overtake or repriva- tize firms are seen as requiring tremendous effort and as capable of fail- ing, leading to a further comparative lack of fear of the state.[206] Azarov was well known for using the Kuchma-era tax administration to attack opponents – a skill that no doubt was deemed useful for Yanukovych, who appointed him prime minister in 2010.[207] Yet even attempts made before the 2004 presidential elections by the outgoing Kuchma regime to use the STA as a political weapon against local firms were not coordi- nated and met strong resistance by firms, which were able to go to law enforcement agencies and to the courts, so that the threats largely were not fulfilled at the stage of implementation.[208]

In the 1990s, as the Ukrainian tax administration developed, it became, in the words of Verena Fritz, a true 'state within the state', which was used to oppress political opponents and media organizations as securing and consolidating power became the focus for the Kuchma regime.[209] At the same time, fictitious export VAT refund schemes were used as the vehicle for rewarding pro-government businesses.[210] In this time period, this author's former office, Freedom House, in Kyiv itself

---

[203] Author's interview with Lavrinenko.
[204] Author's interview with State Tax Inspector, in a Ukrainian oblast, Ukraine, 20 May 2011.
[205] Mollovan, Shevchenko, and Egorova, p. 8.
[206] Author's interview with senior partner, leading local tax and legal firm, Kyiv, 3 August 2006.
[207] D'Anieri, 2011, p. 39.
[208] Author's interview with senior partner, leading local tax and legal firm, Kyiv, August 3, 2006.
[209] Fritz, p. 138.
[210] Author's email correspondence with an anonymous expert who is a tax consultant and professor at the Ukrainian State Trade and Economic University, 1 June 2016.

Building Trust, Instilling Fear: Tax Administration Reform   177

became the focus of the tax authorities with extra inquiries, but ultimately no wrongdoing materialized. The so-called Kuchma tapes, in which a security guard had made secret electronic recordings of Kuchma that were alleged to implicate the Ukrainian president in the disappearance of Internet journalist Georgi Gongadze and which were later sent to Central Europe for authentication by Freedom House, also confirmed that Kuchma had called upon the tax administration to pressure businesses and other groups during the 1999 presidential campaign.[211]

The Media and Public Outreach in Ukraine In Ukraine, the tradition of not communicating with the public did not change after the Orange Revolution.[212] A wide-scale outreach campaign educating the public on how to comply with the tax laws has never really taken place in Ukraine.[213] The introduction of new taxes in the 1990s was quite unlike the rollout in Poland. In Ukraine, there was a lack of such efforts to educate the country on the new taxes.[214] Some seminars on how to pay the new taxes, however, were conducted by firms connected to the STA, which then monopolized the information they gave out.[215] Meanwhile, explanatory letters from the STA were regarded by accountants to be as significant as court decisions.[216] In many ways, as one Ukrainian lawyer put it, the state did not care to explain to citizens how the state and its laws work, indicating an utter lack of concern for citizens.[217]

However, what has changed since the Orange Revolution is that STA officials have been more responsive than in the past in issuing letters explaining their reasoning, which are more useful to taxpayers.[218] In addition, among the aforementioned Ukraine tax administration modernization project programs was included the construction of an information centre, initially in Kyiv and Kyiv oblast, so that taxpayers could call, e-mail, send a facsimile, or directly post questions on the Web regarding the STA's approximately 2,000 tax laws and decrees.[219] A

---

[211] Fritz, p. 164, 176, and 193.

[212] Author's interview with Inna Golodniuk, executive director, Centre for Social and Economic Research, Kyiv, 14 October 2005.

[213] Author's interview with partner, tax and legal services, leading international accounting firm, Kyiv, 1 August 2006.

[214] Author's interview with senior associate, Kyiv office of one of the Big Four international accounting firms, Kyiv, 26 October 2005.

[215] Author's interview with Dubrovsky.   [216] Ibid.

[217] Author's interview with partner, tax and legal services, leading international accounting firm, Kyiv, 2 August 2006.

[218] Author's interview with senior associate, Kyiv office of one of the Big Four international accounting firms, Kyiv, 26 October 2005.

[219] Author's interview with senior tax official, Modernization Department, State Tax Administration of Ukraine, Kyiv, 10 August 2005.

178   Taxes and Trust

series of group seminars to which taxpayers are invited, public speeches by tax officials, and the distribution of brochures and other materials also were seen by the STA as steps forward.[220]

The STA in the mid-2000s also took a keen interest in surveying its employees across the country to discern how workers generally related to their bosses, and it commissioned public opinion surveys to gauge Ukrainians' reactions to its improvements. In particular, the STA points to a survey it commissioned from an independent firm in December 2005 as indicating that it is perceived as doing a better job vis-à-vis taxpayers. Although the survey's exact results, including the starting points of trends, were not released to the public (or to independent researchers!), the STA states that the results show a better relationship between taxpayers and tax workers, an increase in the willingness of taxpayers to make payments, and a slight worsening in the public's perceptions of the STA's fulfilment of laws.[221] The STA also states that payments to the budget increased two and one-half times in 2005, indicating greater trust in the service.[222] Hence, the STA's modernization efforts during the Yushchenko years could have led to a greater increase in trust on the part of ordinary Ukrainian taxpayers that they would be treated fairly by their state.

Nevertheless, in the more recent Yanukovych era, there was some recognition, according to the director of the Department of Interaction with the Media and the Public of the State Tax Service of Ukraine, Olga Semchenko, that it had become 'fashionable for entrepreneurs to brag about who and how cheated the state' and that measures needed to be undertaken through the media to combat such a culture. Such a media outreach program included the printing of materials in the Transcarpathian oblast, the use of billboards and a local public television program in Kharkiv oblast, as well as billboards displaying public service advertisements regarding employment laws in Donetsk oblast.[223] Also, the STA developed a popular tax education program for schoolchildren, complete with colour drawing competitions.

Table 5.2 summarizes the differences in the work philosophies of the three states' tax administrations.

Additional Structural Constraints to Prevent Polish, Russian and Ukrainian Tax Official Corruption

Poland's tax system also appears at first glance to be designed in such a manner as to provide barriers to corruption better than those of

---

[220] Ibid.   [221] Ibid.   [222] Ibid.   [223] Germanova.

Building Trust, Instilling Fear: Tax Administration Reform   179

Table 5.2 *Tax administration work philosophy*

	Poland	Russia	Ukraine
Findings	Compliance-driven: • Treat taxpayers more like clients	Target-driven: • Go after those who have already paid to collect more • 2011 survey: Nearly ½ of tax officials said their job was 'to replenish budget at any cost' and that they were judged by amount collected. Use of tax administration as a strong political weapon	Target-driven: • Go after those who have already paid to collect more even after the Orange Revolution Bureaucratic discretion: • Focus less on compliance Tax police less coercive than in Russia Under Kuchma, VAT schemes to fund campaigns Weak use of tax administration as political weapon in 2004 election
Societal Approach	More citizen-based	More coercive	Weakly coercive

Russia and Ukraine. For example, within the tax chambers and tax offices, many people oversee particular cases. One team working on a case must transfer the paperwork to another unit; cases considered by employees require the director's signature; and taxpayers do not have direct access to the audit organs. In general, the system is designed in a manner that sacrifices some Weberian *autonomy* for the greater cause of uniformity and security. As one tax chamber department head put it, 'Corruption appears where the bureaucrat has discretion in making a decision'.[224] Moreover, the tax chambers conduct their own audits – complex or thematic – of the tax offices that they oversee, and undertake the complex audits every other year.

Another such barrier is the fact that tax allowances (exemptions) are no longer given out at the discretion of the tax offices in Poland. Back in 1995, NIK asserted that the decision-making process in the awarding of tax allowances was conducted in many cases incorrectly, with decisions made without an audit of the taxpayer who was receiving the exemption.

Moreover, a significant number of tax allowances, granted under the influence of recommendations from the Ministry of Finance, were not issued after careful research was conducted to justify such a decision.[225]

---

[224] Author's interview with tax chamber department head, Gdańsk, 26 November 2001.
[225] NIK, May 1995, p. 57.

180   Taxes and Trust

NIK also found it problematic to conduct a review of the size and effect of such allowances owing to the lack of a register of such tax relief decisions, which NIK had earlier proposed that the Ministry of Finance should create.[226] Hence, a change in legislation on tax allowances prevents opportunities from arising whereby taxpayers try to influence tax administration employees to obtain such relief.

What was possible in 2001, however, was that tax office employees could have options for assisting those who incur tax arrears. On an individual basis, the tax office or the tax chamber (but not the tax control office) could change the terms of settlement periods so that the individual could pay in instalments, delay the date of payment or amortize the debt, although the latter was regarded as very rare.[227] Although such assistance was checked by supervisors, NIK found violations of this practice, suggesting that the structural constraints are not as strong as they should be.[228]

A final barrier for the tax bureaucrat with respect to his relation to taxpayers was that new legislation in 2001 stipulated that, unlike in Russia, a bureaucrat could no longer issue a fine or punishment to a taxpayer, but specified rather that only a court can do this.[229]

The controls seemed to have some resonance with taxpayers. A 2003 survey of small and medium-size businesses in three voivodeships found that 98 per cent of respondents stated that they did not have the impression that a tax office worker expected any benefits in exchange for a positive settlement of their case and that 70 per cent viewed officials auditing them as impartial when conducting audits.[230]

In contrast to all these controls placed on a tax bureaucrat's work in Poland, Russia's and Ukraine's tax systems relied heavily throughout the 1990s on individual relations between tax inspectors and taxpayers. This practice, though, has been diminishing. In Russia, in the 1990s, a taxpayer would turn in his or her tax return to a single tax inspector, who would review the accuracy of the documents – a situation that would provide an opportunity for collusion between the two parties.[231] Moreover, according to some, as mentioned above, when a taxpayer would pay his or her tax arrears, the tax inspector would receive a portion of the extra

[226] Ibid.
[227] Author's interviews with vice-director, department of the state budget, NIK, 8 November 2001; manager of a department, tax chamber, Warsaw, 15 November 2001; tax office head, Warsaw, 20 November 2001; and tax control office director, Bialystok, 4 December 2001.
[228] NIK, April 1993, p. 6; and NIK, April 2001, pp. 9–10.
[229] Author's interview with tax office head, Bialystok, 4 December 2001.
[230] Ministry of Finance, 2004b, p. 42.   [231] Ebrill and Havrylyshyn, p. 13.

Building Trust, Instilling Fear: Tax Administration Reform   181

revenue received.[232] However, thanks to the 1999 tax code, a more formal relationship began to develop in some parts of the country.[233] Departments inside the tax administration and tax police departments in all countries do conduct internal audits and checks designed to examine corruption issues.[234] In Poland, an external organization that audits the tax collection process is the NIK, mentioned above as having a historical legacy dating back to the pre-war period. As for analyzing the different organs of the tax administration, NIK conducts thematic audits (analyzing activities of the different tax bodies) and problematic audits (analyzing the computerization of the tax organs, the collection of tax arrears, the installation of the information system POLTAX, the collection of the PIT, etc.) Generally, these reports do not take a broader view and do not suggest alternative structures or practices; they merely judge whether rules or regulations were followed with respect to paperwork filed and decisions made. Indeed, for example, they have found at one time the tax chambers to be too slow and bureaucratic in processing complaints, and at another time that the tax audit offices increased the number of inspectors only to see a reduction in the number of audits.[235] On another occasion, NIK surveyed 38 tax offices from July 1993 to December 1996 with respect to giving VAT refunds back to firms and found that '[i]n three-quarters of tax offices audited tax refunds were completed without being preceded by an audit of the taxpayer in spite of such a responsibility appearing in the guidelines of the Ministry of Finance to the organization of work in tax offices in the framework of the tax on goods and services'.[236] The rise of arrears in the late 1990s led NIK, in another report, to conduct a special audit into whether the tax offices have been using all legal means to obtain tax debts and to prevent them in the first place.[237] Separately, NIK also has found that there appears to be significant variance among the tax offices that collect arrears due to some inappropriate behaviour and ineffective supervision by the tax chambers.[238]

Moreover, despite the fact that NIK is generally respected in the society at large (receiving favourability ratings of 49 to 61 per cent from

---

[232] Interview with Mukhin; and Valencia.

[233] Author's interview with lawyer at Moscow office of international legal firm, Moscow, 7 August 2003.

[234] Author's interview with former assistant to deputy head of Moscow City Tax Police, Moscow, 28 July 2003; interview with former head of a Moscow tax inspectorate, 5 August 2003; and interview with former head of the department of civil service and personnel, Ministry of Taxes and Dues, Moscow, 8 August 2003.

[235] NIK, June 1993, p. 32; and NIK, December 1994, p. 4. Translation from the Polish by the author.

[236] NIK, October 1997, p. 7.   [237] NIK, April 2001.   [238] NIK, May 1997, p. 3.

182   Taxes and Trust

1997 to 2001 in one set of opinion polls[239]), several employees within the tax system find that the work of NIK has no bearing upon their day-to-day work. (Commenting on the relevance of NIK, one manager at a tax chamber even went so far as to joke that 'NIK checks how many published brochures were printed more than needed; they provide a generalized accusation [as to it being so]; and then it is confirmed that too many brochures were printed.'[240]) At times, though, there have been real conflicts between the Ministry of Finance and NIK over a report's results. In May 2001, then Minister of Finance Jarosław Bauc criticized NIK for its report on the collection of tax arrears. According to the report, the tax offices only collected 23 groszy for every złoty of tax arrears in 1999, whereas the Ministry of Finance placed the number at 44 groszy.[241]

Hence, the value of NIK's involvement in the process of tax collection in Poland is mixed. On one hand, NIK does provide for a comprehensive accounting as to whether certain procedures are implemented and how government money was spent by various administrative structures. Occasionally, it will even uncover incidents of malfeasance or corruption. This information, no doubt, is useful for the parliament and for the Ministry of Finance, even if the latter does not always agree with the final assessment. On the other hand, for reasons perhaps due to the methodology of its reports, its mission, and how it is perceived in the bureaucracy, NIK does not appear to be utilized by the tax administrative structures as an aid in evaluating what constructive changes could be made in the system. The extent to which the tax structures actually make use of NIK's reports can be called into question. Because there is room for the maximization of its role as an oversight body, NIK can be deemed to make a positive, but limited contribution to tax administration in Poland, helping to qualify the entire tax collection process in Poland as an example of partial bureaucratic rationalism.

Meanwhile, in Russia, the Accounts Chamber, accountable to the Federal Assembly, conducts mostly financial audits, but not performance audits. (On the basis of personal experience, NIK is a far more transparent organization, accessible to outside researchers, than Russia's Account Chamber.) The regional *upravlenie* (administration) was said to check the tax inspection offices about once every three years, while thematic checks could be ordered by the Ministry of Taxes and Dues at the regional level.[242] The Accounts Chamber appears to be underutilized as

---

[239] CBOS, January 2002.

[240] Author's interview with a Tax Chamber Manager, Gdańsk, 26 November 2001.

[241] K., L., 16 May 2001. One hundred groszy equal one złoty.

[242] Interview with former head of a Moscow tax inspectorate, 5 August 2003.

Building Trust, Instilling Fear: Tax Administration Reform   183

an external inspection agency, as only 12 per cent of tax officials in the 2011 Russian Public Officials Survey stated that their organization had been inspected in the last two years by an Accounts Chamber representative; Russia's tax organs, it seems, appear to be much more likely to be inspected by internal supervisory bodies (see Question #12 in Appendix II). At the same time, Russian tax bureaucrats have been accused in the media of massive corruption through VAT refund claims.[243]

Similarly, in Ukraine, the Accounting Chamber was said in 2006 to have provided little oversight of the STA, because its reports are often only read when members of Parliament can use them to support their points of view.[244] Ukraine's Procuracy and the Accounting Chamber also were said not to have good contact with one another, because the former was not reading the latter's reports. The Accounting Chamber also had been struggling for seven years to gain the right to check income to the state, including, especially, the revenue collected by the STA, but it has only been able to review expenditures made by the state.[245] Meanwhile, the tax administration's oblast-level offices undergo a complex internal audit by the STA once every three years.

Despite some of these administrative controls, over the last decade, society has viewed corruption as a greater problem in all three countries, as detailed in Chapter 3. In spite of the occasional violation at the bottom of the system, there is a greater perception both from within and from outside the tax system that corruption tends to occur to a greater extent at the top of the political system, with laws and tax allowances or exemptions written with special interest groups in mind. As one Polish tax chamber office division manager stated, 'In small offices, small cases of corruption occur; if someone wants to commit a large crime, he begins at the top level.'[246]

Writing generally about the Polish bureaucracy, Antoni Kamiński has stated that 'it appears that many loopholes in Polish law, above all economic, are not found there for no reason, [and] that the only rationale for certain laws are the narrow particular interests promoting them. This results in the covering up of the differences between the public and private spheres.'[247] The public at large also has had the perception that the top of the political system – rather than the middle or bottom – is where selected interest groups receive the most attention. This belief coincides

[243] BBC Monitoring, 4 April 2012.
[244] Author's interview with Lavrinenko.   [245] Ibid.
[246] Author's interview with Tax Chamber Department Manager, Gdańsk, 26 November 2001. Translation from the Polish by the author.
[247] Kamiński, 22 March 1999. Translation from the Polish by the author.

184   Taxes and Trust

Table 5.3 *Structural design and oversight of tax administrations*

	Poland	Russia	Ukraine
Findings	Design aspects: • Rational division and subordination • Constraints against corruption improve	Design aspects: • Poor design and lack of barriers to corruption in '90s • Improving somewhat	STA chief's *zhorstkoyu kontrol'* contributed to less fear of state Local tax offices given more autonomy than in Russia
	Supreme Audit Chamber = watchdog	Accounts Chamber = less transparent; 2011 survey: only 12% tax officials said they were inspected by Accounts Chamber	Little oversight by government, parliament and Accounting Chamber
Societal Approach	More citizen-based	More coercive	Weakly coercive

with a 1999 survey in which 75 per cent of Poles deemed that recent proposed tax law changes were written above all for wealthy taxpayers.[248]

Table 5.3 summarizes the differences in the structural designs and oversight processes with respect to the three states' tax administrations.

Computers as Resource Tools

The computerization of the Polish tax administration in the early days is a perfect example of why the Polish tax system has been an example of mixed bureaucratic rationalism. On one hand, computers and databases have been recognized by the tax system as being necessary to catalogue cases and to speed up coordination between offices regarding audits of taxpayers. Poland successfully developed and implemented in 1996 a taxpayer identification number (NIP) system, by which all entities that possess the status of a taxpayer were assigned numbers. On the other hand, computerization was implemented slowly in the early 1990s. While work on an information system began in 1989,[249] the system was not complete in the early 1990s, necessitating work being done by hand.[250] The tax offices lacked computer programs to handle the data accompanying the introduction of the PIT in 1992.[251] In the

[248] CBOS, 1999.   [249] NIK, October 1994, pp. 14 and 38.
[250] NIK, April 1993, pp. 35–36; and NIK, June 1993, pp. 7 and 43.
[251] NIK, June 1993, p. 8.

Building Trust, Instilling Fear: Tax Administration Reform   185

mid-1990s, tax offices lacked a unified information system, which would provide easier disclosure of tax debtors and a more expedient issue of titles of seizure.[252] A 1997 NIK report on the tax on goods and services attributed the delays in accounting most significantly to the lack of proper preparation of information, with some offices doing bookkeeping by hand and others using different local accounting computer application programs.[253] One tax office department manager remarked in 2001 that full computerization had existed for only two years while, since 1994, only records for a few types of taxes were available on a computer system.[254]

More problematic in 2001 was that the Polish tax audit offices did not have constant electronic access to the significantly larger databases of the tax chambers or even to the Ministry of Finance, despite the fact that the effort to provide access to such data was begun when the tax audit offices were created in 1992.[255] A director of planning, analysis and information at one tax audit office stated that he would go to the tax chamber once a year to obtain data on certain taxpayers, writing down some of the data by hand.[256] (Indeed, the problem concerning the lack of database information was noted in NIK's first evaluation of the then-new tax audit offices in 1992 and 1993.[257]) In addition, nearly three years after the administrative reform combined territorial provinces to lower their overall number, one province's main tax audit office was found in late 2001 still to have problems linking with its branch office, which covers the territory of an entire former province, despite the fact that both offices share the same computer system.[258] Moreover, the tax audit offices also find that they lack funds to buy up-to-date computer programs such as the LEX legal program, used by revenue inspectors of criminal investigations.[259]

Finally, the POLTAX information system still was not completely implemented in 2001, which one expert at NIK pointed to as a reason arrears are not always collected.[260] The delay in the implementation

[252] NIK, May 1997, p. 4.   [253] NIK, October 1997, p. 54.
[254] Author's interview with a Tax Office Division Leader, Warsaw, 21 November 2001.
[255] Author's interview with Tax Audit Office Director, Bialystok, 4 December 2001; and NIK, May 2000, p. 3.
[256] Author's interview with Tax Audit Office Department Leader, Gdańsk, 27 November 2001.
[257] NIK, December 1994, p. 4.
[258] Author's interview with Tax Audit Office Department Leader, Gdańsk, 27 November 2001.
[259] Author's interview with Manager, Department of Criminal Investigations of Tax Revenue, Tax Audit Office, Gdańsk, 27 November 2001.
[260] Author's interview with Marek Trosiński, Vice Director, Department of the Budget, NIK, 8 November 2001. Two other reasons given for arrears not being collected were

186   Taxes and Trust

of the POLTAX system by a French company in the early 1990s was explained in part by NIK as being due to the lack of a leader of the project from the Polish side, the liquidation of a quality control department and the refusal of free assistance from the US and Swedish governments to assess the quality control.[261] NIK viewed the process as being bungled:

> The experience connected with the work of preparing and implementing the complex information system for the service of taxes – within the framework of the contract with the [French] firm BULL S.A. – shows exactly the lack of effectiveness and efficacy of the actions taken in the Ministry of Finance by a series of under-secretaries who coordinated the work of organization of the information system in the department of finances as well as directors of the organizational entities that created the Council of the Program System POLTAX.[262]

In short, there was a lack of a unified conception of the goals of the functioning of the system.[263] Nine years after the process of a creating a unified computerization system for the tax organs, the goals of the project were found not to be fully realized, the system was found not to serve all of the tasks of the tax organs, and individual tax offices were forced to utilize local applications or even to keep records in handwritten ledgers.[264] Hence, for years, full computerization was still a goal to be realized. (And yet, in Poland, a body external to the Ministry of Finance and the tax system investigated the issue and published a report freely available to the public.)

Given the lack of accessible, independent and substantive audits of Russia's tax administration, it is difficult to judge how quickly Russia has computerized its tax administration. While Poland introduced a taxpayer identification number (TIN) system in 1996, Russia had such a system in place from the beginning of the transition period for legal entities, while in 1996–1997, such TIN numbers were distributed for individual persons.[265] However, a single state register of all commercial legal entities, numbering 3.2 million enterprises on 1 July 2002, was not completed until the end of 2002, after some 1.5 million firms had been re-registered.[266] Computerization varied across the country at the beginning of the Putin era, with project regions having more

---

the facts that the tax offices have a lot of work and that many tax cheats work too quickly for the system.

[261] NIK, January 1996, p. 19.

[262] Ibid., p. 20. Translation from the Polish by the author.

[263] NIK, May 2001, p. 10.   [264] Ibid., p. 10.

[265] Interview with acting head of the division of methodology, Department of Modernization of the Tax Organs, Ministry of Taxes and Dues, Moscow, 22 July 2003.

[266] Bureau of Economic Analysis, p. 5. Translation from the Russian by the author.

Building Trust, Instilling Fear: Tax Administration Reform   187

up-to-date equipment and more computers than the others. For Moscow, there was a computer network by the mid-2000s, but the tax administration was said to be still working on such a network across the country.[267] Despite the fact that all tax offices are part of the same federal organization, there have been different computer programs used across the country; at first, within Moscow, for example, different programs were tested at different inspectorates, but now all within the capital have the same program.[268] Another project, the 'System of Electronic Processing of Information of the [Inspection offices of the Ministry of Taxes and Dues] at the local level', had set as its impressive goal the presentation by 50 per cent of taxpayers of their accounts in electronic form by the end of 2003.[269] In 2011, a consultative call centre for Moscow taxpayers was said to have opened; in 2012, individual taxpayers were able to submit their tax documents electronically to the Unified Registration Centre; and in 2014, an electronic submission service was launched for corporate taxpayers.[270]

Former Minister of Taxes and Dues Bukayev also may have been especially interested in automating the tax system, as he introduced an automated system of recording taxpayers, their incomes, their real estate and their personal assets while previously serving as the head of Bashkortostan's Tax Inspectorate in the late 1990s. (Under his direction, the Bashkir tax officials began to complete the tax forms themselves and then send them to taxpayers – all in violation of federal law.[271]) Hence, what evidence does exist on Russia's computerization activities suggest that, as in Poland, the process has not been smooth, but unlike Poland, it is not uniform across the country. And, as success has been made in computerizing taxpayer data, new problems also have arisen for the tax administration. In November 2005, after a leak of some sort from the tax service, a database for 2004 incomes and other personal information of Moscow city and oblast taxpayers began to be sold around the capital for as little as U.S.$50 on a compact disc.[272]

In Ukraine, meanwhile, there is some similarity to the Polish situation with respect to the degree of access to taxpayer databases. The Tax Police have access to all databases, while the tax inspection offices have no access to the Tax Police databases.[273]

---

[267] Interview with former head of a Moscow tax inspectorate, 5 August 2003.
[268] Ibid.   [269] Bureau of Economic Analysis, p. 4.
[270] Prime-TASS News, 23 November 2010; Prime-TASS News, 14 March 2011; and Medetsky.
[271] Kochetov.
[272] RFE/RL Newsline, 15 November 2005; and *Moscow Times*, 17 November 2005.
[273] Author's interview with State Tax Inspector, in a Ukrainian oblast, Ukraine, 20 May 2011.

188   Taxes and Trust

Personnel Resources

The tax administrations in these three countries are large entities. As mentioned in Chapter 3, in Poland, tax administration employees composed 35.3 per cent of all civil servants in the country in 2013.[274] In Russia, the head of the Personnel Directorate of the Federal Tax Service stated in 2015 that the staff limit for the Russian Federal Tax Service was 154,000.[275] In Ukraine, by the end of 2000, the STA already had personnel of 56,500, making it the largest single administrative body in the country.[276] In many ways, to study the state, one has to study the tax administration.

'[R]evenue collection practices are nevertheless by comparison with more advanced countries considerably labour-intensive, which explains in part the very low salaries on offer to tax officials', Highfield and Baer wrote with respect to Russia in 2000. 'Not surprisingly, and in line with experience in other transition and developing economies, this has fuelled an environment for corrupt practices which have served to undermine respect for government and the institutions concerned.'[277]

Part of building an effective civil service within the tax bureaucracies is recruiting state officials in a competitive process to compose impartial personnel. As one Polish tax chamber head put it, 'The role of the bureaucrat in Poland is to be [part of] a cultured, white-collar, merit-based service.'[278] Such personnel are provided in a number of ways in Poland but appear to be lacking in Russia and Ukraine. By 2004, nearly half of the civil service corps in Poland comprises personnel from the fiscal administration.[279]

First, top positions within the Polish tax administration offices are filled by an open, competitive process.[280] (For example, two out of three heads of tax chambers interviewed in 2001 received their positions via such a process; the third had been in the position since a time that

---

[274] Ministry of Finance, 2014, p. 12.

[275] 'Interview with the head of the Personnel Directorate of the Federal Tax Service of Russia Igor Shevchenko', accessed 21 February 2016 at <http://www.fa.ru/faculty/nin/news/Pages/2015–04–02-intervyu-s-nachalnikom-upravleniya-kadrov-federalnoy-nalogovoy-sluzhby-rossii-shevchenko-igorem-viktorovichem.aspx>.

[276] Fritz, p. 163.   [277] Highfield and Baer, p. 10.

[278] Author's interview with a Tax Chamber Director, Warsaw, 15 November 2001.

[279] Ministry of Finance, 2004b, p. 48.

[280] Despite these advances, however, the European Union in its October 2002 report on the progress of EU candidates specifically criticized Poland for suspending a civil service law to permit the recruitment of high-level administrative staff without an open competitive process of selection, which was perceived by some as a direct reference to the ruling coalition's decision earlier in the year to pack the Agency for Restructuring and Modernization of Agriculture with 'political cronies.' (RFE/RL Poland, Belarus and Ukraine Report, 15 October 2002.)

Building Trust, Instilling Fear: Tax Administration Reform   189

pre-dated such competitions.) While required by law in Russia, the hiring of top officials in the tax administration by competition does not exist in practice, with personal connections viewed as the best way to get a job within the tax service.[281] Within one Ukraine oblast, competitions for positions requiring higher education degrees were said to exist in 2011, but all senior managers in the tax administration were said to be appointed solely by connections and in accord with the classical Ukrainian principle of '*kum, brat, svat*', or 'godfather, brother, friend', as one tax inspector relayed:

> For example, the previous chairman of our regional tax administration was a native of Donetsk (like our president [Yanukovych]). When he came to power, the heads of our most 'profitable' departments were dismissed, and were replaced by the relatives and friends of our chairman (for example, they took charge of audit management, legal, personnel, foreign economic activity and other departments.) Also, half of the heads of the regional (*raion*) tax inspection offices were replaced by Donetsk newcomers. In addition, the nephew and brother of the chairman were appointed department heads.[282]

Second, in Poland, in the tax audit offices, inspectors, who usually have a higher education degree, must endure three years of training plus passing an exam before starting work.[283] Moreover, to provide an incentive for the inspectors on the job, a ranking system within each province was established for the inspectors, who numbered 1,519 when the tax audit offices came into existence in 1992 and numbered around 2,500 in 2001.[284]

In Russia, tax administration employees usually come from the military and are used to working for the government, or they are young people who come only for two to three years of experience and then leave for the private sector.[285] Most of the workers in the Russian tax organs had middle (technical) educational backgrounds when the Law on State Service was introduced in 1995, which mandated higher education degrees for high-level positions. Therefore, since 1998, such workers have been

---

[281] Author's interview with former head of a Moscow tax inspectorate, August 5, 2003; Interview with former head of the Department of Civil Service and Personnel, Ministry of Taxes and Dues, Moscow, August 8, 2003; and e-mail correspondence with Moscow-based lawyer on 26 January 2016.

[282] Author's interview with State Tax Inspector, in a Ukrainian oblast, Ukraine, 20 May 2011.

[283] Author's interview with former head of a Moscow tax inspectorate, 5 August 2003; and Interview with former head of the Department of Civil Service and Personnel, Ministry of Taxes and Dues, Moscow, 8 August 2003.

[284] NIK, December 1994, p. 3; and Interview with Senior Specialist, Department of Analysis of Tax Control, Ministry of Finance, Warsaw, 1 October 2001.

[285] Author's interview with former head of the Department of Civil Service and Personnel, Ministry of Taxes and Dues, Moscow, 8 August 2003.

190   Taxes and Trust

given the opportunity to pursue higher education.[286] In the tax administration, employees receive additional training not less than once every five years.[287]

Despite this, the Main Audit Administration of the President evaluated the performance of the Russian tax organs and cited the low qualifications of tax administration employees as the main reason for the poor levels of tax collection in 2002. More than 30 per cent of tax workers in the regions were said to lack higher education.[288] Similarly, while up until 1995 the education level of tax police officers was very high, the quality of the tax police workers became worse and worse with respect to hiring those with higher education as the 1990s wore on.[289]

Tax morality among Russian officials may not be uniformly high across the tax administration. In the 2011 Russian Public Officials Survey, nearly one in four refused to state that they would follow the tax laws even if they did not consider them to be fair (Question #22 in Appendix I). This response from officials working in the tax administration to uphold Russian law and to ensure compliance with the tax laws is even slightly worse than the responses to similar questions asked of Polish taxpayers at large in 2004 and 2010 (also Question #22.) Further, roughly one in five Russian tax officials failed to state in the 2011 survey that they would not evade taxes if they were sure they could get away with it (Question #16 in Appendix I); nearly one in five did not disagree that they could avoid paying taxes if they knew for sure that they would not receive a serious punishment (Question #17); nearly one in five stated either that there were many dishonest tax co-workers or that it was too difficult to say (Question #3); and approximately one in four stated affirmatively that if the state does not fulfil its obligations to its citizens, then tax evasion is justified (Question #28.)

Further, while still significant in 2011, the number of tax officials who recognized a place for dishonesty in the workplace might have gone down over the decade before. In 2001, Pryadilnikov and Danilova found that 46 per cent of Moscow tax inspectors and 56 per cent of Nizhniy Novgorod tax inspectors agreed that it was impossible under current circumstances for tax officials to work honestly.[290]

Third, being impartial also means withstanding outside influence. Of the more than 45 bureaucrats in the Polish Ministry of Finance and tax–related offices interviewed in the fall of 2001, none mentioned any

---

[286] Author's interview with former head of the Department of Civil Service and Personnel, Ministry of Taxes and Dues, Moscow, 21 June 2003.
[287] Ibid.   [288] Lyashenko.
[289] Former assistant to deputy head of Moscow City Tax Police, Moscow, 28 July 2003.
[290] Pryadilnikov and Danilova, pp. 27–28.

Building Trust, Instilling Fear: Tax Administration Reform 191

party affiliation and several stated that as civil servants, their job was to be politically neutral. Neutrality also appeared to mean having no contact with outside groups. Outside of the tax system, tax office and tax chamber heads meet with the local and regional governments regarding economic growth and planning of budgetary income levels, but that appeared to be it. Meanwhile, in Russia, while the 1995 Law on State Service requires political neutrality on the part of officials, in reality, there is no mechanism to prevent political party affiliations.[291] Moreover, the influx of those with military backgrounds is thought to provide a branding of political allegiance of a common sort.

Fourth, a problem for the bureaucracy and for the tax administrative offices is that the level of pay is relatively low compared with job opportunities within the private sector. 'Bureaucrats, who have reached a relatively high position, do not compare their salary with the national average', writes Antoni Kamiński, 'but with the incomes of representatives of the private sector.'[292] Salaries in Poland tend to be similar between the state and the private sector for entry-level positions, but the higher up one goes in the tax bureaucracy, the larger the difference in pay with the private sector.[293] Indeed, accounting firms are able to hire the best people, depleting the tax system of its best and brightest.[294] Often those outside the system know the tax laws better than the bureaucrats, and those who have viewed the system from the outside criticize it for its paucity of good specialized experts on different aspects of tax and financial law.[295] The structure of the system should be altered to allow such specialists to exist.

A related problem, NIK found in the 1990s, at least with respect to those working on the indirect taxes, is that the number of personnel in the tax system is too small to handle the accounting and bookkeeping required to audit those taxpayers declaring a tax refund, especially for taxes such as the VAT.[296] This finding occurred despite the fact that, as mentioned earlier, the number of staff positions had been growing.

---

[291] Author's interview with former head of the Department of Civil Service and Personnel, Ministry of Taxes and Dues, Moscow, 8 August 2003.
[292] Kamiński, 22 March 1999. Translation from the Polish by the author.
[293] Author's interview with a Tax Chamber Department Manager, Warsaw, 15 November 2001.
[294] Author's interview with Robert Gwiadowski, Tax Lawyer, Expert for Adam Smith Centre, 21 September 2001.
[295] Author's interviews with Gwiadowski; and a tax lawyer, Andersen, Warsaw, 18 December 2001.
[296] NIK, October 1997, p. 61.

192   Taxes and Trust

Similarly, in Russia, young people come into the system, get education and then leave for the business world.[297] Turnover of cadre is high everywhere and at all levels of the system, due to the low salaries and the fact that it is hard to find replacements in the more rural areas.[298] As a former head of the Ministry's Department of Personnel put it, 'the salaries do not stimulate the process of preparing smart, driven people to work in the bureaucracy'.[299] Indeed, the 2011 Public Officials' Survey found that 53 per cent and 52 per cent of tax officials viewed insufficient staffing levels and low salaries, respectively, as restricting their organization from working effectively. Combined with insufficient quality of legislation, these were the most popular reasons offered for a less than effective tax administration (Question #11 in Appendix II).

Meanwhile, in Ukraine, despite the fact that Yushchenko was brought to power in large part by hundreds of thousands of protesters clamouring for a more accountable, competent state, the quality, skills, and education of the STA personnel were said in 2006 still to be poor, according to local tax lawyers who interact regularly with tax offices.[300] Few tax officials are regarded by these lawyers as having a good understanding of tax legislation. When invited by local, private accounting firms to seminars on tax legislation and international practices, STA bureaucrats initially say yes, recognizing the educational value of such meetings, but they eventually decline the offers, presumably after speaking with higher officials in their organization.[301] Further, there has been a lack of stable and experienced cadres because most bureaucrats work at the STA for only a year before heading off to higher-paying jobs in the private sector and because those who were present at the start of the transition are not still with the STA.[302] However, in the STA's view, there has been an increase in the quality of tax cadre workers, and there has been a concerted effort in recent years to implement competitions for senior positions within the STA in the provinces.[303]

---

[297] Author's interview with former head of a Moscow tax inspectorate, 5 August 2003.
[298] Author's interview with former head of the Department of Civil Service and Personnel, Ministry of Taxes and Dues, Moscow, 21 June 2003 and 8 August 2003.
[299] Ibid.
[300] Author's interviews with senior associate, Kyiv office of one of the Big Four international accounting firms, Kyiv, 26 October 2005; and with partner, tax and legal services, leading international accounting firm, Kyiv, 27 July 2006.
[301] Author's interview with partner, tax and legal services, leading international accounting firm, Kyiv, 1 August 2006.
[302] Author's interview with tax manager, Kyiv office of one of the Big Four international accounting firms, Kyiv, 26 July 2006.
[303] Author's interview with senior tax official, Modernization Department, State Tax Administration of Ukraine, Kyiv, 10 August 2005.

Building Trust, Instilling Fear: Tax Administration Reform   193

At the same time, the application of Russian tax laws has been deemed to vary so significantly from one office to another that at least one foreign investor, Andrei Movchan, chief executive of the Third Rome Investment Fund, relayed at a conference that his firm discusses with their investors to which tax office they should go.[304]

Similarly, Ukrainian and foreign enterprises often have chosen to locate their main offices in certain districts of a province or in certain sections of a large city such as Kyiv in order to have a constructive and transparent dialogue with better-qualified tax bureaucrats, because there has been a widely held belief that the quality of tax bureaucrats varies widely from one tax office to another.[305] With large numbers of tax returns, the occasional lack of basic stationery goods, and the absence of internationally recognized computer software for tracking tax returns, some local STA offices have given the impression of disorganization behind the counters.[306] The variation across offices is further shown by the fact that in recent years, offices in a few districts have made tremendous improvements through more training of personnel and the procurement of new computer equipment, enabling them to be better equipped to distinguish between fraudulent and legitimate taxpayers and to impress some taxpayers with significant levels of sophistication.[307]

Thus, while in all three countries, low salaries compared with the marketplace hamper the tax systems from performing at their best, the transition has brought higher criteria and impartial measures for hiring personnel that are able to withstand outside influence in Poland to a greater extent than in Russia and Ukraine.

Finally, an organization's internal culture can suppress efforts by employees to make the system work better. One tax inspector in Ukraine complained that initiative is punished, rather than rewarded or encouraged.[308]

Table 5.4 summarizes the human resources available in the three states' tax administrations.

---

[304] Vasilyeva.

[305] Author's interview with senior partner, leading local tax and legal firm, Kyiv, 3 August 2006; and telephone interview with president, leading foreign business association, Kyiv, 10 August 2006. Similarly, judges across the country vary in terms of their expertise in tax legislation. Judges in Kyiv are deemed to be better equipped with handling tax issues due to their higher volume of cases.

[306] Author's interview with partner, tax and legal services, leading international accounting firm, Kyiv, 1 August 2006.

[307] Author's telephone interview with president, leading foreign business association, Kyiv, 10 August 2006.

[308] Author's interview with State Tax Inspector, in a Ukrainian Oblast, Ukraine, 20 May 2011.

194   Taxes and Trust

Table 5.4 *Human resources in tax administrations*

	Poland	Russia	Ukraine

Findings	• Civil service personnel:
	  • Some hired in competition from late 1990s on
	  • High education of tax inspectors
	• Extensive training and planning for new taxes
		• Military/law personnel (especially for tax police):
		  • Into the 2000s: Not hired in competitions
		  • High education problems
		• Poor/moderate training and planning for new taxes
			• Personnel: poor quality, skills and education
			• Yanukovych filled top positions with Donetsk natives
			• Few tax officials understand laws well
			• Firms choose to locate main offices in certain areas as the quality of tax bureaucrats varies

Societal Approach	More citizen-based	More coercive	Weakly coercive

Conclusion

Such a discussion of the structural means of preventing corruption of bureaucrats brings the topic back full circle to the Weberian ideals of a rational bureaucracy staffed by independent, professional employees. In comparing Poland, Russia and Ukraine's tax administrations, we can look at how rational and society-oriented they are with respect to their *historical references, structures, human resources* and *work philosophy*.

• *Historical References*: Poland's rational structural design draws upon its inter-war past for some of its current institutions, whereas Russia and Ukraine, to a lesser extent, appear lately to be drawing on some aspects of Soviet bureaucratic administration in an effort to obtain strong hierarchical control at the expense of bureaucratic autonomy.

• *Structures*: Poland's tax administration has maintained a structure that has direct lines of subordination both between offices and within them. The uniquely separate, but integrated, position of the tax audit offices in Poland, though, does not always provide smooth interactions with the other tax administration components, suggesting that the structure is not completely rational. Meanwhile, throughout the 1990s there appear to have been insufficient barriers placed on Russia and Ukraine's tax inspectors as they interacted with taxpayers. Poland also has an external watchdog organization (NIK) that actually produces critical financial and performance audit reports, available to the public (unlike Russia's and Ukraine's accounts chambers).

- *Human Resources*: Poland's tax administration has utilized different employee training techniques to control how the new taxes were to work.
- *Work Philosophy*: The methods by which the Polish authorities work, and how they educate the public about tax procedures, appear to be more compliance-driven and less focused on reaching a monetary target than in Russia and Ukraine – a philosophy that tends to treat the taxpayers more as clients.

In short, in the model of Poland's tax bureaucracy, a mixture of successes and failures with respect to the use of its *historical reference points, structures, human resources* and *work philosophy* – all oriented towards improving the trust that taxpayers have in the tax administration – combine to produce a case of partial bureaucratic rationalism. Meanwhile, a less successful mix of these Weberian components produced a lower level of bureaucratic rationalism on the part of the Russian tax administration in the 1990s, with some significant reform successes in the past couple of years. Poland has thus opted for *rationalizing* the tax bureaucrats, whereas Russia has sought to *empower* them so that the state can be perceived as holding power over society – ordinary taxpayers and businesses alike. Ukraine has similarly sought to empower the tax bureaucracies with some 'strengthening' of their powers over Ukrainian taxpayers under Yanukovych, but still to a lesser extent historically than in Russia.

Moreover, the Polish model also shows that a state agency not only needs to be internally strong and autonomous from outside groups in order to get the job done; it must also involve society by creating citizens' trust in the tax collection agencies through mechanisms such as 'audit-free' filings, tax office information booths and other means of public outreach. A strong structure alone does not produce effective implementation of tax collection policies. Nor should effective internal oversight or a unified esprit de corps be seen as preferable or contrary to being an outward-focused state agency. The two approaches – internally and externally motivated – go hand in hand.

Finally, the fact that for a short time there was significant progress in two Russian provinces (Nizhny Novgorod and Volgograd) suggests that Russian tax offices can perform in a rational bureaucratic manner once comprehensive reforms are initiated to overhaul the power relationship between tax bureaucrat and taxpayer, from one based principally on coercion to one based largely on trust, through 'audit-free' filings. The Russians clearly are capable of building effective Weberian state agencies as well, provided Moscow allows it.

As the Polish, Russian and Ukrainian paths and methods of governance diverged during the course of the transition – and became more

196 Taxes and Trust

distinct during the Putin era – comparing how bureaucrats collect taxes does help illustrate that a state that seeks to 'impose power' may not be as effective as one that engages with society on more equal terms. 'Empowering' bureaucrats so that the state will be 'strengthened' vis-à-vis society may not provide as successful an implementation of state policy in the long run as an approach based upon 'rationalizing' the state.

With respect to the Russian state, one of course can ponder whether historical patterns of governance from the distant past have any saliency for Russia's more coercive style of governance today. Yanni Kotsonis has described the pressure placed on tax collectors in the early eighteenth century to address the arrears that appeared with the very first poll taxes in the 1720s. The tax collectors, he writes, 'were the only people with whom the government interacted directly. It was easy to not only focus on them but also assume that they were causal factors in the arrears; any other causes were invisible. The collectors in each region and estate were regularly accused of corruption and then arrested, flogged and exiled . . . Empress Anna was especially fond of blaming the collectors, and large punitive detachments rounded up the tax farmers, the bailiffs on state lands, the gentry's managers, and the peasant elder and beat them with whips and birch rods. Some were executed. Even noblemen who withheld their serfs' taxes were arrested, but the practice was discontinued because noblemen tended to die in prison at a high rate.'[309] In spite of such terror, Kotsonis remarks, the arrears under Empress Anna Ivanovna were never collected. While tax collectors are no longer treated in such a manner, the focus on collection target goals appears to be just as strong today.

[309] Kotsonis, pp. 49–50.

6 Citizens, Subjects and Slackers and Paying Taxes

To function properly and to provide for the welfare and security of its citizens, every state must undertake the critical task of raising revenue from its populace. When it comes to collecting taxes, the most critical ingredient, no doubt, is the attainment of a sufficient level of compliance on the part of society. Citizens must agree to the levels of taxation required of them and must file tax returns accordingly. Payment of one's dues to the state is the hallmark of becoming a citizen, and it is a duty that all citizens, including those in the new states that emerged from communism in Eastern Europe and the former Soviet Union, must take up.

In gauging specifically how well residents in new states such as Poland, Russia and Ukraine become true citizens, who are capable of fulfilling their obligations to their governments, it is necessary to measure how compliant the populace is with taxes.

The Taxpayer Compliance Attitudinal Surveys of 2004, 2005, 2010, 2012 and 2015 (see Appendix I), introduced in Chapter 4, indicate not only that the Polish polity is far more willing and compliant in its attitude towards paying taxes than the Russian and Ukrainian polities are, but also that Russians respond to their state with greater fear of deterrence, albeit perhaps more in 2004 than in 2010, while Ukrainians, showing the lowest levels of support for obeying the law, react to state efforts to increase tax compliance with less fear and little trust, especially in 2005.[1]

The important question, then, becomes 'why?' Why are Poland, Russia and Ukraine so dramatically different attitudinally with respect to paying one's share to the government? Where does such tax compliance (or lack thereof) actually come from?

This chapter will address this question. Three main theories of taxpayer compliance will be explained. First, I will consider the deterrence

---

[1] Great care was given to ensure that the Polish, Russian and Ukrainian survey questions were as equivalent as possible in terms of meaning and interpretation. Final versions of the questions were made in consultation with linguistic specialists at each survey firm to make sure that all survey questions were worded naturally for the ears of native speakers and equivalent in meaning to the questions used in the other country surveys.

197

198   Taxes and Trust

theory, which emphasizes that those governments eager to extract tax revenues from society should provide the public with sufficient fear of the consequences if one does not pay. Second, notions of trust in government to provide goods and in other fellow citizens to pay their fair share (also referred to as the theory of 'quasi-voluntary compliance') will be examined. And, third, paying taxes on the basis of prior experience and interaction with the tax authorities will be explained through a theory that suggests that obeying the law is dependent upon prior encounters with the tax bureaucracy.

These theories will be tested utilizing the Polish (2004 and 2010), Russian (2004 and 2010) and Ukrainian (2005, 2010 and 2015) Taxpayer Compliance Attitudinal Survey data. The findings suggest that an important aspect of the theory of 'quasi-voluntary compliance' that relies on taxpayers' trust in their government to fulfil its obligations to society holds up well in all of the surveys. Within the Russian and Ukrainian 2004–2005 surveys (but not the Polish 2004 survey), the deterrence theory, however, was shown to be just as significant, but had an even greater effect in increasing the predicted likelihood of expressing support for tax compliance in the Russian 2004 survey. In the 2010 Polish, Russian and Ukrainian surveys and in the 2015 Ukrainian survey, in contrast, citizens' trust in their states mattered more across the board in accounting for why taxpayers would support complying with tax laws.

Furthermore, with respect to examining the impact of having had prior interaction with bureaucrats, the results are quite different for the three cases and across the multiple surveys, as they show that the nature of the past conduct of the tax officials can make a critical difference in terms of future support for complying with tax laws.

How Do Polish, Russian and Ukrainian Attitudes Differ with Respect to Paying Taxes?

While nearly equivalent percentages of respondents to the Poland and Russia Taxpayer Compliance Attitudinal Surveys conducted in 2004, 79 per cent and 71 per cent, respectively, stated that a citizen should always follow the tax laws even if he or she considers them to be unfair (Question #21), only 57 per cent of Ukrainians in 2005 stated the same. Figures for the 2010 surveys were quite similar: 81 per cent of Poles and 74 per cent of Russians in 2010 stated that a citizen should always follow the tax laws even if he or she considers them to be unfair, while only 64 per cent of Ukrainians in 2010 concurred. (The corresponding figures for Ukraine in 2012 and 2015 were stable at 59 and 61 per cent,

Citizens, Subjects and Slackers and Paying Taxes   199

respectively.) Hence, obligations for citizens are viewed as significantly more limited by Ukrainians.

Interestingly, though, in both Russia and Ukraine (but not in Poland), there is a dramatic difference when it comes to whether individuals state that they would follow the tax laws even if they personally did not consider them to be fair. Whereas 83 per cent of Poles in 2004 (and a similar 77 per cent in 2010) would follow the tax laws in such cases, only 53 per cent of Russians in 2004 (and a nearly identical 52 per cent of Russians in 2010) and 36 per cent of Ukrainians in 2005 (and a somewhat similar 44, 39 and 45 per cent of Ukrainians in 2010, 2012 and 2015) would do the same (Question #22). Expressed another way, and as shown in Appendix III, when compared with the answers to Question #26 regarding whether or not the respondent viewed his or her country's tax laws as fair, in 2010, a minimum of 12 per cent of Poles, a minimum of 21 per cent of Russians and a minimum of 37 per cent of Ukrainians (42 per cent in 2012 and 37 per cent in 2015) did not appear to have any intention of complying with their countries' tax laws. Hence, in both Russia and Ukraine, there appears to be a disconnect between what obligations individuals believe to exist for citizens at large and what individuals state that they would do personally, and this has been sustained throughout the era of President Vladimir Putin in Russia. Such a disconnect between citizens' and one's own personal obligations does not appear to exist in Poland.

Other findings of the surveys indicate that the disconnect between citizens and their state is greater in Ukraine than in Russia. For example, remarkably, according to the survey (Question #36), far fewer Ukrainians (9 per cent in 2005; 10 per cent in 2010; 13 per cent in 2012; and 13 per cent in 2015) than Russians (38 per cent in 2004 and 46 per cent in 2010) stated that they knew the correct personal income flat tax rate, suggesting a populace that is further removed from the activity of the state.[2]

Clearly, Poland's population differs dramatically from those of Russia and Ukraine with respect to attitudes on fulfilling tax obligations to the state, and generally Ukrainians appear to be less compliant attitudinally than their neighbours to both the East and West. It is also extremely important to note that in Ukraine the 2005 survey came exactly one year after the Orange Revolution and that the 2015 survey came some twenty months after the EuroMaidan Revolution. Despite the efforts of those

---

[2] An additional factor might also contribute some lack of knowledge of the PIT rate in Ukraine: Ukrainian legislation allows an 'entrepreneurial' flat tax of as little as 200 hryvnia (or U.S.$40) per month, for which any self-employed individual qualifies.

200   Taxes and Trust

who organized the extraordinary 2004 and 2014 events to bring in a government more accountable to the people, Ukrainian citizens appeared to have the lowest levels of support for paying taxes to their state.[3] This suggests that the efforts to re-make the citizen–state relationship in Ukraine towards more mutually constructive ends for both state and society will remain a tremendous challenge for Ukraine's political leaders.[4]

Obviously, these survey figures are tricky measurements, complicated especially by the fact that this is the first set of survey questions designed to test tax compliance theories in these states, all of which have a history of authoritarian rule. Moreover, the surveys were taken just at two points in time in Poland and Russia and four points in time in Ukraine. Further, any reforms or improvements with respect to tax law or tax procedures undertaken in recent years by the state may not have caught up in the minds of respondents as they form their current overall attitudes towards paying taxes. In addition, while attitudinal decisions are important components of behaviour, surveying attitudes towards compliance is not precisely the same as measuring tax compliance itself.[5] Finally, of course, as discussed in greater length earlier in Chapter 4, the Taxpayer Compliance Attitudinal Survey Question #22, chosen as the main dependent variable for analysis in this chapter, seeks to replicate as

---

[3] The International Finance Corporation (IFC) has found a similar low level of support for paying taxes on the part of Ukrainian firms. Only 16 per cent of respondents in the IFC's 2004 survey of some 2,800 small and medium-sized businesses stated that they paid their taxes in full the previous year, with 20 per cent stating that they underreported their income by more than 20 per cent (IFC, 2004, p. 58). A year later, the IFC found in its 2005 survey that only 18 per cent indicated that companies similar to theirs did not underreport revenue for tax purposes and that one in four respondents who underreported revenue estimated that the amount concealed from tax was more than 50 per cent (IFC, 2005, p. 29).

[4] It should be noted that the survey taken in Ukraine came at a time of relative economic strength compared with the 1990s, but that Ukraine's strong economic growth did slow in 2005. (According to the Economist Intelligence Unit (EIU) website, the rate of GDP growth for Ukraine in 2004 was 12.1 per cent, while in 2005 the rate is estimated to have been 2.4 per cent.) Meanwhile, the stark differences between the Polish and Russian states are even more remarkable considering that the surveys were undertaken at a time in which there was a relative downturn in the Polish economy and a time of relative strength in the Russian economy in comparison with previous years. (According to figures compiled from EIU data, the average GDP growth rate for Poland from 2001 to 2005 was 3.0 per cent, whereas the average for Russia was 6.1 per cent and for Ukraine 7.7 per cent over the same period. This contrasts with average GDP growth rates of 3.73 per cent for Poland from 1991 to 2000, and -3.61 per cent and -7.71 per cent over the same period for Russia and Ukraine.)

[5] The limitations of such survey data should be emphasized here: Survey data reflects what respondents tell interviewers rather than actual compliance; hence, further research such as individual-level data over time constructed from tax returns or audit results would be required to make the link more conclusively.

much of a real world scenario as much as possible, one in which individuals choose every day to follow the tax laws or not, even in cases where they disagree with them.

Nevertheless, it appears that the Russian and Ukrainian publics are with their state to a significant degree less with respect to fulfilling their citizenship obligations and paying their tax dues than the Polish public. The question, then, is why?

Why Do Polish, Russian and Ukrainian Attitudes Differ Dramatically with Respect to Paying Taxes?

Within social science, there is a lack of consensus as to which conceptual model or theory best explains variation in taxpayer compliance. There are few activities that governments engage in that pose more difficulties with respect to issues of trust and compliance than tax collection. States generally can take three main approaches, none of which are mutually exclusive, to improve tax compliance on the part of their citizens – deter taxpayers into complying by fear of punishment, gain citizen trust so that taxpayers will comply quasi-voluntarily, and improve 'customer service' by emphasizing procedural fairness as the tax system interacts with taxpayers. For a compliant society interacting with a citizen-based state, the expectations would be that tax compliance depends largely on trust in the state and/or satisfaction with tax bureaucrats' level of customer service from prior encounters. For a society interacting with a deterrent-based approach to tax collection, tax compliance would be expected to depend largely on citizens' being susceptible to deterrence.

Generally speaking, with respect to the tax policy area, Poland's tax administration has a work philosophy that is more compliance-driven and outward-focused. The tax system there is less focused on reaching a monetary target, which promotes a philosophy that treats taxpayers more like clients. Meanwhile, in Russia and Ukraine, the focus has been more target-driven, which makes tax inspectors merely try to fulfil quarterly or yearly targets and go after those taxpayers who have already paid, as more revenue can be obtained from those known to have it.

The Deterrence Model

Economists, as Joel Slemrod has explained, by and large have viewed the task of tax collection as a problem of 'rational decision making under uncertainty' – one in which 'cheating on your taxes is a gamble that either pays off in lower taxes or, with some probability, subjects you

202   Taxes and Trust

to sanctions'.[6] The assumption, then, within the Hobbesian deterrence model is that the fear of being detected or punished by the coercive powers of government embodied in the tax administration will reduce illegal or noncompliant behaviour for the betterment of society at large. The model also suggests that compliance will increase as the odds of being detected and the penalties for tax evasion also increase. Hence, only out of rational self-interest will citizens comply with the will of their state.

According to the results of the Taxpayer Compliance Attitudinal Surveys, when asked what they would do if the risk of punishment was completely taken away, 53 per cent of Poles in 2004 (47 per cent of Poles in 2010), 40 per cent of Russians in 2004 (45 per cent of Russians in 2010) and 34 per cent of Ukrainians in 2005 (38 per cent of Ukrainians in 2010; 29 per cent of Ukrainians in 2012; and 39 per cent of Ukrainians in 2015) stated that they personally would be more likely to evade paying taxes if they thought they could get away with it (Question #16 in Appendix I.) Hence, more Poles than Russians and Ukrainians seem to indicate that on an attitude basis, at least, they would be more responsive to a relaxation of a punishment risk.[7] Later, I will explore how significant a susceptibility to a relaxation of deterrent measures is in explaining differences in overall attitudes towards tax compliance.[8]

---

[6] Slemrod, p. 2.

[7] When adding in those who stated that it was 'difficult to say', the totals for the Polish, Russian and Ukrainian survey responses to Question #16 are the same. Nevertheless, one possible reason for the disparity between Poles, Russians and Ukrainians on the issue of evasion without risk of punishment might be different connotations of what it means to evade. Perhaps for some Poles 'evasion' could mean hiding some taxable income, while for Russians it might be non-payment altogether. Further surveys testing attitudes towards different gradations of cheating might be beneficial here.

[8] While this Question #16 and that chosen for the dependent variable in the logit analysis (Question #22) both ask respondents about tax evasion, the concepts behind the questions are theoretically distinct. Asking individuals whether they would be more likely to evade taxes if there were no punitive consequences is not the same as asking whether they would evade a tax law personally deemed unfair (or one they disagreed with) regardless of whether the state employed deterrent force or not. The former question asks about individuals' views on the effectiveness of removing the risk of punishment for themselves personally, while the latter asks about the extent to which personal notions of fairness (regardless as to what those personal notions of fairness actually are or how they differ from individual to individual) could outweigh the fulfilment of the civic duty to pay one's share in taxes. Hence, the first question is about deterrence and parses out deterrence as to whether it works at all or not. The model shows the impact of deterrence – how big is that impact on compliance with tax laws that one deems to be unfair, that one disagrees with. Indeed, in examining the distribution of the variables constructed from Questions #16 and 22 to be used in the logit analysis, for example in the 2004–2005 surveys, the responses are not clustered together. Roughly 12 per cent of Russians surveyed would neither obey tax laws nor evade if they knew there would be no punishment, roughly 25 per cent of Russians would not obey tax laws and would evade if they knew there would be no punishment, 38 per cent of Russian would obey tax laws and would not

Citizens, Subjects and Slackers and Paying Taxes

The Two Trusts

Other social scientists have begun to argue within the last twenty years that the payment of taxes constitutes a transaction made on the basis of trust, which comes in two forms: trust of the government to provide goods and services to its citizens and trust in other citizens to also pay their own taxes. Citizens and the state will benefit if such trust can be maintained.

Margaret Levi, in *Of Rule and Revenue*, has introduced the concept of quasi-voluntary compliance with respect to the payment of taxes to the state in a manner that reduces the costs of enforcement. '[Quasi-voluntary compliance] is *voluntary*', she writes, 'because taxpayers choose to pay. It is *quasi*-voluntary because the noncompliant are subject to coercion – if they are caught.'[9] To occur, quasi-voluntary compliance requires the two forms of trust previously mentioned. 'Quasi-voluntary compliance', she continues, 'will occur only when taxpayers have confidence that (1) rulers will keep their bargains and (2) the other constituents will keep theirs.'[10] Hence, taxpayers will comply in a quasi-voluntary manner if they have some confidence and relative certainty that the state will provide the goods (and/or services) that it has promised and if the taxpayers also have similar confidence and certainty that others are also complying with the state so that the goods (and/or services) will be paid for. (An additional, important component of trust in the state is of a more moral, less material nature – trust that the state acts and will act fairly towards its citizens.)[11]

Once quasi-voluntary compliance declines, Levi is very pessimistic about the opportunities to reconstitute and rebuild it. Re-establishing it, she concludes, 'often requires an extraordinary event – such as war, revolution, or depression – that makes people willing to negotiate a new

---

evade if they knew there would be no punishment and 26 per cent of Russian would both obey tax laws and evade if there was no punishment. For the Polish 2004 survey, the corresponding percentages were 2, 5, 38 and 55 per cent, respectively. Similarly, for the Ukrainian 2005 survey, the corresponding percentages were 24, 26, 30 and 20 per cent, respectively. Likewise, the scale reliability coefficients of the variables are very low in the Polish survey (0.1108), low in the Ukrainian survey (0.2263) and still not high enough to form a scale in the Russian survey (0.4103). All of this suggests that the concepts behind the questions were most likely distinct in the minds of the respondents as well as of the author of the survey.

[9] Levi, 1988, p. 52.   [10] Ibid., pp. 52–53.

[11] Similarly, Sheffrin and Triest, in an econometric analysis of the U.S. 1987 Taxpayer Opinion Survey, found that 'attitudes are important determinants of compliance behaviour. They find that having a negative attitude toward the tax system and perceiving other taxpayers as dishonest both significantly increase the likelihood that a person will evade taxes.' (Sheffrin and Triest, cited in Ickes and Slemrod, p. 391.)

204   Taxes and Trust

bargain'.[12] In the aftermath of its 2004 Orange Revolution and 2014 EuroMaidan Revolution, Ukraine, for example, may have been given a rare second and even rarer third shot within a twenty-five year period at rebuilding the state's relationship to taxpayers. (Indeed, in the first few months of 2005, preliminary reports stated that tax and customs revenues were significantly higher than usual there.[13])

Trust in the Government to Provide Goods Leaving aside trust in other taxpayers for the moment, Levi states that the government leaders 'must create confidence in their credibility and their capacity to deliver promised returns for taxes' and 'must convince taxpayers that taxpayer contributions make a difference in producing the desired goods'.[14]

According to the results of the Taxpayer Compliance Attitudinal Surveys, 21 per cent of Poles in 2004 (23 per cent in 2010), 42 per cent of Russians in 2004 (35 per cent in 2010) and 52 per cent of Ukrainians in 2005 (53 per cent in 2010; 55 per cent in 2012; and 47 per cent in 2015) believe that there are many dishonest tax service employees in their country, with nearly a third of respondents in these countries stating that it was difficult to say (Question #3 in Appendix I.) This provides one assessment as to how citizens view bureaucrats at the bottom of the political system with regard to trustworthiness. Clearly, Ukrainians are more distrusting of tax bureaucrats than their neighbours both to the East and to the West, and it appears that there were a bit fewer Russians who distrusted their bureaucrats in 2010 than six years earlier. (Additional assessments as to how trustworthy are actors at the top of the political system – namely, the president in Poland, Russia and Ukraine and the parliament and government in Poland and Ukraine – are included in the analysis of what accounts for differences in overall attitudes towards tax compliance as further proxy measurements for how trustworthy the state is in the eyes of citizens.[15])

---

[12] Levi, 1988, p. 70.

[13] On 18 August 2005, Ukraine's Prime Minister Yulia Tymoshenko stated that Ukraine already has collected 50 per cent more in budget revenue so far in 2005, compared with 2004. 'All of the tax rates are exactly the same, yet the revenue received is 1 1/2 times greater', Tymoshenko said (Reynolds, Garfield).

[14] Levi, 1988, p. 53.

[15] The author does recognize that there are limits in utilizing such measures of trust in individual political personalities such as Presidents Aleksander Kwasniewski, Bronisław Komorowski, Vladimir Putin, Dmitry Medvedev, Viktor Yushchenko, Viktor Yanukovych and Petro Poroshenko, for example, as the survey questions asked do pick up respondents' additional perceptions of their leaders and their politics rather than focusing entirely on their perception of their leaders' honesty or trustworthiness. (This is less the case with measures of trust in institutional bodies such as the parliament or government.) Nevertheless, the questions chosen for analysis here are the same as those

While not available for the Polish and Russian surveys in 2004, additional survey questions do suggest that there is a significant lack of trust in the state. With respect to the provision of goods and services, in 2005 only 9 per cent of Ukrainians believe that their government fulfils its obligations to citizens, in 2010 and 2012 only 10 to 12 per cent believe that their state fulfils its obligations to citizens, and in 2015 only 6 per cent (!) believe that their state fulfils its obligations. From 2005 through to 2015, some 50 to 60 per cent of Ukrainians flatly deny that their state or government fulfils obligations (Question #55). Meanwhile, the figure for Poles and Russians in 2010 who believed their state fulfils its duties to citizens was much higher at 21 and 24 per cent, respectively, and only 26 to 27 per cent viewed their state as not fulfilling its tasks. Clearly, Ukrainians do not believe that they get much from their state, and the downward trend in 2015 is not encouraging for the Ukrainian state.

Moreover, when Ukrainians were asked whether they could trust their government to do what was right in 2005 and their state to do what was right in 2010 and 2012, only 9 or 11 per cent stated that they could (Question #56). Further, the figure was little more than half that in 2015, when only 6 per cent could trust their state to do what was right. Similarly, the 2015 survey saw a drop to 7 of the percentage of those who view the state as relating to all citizens in an equal, fair manner – down from 15 per cent in 2010 and 2012 (Question #57.) Again, Poles and Russians are a bit more trusting of their state, with 21 and 26 per cent, respectively, stating in 2010 that they can trust their state to do what is right, and with 21 and 20 per cent, respectively, stating that they trust their state to treat all citizens in an equal, fair manner. Hence, as trust in the state on the part of citizens involves both a material trust that the state will continue to provide goods and services and a moral trust that the state will treat its citizens fairly, Ukrainians appear to be stating flatly after both revolutions that they cannot trust their state to do either, and the latest data on the levels of Ukrainians' trust in their state are the lowest ever recorded in these surveys.

Trust in Other Taxpayers to Pay Their Fair Share As mentioned, those who view tax compliance as based on a combination of trust relationships also give significant relevance to whether or not taxpayers have confidence that their fellow citizens also will pay their dues to the state. In Poland, Russia and Ukraine, distrust in others paying their fair share in taxes is, perhaps surprisingly, quite high. According to the results of

used regularly by the respective polling firms in their surveys used for tracking changes in such attitudes.

206   Taxes and Trust

the Taxpayer Compliance Attitudinal Surveys, some 69 per cent of Poles in 2004 (65 per cent in 2010), 77 per cent of Russians in 2004 (67 per cent in 2010) and 70 per cent of Ukrainians in 2005 (69 per cent in 2010 and in 2012; and 72 per cent in 2015) believe that there are 'many people', as opposed to 'few people', in their country who evade taxes (Question #13 in Appendix I.)[16] In contrast to some of the other survey data presented in the first part of this chapter, levels of trust in one's fellow citizens, at least with respect to paying one's tax dues, might not be dramatically different in the three states.

Prior Personal Experiences and Interaction with the Tax Authorities

Some theories that explain civic obedience rely on whether citizens have had past interactions with relevant government officials.[17] In the Taxpayer Compliance Attitudinal Surveys, survey questions were utilized to explore whether previous experiences with the tax authorities affect citizen views on complying with the law. According to the surveys, nearly half of all Poles in 2004 (38 per cent in 2010), a quarter of all Russians (in both 2004 and 2010) and only 12 to 19 per cent of all Ukrainians stated that they had dealt with tax service employees within the previous five years on matters of business (Question #6 in Appendix I.) Of these individuals, 51 per cent of Poles in 2004 (50 per cent in 2010), 30 per cent of Russians in 2004 (37 per cent in 2010) and 27 per cent of Ukrainians in 2004 (30 per cent in 2010; 28 per cent in 2012; and 31 per cent in 2015) had overall positive impressions of their individual contact with the tax bureaucrats, while 19 per cent of Poles in 2004 (17 per cent in 2010), 29 per cent of Russians in 2004 (27 per cent in 2010) and 30 to 32 per cent of Ukrainians (in 2005, 2010, 2012 and 2015) had negative impressions (Question #7.) Hence, while Poles overall had more positive impressions, nearly as many Russians and Ukrainians had negative impressions as positive ones.

---

[16] It should be noted that levels of trust in others in Russia generally today are not high, which might also provide some cultural context regarding levels of trust in fellow taxpayers and, in turn, regarding attitudes towards tax compliance generally. For example, according to a poll conducted by the Bashkirova and Partners market research firm in June 2005, only 25 per cent of Russians agreed that, 'generally most people can be trusted.' In addition, while Russia places somewhere in the middle of some 80 nations polled in the World Values Survey as to whether one should trust people in general, Russia and Bulgaria were the only two nations in Eastern Europe where more people said they did not trust 'most people in this country' than said they did, according to a 2004 poll conducted by the Centre for the Study of Public Policy at the University of Strathclyde in Glasgow. (See Fak.)

[17] See, for example, Tyler.

Citizens, Subjects and Slackers and Paying Taxes 207

Testing the Theories of Taxpayer Compliance

How do the different theories on tax compliance, derived largely from the study of the US case, test against data on attitudes associated with tax compliance? As mentioned, the expectations for a compliant society interacting with a citizen-based state would be that tax compliance depends largely on trust in the state and/or satisfaction with tax bureaucrats' level of customer service. For a society interacting with a state that employs a more deterrent-based approach to tax collection, tax compliance would be expected to depend largely on citizens' being susceptible to deterrence.

Appendix IV presents the results of tests of the different variables representing the tax compliance theories discussed through logit analyses of the 2004 and 2010 Poland and Russia and of the 2005, 2010 and 2015 Ukraine Taxpayer Compliance Attitudinal Surveys, respectively. The dependent variable in these tests is whether one agrees to obey the tax laws even if they are personally deemed to be unfair (Question #22 in Appendix I.)[18] Before proceeding, though, it is important to emphasize that the analysis presented here is not an evaluation of the behaviour of Poles, Russians and Ukrainians, but rather an examination of the links in attitudes that are essential part of behaviour decisions whether or not to comply. Moreover, as mentioned earlier, it is important to recognize that there are challenges in conducting quantitative surveys on these sensitive topics in countries with a tradition of authoritarianism. Further, no one, to the author's knowledge, has undertaken such a comprehensive survey on attitudes in these transitional countries to test tax compliance theories. Hence, the data here are suggestive, not definitive.

With regard to the independent variables in the regression analysis, they are divided into four categories.[19] Viewing evasion as OK if one

---

[18] Regarding the choice of the dependent variable, this dependent variable was most favourable to Poles as well as to Russians and Ukrainians. For example, in the 2004 and 2005 surveys, with near even splits (in Russia, 53 per cent of Russians would obey a law personally deemed unfair while 28 per cent would not and 19 per cent were unsure; and in Ukraine, the corresponding figures were 36, 37 and 27 per cent, respectively) provides opportunity to explain Russian and Ukrainian non-compliance. For obvious reasons, respondents were not asked directly about their own payment of taxes, nor were the respondents subject to any type of outside assessment to see if their taxes were paid in full. However, this survey question was the most direct question on what a respondent personally would do with respect to making a choice regarding tax evasion. Hence, despite the limitations of such an exercise, the focus here to examine what impacts attitudes towards tax compliance as a proxy for tax compliance itself.

[19] With the exception of Age and Income, all of the independent variables, as with the dependent variable, are coded 0 and 1. Mean replacement replaces missing values at

208 Taxes and Trust

could get away with it (Question #16) is a proxy variable for the deterrence theory, as it will help examine whether the extent to which one is susceptible to a relaxation of deterrent measures affects attitudes towards tax compliance.

The second category comprises a set of variables that examine the 'two trusts' behind theories of 'quasi-voluntary compliance' – the need both to trust the state to deliver the goods and the requirement to trust others to pay their fair due before one agrees to pay one's own taxes. The first of these variables in this set focus on trust of government – its leaders at the top (Presidents Aleksander Kwaśniewski (2004), Bronisław Komorowski (2010), Vladimir Putin (2004), Dmitry Medvedev (2010), Viktor Yushchenko (2005), Viktor Yanukovych (2010) and Petro Poroshenko (2015)); in Poland and Ukraine, the parliament and the government as a whole; and in Russia (2010), the prime minister (Putin) and parliament (State Duma) – as proxy variables for trust that the government fulfils its obligations to its people.

Meanwhile, for additional versions of the regression analysis, scales were compiled in the Ukraine 2005 surveys and in the Poland, Russia and Ukraine 2010 and 2015 surveys to reflect respondents' general trust in the state at the top of the system. The Trust in the State Scale for the Poland 2010 survey is a composite of trust in the president, the prime minister, the Sejm, the Senate and the government and trust in the state to do what is right and to fulfil its obligations to its citizens. The Trust in the State Scale for the Russia 2010 survey includes trust in the president, the prime minister, parliament (the State Duma) and the government and trust in the state to do what is right and to fulfil its duties. Further, the Trust in the State scale for Ukraine 2005 and 2010 surveys is a composite of trust in the president, the parliament and the state (government in 2005) and trust in the state (government) to do what is right and to fulfil its duties.

Further, for all surveys, the variable 'Many Dishonest Tax Bureaucrats' (Question #3) serves as a proxy for trust in the lower levels of the state bureaucracy, while 'Many People Evade Taxes' (Question #13) is a good proxy for estimating one's views as to whether others pay their dues.

Whether or not one has had contact with tax bureaucrats within the previous five years (Question #6) allows us to test whether prior contact, in and of itself and irrespective of the nature of that

the mean, but mean-replaced variables were not used as the dependent variable in these logit regressions.

Citizens, Subjects and Slackers and Paying Taxes 209

contact or its outcome for some individuals, matters with respect to attitudes towards tax compliance. A final set of control variables also are considered.[20]

Poland 2004 As Appendix IV illustrates, the logit regression provides evidence to suggest that the Polish public does not react significantly to the first approach option for the state (deterrence) in 2004, but does to the second approach through 'trust in government'. First, the deterrence theory, as measured by the proxy variable regarding what one would do if the risk of punishment were taken away, is shown to be insignificant. How one would respond to the withdrawal of the risk of punishment does not appear to have anything to do with whether one would say they would obey the tax laws. Second, prior contact with the tax bureaucrats also does not appear to matter significantly – although the analysis presented here does not separate out the impact of having had *unsatisfactory* prior contact on tax compliance. Moreover, income and being male are shown to be significant. (The fact, though, that the higher the income, the less willing Poles appear to be compliant suggests that compliance does not depend upon an individual's ability to pay.) In addition, age and having graduated from a higher education institution do not matter (although the latter's substantive effect, described below, does show some slight significance).

While binominal logit analysis is an appropriate method for analyzing dichotomous dependent variables, coefficients in such analysis – at least compared to those in ordinary least-squares regression – lack substantive meaning. To remedy this, a measure of the substantive effect of each variable is made by calculating what is referred to as a 'first difference' of the change in the predicted probability in the dependent variable. Here, the 'substantive effect' is the change in likelihood of declaring that one would obey tax laws even if personally viewed as unfair when the variable in question is shifted from its minimum to its maximum and all other independent variables are held even at their means.[21] Such estimates for

---

[20] Those control variables concern socio-economic and additional effects and include the monthly income one declared as part of the omnibus survey, who actually files one's personal income taxes (Question #2), whether one is male, one's age and what is the highest education one has achieved.

[21] The substantive effects presented in Appendices IV, V, VI and VII reflect the change in likelihood of declaring that one would obey tax laws personally viewed as unfair when shifting the variable in question from its minimum to its maximum for all variables with the except of 'Age', which is varied from one standard deviation below the mean to one standard deviation above the mean.

210   Taxes and Trust

the variables (with substantive effects that have p-values estimated to be ≤ 0.05) are depicted graphically in Table 6.1.[22]

The variable with the most significance and with the largest substantive effect in the Polish survey was a proxy variable for 'quasi-voluntary compliance'. Namely, obeying tax laws appears to depend more than any other variable in Poland on whether one trusts the government – which in Poland's system of government directs, leads and bears the most direct responsibility for policy making in the country (as opposed to the president or the parliament at large). The other proxy variables for the main theories tested were not that significant, and hence do not appear in Table 6.1 for Poland. Noticeably and peculiarly, trust in other citizens is not significant.

Poland 2010 As Appendix IV also illustrates, the logit regression suggests that six years later the Polish public did react to the deterrence measures taken by the state in balance with a number of other variables that assess 'trust in the state', both at the higher and lower levels in the state, measured either individually (Versions 1 and 2) or as part of a Trust Scale (Versions 3 and 4). (Versions 3 and 4 are, perhaps, a more complete assessment of Trust in the State, as they encompass a variety of trust questions regarding one's view of the state at large and is comparable with regressions undertaken in the 2005 Ukraine, 2010 Russia and 2010 Ukraine surveys, but as some of these questions were not asked in 2004, Versions 1 and 2 are provided to make possible a comparison between the 2004 and 2010 Poland surveys.) Collectively these 'trust in the state' variables – either the measurements for trust in the president or the parliament or those for the Trust in the State scale of seven variables and the separately measured trust/distrust of tax bureaucrats – do have greater substantive impact on one's willingness to obey tax laws than the deterrence measure alone. As before, prior contact with tax bureaucrats

---

[22] The substantive effects presented in Appendices IV, V, VI and VII contain an indicator of statistical significance but no standard errors. While it is not possible to calculate a probability distribution of a first difference, we can simulate this distribution using stochastic simulation as described in King, Tomz and Wittenberg. Therefore, instead of calculating one estimate of each first difference, 1,000 estimates of the first difference are calculated using the program Clarify, Version 2.1, Tomz, Wittenberg and King, 5 January 2003. The value listed for the substantive effect is the mean of those simulations. To provide a measure of uncertainty in deriving the substantive effects, the p-value is estimated by the proportion of simulations that are greater (or less, if the mean is negative) than zero. So $p \leq 0.01$ means that at least 990 of the simulations were greater than zero for a positive variable, $p \leq 0.05$ means at least 950, etc. One article that employs such a method of estimating substantive effects is Markowski and Tucker, 2005.

Table 6.1 *Citizens, subjects and slackers: Substantive effects that are significant in the Poland, Russia and Ukraine 2004–2005 Taxpayer Compliance Attitudinal Surveys*

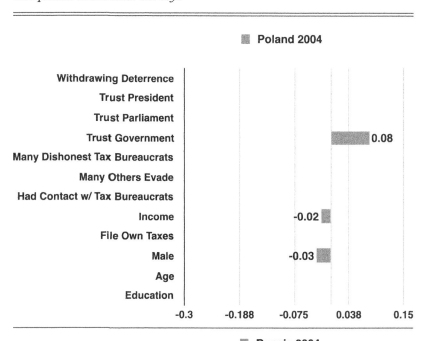

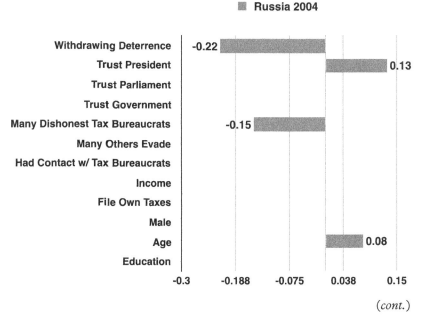

(*cont.*)

Table 6.1 (cont.)

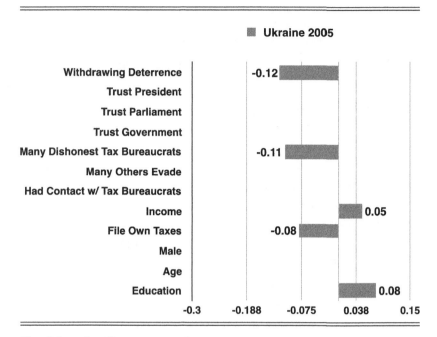

Note: Substantive effects possess *p*-values ≤ 0.05.

does not appear to matter significantly. Moreover, being male again is shown to be significant, as now is education.

Hence, as shown in Appendix IV, the variables that together have the most significance in both the Polish 2004 and 2010 surveys were the proxy variables for 'quasi-voluntary compliance'. By and large, obeying tax laws even if they are considered unfair appears to depend more than any other variable in Poland on whether one trusts the state. Therefore, if, as has been shown in the first part of this chapter, the Polish polity is viewed as more compliant with respect to taxes, it might very well be because the Polish state has maintained some degree of trust with its citizens that it will continue to fulfil a significant proportion of its obligations to its citizens to ensure that life will be still be better – despite voter apathy, corruption scandals and the rapidly changing nature of the Polish political party system.

One of the implicit assumptions regarding these countries is that Poland, unlike its eastern neighbours, has developed a civil society that possesses citizens who are more politically active and demand greater

Citizens, Subjects and Slackers and Paying Taxes   213

openness and transparency on the part of the state. This is deemed to have come about, in significant part, due to the historical role the Catholic Church played in the Polish People's Republic and its collapse in 1989. Once a regime established by outside forces met its demise and a new state was built by, for and of Poles, citizens then could place greater trust in their state, allowing development of the particular type of civil society that is, perhaps, familiar in more consolidated democracies. As such, this greater trust in the state aids societal compliance.

Russia 2004 As for the results of regression analysis of the Russian 2004 survey, shown in Appendix V, the contrast with the Polish 2004 and 2010 survey results is quite striking. The logit regression provides evidence to suggest that deterrence theory does hold significant weight among the Russian public. Meanwhile, the theory of 'quasi-voluntary compliance' appears to be applicable in part, as proxy variables for trust in the president but not for trust in other citizens are quite significant. As for prior contact, it was not very significant in the regression, although it was somewhat close to significance. (The p value was 0.166.) Additionally, age seems to be significant. Like prior contact, possessing high education was not very significant in the regression, but its substantive effect picks up slight significance. Interestingly, income has no effect at all in Russia, while having filed one's taxes oneself only has slight significance (the p value was 0.193).[23]

For Russia, the independent variable with the largest 'substantive effect', as shown in Table 6.1, is the proxy variable for the deterrence theory. However, somewhat close behind with respect to size of 'substantive effect' are several of the variables that are part of the 'quasi-voluntary compliance' theory, such as, among others, trust in the president and distrust in tax bureaucrats, suggesting that Russian tax compliance may very well hinge somewhat on the degree to which citizens trust the state.

Russia 2010 Six years farther along into the Putin-Medvedev era of governance, Russians show that they are no more supportive of obeying tax laws even if they find them to be unfair. The logit regression shows that the deterrence proxy variable continues to hold significant weight among the Russian public. Meanwhile, the theory of 'quasi-voluntary compliance' is applicable, as proxy variables for trust in Putin

---

[23] As income and education variables do possess some strong relations to one another, additional regressions were run to show whether income would matter if education were dropped out (it did not) and to see whether possessing high education would still matter without including income (it did and became stronger.)

214   Taxes and Trust

(as prime minister, this time), trust in the State Duma and trust in tax bureaucrats are quite significant (Versions 1, 2, 5 and 6). A 'trust in the state' scale, composed of five questions, also was found to be quite significant in a separate regression (Versions 7 and 8).

However, what is interesting to note is that (in Versions 5 and 6) trust in the president (Medvedev in 2010) now appears to have the opposite sign from 2004. That is, the more one trusts Medvedev, the more one is less likely to support complying with tax laws with which one disagrees. Having had prior contact was not that significant in the regression, nor was filing taxes oneself.

In 2010, the independent variables with significant substantive effects are the proxy variable for the deterrence theory and those for the theory of quasi-voluntary compliance. Unlike in 2004, the deterrence variable, while sizeable, is smaller than that the variable for trust at the bottom of the state system (the tax bureaucrats). In short, when the 2004 and 2010 Russian surveys are compared, what has really changed – besides the change in the effect of trust in the new Russian president – is that the coercive threat of the state does not have as strong an effect as before. This raises the question of whether the Russian state is 'feared' just a bit less than earlier in the Putin era.

Further, with respect to socio-economic variables, the Polish 2004 and Russian 2010 surveys also give support to the theory, derived from the study of tax compliance in the United States, that men are less compliant than women. In Russia 2010, being male meant that, other things being equal, you were nearly 4 per cent less likely to state that you would obey tax laws. The 2010 Russian survey also showed that the older you are, the more likely you were to state that you would be compliant.

Ukraine 2005 Although Ukrainians in 2005 appear to have somewhat lower levels of support for tax compliance than Russians, the results from the regression analysis examining why Ukrainians support obeying a tax law even if it is personally deemed unfair suggest that Ukrainians are influenced almost equally by their reactions to the state's deterrent measures and by their own trust in government. With respect to the three main theories on how citizens respond to state efforts to increase tax compliance, two sets of variables stand out as strongly significant and nearly as great in terms of 'substantive effect'.

Table 6.1 illustrates that alternating the proxy variable for the deterrence theory (whether one would respond to relaxation of the coercive threat to pay) from its lowest to its highest values while maintaining the other independent variables at their means decreases the likelihood that a Ukrainian respondent would state that he or she would obey tax laws by about 12 per cent. Meanwhile, as is shown in Appendix VI, alternating the trust in state scale variable from its lowest to its highest values increases the likelihood of saying that one would obey such a law by 2 per cent. Similarly, distrusting tax bureaucrats decreases the likelihood of stating that one would obey tax laws by 9 to 11 per cent (depending on whether the Trust in the State scale is used in the regression). Hence, such numbers indicate that unlike Poland in 2004, deterrent measures do matter and unlike Russia in 2004, trusting government matters nearly as much.

Interestingly, like the Polish 2004 and 2010 and the Russian 2004 surveys, the secondary type of trust that is part of the theory of quasi-voluntary compliance, trust in other citizens to pay their taxes, does not matter at all for Ukrainians in 2005. This suggests that, for the most part, Poles, Russians and Ukrainians do not place themselves in relation to others in society when deciding whether to agree to obey a tax law even if it is personally deemed unfair and that citizens of all three countries do not respond as 'rationally' in terms of estimating whether the state has enough tax revenue from others to be able to deliver goods and services back to its citizens.

Having had any previous contact with tax bureaucrats, regardless of whether the interaction was good or bad, does not appear to have any impact whatsoever on whether Ukrainians state that they would obey a tax law that they personally deem to be unfair.

With respect to the socio-economic variables tested, whether or not one files one's own taxes appears to be significant but has a negative sign, suggesting that those who file their own taxes in 2005 are less likely to be observant of tax laws than those who do not. Also, education appears to be significant. As in Poland in 2004, levels of income matter with respect to tax compliance attitudes in Ukraine. However, unlike the case with Poles, the higher the income of Ukrainians, the more likely they are to agree to obey tax laws. This finding conflicts with some theories from the study of tax compliance patterns in the United States, but suggests that wealthier individuals in Ukraine can afford to pay their taxes. Curiously, while those with more income in Ukraine might be more likely to pay taxes in Ukraine themselves, those who stated that they do file taxes on their own actually are less likely to state that they would obey tax laws even if they considered them unfair. As for education, the findings are more consistent with the Russian 2004 case than with the Polish one – that is, lower levels of education correspond with lower levels of support for tax compliance.

Overall, the mixed nature of the survey results in Ukraine for 2005 – that is, the fact that proxy variables for reacting to state deterrence and

216   Taxes and Trust

for trusting the state matter with respect to attitudinal support for tax compliance in near equal amounts – does suggest that Ukraine does not strictly follow the pattern of either Poland or Russia. Poland appears to be a case that possesses a compliant society interacting with a citizen-based state such that tax compliance depends largely on trust in the government. Russia, on the other hand, has a society interacting with a state that strongly employs a deterrence-based approach to tax collection, where the significance of the effect of coercive measures is still strong in 2010, albeit with perhaps a bit smaller effect.

Ukraine is a different case altogether. The employment of deterrence – perhaps to an extent that is not as great as in Russia – is the state's primary tool for ensuring tax compliance through the State Tax Administration of Ukraine. Yet the greater freedom of information on the shortcomings of the state and its political leaders in Ukraine in November 2005 might have allowed Ukrainians as a whole to balance their support for tax compliance between reactions to deterrent measures of the state and their trust in the state. The fact that deterrent force might not be as great in Ukraine as in Russia might be due to the fact that in late 2005, when the poll took place, Ukrainians were better informed about their state's government and politics. (In addition, it has been suggested by several experts in Kyiv that the dynamic of corruption on the part of state workers changed after an Orange Revolution 'honeymoon' period from January through August 2005, increasing around the time of Yulia Tymoshenko's dismissal as Prime Minister in September 2005, if not a bit before.[24])

Moreover, the fact that Ukrainians might not be as trusting of their state as Poles are of theirs might account for the fact that Ukraine had the lowest rate of support for obeying a tax law deemed unfair among the three states surveyed. Indeed, as Questions #55 and #56 in Appendix I illustrate, only 9 per cent of Ukrainians in 2005 feel that the government fulfils its obligations to its citizens, and similarly, only 9 per cent of Ukrainians agree that their government can be trusted to do what is right. Clearly, Ukraine's post-Orange transition from a coercive and corrupt state to a more open, democratic one has come about without rebuilding citizens' trust that their state can act fairly and can deliver goods and services, and the failure to create and draw upon such trust may very well curtail the state's capacity to administer its own policies.

---

[24] Interview with Igor Lavrinenko, Centre for Political and Legal Reforms, Kyiv, 24 July 2006; and interview with a director at an international business association, Kyiv, 8 August 2006.

As shown in Table 6.1, the substantive effects from the analysis of the first, basic surveys from 2004–2005 suggest that the three cases can be labelled 'Citizens, Subjects and Slackers' in terms of the citizen–state tax relationship. Ukrainians acted neither as true 'citizens' (i.e., out of trust, like the Poles) nor as 'subjects' of their state (i.e., out of fear, like the Russians), but rather sought to avoid interacting with their state altogether, as tax 'slackers'.[25] That is, Poles in 2004, who possessed a high willingness to obey the tax laws, reacted more out of trust towards government when expressing support for obeying tax laws even if they disagreed with them. Russians in 2004 showed that their fear of being caught had more of an effect on their willingness to obey tax laws than their trust in the state. And, Ukrainians, with effects for trust and fear in balance coupled with low levels of support for obeying tax laws even if they are deemed unfair, can be termed 'slackers' with respect to observing tax dues.

Ukraine 2010 The big story for the Ukraine 2010 survey is, as for Russia, that trust variables matter more than they did in the earlier survey, but unlike the case in Russia, deterrence matters far less. As shown in Appendix IV, alternating the proxy variable for the deterrence theory (whether one would be respond to the relaxation of the coercive threat to pay) from its lowest to its highest values while maintaining the other independent variables at their means decreases the likelihood that a Ukrainian respondent would state that she or he would obey tax laws even if deemed unfair by about 3 per cent. Meanwhile, alternating the 'trust in the state' variable (Versions 3 and 4) from its lowest to its highest values increases the likelihood of saying that one would obey such a law by 8 per cent. (Trust in the government and trust in the parliament, when shown separately in Versions 1 and 2, have somewhat high levels of predicted likelihood as well.) Similarly, distrusting tax bureaucrats decreases the likelihood of stating that one would obey tax laws by 10–11 per cent, nearly identical to the decrease in 2005.

Hence, five years after the Orange Revolution, the 2010 Ukraine survey indicates that trusting the state may matter the most when it comes to explaining why Ukrainians continue to demonstrate the lowest levels of support for paying taxes among citizens in all three countries.

---

[25] It is important to emphasize that the selection of the term 'slackers' is applied to Ukrainians only within the context of taxpaying and does not imply in any way that Ukrainians 'slack' in any other particular sphere of activity; moreover, given their environment and state–society relations, it may even be considered to be quite 'rational' on an individual-level basis for Ukrainians to 'slack' in the area of tax compliance at different points in time.

218   Taxes and Trust

Ukraine 2015 Some twenty months after the EuroMaidan revolution, the Ukrainian public, perhaps due to the departure of Yanukovych's regime, appears to be reacting out of trust concerns as demonstrated by strong substantive effects in the logit regression. Namely, while taking away the deterrent threat completely may make Ukrainians 9–10 per cent less likely to state that they would obey tax laws, altering trust in Poroshenko from its lowest to its highest levels has a larger impact of 18 per cent. Distrusting the tax bureaucrats in 2015 also made Ukrainians 10–11 per cent less likely to obey the tax laws. Additionally, distrusting other taxpayers by confirming that many people evade taxes has an almost equal impact of 17–18 per cent, but the effect is positive – quite the opposite of what Margaret Levi would predict. That is, the more Ukrainians in 2015 recognized that others evade taxes, the more likely they were to state that they themselves would be compliant. This phenomenon did not occur in any of the other surveys, and is, perhaps, due to a desire on the part of Ukrainians in 2015 to distinguish oneself as being and behaving differently from perceived lawlessness and improper behaviour elsewhere. Finally, while filing one's own taxes appears to have no effect, having more income and being older were factors associated with a greater willingness to obey.

Why Focus on Individual Attitudes and Not Those of Businesses? Before moving on, it is important to observe that the results from the analysis of these surveys likely would not have been much different if these respondents were solely managers, business owners, individuals who file taxes themselves (because they have more than one source of income or more complicated tax returns) and/or individuals who interact with tax bureaucrats (even if most Russians and Ukrainians, at least, do not.) While conducting a survey of business attitudes (or especially of the attitudes of those within businesses that are directly responsible for the paying of taxes) in transition environments is especially challenging, as mentioned in Chapter 4, these public opinion surveys actually do include the attitudes of those in business in Poland, Russia and Ukraine.

Moreover, three questions included in the analysis highlight factors attributable to those in business. Namely, the survey – and the logit regressions analyzed above – did ask respondents whether they were a company director, top manager or entrepreneur or not (highlighted in the variable 'occupation'); whether they have had previous contact with tax bureaucrats (more common for those involved in business than ordinary citizens); and whether they filed their taxes themselves (rather than had their employer do so for them, which is more common for employees than it is for entrepreneurs or executives).

Citizens, Subjects and Slackers and Paying Taxes 219

In none of the eight surveys was 'occupation' deemed to be significant at $p \leq 0.10$, either in the logit regression or as shown by the p-values for the substantive effects, although one, but not all, of the Ukraine 2005 regressions (Version 4 in Appendix VI) did have some slight negative significance. (If significant, for those Ukrainians with higher-status jobs, the likelihood that one would obey tax laws deemed unfair decreases about 6 per cent.) Having had previous contact with the tax bureaucrats also never appeared to be significant in any logit regression at $p \leq 0.01$, $p \leq 0.05$ or $p \leq 0.10$, although the substantive effects for having had prior contact did pick up slight significance at $p \leq 0.10$, a broader confidence interval, for some versions of the Russia 2004 and 2010 and the Ukraine 2010 regressions.

Similarly, filing one's own taxes was not a significant factor in any of the Polish and Russian survey regressions, but substantive effects for this variable did pick up similar slight significance at $p \leq 0.10$ in the Polish 2010 and Russian 2004 regressions. Where filing one's own taxes mattered significantly was in the Ukraine 2005 and 2010 surveys (but not in the 2015 survey). In these cases, the influence was negative – that is, the more Ukrainians were likely to have filed their own taxes, the less likely they were to state that they would comply with tax laws even if considered unfair. Further, the size of the substantive effect for this variable was smaller than for others that were significant – especially in the 2010 survey. Hence, for these years, needing to file one's own taxes was associated with even less willingness to obey than the already low levels offered by Ukrainian respondents as a whole (36 and 44 per cent in 2005 and 2010).

Thus, with respect to the dependent variable in question, the level of support for obeying tax laws expressed by individuals who share 'business-like' factors appears to be broadly similar to the level of the public at large across all eight surveys, with the slight possibility that the support for tax compliance might even be a bit lower than for the general public in 2005 and 2010 in Ukraine.

Finally, as other socio-economic variables were selected as control variables based on their significance in explaining taxpayer compliance, largely in US studies, it is important to observe that none of these additional variables uniformly had influence or lacked influence in the Polish, Russian and Ukrainian surveys. With respect to income, having more income was correlated with less willingness to obey tax laws in Poland in 2004, but not in 2010; had no effect in either Russian survey; and was associated with greater willingness to obey in Ukraine in 2005 and 2015, but not in 2010. This finding does not, therefore, help resolve the question of whether wealthier taxpayers are more willing to be compliant (because they have more money to offer the state) or less

220   Taxes and Trust

willing to be compliant (because they are more reluctant to relinquish money the more they acquire it).

Being male made one less likely to support tax compliance in Poland in 2004 and 2010 and in Russia in 2010, but had no effect in Ukraine in any year. Such results suggest that men are unlikely to be more supportive of tax compliance than women, but do not definitively find that they are always less likely to be supportive of compliance. Being older was associated with less willingness to comply in Poland only in 2010, but had a positive effect on supporting compliance in Russia in 2004 and 2010 and in Ukraine in 2015, with no effect in other years. Education also produced mixed results, with the more educated possibly being willing to support tax compliance more in 2004 in both Poland and Russia and in 2005 in Ukraine. Being more educated, however, was associated with less support for compliance in Poland in 2010 and had no effect in other years. Hence, with respect to other socio-economic variables, the Taxpayer Compliance Attitudinal Surveys only give support to the theory that men are likely to be less supportive of compliance than women.

Testing Tyler's Theory for Those Who Had Prior Encounters with Tax Bureaucrats

Some of the questions for the Taxpayer Compliance Attitudinal Surveys are adaptations of survey questions used by Tom Tyler in his book *Why People Obey the Law*, which argues that the procedural aspects (conduct of the government officials) of prior previous experiences with the law affect citizen views of the legitimacy of the authorities, which in turn affect the degree of compliance. Likewise, in the survey questions developed for Poland, Russia and Ukraine, inquiries are made not only as to what the citizens' views are with respect to why people pay taxes but also about their previous experiences with the tax authorities and personal assessments of the tax administration's work.[26]

---

[26] Tyler measures support for legitimacy in two ways: as the perceived obligation to obey the law and as support for legal authorities. Perceived obligation to obey the law was measured as the percent of people who agreed that 'a person should obey the law even if it goes against what they think is right' and other such statements. (See, especially, Tyler, pp. 40–56.) Such a measure of legitimacy, at least with respect to perceived obligation, is very similar to the dependent variable selected here in this chapter's analysis of attitudes towards tax compliance regarding whether one would obey tax laws even if they were perceived personally to be unfair. As mentioned earlier, a direct measure of compliance (i.e., did you pay your taxes?), or preferably, an outside assessment of whether taxes were paid in full, is not presented here. Hence, the dependent variable selected is an attitudinal proxy for tax compliance. While it would be enormously helpful and ideal to have a separate measure of compliance, for now, the measure chosen, which does shares

Citizens, Subjects and Slackers and Paying Taxes 221

In the 2004–2005 Taxpayer Compliance Attitudinal Surveys, 470 Poles – practically half of all those surveyed in Poland; 410 Russians – about a quarter of all surveyed in Russia; and 583 Ukrainians – about 15 per cent of all polled in Ukraine – had contact with members of the tax administration during the previous five years. In 2010, 760 Poles – 38 per cent of those surveyed, 707 Russians – still just a quarter of all surveyed, and 489 Ukrainians – about 12 per cent of those surveyed – stated that they had contact with tax bureaucrats. Meanwhile, in 2012, 232 Ukrainians – 11 per cent of those surveyed – and, in 2015, 746 Ukrainians – 15 per cent of those surveyed – stated that they had met with tax officials.

What is interesting is when specific close tests are undertaken of the two Tyler specific variables (Conduct and Result) to establish whether it is the judgements about the justice or injustice of past experiences – the procedures and/or the outcomes of these experiences – that influence attitudes towards tax compliance. Question #9 in Appendix I asks respondents who had prior contact with the tax administration whether or not they were satisfied by how the tax service employees spoke with and treated them. Similarly, Question #8 inquired whether respondents were satisfied with the results of their meetings with tax service employees.

A closer examination of the interaction of the responses to these questions is provided in Table 6.2, which presents charts of the percentages of those who stated that they would obey tax laws deemed unfair. In the Poland 2004 case, any combination of being satisfied or unsatisfied with respect to Conduct or Result does not seem to impact whether one would obey tax laws even if one considered them unfair. (Indeed, the percentages of those who would obey in the different boxes of the table vary only from 88 to 96 per cent.) Meanwhile, the Russian 2004 survey yields entirely different results. For Russians, in 2004, if one is satisfied with either Conduct or Result or with both, then the percentages of those who would obey tax laws is about the same (72 to 76 per cent.) However, if one is dissatisfied with both the Conduct and the Result, the percentage of those who would obey drops down to 56 per cent.

For the Russia 2004 survey, it appears that it is the interaction of bad Conduct and bad Result that depresses compliance. (In contrast, in Poland, bureaucratic conduct may be important to taxpayers, but does appear to affect attitudes towards compliance.) Satisfaction with

a great deal with Tyler's concept of legitimacy, will have to do. Thus, due to the lack of a direct measure of compliance, a true, two-step model approach replicating Tyler exactly cannot be followed for now.

222   Taxes and Trust

Table 6.2 *Taxpayer Compliance Attitudinal Surveys: Percentage of prior tax bureaucrat contact respondents who would follow the tax laws even if personally considered to be unfair*

		Poland 2004 Taxpayer Compliance Attitudinal Survey	
		Were You Satisfied with the Result of Your Contact with the Tax Bureaucrats?	
		No	Yes
Were You Satisfied with the Conduct of the Tax Bureaucrats?	No	96% $N = 79$	88% $N = 25$
	Yes	93% $N = 29$	94% $N = 330$

		Poland 2010 Taxpayer Compliance Attitudinal Survey	
		Were You Satisfied with the Result of Your Contact with the Tax Bureaucrats?	
		No	Yes
Were You Satisfied with the Conduct of the Tax Bureaucrats?	No	74% $N = 84$	87% $N = 68$
	Yes	83% $N = 36$	85% $N = 500$

		Russia 2004 Taxpayer Compliance Attitudinal Survey	
		Were You Satisfied with the Result of Your Contact with the Tax Bureaucrats?	
		No	Yes
Were You Satisfied with the Conduct of the Tax Bureaucrats?	No	56% $N = 95$	76% $N = 25$
	Yes	72% $N = 29$	75% $N = 213$

		Russia 2010 Taxpayer Compliance Attitudinal Survey	
		Were You Satisfied with the Result of Your Contact with the Tax Bureaucrats?	
		No	Yes
Were You Satisfied with the Conduct of the Tax Bureaucrats?	No	63% $N = 135$	63% $N = 43$
	Yes	66% $N = 50$	68% $N = 364$

Citizens, Subjects and Slackers and Paying Taxes 223

Table 6.2 (cont.)

Ukraine 2005 Taxpayer Compliance Attitudinal Survey

		Were You Satisfied with the Result of Your Contact with the Tax Bureaucrats?	
		No	Yes
Were You Satisfied with the Conduct of the Tax Bureaucrats?	No	45% $N = 154$	42% $N = 31$
	Yes	42% $N = 31$	51% $N = 184$

Ukraine 2010 Taxpayer Compliance Attitudinal Survey

		Were You Satisfied with the Result of Your Contact with the Tax Bureaucrats?	
		No	Yes
Were You Satisfied with the Conduct of the Tax Bureaucrats?	No	42% $N = 137$	56% $N = 25$
	Yes	55% $N = 33$	54% $N = 187$

Ukraine 2012 Taxpayer Compliance Attitudinal Survey

		Were You Satisfied with the Result of Your Contact with the Tax Bureaucrats?	
		No	Yes
Were You Satisfied with the Conduct of the Tax Bureaucrats?	No	33% $N = 58$	40% $N = 12$
	Yes	67% $N = 12$	59% $N = 96$

Ukraine 2015 Taxpayer Compliance Attitudinal Survey

		Were You Satisfied with the Result of Your Contact with the Tax Bureaucrats?	
		No	Yes
Were You Satisfied with the Conduct of the Tax Bureaucrats?	No	48% $N = 242$	59% $N = 32$
	Yes	50% $N = 42$	70% $N = 284$

224   Taxes and Trust

Conduct is important. But how important depends upon its interaction with another variable (Result). As Tyler delineated, there are, indeed, two types of negative experiences associated with contact with the law. Attitudes towards tax compliance when Result is negative, or unsatisfactory, can be significantly affected by what Conduct is. Hence, in the Russian 2004 case, for those who had such prior contact with the tax administration, it is the interaction of Conduct and Result that makes a difference.

The Poland 2010 and Ukraine 2010 surveys follow a similar, albeit less pronounced, pattern. That is, for Poles, in 2010, of those who are satisfied with either Conduct or Result or with both, the percentages of those who would obey tax laws even if deemed unfair is about the same (83 to 87 per cent.) However, of those dissatisfied with both the Conduct and the Result, the percentage who would obey drops to 74 per cent. For Ukrainians, in 2010, the corresponding figures were 54 to 56 per cent of those who would obey tax laws if they were satisfied with the Conduct or Result or both, dropping to 42 per cent if they were dissatisfied with both Conduct and Result.

The patterns with the Russians in 2010 and the Ukrainians in 2005 are relatively flat, and it is difficult to discern significant differences. However, what differences there are illustrate that if the 2005 sample of Ukrainians and the 2010 group of Russians are satisfied with both Conduct and Result, they are a bit more likely to obey tax laws, whereas if they are dissatisfied with Conduct, with Result or with both, the percentage who would obey drops a bit. This would imply that tax officials would have to offer *both* satisfying Results *and* satisfactory Conduct when interacting with Ukrainians and Russians today in order to raise levels of taxpayer compliance – a greater burden to hurdle than that of the Polish tax administrations. Further, it is also interesting to note that Russians who *are dissatisfied* with both Conduct and Result still respond favourably to obeying the tax laws to a greater extent (56 per cent in 2004 and 63 per cent in 2010) than of those Ukrainians who *are satisfied* with both Conduct and Result in the 2005 and 2010 surveys (51 and 54 per cent, respectively.)

In the much smaller 2012 Ukraine survey, fewer respondents answered these questions with respect to prior tax bureaucrat interaction. Nevertheless, the survey marked the first time that Ukrainians with positive prior experiences expressed a willingness to obey that was higher than that of the Russians who were dissatisfied with both Conduct and Result in 2004. Moreover, the percentage of Ukrainians who stated that they would obey tax laws even if deemed unfair after having experienced both unsatisfying Conduct and Result was the lowest – 33 per cent.

Citizens, Subjects and Slackers and Paying Taxes 225

Finally, the 2015 survey strongly shows that Ukrainians who are satisfied with both how they are treated and the result of meeting a tax bureaucrat will be much more likely than not to obey tax laws even if they are personally considered unfair.

Why Ukrainians Who Pay Taxes Choose to Be Compliant

The blatantly transparent schemes whereby Ukrainians attempt to avoid taxes have amazed the Western executives who work in the country. One foreign lawyer was stunned to learn that a car dealer would opt for a 'power of attorney' document instead of taking title on a U.S.$80,000 vehicle that was being traded to him in order to avoid paying a tax of 1,000 hryvnia (U.S.$200) on the title ownership.[27] There is also a wide perception that more salaries are paid in envelopes under the table in Ukraine than in Russia.[28]

Some have surmised that less fear of the state, compared with that in Russia, has existed in Ukraine since the start of the 1990s, in large measure due to a general weakness of the state and the disorganization of policies from the start of the transition to democracy. More recently, during the prolonged period from March to August 2006, when a new government coalition had yet to appear, there was a decrease in the functioning of the tax system because of great uncertainty as to what policies would emerge from rapidly changing but indefinite political developments and the lack of political will to implement current policy in general.[29] In addition, the greater lack of faith in the government than in other post-communist states may also be due in part to the fact that Ukraine has lacked an 'imperial mentality', which has contributed to a lack of desire on the part of Ukrainians for their state to be 'great' and 'strong'.[30] Further, Ukrainians are said to have a more deeply held belief that they should try to solve their own problems without the help of the state and judge for themselves what is fair and reasonable rather than accept the state's word on obligations of citizenship.[31] Indeed, the

---

[27] Author's interview with partner, tax and legal services, leading international accounting firm, Kyiv, 27 July 2006.
[28] Author's interview with Valeriy Kochetov, director, National Centre of Monitoring of Compliance and Defence of the Constitutional Rights and Basic Freedoms of People, Kyiv, 26 July 2006.
[29] Author's interview with senior partner, leading local tax and legal firm, Kyiv, 3 August 2006.
[30] Author's interview with Kochetov.
[31] Author's interviews with senior STA official and with partner, tax and legal services, leading international accounting firm, Kyiv, 2 August 2006; and with senior partner, leading local tax and legal firm, Kyiv, 3 August 2006.

226   Taxes and Trust

findings on Ukraine tax compliance correlate with an observation of John Lough and Iryna Solonenko, who remarked that, 'In contrast to their counterparts, Ukrainians do not have a historical experience of successful identification with the state despite depending on it. As a result, they tend to distrust the government and seek ways to work around it.'[32]

Just as those who evade taxes do so without fear of the state, in many ways, those who do comply with the state do so without regard for what the state does or does not do. Some tax lawyers argue that Ukrainian firms are today more likely to comply not out of either fear of or trust in the state but because of external competitive pressures. These pressures include the need to gain access to capital markets abroad in order to find foreign investors, which before investing will hire auditors to verify that a Ukrainian firm has its accounts in order.[33] Additionally, local banks require proof of income earned officially from their clients who wish to take out loans and receive financing for cars and mortgages, providing a further incentive for firms to place everything on their books.[34] Others have attributed post–Orange Revolution increases in tax compliance not to any changes in the STA's interaction with the public but to amendments in tax legislation that have led to decreases in tax rates.[35] Finally, the trust that has existed in the state, as one tax lawyer surmised, has been due to a trust that things will get better in the future, that better laws will be adopted, and that the state will be more responsive to its citizens.[36] Hence, in the opinions of those who work with leading firms in Ukraine, neither a stick nor a carrot provided by the state is the underlying motivating factor that influences decisions by companies to comply with the tax laws. One local tax lawyer has summed up the state's relationship with society in the arena of tax collection as 'not so much *strakh*, but *bezsyllya*' ('not fear, but impotence').[37]

Conclusion

A strong belief in the limitations of duties to the state and a firm trust in the government seem to suggest that in both 2004 and 2010 Poles are

---

[32] Lough and Solonenko, p. 13.
[33] Author's interviews with partner, tax and legal services, leading international accounting firm, Kyiv, 27 July 2006; and with partner, tax and legal services, leading international accounting firm, Kyiv, 1 August 2006.
[34] Author's interview with partner, tax and legal services, leading international accounting firm, Kyiv, 1 August 2006.
[35] Author's interview with tax manager, Kyiv office of one of the Big Four international accounting firms, Kyiv, 26 July 2006.
[36] Ibid.
[37] Author's interview with partner, tax and legal services, leading international accounting firm, Kyiv, 2 August 2006.

Citizens, Subjects and Slackers and Paying Taxes 227

paying their taxes out of notions consistent in part with quasi-voluntary compliance.

With respect to Russia and Ukraine, there is support within the analysis of the Taxpayer Compliance Attitudinal Surveys for at least two of the three main theories of tax compliance discussed here, suggesting a much more complicated path towards becoming citizens. Russians appear to have reacted significantly to the 'deterrence' method of tax collecting in 2004 and continue to react more strongly to the 'deterrence' method than Poles and Ukrainians in 2010. The fact that citizens are susceptible to deterrence in Russia is indicative of a society interacting with a relatively more deterrent-based approach to tax collection. Russians may actually react more to deterrent measures – or to the removal of such measures – when it comes to shaping their attitudes as to whether to comply with their state's tax laws. This scenario, though, becomes a bit more complex for Russia as the Putin era progresses, with overall support for tax compliance appearing to be identical to that in 2004, but with deterrence having less of an impact than before in motivating those who choose to support compliance. Nevertheless, 'deterrence' still maintains a significant role in motivating Russians to pay.

Meanwhile, the fact that, in the Ukrainian surveys, the 'trust in the state' variables are estimated to predict an increase in the likelihood of expressing attitudes in support of tax compliance about as large as the 'deterrence' proxy variable in 2005 and are significantly more substantive in impact in 2010 and 2015 does suggest that the deterrence efforts of the Ukrainian state may not have had as strong an impact on its populace as those of the Russian state did on its taxpayers earlier on under Putin. Ukrainians' attitudes towards paying taxes are based almost equally on their degree of fear of the state and their lack of trust in it in 2005. And 2010 and 2015 attitudes towards taxes are based almost solely on their lack of trust in the state in those years. Thus, while the legitimacy of the state matters for Poles, Russians and Ukrainians as they begin to fulfil their duties of citizenship by paying their dues, precisely how Russians and Ukrainians as a whole view and comprehend that legitimacy might be more varied and much more complicated than the manner in which the Polish polity views its state.

Therefore, the implications from this research are twofold. First, post-transition governments and their tax administrations must find ways to create and build up levels of trust on the part of citizens in their state. How government behaviour impacts upon societal trust – that is, how the state maximizes or minimizes the levels of trust that society has – will affect, then, how well the state goal of ensuring the public's tax compliance is accomplished. And, second, these governments and tax administrations must also emphasize 'procedural fairness' in order to improve compliance with state regulations. Good 'customer service' can make a real difference.

The survey of Russian tax officials that was undertaken in the fall of 2011 reveals that, in many ways, tax officials share similar attitudes towards taxes, the tax system and the state to those of Russian citizens, highlighting how even those working in the tax system must be aware of such trust issues and the need to emphasize good 'customer service'. Namely, as shown in survey Questions #21 and 22 in Appendix I, like their citizen counterparts, Russian tax officials are more solidly behind supporting the notion that citizens should follow the tax laws than they are in upholding the view that they themselves should do so (91 versus 75 per cent). Moreover, only 47 per cent of Russian tax officials agreed that the state fulfils its obligations to its citizens (Question #55), 50 per cent can trust their state to do what is right (Question #56), some 23 per cent (with 7 per cent declining to reply) stated that if the state does not fulfil its obligations to its citizens then tax evasion is justified (Question #28), and 51 per cent stated that the state treats all citizens equally fairly (Question #57). While the numbers differ from those for citizens, many officials appear to have a trust gap with the state themselves. Further, more than one in five recognized that if an enterprise were to follow all the demands of the tax organs then it would be ruined (Question #2, in Appendix II) and about a third of all tax officials stated that inspectors were unable to catch out all who fail to comply (Question #3, in Appendix II), indicating that there may be some uncertainties as to how the system treats citizens in practice.

But how can states accomplish the two policy objectives – to build up trust and to emphasize 'procedural fairness'? Specific suggestions are offered in Chapter 8. In general, though, the post-transition tax administrations should look for ways to rationalize their bureaucracies and to make them more society- and outward-oriented. Locating and implementing policies that both build levels of public trust in the state and increase the level of customer service provided by the tax administration personnel can help taxpayers become true citizens, who are capable of fulfilling their obligations to their governments.

7 All Together?
Lack of Trust in the Tax State Unifies Ukraine

The post-communist transition began with a large state–society disconnect. In the aftermath of the 1989 and 1991 revolutions, societies across the region shared a deep disillusionment with their bureaucratic states, now viewed as dishonest and untrustworthy.[1] At a time in which much was required of both state and society, such inherited distrust of the state on the part of society made the tasks at hand more difficult. And, nowhere, perhaps, were they more difficult than in Ukraine.

Ukraine, which demonstrates the lowest support for paying taxes in the Taxpayer Compliance Attitudinal Surveys, becomes a critical case and is the focus of this chapter. The country's regional, linguistic and religious diversity; its location between largely Catholic Poland and Orthodox Russia; and its relatively stable and consistent state institutional structure across the country provide an excellent testing ground for discerning how much religion matters with respect to fulfilling an obligation to the state.

Further, the unique presence of a socio-political cleavage between Ukraine's provinces, some of whose histories trace back to Polish or Russian rule or both, allows a more focused study on how such differences, which are not as easily discernible in Poland or Russia, can make an impact on state–society relations. Similarly to the red–blue state divisions in recent US presidential elections, the provinces of Ukraine in recent years have divided themselves starkly between the 'orange' (or 'yellow') west and the 'blue' east. If attitudes and levels of trust towards the state can vary because of different types of society–state relations, born out of different legacies of civil society traditions and church–state relations, then the Ukraine case, with consistently similar state institutions throughout the country, should illustrate this.

Yet, in additional comparative analysis of different regions of the country, what emerges as surprising, perhaps, is that not only do the respondents from the four main regions of the country – East, West, Centre and

[1] Rose-Ackerman, 2004a, p. 1.

Table 7.1 *Ukraine Taxpayer Compliance Attitudinal Surveys 2005, 2010, 2012 and 2015:*
Question: Would you follow the tax laws even if you do not consider them to be fair?

	Poland	Russia	All of Ukraine	West Ukraine	Far West Ukraine	Central Ukraine	Kyiv Ukraine	East Ukraine	Donbas Ukraine	South Ukraine	Crimea Ukraine
% would obey 2004	83	53									
% would obey 2005			36	36	37	36	47	38	43	32	26
% would obey 2010	77	52	44	43	47	44	50	39	47	49	57
% would obey 2012	na	na	39	33	36	38	43	39	44	39	58
% would obey 2015	na	na	45	46	50	46	44	44	43	39	na

Note: Appendix II: Question #22, percentage of responses.

All Together? Lack of Trust in the Tax State Unifies Ukraine   231

South (not including Crimea) – not differ greatly when it comes to over-all support for obeying tax laws, but the rationale for doing so also does not differ greatly between the otherwise seemingly different eastern and western parts of Ukraine with respect to how deterrence and trust issues impact individual-level decisions to support tax compliance. When they are paired alongside each other, the support for obeying tax laws, even if considered unfair, on the part of the Ukrainian regions is more similar to each other than to either Poland or Russia.

Moreover, what is also striking is the relatively modest, but significant difference in the level of support for tax compliance between Catholics and Slavic Orthodox Ukrainians in 2005, which appears to fade away by 2015. There are noticeable differences between those with different religious backgrounds in the earlier Ukraine Taxpayer Compliance Attitudinal Surveys, but the differences are not great and certainly not nearly as great as those between largely Catholic Poland and mostly Slavic Orthodox Russia. All of this suggests that differing societal and religious beliefs and values regarding state–society interactions do not hold predominant explanatory weight for variations in post-communist state–society interactions. Rather, trust – or lack of trust – in the state appears to matter more across critical Ukraine.

Brief Results for Ukraine Regions

As shown in Table 7.1, when broken down into the different regions of Ukraine, including the main East, West, Central and South divisions,[2] the 2005, 2010, 2012 and 2015 Ukraine Taxpayer Compliance Attitudinal Surveys illustrate that the percentage of those who responded affirmatively to the question 'Would you follow the tax laws even if you do not consider them to be fair?' varies little across the country. And, with the exception of Crimea in 2010 and 2012, such support for obeying the tax laws even if considered unfair is consistently lower than the overall levels of support in Poland and Russia.

---

[2] 'West Ukraine' is represented by Chernovitskaya, Ivano-Frankivsk, Lviv, Rivne, Ternopil, Volnysk, and Zakarpat Oblasts; Central Ukraine by Kyiv (city), Kyiv Oblast, Vinnitsk, Zhitomyr, Kirovograd, Poltava, Suma, Khelmnitskie, Cherkassa, and Chernigovskiye Oblasts; 'East Ukraine' by Dnepropetrovsk, Donetsk, Kharkov, Luhansk and Zaporizhskye Oblasts; and 'South Ukraine' by Kherson, Mykolaev and Odesa Oblasts. The Razumkov Centre, which carried out the survey, divides the country into these four main divisions, although for analysis here I have taken Crimea out of the 'South Ukraine' region. In addition to 'West Ukraine', 'Central Ukraine', 'East Ukraine' and 'South Ukraine', I have also conducted analysis on four additional, smaller regions: 'Far West Ukraine' represented by Ivano-Frankivsk, Lviv, Volnysk and Zakarpat Oblasts; 'Kyiv Ukraine' by Kyiv (city) and Kyiv Oblast; 'Donbas Ukraine' by Donetsk and Luhansk Oblasts; and 'Crimea Ukraine' by the Autonomous Republic of Crimea.

Table 7.2 *Suggestions of minimal tax non-compliance levels in Ukraine regions in 2010, 2012 and 2015**

	Poland	Russia	All of Ukraine	West Ukraine	Far West Ukraine	Central Ukraine	Kyiv Ukraine	East Ukraine	Donbas Ukraine	South Ukraine	Crimea Ukraine
2010	12%	21%	37%	40%	40%	37%	37%	43%	35%	29%	14%
2012	Na	na	42%	46%	42%	49%	53%	40%	39%	26%	27%
2015	Na	na	37%	38%	37%	35%	39%	37%	34%	43%	na

* Percentage of those answering the questions 'Would you follow the tax laws even if you do not consider them to be fair?' and 'Are the tax laws in your country fair?' who answered both negatively.

No Mean Replacement: Not included in the percentage calculations are respondents who did not provide an answer to either one or both of these two questions.

All Together? Lack of Trust in the Tax State Unifies Ukraine   233

As the 2010, 2012 and 2015 surveys also asked respondents, in a separate section of the survey, whether they viewed the tax laws in their country as fair, it is possible to determine what percentage of Ukrainians in each region both found the tax laws to be unfair and stated they would not obey the tax laws even if deemed personally unfair. This provides a suggested minimum level of tax non-compliance in each region, as shown in Table 7.2.

Again, the entire country of Ukraine and the different regional divisions all show much higher support for non-compliance than in Poland and Russia, with the exception of Crimea in 2010. Hence, with respect to attitudinal support for tax compliance, the regions of the country – even in the Far West and Far East – resemble each other much more than emulating bordering Poland and Russia. The country is largely united – in a relatively high lack of support for paying taxes.

Testing the Theories of Taxpayer Compliance on Ukraine's Regions

Ukraine is divided into four main regions to test the significance of residing in Ukraine's western, eastern, central or southern parts. Crimea also is separated out in its own analysis, albeit with a large caveat regarding the number of respondents in the surveys there. In addition, to assess the impact of two extremes of differing civil society outlooks within the same country, the two Donbas provinces (Donetsk and Luhansk oblasts), which share borders with Russia, and four of the seven western provinces (Lviv, Ivano-Frankivsk, Volynsk and Zakarpatia oblasts), which are the most western oblasts and are located along the western border, are selected as representatives of the far east and far west regions of the country for comparative analysis. (The findings for the larger 'West' versus 'East' parts of the country were largely similar to those for the Far West and Donbas regions, as shown in Appendix VII, but the latter two will be the main focus of analysis for clarity. Additional analysis is also conducted on the Kyiv region as well.)

Far West and Donbas

Western Ukraine strongly supported President Viktor Yushchenko during the 2004 Orange Revolution and President Viktor Yanukovych's ouster during the 2014 EuroMaidan Revolution, and looks towards Poland and the West for future collaboration. Meanwhile, Eastern Ukraine actively supported Yanukovych prior to the 2013–2014 demonstrations, and its Donbas region became involved in a Russia-backed secessionist conflict in mid-2014. Eastern Ukraine is where Russian is

234   Taxes and Trust

most commonly spoken and has strong trade and cultural links to Russia. Most of the country had been under Russian control except for portions of western Ukraine prior to 1945.

Eastern Ukraine has large firms, many of which have been tied to the gas and coal sectors, while Western Ukraine's economy is composed mostly of small and medium-sized businesses. These differences are borne out a bit in the 2010 survey (four years before the Donbas region was partially occupied), where five times more Far West Ukrainians regarded themselves as 'upper class' than Donbas Ukrainians did (1.14 per cent versus 0.21 per cent). Meanwhile, the proportion of respondents who stated that they were enterprise or institution division heads or entrepreneurs was nearly 32 per cent greater in the Far West than in the Donbas (6.08 per cent of Far Westerners considered themselves as such versus 4.62 per cent of Donbas interviewees.) The proportion of respondents who identified themselves as employees or workers (skilled or unskilled) was 28 per cent more in the Donbas than in Far Western Ukraine (30.12 per cent of the Donbas respondents as opposed to 23.57 per cent of the Far West respondents.) However, the proportion of individuals who regarded themselves as agricultural workers or farmers (1.47 per cent of Far Westerners surveyed and 1.20 per cent of Donbas interviewees) and pensioners (27.81 per cent of Far Westerners and 28.51 per cent of Donbas respondents) was more similar.

In comparing the regression analysis of the question regarding whether one would obey tax laws even if personally considered unfair for the selected far eastern oblasts (the two Donbas provinces of Donetsk and Luhansk) with the far western oblasts (Ivano-Frankivisk, Lviv, Volnysk and Zakarpat), as shown under the labels 'Donbas' and 'Far West' in Appendix VII, one finds that the trust variables (trust in the president, parliament and government and distrust in tax bureaucrats) predominate for both groups in the 2005, 2010 and 2015 surveys (except for Far West Ukraine in 2010, when neither deterrence nor trust issues were very significant but previous contact with tax bureaucrats was.) In other words, when all of the independent variables are held even at their means and the proxy variables for trust in the state were individually altered from their lowest levels to their highest levels, the trust variables had much higher substantive effects than the proxy variable for the deterrence-based approach to ensuring tax compliance.[3] Hence, Ukrainians in the far eastern portion of the country (where fewer Catholics live) have the same primary, underlying motivations (the degree of trust in the state) as Poles and western Ukrainians in deciding whether or not

---

[3] On substantive effects, see Chapter 6, Footnotes 21 and 22.

All Together? Lack of Trust in the Tax State Unifies Ukraine 235

Table 7.3 *Ukrainian trust in the state by region*

	All of Ukraine	West Ukraine	Far West Ukraine	Central Ukraine	Kyiv Ukraine	East Ukraine	Donbas Ukraine	South Ukraine	Crimea Ukraine
Does your state/government fulfil its obligations to citizens?									
2005	10%	17%	15%	11%	10%	3%	2%	9%	8%
2010	11%	10%	6%	13%	7%	9%	13%	15%	6%
2015	7%	5%	5%	9%	8%	6%	5%	5%	na
Do you think you can trust your state/government to do what is right?									
2005	10%	18%	14%	12%	13%	3%	2%	7%	6%
2010	11%	7%	5%	11%	7%	12%	21%	16%	2%
2015	7%	6%	6%	10%	9%	5%	3%	6%	na

No Mean Replacement.

to be supportive of tax compliance. Generally speaking, trust is the more important ingredient for compliance with the state in both East and West Ukraine.

And trust in the state was lacking in both Far West and Donbas regions, just not at the same time in 2005 and 2010. In the 2005 survey, the trust divide between the two regions was stark. Some 78 per cent of Far Western Ukrainians trusted Yushchenko versus just 9 per cent in the Donbas. Similarly, 24 per cent of Far Westerners trusted the parliament as opposed to just 5 per cent of those in the Far East Donbas region. And 35 per cent of Far Westerners as opposed to 4 per cent of Donbas respondents trusted the government. Meanwhile, the next survey five years later yielded nearly opposite responses. In 2010, some 58 per cent of Donbas Ukrainians trusted Yanukovych, whereas only 16 per cent of Far Western Ukrainians did. Similarly, 37 per cent of Donbas Ukrainians trusted the parliament versus 7 per cent of Far Westerners, and 45 per cent of individuals in the Donbas trusted the government as opposed to 10 per cent of those in the Far West. (Trust in the tax bureaucrats and in fellow taxpayers was roughly the same across all regions of the country.)

Such a pattern for 2005 and 2010 also is mirrored in how East and West replied to questions regarding whether their state fulfilled its obligations to citizens and whether their state could be trusted to do what is right, as shown in Table 7.3. In replying to both of these questions, the East and particularly the Donbas region show the lowest support for the state in 2005 and among the highest in 2010. Similarly, Western and Far Western Ukrainians show the highest levels of trust in their state fulfilling its obligations and doing what is right in 2005, but among the lowest in 2010.

236   Taxes and Trust

Meanwhile, with a new president, parliament and government, the 2015 survey saw trust in the state similar – and dramatically low – across both the Far West and Far East of the country, as only 18 per cent and a nearly identical 16 per cent of Far Westerners and of Donbas residents, respectively, trusted President Petro Poroshenko. Similarly, trust in the parliament was 5 and 2 per cent in the Far West and Donbas regions, respectively, and trust in the government was 6 per cent in the Far West and 2 per cent in the Far East. Thus, not only are both extreme sides of the country responding to questions regarding motivations for tax compliance similarly and in correlation with similar trust concerns, but also, by 2015, both far western and far eastern regions are unified in their high distrust of the new, post-EuroMaidan regime in Kyiv.

Moreover, in the logit regressions in Appendix VII, two very interesting anomalies can be observed that illustrate a negative attribute of having trust in the state. First, for Donbas Ukrainians, in 2005, the more one trusts the government, the less likely one would be to express support for obeying the tax laws – and the substantive effect for this was −76 per cent. Second, for Far Western Ukrainians, the more one trusted the president in 2005, the less likely one was to give support for tax compliance – the substantive effect for this was −41 per cent. This was repeated in 2015, when the substantive effect for trust in the president was −22 per cent. These two effects suggest that trust in the state matters, but it also can act negatively upon state–society relations. Why? One possibility is that if one identified with a particular branch of government (in 2005, western Ukraine was more supportive of the president while eastern Ukraine, perhaps, was more supportive of those in the government), then one might feel as if one would not need to be as strict when it came to paying taxes because 'your guy' or 'guys' was in control at the top.

Comparing the Donbas with the four most western provinces shows that trust – or lack of trust – in the state is the prime motivation associated with deciding whether to support tax laws, even those personally deemed to be unfair.

Centre and South

Akin to the Far West–Far East comparison, Ukrainians in the Central part of the country, generally speaking, were more trusting of the president in 2005 than those in the Southern part of the country, with the reverse being the case in 2010 after the change in government. However, the differences are less stark than those above between East and West. In 2005, 49 per cent of Central Ukrainians and 32 per cent of Southern Ukrainians expressed trust in Yushchenko, whereas in 2010, 28 per cent of Central Ukrainians and 55 per cent of Southern Ukrainians trusted Yanukovych and in 2015, 22 per cent of Central Ukrainians and 15 per cent of Southern Ukrainians trusted Poroshenko. With respect to trust in the parliament and the government, though, support was largely constant across both the Centre and the South. In 2005, 18 and 20 per cent of the Central Ukrainians surveyed trusted the parliament and the government, respectively, and the corresponding figures were 21 and 22 per cent in 2010 and 9 and 9 per cent in 2015. Meanwhile, in 2005, 18 and 21 per cent of Southern Ukrainians expressed trust in the parliament and government, respectively, while the figures rose slightly to 34 and 38 per cent, respectively, in 2010 before falling again to 6 and 8 per cent in 2015.

The logit regression analyses of the question 'Would you obey tax laws even if you considered them unfair?' for the Central and Southern regions of Ukraine both broadly mirror the surveys for the country as a whole, especially the overall 2005 result, where Ukrainians reacted largely and relatively equally in response to both coercive and trust-building measures.

For Central Ukraine, the 2005 survey finds that withdrawing the deterrent threat of punishment and a lack of trust in street-level tax bureaucrats have nearly equally strong substantive effects. Withdrawing deterrence fully made respondents 16 per cent less likely to voice support for obeying unfair laws, whereas distrusting tax bureaucrats made them 15 per cent less likely to do so. For the 2010 survey, Central Ukrainians reacted a bit more strongly to trust-building measures. Affirming full trust in Yanukovych corresponded with being 14 per cent more likely to be supportive of compliance, and voicing complete trust in the government corresponded with being 20 per cent more likely to be supportive of compliance. Meanwhile, trusting the parliament and distrusting tax bureaucrats corresponded with being 26 and 22 per cent less likely to obey the tax laws, respectively. Withdrawing the deterrent threat in 2010, interestingly, also made one more likely to support compliance with the tax laws. In 2015, for Central Ukrainians, both withdrawing deterrence and the 'trust in the state' variables had strong significance in explaining why some individuals decided to support obeying tax laws even if deemed unfair, but the substantive effects for the trust variables, which ranged from 18 to 24 per cent, were slightly greater in magnitude than the substantive effect for withdrawing deterrence, which had a value of 12 per cent.

For South Ukraine, the 2005 survey finds that Ukrainians are nearly equally influenced by the withdrawal of deterrence and by their trust in parliament with respect to deciding whether to be supportive of complying with the tax laws even if deemed unfair. Trust in government, though, had the biggest substantive effect. If Southern Ukrainians stated that they trusted government, they were 41 per cent more likely to agree to comply with tax laws they deemed personally to be unfair. In 2010, trust variables had slightly greater impact, as fully trusting the government made one 38 per cent more likely to support compliance while withdrawing deterrence made one 31 per cent less likely to voice a willingness to obey. Ironically, not trusting other taxpayers to comply coincided with a 40 per cent increase in the likelihood of voicing support for obeying the tax laws, perhaps because Southern Ukrainians may have been more willing to distance themselves from the 'bad' behaviour around them. The 2015 survey shows a very different result for Southern Ukrainians, whose decision to support obeying tax laws even if deemed to be unfair only had one significant explanatory variable – the 'trust in the president' variable, which held a large substantive effect of 51 per cent.

Generally speaking, southern Ukraine has been more distrusting of the government in Kyiv (with an exception when Yanukovych was in power, as shown in the 2010 survey) than central Ukrainians. Further, when it comes to explaining why some citizens choose to obey tax laws even if deemed unfair, those in the South were more responsive to 'trust in the state' variables than their fellow citizens in the Centre. The comparison, therefore, highlights the extra importance for the central state to pursue the trust of citizens in the South, even considering that trust in Kyiv is low across the entire country.

Crimea

Crimea is a different case altogether. Unlike the other regions of Ukraine, it is the only one with a majority ethnic Russian population and, of course, it was annexed by Russia in the spring of 2014. And, while the sample size drawn from Crimea was the smallest, the overall support for complying with the tax laws was more similar to that of Russia in 2010 and 2012 (but not in 2005). Compared with the other regions above, the 2010 survey sample from Crimea had the lowest percentage of the population with a higher education (24 per cent) and the lowest percentage who identified themselves as being 'upper class' (0 per cent), but, contrary to being described often as a retiree area, the region did not have the greatest number of individuals above 60 years of age, as the Central, East and Donbas region samples had slightly larger numbers of respondents in that age group. Further, in addition to having a percentage of those who were employees or workers (skilled or unskilled) that

All Together? Lack of Trust in the Tax State Unifies Ukraine   239

was among the highest of the regions, Crimea also had the highest number of those employed in the agricultural sector (7 per cent, over double the national average.) Meanwhile, the number of enterprise or institution division heads or entrepreneurs was the lowest in the country, at 3 per cent, half that of Far Western Ukraine.

'Trust in the state' levels (president, parliament and government) were the lowest of the Ukrainian regions in 2005 – with trust in the president at 13 per cent, in the parliament at 9 per cent and in the government at 11 per cent – and the highest in 2010 – with support at 77, 74 and 76 per cent, respectively. Yanukovych, after all, owes his 2010 victory to the support he received in Crimea. This support contributed directly to high levels of compliance in Crimea in 2010 and 2012 compared with the rest of the country.

Unsurprisingly, then, trust plays the strongest role for Crimea in both the 2005 and 2010 logit regressions. In 2005, Crimeans were 31 per cent less likely to express support for obeying tax laws if they trusted Yushchenko (although this particular finding was not significant) and 54 per cent more likely to obey if they trusted the government. In 2010, only one respondent out of 199 had previous contact with a tax bureaucrat, causing that variable to drop out in the regression. In a regression that excludes prior contact with a tax bureaucrat, Crimeans were 33 per cent less likely to state that they would obey the tax laws if they said their behaviour was affected by the withdrawal of deterrence and were 66 per cent less likely to do so if they trusted Yanukovych. Trusting the parliament in 2010, however, made them 94 per cent more likely to voice support for compliance. Hence, in Crimea, the lack of popularity of Yushchenko and the stronger support a few years later for parliament – balancing along with the effects of increased support for a new president and government – likely account for the dramatic shift in willingness to support tax laws even if deemed unfair from 2005 to 2010 and 2012.

Bureau Contact for Ukraine Regions

In the logit regressions of the 2005, 2010 and 2015 surveys for the Ukraine regions, having had contact with a tax bureaucrat during the previous five years only mattered significantly for East and Donbas Ukrainians in 2005 and for West and Far West Ukrainians in 2010 with respect to the question of whether one would obey the tax laws even if they were considered unfair. For the rest of the country, and for East and Donbas in 2010 and West and Far West in 2005, previous bureaucrat contact did not appear to have any impact on decisions to support complying with the tax laws in the regressions. Moreover, the impact

240　Taxes and Trust

Table 7.4 *Nature of contact with Ukrainian tax bureaucrats by region: Those who stated that they would obey tax laws even if personally considered unfair as a percentage of those who were satisfied with both the conduct and the result of their previous meetings with tax bureaucrats*

	All of Ukraine	West Ukraine	Far West Ukraine	Central Ukraine	Kyiv Ukraine	East Ukraine	Donbas Ukraine	South Ukraine	Crimea Ukraine
2005	51%	48%	53%	47%	75%	40%	29%	79%	na
2010	54%	38%	33%	56%	60%	63%	54%	59%	na
2012	59%	69%	77%	51%	50%	63%	50%	62%	na
2015	70%	65%	67%	73%	91%	72%	68%	64%	na

No Mean Replacement: na = too low number of respondents with prior contact in Crimea in 2005–2012 surveys; Crimea not surveyed in 2015.
Light grey shaded = lower than 50 per cent.

of having had such contact, where it mattered, was negative, except in South Ukraine, where, while insignificant in the regression in 2005, the substantive effect showed slight significance.

Table 7.4 depicts the impact of having met with a tax bureaucrat previously by showing the willingness to obey tax laws even if deemed personally unfair of those who had good experiences with tax bureaucrats (being satisfied both with how one was treated and with the result one received.) Shaded in light grey are the regions where more than half of the respondents still would not agree to obey the tax laws even after such good encounters with tax bureaucrats.

Further, the difference in the willingness to obey tax laws between those who did not have prior contact and those who did was most negative in the East and, especially, in Donbas Ukraine in 2005, but in the West and, especially, in Far West Ukraine in 2010. In those areas, one was more likely to agree to obey tax laws if one did not have interaction with bureaucrats than if one did have such interaction and the experience was satisfactory all around.

These results, shaded in grey in Table 7.4, seem a bit counterintuitive. As examined in Chapter 6 and based on the work of Tom Tyler, it is the nature of previous interactions with authorities that can have a positive or negative effect on one's willingness to obey the state in the future. Given that East and Donbas Ukrainians in 2005 and West and Far West Ukrainians in 2010 who had previous contact with tax bureaucrats were less likely to be supportive of compliance than those who did not have such contact, does this mean that the nature of the interactions with tax bureaucrats in these regions was somehow more negative?

All Together? Lack of Trust in the Tax State Unifies Ukraine   241

Table 7.5 *Percentage of those with good prior tax bureaucrat experience who trust the Ukrainian president (Yushchenko in 2005, Yanukovych in 2010 and Poroshenko in 2015)*[a]

	All of Ukraine	West Ukraine	Far West Ukraine	Central Ukraine	Kyiv Ukraine	East Ukraine	Donbas Ukraine	South Ukraine	Crimea Ukraine
2005	51%	79%	67%	55%	67%	28%	19%	50%	na
2010	59%	47%	41%	64%	63%	60%	78%	65%	na
2015	42%	50%	52%	51%	47%	33%	44%	32%	na

[a] Percentage of those who had prior interactions with tax bureaucrats that were found both to be satisfactorily conducted and to have produced satisfying results who trust the Ukrainian president.

No Mean Replacement: Calculations were made only of those who had stated that they had had contact with a tax bureaucrat in the previous five years and had provided answers for the following three questions: 'Do you trust the president of Ukraine?' 'Were you satisfied with the results of your meeting with the tax service employees?' and 'Were you satisfied by how the tax service employees spoke with and treated you?'

na = too low number of respondents with prior contact in Crimea in 2005–2012 surveys; Crimea not surveyed in 2015.

Light grey shaded = lower than 50 per cent.

Actually no, in all of these four cases, more respondents were satisfied both with how they were treated in such past interactions and with the results of such interactions with the tax bureaucracies. Rather, in these particular regions, even those who were satisfied with both the conduct and the result of meeting tax bureaucrats in the past were more likely to be unsupportive of complying with the tax laws. In fact, this is a finding that is unlike the other regions or in Poland and Russia as a whole, where previous positive interactions (in terms of satisfied conduct and results) always coincided with support for compliance at a level above 50 per cent. Clearly, something other than the nature of these tax encounters in East and West Ukraine is having an impact here.

Given that Yanukovych replaced Yushchenko in 2010 and that the East broadly supported the former and the West the latter (with little support for Poroshenko across the country in 2015), Table 7.5 explores the trust levels for the president across the different regions of Ukraine in the 2005, 2010 and 2015 surveys for all respondents, as well as for those who had previous contact with tax bureaucrats and were satisfied with both the conduct and the result of such interactions.

What emerges is that, in 2005, less than 50 per cent of Ukrainians who had good prior bureaucratic contact in the East and the Donbas (and in Crimea) expressed trust in Yushchenko; elsewhere in the country, those

Table 7.6 *Tax awareness across Ukraine regions*

	Poland	Russia	All of Ukraine	West Ukraine	Far West Ukraine	Central Ukraine	Kyiv Ukraine	East Ukraine	Donbas Ukraine	South Ukraine	Crimea Ukraine
During the past five years, have you had business with employees of the tax service? (% Yes)											
2004	49%	23%	na	na	na	na	na	na	na	na	na
2005	na	na	15%	12%	11%	17%	14%	12%	9%	20%	11%
2010	38%	24%	12%	16%	15%	12%	13%	12%	11%	12%	0.5%*
2012	na	na	12%	12%	11%	13%	7%	9%	8%	13%	14%
2015	na	na	19%	16%	15%	21%	20%	19%	14%	17%	na
What is the personal income tax rate in your country today? (% correct answer)											
2004	na	38%	na	na	na	na	na	na	na	na	na
2005	na	na	9%	9%	10%	8%	4%	12%	12%	9%	7%
2010	22%	46%	10%	13%	17%	7%	9%	7%	9%	6%	50%
2012	na	na	13%	12%	14%	8%	6%	14%	20%	17%	28%
2015	na	na	13%	13%	15%	15%	18%	11%	13%	9%	na

* In the 2010 survey, only one respondent out of 199 in Crimea stated that he or she had had contact with a tax bureaucrat in the previous five years.

Light grey shaded = lower than Ukraine average

All Together? Lack of Trust in the Tax State Unifies Ukraine   243

who had good prior interactions with tax bureaucrats voiced trust in Yushchenko to a greater extent. Similarly, in 2010, less than 50 per cent of Ukrainians who had satisfactory prior interactions with tax bureaucrats in the West and Far West regions affirmed trust in Yanukovych, whereas elsewhere in the country that year those who had good prior bureaucrat contact were more trusting of Yanukovych. Finally, while support was low across the country in 2015 for Poroshenko, the lowest levels of support – even from those who approved of their interaction with the tax bureaucracy – were in the East and South.

Hence, it is likely that it was the nature of the extreme lack of trust among these populations that overrode even satisfying past experiences to account for a low willingness to comply with the state's tax laws. Thus, trust – or lack thereof – in the state, as represented by who was president at the time, trumps good street-level interactions across both East and West. Trust matters most of all, but for who and when, depends upon who is in charge of the state.

Tax Awareness across Ukraine Regions

While a more thorough and vastly more intensive study would be required to assess whether the tax system interacts with taxpayers consistently across the unitary state of Ukraine, the Taxpayer Compliance Attitudinal Surveys do illustrate to what extent awareness of and interaction with the tax system vary across the country. Table 7.6 illustrates what percentage of the Ukrainian public interacted with the tax bureaucracy nationally, across the regions, and in comparison with Poland and Russia, and what percentage of the public knows the correct personal income tax rate.

Compared with their neighbours to the East and West, Ukrainians have been the most disconnected from their tax regime, with less knowledge of and less interaction with the tax system. Yet, across the country, that disconnection was fairly similar, without great disparities from the national average in any region. True, Ukrainians in both the Far West and the Donbas areas were less likely than the country as a whole to have had previous meetings with tax bureaucrats, but such interactions were generally no more than one-third less than the already low national average. Western Ukrainians were more likely than their fellow countrymen in the Centre, East and South to know the correct personal income tax rate, but no region had a level of knowledge of the tax rates approaching that of Poland or Russia. In short, no single region of Ukraine can be shown to be either consistently more or less aware of the tax regime than other parts of the country – suggesting that efforts that

244   Taxes and Trust

try to raise tax awareness among citizens should not be restricted to any particular region. Such a finding related to governance is different from other research, such as that of Ralph De Haas, Milena Djourelova and Elena Nikolova, who have found stark differences between East and West Ukraine when it comes to attitudes supporting market-based economies and democracy.[4]

Religion and Civil Society

In recent years, explanations for why some post-communist states have been able to govern their peoples better than others have pointed to differing conceptions of what constitutes a civil society. Such competing visions of civil society are perceived to have been mediated through both long and short-term relationships between states and societies. John Elster, Claus Offe and Ulrich K. Preuss, among others, have argued that the conditions that favoured consolidation of the post-communist transition in Central and Eastern Europe are those relating to a set of values and beliefs, or 'inherited world views', that are shared within a society that were formed in the past, which carries the transition forward in different ways.[5] So, do country-specific values and beliefs matter with respect to state–society relations?

With respect to post-communist Europe, there is a much-observed religious divide corresponding roughly to that between Catholicism in Central Europe, including Poland, on one side, and Slavic Orthodoxy in the former Soviet Union states, including Russia, on the other. Poland has developed a civil society that possesses citizens who are more politically active and demand greater openness and transparency on the part of the state than the countries to its east. This is deemed to have come about, in significant part, through the historic role the Catholic Church played during the Polish People's Republic and its collapse in 1989. Once the regime established by outside forces met its demise and a new Polish state was built, citizens then could place greater trust in their state, allowing the development of the particular type of civil society that is, perhaps, familiar in more consolidated democracies.

Juan Linz and Alfred Stepan also have sought to explain how the different natures of branches of Christianity can impact the type of support given to nascent democratic groups, while carefully recognizing that Orthodox Christianity is not inherently anti-democratic. They argue that 'Roman Catholicism as a transnational, hierarchical organization can potentially provide material and doctrinal support to a local Catholic

[4] De Haas, Djourelova and Nikolova, pp. 92–107.   [5] Elster, Offe and Preuss.

All Together? Lack of Trust in the Tax State Unifies Ukraine   245

church to help it resist state opposition.'[6] Hence, the Catholic Church could be considered as supporting 'a more robust and autonomous civil society'.

With respect to the nature of the transition's aftermath, the 1989 transition was perceived in Poland dramatically differently by the state and the society than the 1991 transition in Russia, as noted earlier. The Catholic view of civil society, Oleg Kharkhordin has argued, can be found in Polish Solidarity literature. 'Solidarity spoke about the conflict between civil society and the state, while in practice it followed the example of the Catholic Church – a most serious stronghold of Polish national liberation in the 19th and 20th centuries and the only real bulwark of resistance after the imposition of communist rule.'[7] Hence, the vision of civil society from which the new Polish state was born in 1989, was based in some significant part upon the Catholic foundations of Polish society.

The Orthodox Church, on the other hand, does not stand as much in opposition to the state, providing a different outlook as to how an ethical society should be constructed. 'Concerning civil society and resistance to the state, Orthodox Christianity is often (not always) organizationally and doctrinally in a relatively weak position because of what Max Weber called its "caesaropapist" structure, in which the Church is a *national* as opposed to a *transnational* organization', Linz and Stepan have written. 'In caesaropapist churches, the national state normally plays a major role in the national church's finances and appointments. Such a national church is not really a relatively autonomous part of civil society.'[8] How the state's bureaucrats behave towards citizens in society would appear to depend upon how committed state leaders and the Orthodox Church are to greater transparency and civic oversight.

Along the same lines, Russia's society some two decades after communism often has been described as one in which citizens are less prone to be active in demanding transparency on the part of the state and less trusting of it. The development of Russia's civil society, in particular, could be seen to be due in part to a different type of long-term historic church–state relationship, which has complemented a more subject–ruler relationship in everyday governance.

The absence in the Soviet Union of a non-state institutional actor that would play an oppositional role to the state like the role the Catholic Church played in Poland could be seen as having prevented greater transparency and openness from developing. And, because Russians do not view themselves as participating in political life, they would be more

[6] Linz and Stepan, p. 453.   [7] Kharkhordin, pp. 954–955.   [8] Ibid., p. 453.

246 Taxes and Trust

likely to have greater distrust of the state and negative views of the bureaucrats that interact with them. So, differences in religion, or even, perhaps, in religious-based conceptions of state–society relations, may help explain from where long-term distrust of the state can come.

Thus, to aid in the re-creation of a constructive state–society relationship, differing religious conceptions of civil society can help explain the nature of and fundamental basis for society's trust in the state and the state's trust in society. The implication of these distinct outlooks would be that Catholicism, through the Church, promotes an associational life in society that is more independent from the state and that associations, including the Church itself, challenge the state from the outside. This implies that a civil society will respond to the state when individuals trust the state and are in tune with its objectives. In contrast, an Orthodox outlook implies that the state and society should be unified for a civil, ethical life to be achieved.

In order to examine the extent to which the relative legacy of particular religious viewpoints on civil society in post-communist Europe matters for explaining long-term trust/distrust in the state and how they affect state–society interactions on the ground, a close examination of the Ukrainian case is necessary. Whereas Poland and Russia are predominantly Catholic and Slavic Orthodox, respectively, in religious make-up, Ukraine maintains a population that is nearly 10 per cent Catholic, most of whom are geographically concentrated in western Ukraine.

Moreover, while the majority of Catholic Ukrainians are Greek Catholics and Poles are Roman Catholics, one can still regard Ukrainian Catholics as holding a distinctly different outlook on civil society than their Orthodox compatriots and one that is more in line with that of Polish Catholics. The Greek Catholic Church in Ukraine is subordinated to the Pope in Rome, has been influenced heavily by the Polish Catholic Church over the centuries, follows the same doctrine (but not rites) of all Catholics, and stood in opposition to the Soviet state, which persecuted it much more than Orthodox Ukrainians and Catholic Ukrainians who converted to Orthodoxy. Therefore, the distinctions between branches of Catholicism should not have significant impact on utilizing Ukraine as a testing ground for differing religious perspectives on state–society relations.

Tax Compliance and Religion in Ukraine

Further analysis along the East–West political and economic divide of Ukraine and along the mostly coinciding societal cleavage between Catholics and non-Catholics (almost entirely Slavic Orthodox) in the

All Together? Lack of Trust in the Tax State Unifies Ukraine   247

country – a religious mix that does not exist in the neighbouring states – can provide insight as to whether different religious outlooks on civil society provide a background for how citizens react to their states. In comparing the willingness of Catholic and non-Catholic Ukrainians to obey tax laws, there are differences, as shown in Appendix VII, suggesting that the culture and practice of different religions lead to the construction of very different relationships between citizens and their states. The four far western oblasts of Ukraine (grouped together as 'Far West Ukraine') are as a whole nearly split equally between Catholics and non-Catholics. Trust matters more for both Catholic and non-Catholic Ukrainians in the west than the proxy variable for being motivated more to support tax compliance by the state's deterrence approach in 2005, 2010 and 2015 (with the exception of Catholic Ukrainians in 2010, for whom neither trust nor deterrence variables mattered), but as with this regional area as a whole, in 2005, trusting the president makes Catholics as well as non-Catholics less likely to support obeying tax laws.

Whereas the trust variables and the deterrence variable all had about equal weight, in terms of substantive effect (the change in likelihood that one would obey tax laws even if deemed unfair) in the overall Ukraine regression for 2005, trust issues matter most for Catholic Ukrainians in 2005, 2010 and 2015, as Appendices VI and VII illustrate. That is, if all of the independent variables are held even at their means and trust in parliament is varied from its lowest to its highest levels, Catholic Ukrainians were 54 per cent in 2005, 25 per cent in 2010 and 41 per cent in 2015 more likely to be in favour of compliance.[9] Hence, Catholic Ukrainians do appear to respond to the state more out of trust – similar to Poles in 2005 and 2010.

While not entirely surprising, given that 91 per cent of the country is not Catholic, non-Catholic Ukraine's attitudinal behaviour towards tax compliance is shown to be nearly identical to that of Ukraine as a whole in 2005, 2010 and 2015 – 'trust in the state' variables are practically

---

[9] The Ukrainian regressions utilized a trust scale, which is a composite of trust in the president, the parliament and the government and trust in the state to do what it right and to provide goods and services, but when trust in the parliament is disaggregated out it becomes very, very much more significant, with a strong substantive effect. Further, interestingly, about 97 per cent of those Catholic Ukrainians in 2005 who trusted the parliament also trusted the president and the government (but nowhere near the other way around). For a Catholic Ukrainian, then, to be trusting of the parliament, which at the time was very fractious and not aligned with the west-leaning president, who was the choice of the Catholic vote, he or she must have been more trusting overall of the state. (Also interesting to note is that if Catholic Ukrainians voted for president in 2004 Orange Revolution election, they were 31 per cent more likely in 2005 to support complying with the tax laws.)

248   Taxes and Trust

equivalent in substantive effect to the deterrence proxy variable in 2005, but such trust variables have stronger substantive effects than deterrence does in the 2010 survey, while they are broadly all similar in the 2015 survey.

Perhaps these differences between Catholics and non-Catholics in Ukraine help elucidate further the differences between largely Catholic Poland and largely Slavic Orthodox Russia with respect to attitudes towards tax compliance. However, one should be cautious in making such claims. Nationally, in 2005, Catholic Ukrainians were only nearly 13 per cent more likely to state that they would obey tax laws even if deemed unfair than their Slavic Orthodox countrymen (47 per cent to 35 per cent)[10] whereas Poles were 27 per cent more likely to state that they would obey such a law than Russians (83 per cent to 56 per cent.) Meanwhile, by 2010, the gap was even narrower, as Catholic Ukrainians nationally were only 5 per cent more likely to state that they would obey the tax laws than their fellow Orthodox citizens (48 per cent to 43 per cent), whereas Poles were more likely to state that they would obey than Russians by 25 per cent (77 per cent to 52 per cent). And, in 2015, the gap was just 2 per centage points in Ukraine. Catholicism, in and of itself, may account for contributing to a more compliant population, but it does not appear to be enough to explain the entire cross-national differences.

Perhaps, though, the degree to which one is committed to (or indoctrinated by) a particular religion might make one be more in line with a particular religious outlook on civil society interaction, affecting how one reacts to the state. This could be measured through assessing the impact on compliance of attending church frequently. However, this does not appear to be the case in Ukraine. Only 36.22 per cent of all Ukrainians in 2005 who told pollsters that they attend church once a week or more also stated that they would obey tax laws even if considered unfair – compared with 35.70 per cent of Ukrainians who attended church less often. In 2010, the corresponding figures also were nearly identical, at 43.44 per cent and 44.97 per cent, respectively. Moreover, both Catholics and Orthodox who stated that they attended church once a week or more were less likely (by a slight margin) to state support for tax compliance than those who attended less often. Only 42 per cent of frequent Catholic churchgoers (as opposed to 47 per cent of all Catholics) stated that they would obey the tax laws and only 31 per cent

---

[10] This figure does not change regardless of whether we are speaking of Greek or Roman Catholic Ukrainians, as 47 per cent of Greek Catholics (who overall represent 8.23 per cent of those participating in the Ukraine 2005 survey) and a similar 48 per cent of Roman Catholics (0.83 per cent of the Ukraine 2005 survey) stated that they would obey the tax laws.

All Together? Lack of Trust in the Tax State Unifies Ukraine   249

Table 7.7 *Religion and the Ukraine Taxpayer Compliance Attitudinal Surveys*

	Would Obey Tax Laws Even If Considered Unfair 2005	Would Obey Tax Laws Even If Considered Unfair 2010	Would Obey Tax Laws Even If Considered Unfair 2012	Would Obey Tax Laws Even If Considered Unfair 2015
Ukrainian Catholics (9 to 10% of survey)	47%	48%	na	46%
Ukrainian non-Catholics (90 to 91% of survey)	35%	43%	na	44%
Ukraine (all respondents) (100% of Survey)	36%	44%	38%	45%
Far Western Ukrainian Catholics (51 to 56% of Far Western Regions are Catholic)	45%	53%	na	48%
Far Western Ukrainian non-Catholics (44 to 49% of Far Western Regions are non-Catholic)	30%	42%	na	51%
Far West Ukraine (all respondents)	37%	47%	36%	50%

of frequent Orthodox churchgoers (as opposed to 35 per cent of all Orthodox) expressed similar support for complying with the tax laws. (In 2010, only 46 per cent of frequent Catholic churchgoers (as opposed to 48 per cent of all Catholics) and only 43 per cent of frequent Orthodox churchgoers (as opposed to 45 per cent of all Orthodox) supported obeying the tax laws.) Hence, it appears that the *degree* of 'exposure' to a religious outlook on civil society may not matter directly on an individual level.

Therefore, in testing how much weight religious background within a society holds in explaining governance issues, the research here also suggests several findings that give great caution when associating the ability and methods of governance with the existence of a Catholic/Orthodox divide across Eastern Europe. First, namely, as mentioned, the Orthodox–Catholic gap in Ukraine in support for tax compliance narrows to 5 per cent in 2010 and to 2 per cent in 2015, as shown in Table 7.7. Similarly, trust issues mattered more for non-Catholic Ukrainians in 2010 than they did in 2005.

Second, the fact that a majority of Ukrainian Catholics in 2005 (and 2010 and 2015) did not state that they would be compliant with any

250   Taxes and Trust

tax law suggests that religion does not alone (or predominantly) make for 'better citizens'. Such a 'Catholic effect' – even if stronger in 2005 than in 2010 and 2015 – is insufficient to cause a majority of Catholic Ukrainians to support abiding by the tax laws even if deemed unfair.

Third, the fact that the differences in attitudinal support for tax compliance within Ukraine were much smaller than the differences between neighbouring Catholic Poland and Orthodox Russia also suggests a weak relationship between religious preferences and governance. Hence, the significantly higher support in willingness to obey the tax laws of Poles than of Russians, previously observed in other surveys, would not likely be due to the largely Catholic makeup of Poland or the Slavic Orthodox composition of Russia.

Moreover, the fact that the underlying motivations for obeying or not obeying are quite similar between the far eastern and far western portions of Ukraine, as shown at the beginning of this chapter – that is, that at both sides of the country those motivations are based on issues related to trust – also suggests that underlying religious differences across Eastern Europe might not matter greatly.

Finally, as shown in Table 7.7, within the Far Western regions of Ivano-Frankivsk, Lviv, Volnysk and Zakarpat Oblasts, where the population was almost equally divided between Catholics and non-Catholics, there are sizeable differences between the two groups' willingness to obey tax laws even if deemed unfair that are even larger than the differences between Catholics and non-Catholics in the country as a whole in 2005 and 2010. This suggests that the differences noted here are associated less with some aspect of being of one religion or another than with being in one particular area of the country or another. On the other hand, of course, such differences between Catholics and non-Catholics in the Far Western regions are nearly bridged in the 2015 survey, as they are for the country as a whole. Moreover, even though the Far Western region contains more Catholics than elsewhere, comparing the overall results for the Far Western Region with the overall results for all of Ukraine finds that in 2005, 2010 and 2012 the differences between that region and the country as a whole are not that large, suggesting that regardless of internal differences within this part of the country, overall the effect compared to the nation as a whole is limited.

Tax Compliance, Nationality Self-Identification and Language in Ukraine

In addition to religion, Ukraine has been said to be divided both by nationality and by language. In the 2015 survey, additional questions

All Together? Lack of Trust in the Tax State Unifies Ukraine 251

Table 7.8 *National self-identification and the Ukraine Taxpayer Compliance Attitudinal Surveys*

	Would Obey Tax Laws Even If Considered Unfair 2015
Russian Nationality (8% of survey)	47%
Ukrainian Nationality (89% of survey)	44%

were asked of respondents to discern their impact on willingness to obey a tax law even if one considers it to be unfair. When asked which nationality they considered themselves to be, 8 per cent stated 'Russian' while 89 per cent identified themselves as 'Ukrainian'. Yet, as Table 7.8 shows, stating that one was 'Russian' correlated only with a minimal difference (3 per cent) in willingness to show support for tax compliance than if one identified more with being 'Ukrainian'. Hence, it would seem that even if one identified more with being 'Russian', one was just as willing, or perhaps a bit more, to follow Ukraine's tax laws than if one identified as 'Ukrainian'.

Similarly, respondents in 2015 were asked about the languages they mainly speak at home, and Table 7.9 shows that the differences between those who favoured one language or the other are not great. In fact, it made no difference whether respondents said they spoke Russian or both Russian and Ukrainian equally at home. And those who said they spoke Ukrainian at home were just 6 per cent more likely to voice support for obeying tax laws, even if they disagreed with them. Hence, language does not appear to be a significant variable that dramatically divides the Ukrainian public with respect to their personal views on tax compliance.

Thus, even if there is some evidence for the existence of a religious or language effect, there may well be limits to the impact of religious outlooks and language on post-communist governance. It may, in fact, not matter greatly how or whether long-held and local religious, regional or

Table 7.9 *Language and the Ukraine Taxpayer Compliance Attitudinal Surveys*

	Would Obey Tax Laws Even If Considered Unfair 2015
Russian speakers (29% of survey)	42%
Ukrainian speakers (42% of survey)	48%
Speakers of both (28% of survey)	42%

252   Taxes and Trust

cultural outlooks on civil life play a significant role today in how society frames its trust (or distrust) of the state. Instead, the answers as to where that deep societal distrust in the state in Russia and, even more significantly, across all of Ukraine, comes from would appear to be found in more recent and current interactions that citizens have with their states, as shown in Chapter 6 and the first half of this chapter.

Given that neither religious, nationality, linguistic, nor regional differences are that salient across Ukraine with respect to explaining citizen willingness to undertake a critical obligation towards their state, Ukraine appears to be a much more unified country than is expected. That is, trust, or rather the lack of it, across the country appears to account greatly for the very low levels of tax compliance. Trust in the state may vary by region with respect to who is in power in Kyiv, but the entire country is vulnerable to low levels of compliance based on low levels of trust. To improve the government's ability to implement policy, increased confidence in the state is needed across the board, all together.

To address that great need, the next chapter concludes with some tax administration policy suggestions by which transitional states such as Ukraine can create and build up levels of trust on the part of citizens in their state so that greater tax compliance can be achieved.

8 Towards Greater Trust and Tax Compliance

Coercive states may be successful in getting some things done (and clearly even the Russian government functions well enough so that it is not in danger of collapsing in the near future). However, the Polish–Russian–Ukrainian comparison suggests that a state that seeks to build up and to maintain trust with its citizens will be more effective than one that treats its citizens in a more coercive manner. And studying the origins of tax compliance in these countries shows that political parties, the relative strength of society versus the state, religious culture, legacies of corruption or the presence of a federalist structure do not exclusively explain why some transitional states are more capable of administering policy than others. Rather, it is the construction of a bureaucratic rational state oriented towards society, the use of constructive historical legacies when available and a focus on mutually cooperative citizen–state interactions that enable trust to build up between citizen and state so that state activity will be accomplished more successfully.

To alter fundamentally a legacy of poor state–society relations, a break from the past, afforded by a dramatic transition such as the 1989 and 1991 revolutions in Eastern Europe, provides a fresh opportunity for the state to construct a newer, healthier relationship built on mutual trust between state and citizen. States such as Russia in the 1990s that did not fully take advantage of such a unique opportunity may find that coercive measures suffice in the short term, but a fundamental overhaul of state–society relations may be necessary so that the state will function effectively for years to come. Authoritarian rule ended up not working out well for Russia in 1917 and in 1991. A return to more coercive measures today will not work out for Russia in the long run either.

In reaching such conclusions, this book has been about both *testing* existing theories on state capacity, drawn largely from the comparative politics literature, and *building* a new theory on state capacity, specific to post-communist states on both theoretical and empirical grounds. It also serves as a call for political scientists to engage in the study of economic activities within states, specifically those that seek to evaluate how economic policies are implemented.

This project, thus, not only contributes to theoretical debates regarding the origins of capable states, but also discerns where, given limited resources, transitional states should focus their efforts in re-creating themselves in order to implement their own policies successfully.

Moreover, as Poland and Russia symbolize two contrasting routes of post-communist development and as Ukraine lies in the crossroads between the two (figuratively as well as geographically), this book takes up cases that are not just theoretically justified but also critically important for the global study of governance and development.

When governments are perceived as treating citizens unfairly and unequally, citizens' faith in the state is undermined. State and society need to be wedded to each other. Broader, mutually cooperative relationships between state and society lead to the accomplishment of state goals. In short, by focusing on taxation, this book seeks to make sophisticated analytical connections between the levels of civil society and the type of post-communist state that has emerged.

The aims of the research presented in this book have been threefold: At the meta-level, this study has sought to discern how a state transitions from a coercive state to a legal, legitimate tax state; at the macro-level, it has sought to determine how the Polish, Russian and Ukrainian states implement policies to ensure tax compliance; and at the micro-level, it has sought to establish what exactly is going on inside these countries that affects tax collection and, more broadly, governance.

In evaluating tax compliance, the project has employed qualitative process-tracing research methods – such as extensive documentary research and interviews with key informants to assess institutional design, organizational history and reform paths of bureaucracies – as well as unprecedented quantitative survey methods – through eight Taxpayer Compliance Attitudinal Surveys in Poland, Russia and Ukraine and the Public Officials Survey in Russia. While governments of all stripes can be very reluctant to provide data to independent researchers, the process of analyzing how institutions function on the ground can be particularly difficult in countries such as today's Russia, where bureaucracies are not especially transparent regarding what they do or how and why they do it. Nevertheless, this project has succeeded in obtaining data in such environments.

Comparing the origins of tax administration capacity for post-communist Poland, Russia and Ukraine clarifies the importance of building and maintaining a mutually trusting relationship between the state and its citizens. To be deemed trustworthy, the state must be viewed by its citizens as being capable of fulfilling its obligations through the provision of goods and services and of treating citizens in a fair manner. Further, for citizens to be deemed trustworthy by their state, they not only must recognize what the duties of being a good citizen are, such as complying with tax laws, but also must individually be willing to carry such tasks out. Trust in the governed on the part of the government can build up as citizens respond to the state constructively when they deem the state to be trustworthy (and vice versa.) Further, such mutual trust will provide successful policy implementation to the benefit of all. Good governance requires both good citizens and a trustworthy state.

Testing the Three Theories on State Capacity

In comparing the collection of taxes, three main theories on state capacity, drawn largely from the comparative politics literature – state capacity as a function of either political institutions such as parties, state–society relations or state structures – have been tested with respect to post-communist Poland, Russia and Ukraine. The first, regarding political parties, was shown not to be relevant. State–society relations and the structure of the state were found to be important for building state capacity in these three countries, but not precisely in the ways predicted by the second and third theories.

State Capacity as a Function of Political Parties

Chapter 3 showed, somewhat surprisingly, that political parties – how well they direct attention to the post-communist state organizations and civil service – need not play a substantial role in the construction of the capacity of state bureaucracies. With respect to examining the relevance of political parties to shaping the agenda and impacting the administrative structures significantly so that policy can be administered, Poland's relatively greater state capacity has not been due to a competitive political party system. While no governing party was re-elected in Poland from the first post-communist election in 1991 up until 2011, the party battles back and forth over civil service reform were not overly productive even as the tax service took shape.

Further, as described in Chapter 5, in interviews with several Polish personnel within six tax offices, three tax chambers, three tax audit offices and the finance ministry, bureaucrats continuously stated, 'We are civil service. We are not allied to parties.' Hence, the differences in governance levels in the three post-communist states are not due to the presence of stable, competitive political parties in Poland and the lack

256   Taxes and Trust

of them in Russia and Ukraine. Strong political party influence is not necessary for constructing an effective bureaucratic rational state.

State Capacity as a Function of State–Society Relations

Among the core intuitions of the standard state–society literature is that governance depends on whether the society can be subordinated to the state or society is strong enough to resist or co-opt the state. Yet, despite the efforts at increased state control at the expense of society in Russia under President Vladimir Putin, governance is not stronger there than in Poland, where there are less of a divide between citizens and their government and less coercion.

In addition, certain cultural aspects also have been commonly viewed as important in distinguishing Russia's state–society relationship from Poland's. Yet, with respect to tax collection, the success of the Tax Administration Modernization Project in Nizhny Novgorod and Volgograd oblasts, as discussed in Chapter 5, indicated that once a part of the Russian tax service is given permission from Moscow to reform, renounces targets and introduces an audit-free tax collection system that requires greater trust of citizens, tax arrears can decline dramatically. Hence, utilizing less coercion works in Russia, too!

Moreover, as shown in Chapter 7, at least with respect to the case of Ukraine, religion, self-identified nationality and language had very little impact on tax compliance, suggesting that getting the right 'software' rather than possessing the right 'culture' is what matters.

Therefore, mutually constructive state–society relations are necessary for good governance – just not in a manner in which a society is pitted against the state. Indeed, the post-communist transition began with a large disconnect between state and society in all the East European and Eurasian countries that simply had to be overcome. In fact, in spite of an ongoing and, perhaps, increasing dislike for corruption scandals, party politics and politicians, Poles, as shown in Chapter 6, after the transition, have maintained general support for the new system and for those more directly responsible with governing. Thus, trust in the state by society is the foundation for a constructive and non-zero-sum state–society relationship.

State Capacity as a Function of the Structure of the State

While the third theory on state capacity plays down the relevance of state–society interactions, the state structural argument does hold well for explaining, in part, the dynamics that accounts for effective governance. As shown in Chapter 5, the design of *administrative structures,* the *human and technological resources* afforded to bureaucracies and the *work philosophy* among bureaucrats are necessary to provide for effective policy outcomes.

However, the existing theory that links state capacity to the structure of the state fails to account for two important provisions for better governance. First, *historical reference* points, such as the use of previous institutional structures, should be utilized, whenever possible, to link back to healthier state–society interactions. History matters, but it matters in terms of how it is used and applied in the present as a model for current, constructive state–society relations. Previous paths towards creating cooperative state–society interactions that were laid down by earlier state–society efforts should be continued. Second, the *state structures, human and technological resources* and *work philosophy* must be directed towards society so that trust in their state is built up among citizens.

The research presented here provides some evidence to refute the notion that the structure of the Russian state, particularly federalism, accounts principally for the relatively poor implementation of policy. The Nizhny Novgorod and Volgograd tax modernization programs, mentioned above, show that once Moscow allows a target-based approach to tax collection to be eased, regions can perform in a manner more similar to that in, say, Poland. In addition, under Putin, the Russian Federation has become much more like a unitary state than it was under President Boris Yeltsin and is governed as such. Putin's expressed desire for a strict 'power vertical' is not compatible with notions of federalism. There also has been a lack of clear provision for the rights of the regions in the federal structure, and sovereignty has not been shared at different levels of government in Russia. Thus, state structure matters, as do state–society relations, but an exclusive focus on either one or the other misses out on the important links between the two theoretical approaches.

A New Model of State Capacity for the Post-communist States

Analyzing the Polish, Russian and Ukrainian cases makes possible proposing revisions to the second and third theories in order to build a new theoretical model for state capacity that better explains how post-communist governments govern. In Chapter 2, I constructed a new model for state capacity, which focuses on the extent to which the state is organized in a Weberian sense and focuses on the manner in which society is ready to be a willing partner in state activity. The role of citizens' trust in the state and the state's trust in citizens to comply with the state without overuse of coercion is also emphasized.

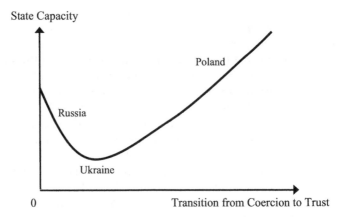

Figure 8.1 State capacity in transition from coercion to trust

This study distinctively has underlined the construction and accumulation of *trust* as state and society engage with one another as the primary instrument for transitioning from a coercive tax state to a modern, legal and legitimate one. Trust is inherent in the revenue collection process.

In essence, the new model suggests that where a state is bureaucratically rational – embodied with well-organized *structural designs, human and technological resources* and a *work philosophy* all oriented towards involving society – and a society is able and willing to be compliant, trust will develop as the two interact so that state goals can be realized more successfully.

This book has provided an evaluation of this new model by viewing more closely how state and society interact to ensure tax compliance in Poland, Russia and Ukraine. Good tax compliance was shown to be a product of a bureaucratic rational state, necessary for building up societal trust on taxes, and a society of individuals, shown to be willing to partner with the state more because of their *trust* in the state (rather than because of their *fear* of the state.)

An effective tax state is one that provokes some fear as a higher authority – all states need to rouse some fear in order to get people to comply with paying taxes – but does not employ the extreme coercion that limits state effectiveness in the long run. Russia is at that sub-optimal level, with a state often evoking more fear than trust, while Ukraine is at the bottom of the trough, trying to transition, if you will, from Russia to Poland. (See Figure 8.1.) Meanwhile, of the three, Poland is the case that has transitioned successfully from coercion to trust and, as a result, enjoys the highest state capacity.

For the state to be trustworthy before its citizens in order to receive cooperation and compliance so that state policy can be administered effectively, how street-level bureaucrats treat citizens – whether they treat them more like clients – matters with regard to whether or not the state can build up its trust to function properly. This was shown most clearly in Chapters 6 and 7 with the Taxpayer Compliance Attitudinal Surveys. To strengthen the state's legitimacy, then, improving the quality of street-level bureaucracies is vital. The provision of poor 'customer service' by bureaucrats has a negative effect on society, which may decline to fulfil its obligations to obey the state, whereas good 'customer service' can mitigate the impact of bad 'outcomes' that can emerge from interactions with the tax authorities.

To make such dramatic increases in citizens' trust in the state generally and in street-level bureaucracies in particular, states need to update, if not overhaul, their administrative structures so that they are directed at society. Transitioning from communism allows the state to re-create such citizen–state trust radically not only because the 1989 and 1991 revolutions were dramatic events but also because the communist legacy of socio-economic equality makes it easier for the state to focus on building trust in society generally rather than focusing exclusively on one sector of society at the determent of others. The fact that the legitimacy of the transition itself was less certain in the minds of Russians than in those of Poles or even Ukrainians, however, has posed a greater hurdle for the post-Soviet Russian state.

To aid in the re-construction of a healthy state–society relationship, past legacies have been shown through the evidence presented in Chapter 3 to be very beneficial. Which historical reference points post-communist states choose to utilize to transform partly into a version of their former selves, modelled on a time when the state is perceived to have been quite capable, can give a substantial boost to society's perception of the legitimacy of the state. Hence, the book contributes to the study of comparative bureaucracy by introducing the argument that reforming bureaucracies – especially those caught up in regime change – will be shaped by historical models from decades past via 'model transference'.

Moreover, as evidence from the Taxpayer Compliance Attitudinal Surveys confirms, trusting the state to provide goods and to treat others fairly is not related to citizens' trust in one another. State–societal trust requires a unique and special relationship, irrespective of levels of social capital within society itself. A powerful interplay directly between citizens and their government will enable both state and society to mutually reinforce each other's capacities so that policies can be implemented successfully.

260   Taxes and Trust

For Poland, as time elapses from the start of the transition and as politics takes a more nationalist turn, the question remains whether and how such mutually reinforcing trust between citizen and state – created in great part during a post-1989 period of extraordinary politics – will be maintained. For Russia, with few signs of economic recovery appearing in the near future due to the decline in global oil prices, economic sanctions imposed by the West after the Crimean invasion and a downturn in investment, among other things, the question becomes whether Russia will be even more coercive in the future to achieve state tasks. And, for Ukraine, the question, of course, remains whether it will gain enough trust from the public to transition to a stable rule-of-law democracy.

State Capacity Puzzle Posed by Ukraine

One of the questions at the core of this project has been whether the changes that Ukraine has undergone have increased the propensity of citizens to trust their state. The past couple of years alone have witnessed significant change in Ukraine: the 'EuroMaidan' uprising, the departure of Viktor Yanukovych from power, the extraordinary presidential and parliamentary elections in 2014, the catastrophic loss of control over territory in Crimea and the Donbas, a seemingly intractable low-grade war with Russia, the conclusion of a deep and comprehensive Free Trade Agreement with the European Union, and a spiral of economic destruction. The question is whether these changes will be truly transformational. Earlier episodes of heightened political contestation in Ukraine – from 'Kuchmagate' to the Orange Revolution – failed fundamentally to alter the nature of the relationship between Ukrainian citizens and their state: citizens retreated into angry disaffection, and leaders took corruption to new heights, as evidenced not only by a gilded presidential palace but also by the glittering and golden spa rooms, salt therapy room, cryonic saunas and special interrogation facilities hidden deep inside the tax administration's main Kyiv headquarters on *L'vivs'ka Ploshcha* (Lviv Square). More recent issues – such as the release of the Panama papers in the spring of 2016 and the ensuing allegations that President Petro Poroshenko had sought the restructuring of his assets abroad with the intention of decreasing taxes paid in Ukraine (a *Kyiv Post* editorial cartoon depicted Poroshenko telling others, 'Pay your own taxes or get your own offshore company!'[1]), the July 2016 protest in the occupied Donetsk city of Horlivka against the Donbas separatist militants' methods of collecting taxes, which required everything to be inventoried, in

---

[1] Published in *Kyiv Post*, 8 April 2016, p. 5.

Towards Greater Trust and Tax Compliance 261

preference for Ukraine's simplified tax system for small entrepreneurs[2]; and the persistent possibility that southeast Ukraine might support pro-Russian political parties – all highlight the challenges of building trust in the state.

The EuroMaidan – a revolution staged by a public that had had enough of a corrupt leader who had used public revenue (and taxes) for private gain – was meant to put an end to that cycle, by so radically altering the incentives of politicians that they would have no choice but to work for the trust of the people. If the changes in Ukraine are to be truly transformational, they will have to lead to new levels of trust – a willingness on the part of citizens to move from ad hoc, individualized strategies towards engagement with formal institutions and rule-based mechanisms.

No more than 7 per cent of Ukrainians in November 2015 felt that their state fulfils obligations to its citizens and provides them with goods and services, that their state can be trusted to do what is right and that their state treats individual citizens fairly – much lower than in Poland and Russia. This finding represented a significant decline from pre-EuroMaidan levels and found trust at its lowest level since the Ukraine Taxpayer Compliance Attitudinal Surveys began in 2005.

The research findings, however, highlight important opportunities for the Ukrainian government to rebuild its relationship with its citizens through key reforms to taxation. Overcoming distrust of the state is a difficult, but common task for any society, especially Ukraine. 'In sum, it makes far readier sense to distrust government than to trust it', writes Russell Hardin. 'The kinds of understanding necessary for trusting government are almost logically ruled out for typical citizens, while the kinds necessary for distrusting it are commonplace and resonant with ordinary life experience.'[3]

Ukraine does not adhere exactly to the model of either Poland or Russia. Poland is a case that enjoys a compliant society cooperating with a citizen-based state so that tax compliance depends greatly on trust in the government. Russia, meanwhile, has a society interacting with a state that strongly employs a coercion-based approach to tax collection in an environment with decreasing opportunities to be critical of the state through the media and through political contestation, or even to become aware of the state's shortcomings. There, tax compliance appears to depend largely on citizens' being susceptible to coercion and deterrence.

---

[2] Coynash.   [3] Hardin, 2002, p. 167.

262 Taxes and Trust

Ukraine is a different case. The use of coercion – to a degree that is not as extensive as in Russia – has been the state's primary method for securing tax compliance through its State Tax Administration, now renamed the State Fiscal Service. Yet the prevalence of greater media freedom than in Russia, which helps expose the failings of the state and its leaders, might have allowed Ukrainians as a whole to square their support for tax compliance between reactions to coercive measures of the state and their trust in the state.

Ukrainians are not as trusting of their state as Poles are of theirs, and with such low levels of trust in the state, Ukraine demonstrates the lowest support for obeying tax laws among the three states surveyed. Clearly, Ukraine's transition from a coercive, corrupt state to a more open, democratic one has taken place without (re-)establishing citizens' trust that their state will act fairly and will supply goods and services; the failure to build and draw upon such trust may very well limit the state's ability to administer its own policies.

Hence, the Ukraine Taxpayer Compliance Attitudinal Surveys suggest that the state probably needs to continue to undertake its own revolution and to embark on an overhaul of its own relationship with its citizens in order to gain (if not regain) their trust. The tentative position of critical state reforms in the aftermath of the Orange and EuroMaidan Revolutions raises the question of whether Ukraine's political leaders will lose a great opportunity to undertake such an overhaul so that the Ukrainian state actually will be able to govern on the ground to a greater extent. In Ukraine, you have the worst of both – a society that neither trusts nor fears the state, and one that is very capable of shunning obligations anyway and getting away with it. Twenty-five years after Ukraine secured its independence, Ukraine's statehood is no longer questioned by its citizens, but the Ukrainian state itself is.

Clearly, the trust that a bureaucratic rational state and a compliant society have in each other, as shown in the case of Poland, provides for greater implementation of state policies than the fear and distrust that exist between a more coercive state and its society, as demonstrated in Russia. Ukraine's present difficulties in building trust in the state rightly raise the question of how possible making such a transition can be without a short-term loss in the capacity of the state to function becoming permanent. Ukraine has never been able to reconcile a state–society divide, and this has been a mutually reinforcing process, fuelling antagonism between state and society. Yet, if the immediate hurdles can be overcome, a successful re-creation of the state will yield far more stable and successful governance, mutually empowering both state and society.

Towards Greater Trust and Tax Compliance 263

To build trust across the state–society divide, there also needs to be an enlarged, spirited intellectual and political debate over the future of Ukraine – not just regarding its independence, but as to what type of state and what type of society should develop there. Admittedly, most of the conversation recently has been about the war in the East, whether and how the state should be decentralized and the desired return of Crimea. But there has been little intellectual debate among prominent civil society members with respect to where Ukraine is going and how the old regime's void should be filled. Ukraine needs a much more vibrant debate regarding its future direction, what type of democracy should develop and how the society should interact with the state.

Despite the absence of such discussion, there has been much – and perhaps surprising – consensus within Ukraine and its parliament, the *Verkhovna Rada*, regarding the need to push further with reforms, as well as lively discussion as to whether the Yanukovych-era elites should be allowed to work for the state. A legal basis also has been created to push forward the process of decentralization, by allowing local taxes and granting budgetary powers to local governments.

Tax administration reform is currently also on Ukraine's reform agenda.[4] In addition to the efforts of key members of the *Rada* and the government, both the IMF and the OECD have been pushing Ukraine to make progress in this arena in order to help restore the country's financial stability and investment climate.[5] In the autumn of 2016, Ukraine and the IMF signed a Memorandum of Economic and Social Policy that included a commitment to reduce the tax administration staff from about 58,800 to about 44,000; to dissolve the tax police and, in consultation with IMF staff, establish 'a new civil service with new staff under the Ministry of Finance that will be responsible for investigation of financial and economic criminal offenses against the State, including tax-related offenses, while removing the role of other government agencies in this area'; to implement targeted compensation reform at the State Fiscal Service, in order to make salary levels comparable with those in other reformed government agencies, such as the new National Patrol Police in many Ukrainian cities; to establish a new internal investigation division at the State Fiscal Service with new staff who will assess risks, analyze reports on assets of high-ranking State Fiscal Service officials, and carry out investigations as part of efforts to tackle corruption – all under the control of a recently established independent expert group; and to conduct regular independent surveys to monitor public perception.[6]

---

[4] Interfax-Ukraine.   [5] Talant.   [6] IMF, 1 September 2016.

264   Taxes and Trust

Such recent reform efforts highlight that a discussion has begun as to how the state institutions, agencies and bureaucracies – the real guts and heart of the state apparatus that sit below the elites and interact at the street level with citizens – should be reformed and made less corrupt in Ukraine.

Policy Recommendations for Tax Administrations Transitioning to Trust

Transitioning from fear and distrust to trust can provide greater state viability. How to create 'good governance' and especially how to create a high level of administrative capacity after regime change is very high on the academic and global policy agendas. While the book has focused on former communist 'transition' countries, the approach taken and the results obtained are very likely to have 'universal' value, applicable to others who study, work in and advise developing countries.

Transitional states such as Ukraine must find ways to create and to build up levels of trust in the state on the part of citizens and to focus on 'procedural fairness' in order to improve compliance with state regulations within the tax administration and across other government agencies and services. How government behaviour impacts societal trust – that is, how the state maximizes or minimizes the levels of trust that society has – will affect, then, how well the state goal of ensuring the public's compliance is accomplished.

But how can states accomplish the two policy objectives – to build up trust and to emphasize 'procedural fairness'? The most fundamental question of all, perhaps, is how the tax administration officials identify who the client is. Is the client the government or the taxpayers? In Russia and Ukraine, the tax administration was established to serve the authorities in power, not the people. Going forward, the success of the reforms will depend on to what extent 'taxpayers' become the answer to that basic question, in recognition that the state bureaucracy should be 'rationalized' in a Weberian sense rather than 'empowered'.

More broadly, though, in the tax arena, the post-transition tax administrations should look for ways to rationalize their bureaucracies and to make them more society- and outward-oriented. Further, detailed suggestions on how to create trust and improve 'customer service' might include utilizing constructive *historical references*, *structures*, *human and technological resources* and *work philosophies*, which are all oriented towards society.

A. Historical References

How the state has treated citizens in the past and how the state and society view past state activity vis-à-vis citizens are important in determining how well citizens currently fulfil their obligations. Therefore, what may matter in terms of helping create better citizens is which historical model a current state applies or references when attempting to make itself capable and legitimate before society. At the crux is a need to focus on repeating and routinizing past and current experiences of well-perceived procedural fairness whenever and wherever possible, even for those states that may have a scarcity of such experiences in the past. Specific policy activities might include the following:

- Good governance at the street level can yield greater citizen trust and a greater ability to implement policy across transitional states like Ukraine – both across the state and within its tax administration.
- Improving trust on the part of all citizens and taxpayers toward the state, which has been low, for example, throughout post-Soviet Ukraine's history, must be deemed a prime, focal point for the entire state – including leading politicians, political leaders, administrative agencies and government bureaucracies alike. Indeed, as the findings from Chapter 7 showed that Ukrainian willingness to pay taxes can be highly dependent upon individual attitudes towards the president – even more than past positive experiences with the tax authorities – it is incumbent upon all political leaders to seek out and maintain long-term trust among citizens.
- Building upon good, healthy experiences – even if they are relatively new – should be a key focus. For example, Ukrainians, who have very low expectations that the state will treat them fairly, need to experience and witness first-hand that the post-2014 state will interact with them differently henceforth. Just as the public relations surrounding the National Police of Ukraine, launched in July 2015 by Poroshenko, has showcased a new manner of state authorities relating to the public, so, too, must other administrative services, including the tax administration, be re-launched to highlight a new manner of working with citizens at the ground level. The police reform in cities across Ukraine shows that the state can overhaul an agency and gain trust at the grassroots level. Good 'customer service', copied and mimicked from other state agencies, can make a real difference.
- Create new historical trends. When tax policy reforms are changing how much citizens are paying, it is also vital to make public spending and budget expenditures effective, less costly, transparent and visible.

266   Taxes and Trust

Since 2014, Ukrainians have been voluntarily giving money to their state's military directly or through friends even while they do not trust the state itself to allocate tax revenue effectively to the military. In other words, Ukrainians are voluntarily giving if they know such contributions will be targeted and go to the right place, but they do not trust the state to fund those places directly through taxes.[7] 'In this kind of situation, even ideal tax reforms will not succeed if the state fails to learn to manage taxpayer contributions in an efficient, thrifty manner', Lyubomyr Shavalyuk has written, 'because ordinary Ukrainians will continue to distrust it and not pay taxes.'[8] The lower the tax compliance, the greater the need for the state to show it is spending tax revenue wisely.

B. Structures

A rational structural design is one that is infused with both flexibility and constraints. In general, it is critically important to limit the degree of discretion afforded to tax officials in order to constrain corruption so that citizens can trust the system. This can be done, in part, through an organizational structure that has direct lines of subordination both between offices and within them, eliminating all forms of opportunity for partiality as much as possible. Suggested policy activities in this area might include the following:

- In transitional states such as Ukraine, reform of the tax bureaucracy needs to happen at the top, bottom and middle layers of the administration – simple lustration for a few is not sufficient. Such thorough reforms would empower tax officials and employees to behave more like true Weberian bureaucrats in a more publicly transparent organization.
- Monitoring activities need to be undertaken as new procedures, activities and reforms are carried out.
- Further, the establishment of departments inside the tax administration to conduct internal audits and checks and the establishment of an external watchdog – such as an empowered, independent national accounting chamber like Poland's Supreme Audit Chamber (*Najwyższa Izba Kontroli*, or NIK) – to produce critical financial and performance audit reports, available for the public, are critical to providing for a more effective administration and for gaining citizen trust in government activity.

---

[7] Bychenko.   [8] Shavalyuk.

C. Human and Technological Resources

In addition to seeking out and employing professional, capable personnel and new, cost-efficient technologies, the tax administrations can employ a variety of employment training techniques and outreach activities to help bureaucrats better interact with the public in explaining how the (new and old) taxes work. Such public-outreach procedures taken up by tax administration personnel might include the establishment within local tax offices of low-tech 'information checkpoints', staffed by employees who know the tax laws well; a more high-tech mass media campaign, in which local tax bureaucrats appear on radio, television, web and social media to explain new laws and procedures; and the maintenance of websites, which enable taxpayers to write to their own tax offices, as detailed below:

- Real taxpayer outreach programmes (such as those that took place in Poland in the 1990s when that country rolled out its new tax system) need to be undertaken in transitional countries. In the early 1990s, Poland truly was unique among the three countries in this study in that tax bureaucrats really went out into the public to educate people as to what these newly founded things called taxes were. The Polish experience, which saw ordinary, local tax bureaucrats go on local television and radio programmes and open special tax assistance booths inside the tax offices in order to explain what the new tax system was all about, did help improve citizen perception of the state and increase the numbers of those filing taxes. By the end of the 1990s, Poles rated the tax administration – yes, the tax administration! – as *the* most favoured state agency due to this type of outreach.[9] That type of public interaction did not take place farther to the East, but states such as Ukraine now have the opportunity to re-boot their tax outreach reforms alongside tax policy reforms. One of the Ukraine Tax Administration's more successful civics activities has been colour drawing competitions for elementary schoolchildren, but outreach can be much more than that.
- In lieu of individual personal income tax filing, employees should be made much more aware of the fact that they are paying taxes, what their pre-tax and post-tax salaries are, the tax rate and the withholding process in general, even if their employers file for them. By being informed how much and at what rate employers are deducting, citizens will become more aware that they actually are paying taxes and that the state should be accountable to them.

[9] Wrobel.

268   Taxes and Trust

- An advertising campaign employing websites and social media, as well as literature distributed along with monthly pay cheques, should be targeted at all citizens who pay taxes to inform them of the new tax changes regardless of who files taxes. At times when there are changes in tax rates, especially a lowering of rates, it is not sufficient that the tax policy reforms simply yield larger pay cheques. Citizens and employees should also be made aware of what the old tax policy was and what the new tax policy is. (In Ukraine's case, only some 9 to 13 per cent of Ukrainians knew the correct personal income tax rate.)
- In countries where individuals file their own personal income taxes, the taxpayer takes on a greater role as a citizen by completing self-assessments and tax declaration forms. Such an interactive mode of paying taxes was even understood by Imperial Russian tax authorities, as Yanni Kotsonis has described, as a way of making citizens out of them. Such an assessment process 'produced the notion that the citizen, not the state, was doing the taxing or that the state was taxing only to the extent that it comprised the citizenry. The mode of thinking was expressed in taxation as "self-assessment."'[10] While more complicated, individual filing of taxes has been shown to increase citizens' interest in and sense of accountability over the state; by simply recognizing that they are paying for the state's income, individual filing encourages citizens and society to take a more accountable view of the state.
- Citizens must become more aware of the availability of reimbursements through the tax system for items such as medical, prescription and/or education expenses, and the tax administration should be encouraged to make such 'tax refunds' easier to claim with new technologies. Being able to claim money back from the state will encourage greater interaction with the state and encourage compliance, as was the case in Poland in the 1990s when within a period of about five years the number of citizens filing taxes in order to get reimbursements from the state increased dramatically.
- Surveys should constantly be undertaken by tax administration staff of those directly affected by reforms in order to get feedback and to fine tune reform actions to get best results, as well as to showcase wins and to demonstrate that the state is listening to public.

D. Work Philosophy

A primary basis for differences in the degree of discretion given to tax officials often can be accounted for by the overall work philosophy (esprit

[10] Kotsonis, p. 16.

de corps) of the tax system – specifically, whether the system focuses to a greater extent on compliance than on reaching collection target goals:

- A compliance-driven approach promotes a work ethic that tends to treat the taxpayers more like clients, which can encourage good citizenship. Further, whether a system is compliance- or target-driven provides different incentives for tax inspectors. A more target-driven approach can lead the focus away from ensuring compliance with tax laws and towards making tax inspectors merely try to fulfil quarterly or yearly targets, and to seek additional payments from those firms and individuals who have paid their dues rather than to locate those who have not paid at all. In Russia and Ukraine, such internal target levels have never really gone away. A system built on incentives and bonuses for collecting revenue – and for levying more fines on taxpayers – leads to firms being pressured to pay taxes in advance and takes away from the prime tax collection function of aiding and helping taxpayers to comply with the law.

In short, the extent to which state tax administrations utilize *historical reference points, structures, human and technological resources* and a *work philosophy* that are oriented outward towards the public may well impact the extent to which taxpayers can trust their tax system, leading them to be more compliant. Identifying and implementing policies that raise both levels of public trust in the state and the level of 'customer service' offered by the tax administration does assist taxpayers in becoming true citizens, who then can follow through on their obligations to their state. By making changes and adopting some of the above policy prescriptions, tax administrations will find that their personnel's mentality will change as well.

Borderland states are always concerned that their friends one day will abandon them. And, with agendas of those in the European Union and North America always susceptible to adjustments, whether out of fatigue or in pursuit of new interests elsewhere, it is important to recognize that transition states are not failed states, but simply weak ones, requiring effective guidance and support to see the transformation through. By being at the heart of the state, the tax administration becomes the epicentre of this state transformation process.

So how does a state transition from a coercive state to a legal, legitimate tax state? Poland's path, of course, is the ideal one, but Ukraine's protracted route is the reality for too many states – including one day, perhaps, Russia.

Those interested either in the establishment of an accountable, highly capable state or in the transition of any coercive state to a more compliance-oriented one must be concerned with states such as Ukraine, caught in the middle. Ukraine matters not just because of its location and geography, but also because its development will show whether a state can transition successfully from post-Soviet rule to the rule of law relatively late in the game – and tackling such a task is in the interest of the West.

Appendix I: Poland, Russia and Ukraine Taxpayer Compliance Attitudinal Surveys 2004–2015 and the Russian Tax Officials Survey 2011

In Poland, the CBOS Public Opinion Research Centre conducted the 2004 survey, designed by this author, on 5–8 November 2004. The sample size was 988 respondents. The method employed was face-to-face PAPI, in which the interviewer filled out a paper questionnaire. The margin of error did not exceed 3.2 per cent. The Polish 2010 survey was conducted in September 2010 on 2,021 Poles nationwide by the PBS DDG Market Research firm, based in Sopot.

For the Russian 2004 survey, carried out by the Public Opinion Foundation on 23–24 October 2004, nationwide home interviews were conducted in 44 regions. The sample size was 1,500 respondents. Additional polls were made of the Moscow population, with a sample of 600 respondents. The margin of error did not exceed 3.6 per cent. The Russian 2010 survey also was carried out by the Public Opinion Foundation on 7–12 July 2010 with a nationwide sample size of 3,000 respondents.

In Ukraine, the survey was carried out nationwide on 3,995 Ukrainians on 20–29 November 2005 by the Razumkov Centre for Economic and Political Studies. The method employed was face-to-face interviews. The response rate was 70.6 per cent. The margin of error did not exceed 2.3 per cent. The Ukrainian 2010 survey was also carried out by the Razumkov Centre on 4,015 Ukrainians nationwide from 10 August to 5 October. The Ukrainian 2012 survey also was carried out by the Razumkov Centre on 2,008 Ukrainians nationwide in April 2012. The Ukrainian 2015 survey also was carried out by the Razumkov Centre on 4,025 Ukrainians nationwide (excluding Crimea and areas of occupied Donetsk and Luhansk oblasts that were inaccessible to researchers) on 30 October–7 November 2015.

In Russia, the Public Opinion Foundation carried out a survey, also designed by this author, from 15 September to 31 October 2011, of 1,015 public officials, of whom 39.5 per cent, or 401 individuals, were tax officials.

All survey responses are rounded to the closest per cent.

Blank = not asked

272 Appendix I

1. Do you consider yourself to be a taxpayer?

	Poland 2004	Poland 2010	Russia 2004	Russia 2010	Ukraine 2005	Ukraine 2010	Ukraine 2012	Ukraine 2015
Yes		83	66	75	61	59	59	60
No		15	30	22	30	35	35	33
Difficult to say		2	4	3	9	6	7	6

2. Who files your personal income taxes?

	Poland 2004	Poland 2010	Russia 2004	Russia 2010	Ukraine 2005	Ukraine 2010	Ukraine 2012	Ukraine 2015	Russian tax officials 2011
I, myself, do	54	22	13	17	7	7	8	9	
My employer does	5	44	47	50	46	44	43	43	
No one does		6	6	7	13	13	12	12	
Somebody else does	19		4	6	6	8	9	7	
I don't have to pay taxes	19	6	24	16	17	19	20	18	
Other situation	3	22							
Difficult to answer	1	2	6	5	11	9	8	10	

3. Are there many dishonest people who work in the tax service?
Russian Tax Officials Survey 2011: In present conditions is it difficult for tax service co-workers always to work honestly?

	Poland 2004	Poland 2010	Russia 2004	Russia 2010	Ukraine 2005	Ukraine 2010	Ukraine 2012	Ukraine 2015	Russian tax officials 2011
Yes, there are many dishonest tax service employees	21	23	42	35	52	53	55	47	14
No, there are few dishonest tax service employees	43	53	25	32	20	27	21	26	81
There are no such people	2	4	2	2	1	1	1	1	
Difficult to say	33	20	31	30	28	20	24	26	5

Appendix I 273

4. How, in your opinion, do the tax service employees cope with their responsibilities – excellent, good, fair, bad or very bad?

	Poland 2004	Poland 2010	Russia 2004	Russia 2010	Ukraine 2005	Ukraine 2010	Ukraine 2012	Ukraine 2015	Russian tax officials 2011
Excellent	2	2	3	2	2	2			1
Good	26	33	15	19	15	16			14
Satisfactorily	27	35	29	42	34	40			35
Bad	17	10	14	9	16	12			17
Very bad	4	3	5	3	4	3			4
Difficult to answer	24	16	33	25	29	27			30

5. Do you think the taxpayers who have had to deal with tax service employees are satisfied or not satisfied with how tax service employees talked and interacted with them?

	Poland 2004	Poland 2010	Russia 2004	Russia 2010	Ukraine 2005	Ukraine 2010	Ukraine 2012	Ukraine 2015	Russian tax officials 2011
Taxpayers are satisfied					17	21		23	
Taxpayers are not satisfied					37	34		34	
Difficult to Answer					46	45		43	

6. During the past five years, have you had business with employees of the tax service?

	Poland 2004	Poland 2010	Russia 2004	Russia 2010	Ukraine 2005	Ukraine 2010	Ukraine 2012	Ukraine 2015	Russian tax officials 2011
Yes	49	38	23	24	15	12	11	19	
No	50	61	73	75	82	85	85	79	
Difficult to say	1	2	4	1	4	3	4	3	

274 Appendix I

7. **What was your impression of the individual contact you had with the tax service employees?**
(For those saying 'Yes' in question #6.)

	Poland 2004	Poland 2010	Russia 2004	Russia 2010	Ukraine 2005	Ukraine 2010	Ukraine 2012	Ukraine 2015	Russian tax officials 2011
Positive	51	50	30	37	27	30	28	31	
Neutral	30	32	38	34	35	38	40	36	
Negative	19	17	29	27	31	30	31	32	
Difficult to say	0	1	3	2	6	2	2	1	

8. **Were you satisfied with the results of your meeting with the tax service employees?**
(For those saying 'Yes' in question #6.)

	Poland 2004	Poland 2010	Russia 2004	Russia 2010	Ukraine 2005	Ukraine 2010	Ukraine 2012	Ukraine 2015	Russian tax officials 2011
Satisfied	76	79	58	66	47	52	56	49	
Not satisfied	23	17	33	31	40	41	37	44	
Difficult to say	1	4	10	3	13	7	7	6	

9. **Were you satisfied by how the tax service employees spoke with and treated you?**
(For those saying 'Yes' in question #6.)

	Poland 2004	Poland 2010	Russia 2004	Russia 2010	Ukraine 2005	Ukraine 2010	Ukraine 2012	Ukraine 2015	Russian tax officials 2011
Satisfied	77	75	63	67	49	54	56	52	
Not satisfied	22	21	34	29	41	40	40	42	
Difficult to say	1	4	3	4	11	6	4	6	

10. **Are the procedures and basis of the tax service understandable to you?**
(Poland 2010, Russia 2010, Ukraine 2010 Surveys: Only asked of those who answered yes to Question #6.)

	Poland 2004	Poland 2010	Russia 2004	Russia 2010	Ukraine 2005	Ukraine 2010	Ukraine 2012	Ukraine 2015	Russian tax officials 2011
Yes		48		58		49		24	
No		48		38		47		55	
Difficult to answer		4		4		5		22	

Appendix I

11. Can one always count on the assistance of bureaucrats in the tax office?
(Poland 2010, Russia 2010, Ukraine 2010 Surveys: Only asked of those who answered yes to Question #6.)

	Poland 2004	Poland 2010	Russia 2004	Russia 2010	Ukraine 2005	Ukraine 2010	Ukraine 2012	Ukraine 2015	Russian tax officials 2011
Yes		64		36		31		25	
No		31		54		63		44	
Difficult to answer		5		10		7		32	

12. Does contact with the tax service take up a lot of time?
(Poland 2010, Russia 2010, Ukraine 2010 Surveys: Only asked of those who answered yes to Question #6.)

	Poland 2004	Poland 2010	Russia 2004	Russia 2010	Ukraine 2005	Ukraine 2010	Ukraine 2012	Ukraine 2015	Russian tax officials 2011
Yes		37		73		75		37	
No		62		23		20		16	
Difficult to answer		1		4		5		37	

13. Do many or few people evade taxes in your country?

	Poland 2004	Poland 2010	Russia 2004	Russia 2010	Ukraine 2005	Ukraine 2010	Ukraine 2012	Ukraine 2015	Russian tax officials 2011
Many	69	65	77	67	70	69	69	72	74
Few	17	21	8	18	14	21	16	16	21
There are no such people	1		0	1	1	0	1	1	0
Difficult to answer	13	14	15	15	16	10	14	11	4

276   Appendix I

14. What do you think encourages people more to pay taxes: a sense of civic responsibility or fear of punishment for evasion?

	Poland 2004	Poland 2010	Russia 2004	Russia 2010	Ukraine 2005	Ukraine 2010	Ukraine 2012	Ukraine 2015	Russian tax officials 2011
A sense of civic responsibility	27	22	36	40	38	35		40	
A fear of punishment	69	73	49	52	49	54		50	
Difficult to answer	5	5	15	8	14	11		11	

15. Some people believe that tax evasion is unacceptable in any case. Others believe that there are situations in which it is permissible to evade taxes. With which opinion – the first or the second – do you agree?

	Poland 2004	Poland 2010	Russia 2004	Russia 2010	Ukraine 2005	Ukraine 2010	Ukraine 2012	Ukraine 2015	Russian tax officials 2011
With the first	49	53	30	53	47	53		48	
With the second	37	35	50	34	33	30		34	
Difficult to answer	14	12	20	14	20	17		18	

16. Is it possible that you would evade taxes if you were sure that you could get away with it?

	Poland 2004	Poland 2010	Russia 2004	Russia 2010	Ukraine 2005	Ukraine 2010	Ukraine 2012	Ukraine 2015	Russian tax officials 2011
Yes	53	47	40	45	34	38	29	39	14
No	34	45	38	40	40	43	47	41	81
Difficult to say	14	8	22	15	26	19	24	20	5

Appendix I   277

17. Is it possible that you could avoid paying taxes if you knew for sure that you would not receive a serious punishment?
(Ukraine 2005: Is it possible that you could avoid paying taxes if you knew for sure that you would not have to go to jail and would not have to pay a large fine?)

	Poland 2004	Poland 2010	Russia 2004	Russia 2010	Ukraine 2005	Ukraine 2010	Ukraine 2012	Ukraine 2015	Russian tax officials 2011
Yes		44		42	30	35	28	36	14
No		49		40	43	47	47	42	81
Difficult to say		8		17	29	19	26	22	4

18. Do you pay taxes only because you know that you will be punished by the state if you don't?

	Poland 2004	Poland 2010	Russia 2004	Russia 2010	Ukraine 2005	Ukraine 2010	Ukraine 2012	Ukraine 2015	Russian tax officials 2011
Yes		55		47	38	44	35	43	
No		37		39	40	41	43	40	
Difficult to say		8		14	22	16	22	17	

19. Is it possible that you could avoid paying taxes, if you were sure, that there would be no punishment, but your friends, acquaintances and co-workers would know and wouldn't approve?

	Poland 2004	Poland 2010	Russia 2004	Russia 2010	Ukraine 2005	Ukraine 2010	Ukraine 2012	Ukraine 2015	Russian tax officials 2011
Yes		40		36	24	30	25	32	9
No		50		46	45	50	48	45	84
Difficult to say		10		19	31	20	27	23	6

20. Would a majority of people avoid paying taxes, if they thought that they would not receive any punishment?

	Poland 2004	Poland 2010	Russia 2004	Russia 2010	Ukraine 2005	Ukraine 2010	Ukraine 2012	Ukraine 2015	Russian tax officials 2011
Yes	88		71	75	63	66		65	73
No	6		14	15	19	21		18	25
Difficult to say	6		15	10	19	14		14	2

278   Appendix I

21. Should a citizen always follow the tax laws, even if s/he considers them to be unfair?

	Poland 2004	Poland 2010	Russia 2004	Russia 2010	Ukraine 2005	Ukraine 2010	Ukraine 2012	Ukraine 2015	Russian tax officials 2011
A citizen should always follow the tax laws	79	81	71	74	57	64	59	61	91
A citizen should not always follow the tax laws	14	12	17	18	28	24	25	25	7
Difficult to say	7	7	12	8	15	12	16	14	2

22. Would you follow the tax laws even if you do not consider them to be fair?

	Poland 2004	Poland 2010	Russia 2004	Russia 2010	Ukraine 2005	Ukraine 2010	Ukraine 2012	Ukraine 2015	Russian tax officials 2011
Yes, I would follow the tax laws	83	77	53	52	36	44	39	45	75
No, I would not follow the tax laws	6	15	28	30	37	37	36	34	22
Difficult to say	10	18	19	18	27	20	25	22	3

23. Would a majority of taxpayers follow the tax laws even if they did not consider them to be fair?

	Poland 2004	Poland 2010	Russia 2004	Russia 2010	Ukraine 2005	Ukraine 2010	Ukraine 2012	Ukraine 2015	Russian tax officials 2011
Yes									63
No									31
Difficult to say									5

Appendix I 279

24. Are you confident that the tax service would never try to take more money from you than it should?

	Poland 2004	Poland 2010	Russia 2004	Russia 2010	Ukraine 2005	Ukraine 2010	Ukraine 2012	Ukraine 2015	Russian tax officials 2011
Yes		56		40	33	27	24	24	
No		31		40	35	51	48	50	
Difficult to say		14		20	32	22	28	26	

25. How do you suppose, does the ordinary citizen have a possibility to defend his or her interests before the co-workers of the tax service or does he or she not have such a possibility?

	Poland 2004	Poland 2010	Russia 2004	Russia 2010	Ukraine 2005	Ukraine 2010	Ukraine 2012	Ukraine 2015	Russian tax officials 2011
Yes		34	37	35	33	20		19	
No		53	43	45	45	60		56	
Difficult to say		13	19	20	22	20		26	

26. Are the tax laws in your country fair?

	Poland 2004	Poland 2010	Russia 2004	Russia 2010	Ukraine 2005	Ukraine 2010	Ukraine 2012	Ukraine 2015	Russian tax officials 2011
Yes		21		32		19	16	12	72
No		62		45		61	63	68	18
Difficult to Say		14		23		21	21	20	10

27. Is your country's tax system simple or complicated?

	Poland 2004	Poland 2010	Russia 2004	Russia 2010	Ukraine 2005	Ukraine 2010	Ukraine 2012	Ukraine 2015	Russian tax officials 2011
Simple		18		18		13		7	19
Complicated		72		57		67		70	77
Difficult to Say		10		25		20		23	4

280   Appendix I

28. If the state does not fulfil its obligations to its citizens, then is tax evasion justified?

	Poland 2004	Poland 2010	Russia 2004	Russia 2010	Ukraine 2005	Ukraine 2010	Ukraine 2012	Ukraine 2015	Russian tax officials 2011
Yes	40	44	60	52	47	51		48	23
No	44	44	23	33	31	33		35	69
Difficult to Say	16	12	18	14	21	16		17	7

29. Do you feel that when you pay taxes, the money is returned to you and your close ones through government expenditures?

	Poland 2004	Poland 2010	Russia 2004	Russia 2010	Ukraine 2005	Ukraine 2010	Ukraine 2012	Ukraine 2015	Russian tax officials 2011
Yes		45		43	15	41		41	
No		46		43		42		40	
No answer		9		14		17		19	
No/no answer					85				

30. Do you feel that when you pay taxes, honestly earned wages are seized from you?

	Poland 2004	Poland 2010	Russia 2004	Russia 2010	Ukraine 2005	Ukraine 2010	Ukraine 2012	Ukraine 2015	Russian tax officials 2011
Yes		60		52	19	41		41	
No		32		30		40		37	
No answer		8		18		19		22	
No/no answer		.			81				

31. Do you feel that when you pay taxes, you are supporting those who need such money more?

	Poland 2004	Poland 2010	Russia 2004	Russia 2010	Ukraine 2005	Ukraine 2010	Ukraine 2012	Ukraine 2015	Russian tax officials 2011
Yes		49		45	14	44		45	
No		42		39		40		35	
No answer		9		15		15		19	
No/no answer					86				

Appendix I 281

32. When you pay taxes, are you proud to be a part of the financial power of the state?

	Poland 2004	Poland 2010	Russia 2004	Russia 2010	Ukraine 2005	Ukraine 2010	Ukraine 2012	Ukraine 2015	Russian tax officials 2011
Yes		43		40	12	35		32	
No		48		40		45		45	
Difficult to answer		10		19		20		23	
No/no answer					88				

33. When you pay taxes, do you think that all the money will be stolen by bureaucrats anyway?

	Poland 2004	Poland 2010	Russia 2004	Russia 2010	Ukraine 2005	Ukraine 2010	Ukraine 2012	Ukraine 2015	Russian tax officials 2011
Yes		39		52	22	52		55	
No		52		30		28		24	
Difficult to answer		9		18		20		21	
No/no answer					76				

34. When you pay taxes, do you think that while taxpayers' money is not stolen, it is not distributed as you would like?

	Poland 2004	Poland 2010	Russia 2004	Russia 2010	Ukraine 2005	Ukraine 2010	Ukraine 2012	Ukraine 2015	Russian tax officials 2011
Yes		70		61	22	60		53	
No		19		19		21		23	
Difficult to answer		11		20		19		23	
No/no answer					78				

282 Appendix I

35. How satisfied are you with how the state spends taxpayers' money?

	Poland 2004	Poland 2010	Russia 2004	Russia 2010	Ukraine 2005	Ukraine 2010	Ukraine 2012	Ukraine 2015	Russian tax officials 2011
Satisfied		18		18		9		6	
Not satisfied		70		61		75		77	
Difficult to say		12		21		17		17	

36. What is the personal income tax (PIT) rate in your country today?

	Poland 2004	Poland 2010	Russia 2004	Russia 2010	Ukraine 2005	Ukraine 2010	Ukraine 2012	Ukraine 2015	Russian tax officials 2011
Correct answer*	22	38	46	9	10	13	13		
I don't know	63	21	52	39	73	68	68		
Incorrect answer	16	5	3	30	16	20	8		
Difficult to say	0	11	0	28	0	0	12		
No response		24							

* 13% for Russia in 2004 and 2010 and for Ukraine in 2005. 15% for Ukraine in 2010 and 2012. Either 15% or 20% for Ukraine in 2015 (15% for monthly income not exceeding 10 minimum salaries (UAH 12,180) and 20% for income that exceeds that amount.) For Poland in 2010, responses of 18, 19 or 32% or a combination thereof were considered 'correct,' as PIT is progressive with an individual rate of 18% or 32%. Individuals also can choose, under certain conditions, to pay a flat rate of 19% on business income.

37. What is the value-added tax (VAT) rate in your country today?

	Poland 2004	Poland 2010	Russia 2004	Russia 2010	Ukraine 2005	Ukraine 2010	Ukraine 2012	Ukraine 2015	Russian tax officials 2011
Correct answer*		34		12		32		23	
I don't know		45		74		63		61	
Incorrect answer		22		13		5		5	
Difficult to say				0		0		11	
No response									

* In 2010, it was 22% in Poland, 18% in Russia and 20% Ukraine. In 2015 it was also 20% in Ukraine.

Appendix I 283

38. Is it necessary to increase, reduce, modify or outright cancel the personal income tax on individuals?

	Poland 2004	Poland 2010	Russia 2004	Russia 2010	Ukraine 2005	Ukraine 2010	Ukraine 2012	Ukraine 2015	Russian tax officials 2011
Need to increase		1		3		2		1	
Don't need to modify		30		38		21		15	
Need to reduce		48		38		44		52	
Need to cancel outright		7		6		6		8	
I don't know this tax		6		2		5		6	
Difficult to answer		8		13		21		19	

39. Is it necessary to increase, reduce, modify or outright cancel the company payroll charges?
(Poland 2010 Survey: 'Company contributions to social, pension and medical insurance (ZUS)'; Russian 2010 Survey: 'Company deductions for social, pension and health insurance.')

	Poland 2004	Poland 2010	Russia 2004	Russia 2010	Ukraine 2005	Ukraine 2010	Ukraine 2012	Ukraine 2015	Russian tax officials 2011
Need to increase		7		29		7		6	
Don't need to modify		34		40		20		17	
Need to reduce		41		12		40		44	
Need to cancel outright		6		2		4		6	
I don't know this tax		3		2		7		7	
Difficult to answer		9		15		22		21	

284   Appendix I

40. Is it necessary to increase, reduce, modify or outright cancel the single tax for individual entrepreneurs?
(Poland 2010 Survey: 'Uniform tax for individuals engaged in economic activities (PIT 5L).')

	Poland 2004	Poland 2010	Russia 2004	Russia 2010	Ukraine 2005	Ukraine 2010	Ukraine 2012	Ukraine 2015	Russian tax officials 2011
Need to increase	3		15		9		7		
Don't need to modify	32		36		27		21		
Need to reduce	29		18		32		37		
Need to cancel outright	3		2		3		4		
I don't know this tax	20		5		6		8		
Difficult to answer	13		24		23		23		

41. Is it necessary to increase, reduce, modify or outright cancel the corporate income tax (CIT)?

	Poland 2004	Poland 2010	Russia 2004	Russia 2010	Ukraine 2005	Ukraine 2010	Ukraine 2012	Ukraine 2015	Russian tax officials 2011
Need to increase	11		18		12		12		
Don't need to modify	30		37		21		20		
Need to reduce	19		14		31		33		
Need to cancel outright	3		2		3		4		
I don't know this tax	24		4		8		7		
Difficult to answer	13		26		25		25		

Appendix I

42. Is it necessary to increase, reduce, modify or outright cancel the value-added tax (VAT)?

	Poland 2004	Poland 2010	Russia 2004	Russia 2010	Ukraine 2005	Ukraine 2010	Ukraine 2012	Ukraine 2015	Russian tax officials 2011
Need to increase	1		3		2				1
Don't need to modify	29		31		16				14
Need to reduce	53		23		37				45
Need to cancel outright	6		7		15				15
I don't know this tax	4		6		7				3
Difficult to answer	6		30		23				21

43. Is it necessary to increase, reduce, modify or outright cancel the excise duties on alcoholic beverages and tobacco?

	Poland 2004	Poland 2010	Russia 2004	Russia 2010	Ukraine 2005	Ukraine 2010	Ukraine 2012	Ukraine 2015	Russian tax officials 2011
Need to increase	28		37		26				23
Don't need to modify	33		30		22				23
Need to reduce	26		14		28				29
Need to cancel outright	5		3		6				6
I don't know this tax	3		3		3				2
Difficult to answer	7		13		15				17

286   Appendix I

44. Do you trust the president?

	Poland 2004	Poland 2010	Russia 2004	Russia 2010	Ukraine 2005	Ukraine 2010	Ukraine 2012	Ukraine 2015	Russian tax officials 2011
Yes, I trust	56	43	54	63	29	37		18	70
Sometimes I trust, sometimes I don't		27	29	23	50	45		53	20
No, I don't trust	37	27	13	12	17	16		26	5
Difficult to answer	7	4	4	2	5	3		4	4

45. Do you trust parliament?
(Poland: 'Sejm'; Russia: 'State Duma'; Ukraine: 'Verkhovna Rada.')

	Poland 2004	Poland 2010	Russia 2004	Russia 2010	Ukraine 2005	Ukraine 2010	Ukraine 2012	Ukraine 2015	Russian tax officials 2011
Yes, I trust	17	25		26	16	24		7	55
Sometimes I trust, sometimes I don't		32		31	64	55		56	27
No, I don't trust	71	40		36	14	18		35	12
Difficult to answer	12	3		7	6	3		3	6

46. Do you trust the upper house of parliament?
(Poland: 'Senate'; Russia: 'Federation Council.')

	Poland 2004	Poland 2010	Russia 2004	Russia 2010	Ukraine 2005	Ukraine 2010	Ukraine 2012	Ukraine 2015	Russian tax officials 2011
Yes, I trust		31		33					59
Sometimes I trust, sometimes I don't		29		30					23
No, I don't trust		35		21					9
Difficult to answer		5		15					9

Appendix I 287

47. Do you trust the government?

	Poland 2004	Poland 2010	Russia 2004	Russia 2010	Ukraine 2005	Ukraine 2010	Ukraine 2012	Ukraine 2015	Russian tax officials 2011
Yes, I trust	21	28		42	18	28		7	62
Sometimes I trust, sometimes I don't		32		33	36	29		24	23
No, I don't trust	70	37		19	37	39		66	9
Difficult to answer		3		6	8	4		1	6

48. Do you trust the head of the government (premier)?

	Poland 2004	Poland 2010	Russia 2004	Russia 2010	Ukraine 2005	Ukraine 2010	Ukraine 2012	Ukraine 2015	Russian tax officials 2011
Yes, I trust		34		62					70
Sometimes I trust, sometimes I don't		27		22					20
No, I don't trust		36		13					6
Difficult to answer		3		3					4

49. Do you trust the procuracy?

	Poland 2004	Poland 2010	Russia 2004	Russia 2010	Ukraine 2005	Ukraine 2010	Ukraine 2012	Ukraine 2015	Russian tax officials 2011
Yes, I trust		33		26		13		6	60
Sometimes I trust, sometimes I don't		26		29		25		19	24
No, I don't trust		29		31		50		69	10
Difficult to Answer		12		14		11		6	6

288 Appendix I

50. Do you trust the police?
(Poland 2010 Survey: 'Policja'; Russia 2010, Ukraine 2010 and 2015 Surveys: 'Militsiya'; Russian Tax Officials Survey: 'Politsiya')

	Poland 2004	Poland 2010	Russia 2004	Russia 2010	Ukraine 2005	Ukraine 2010	Ukraine 2012	Ukraine 2015	Russian tax officials 2011
Yes, I trust		44		19		13		8	50
Sometimes I trust, sometimes I don't		28		30		26		23	28
No, I don't trust		24		44		53		64	16
Difficult to answer		3		8		7		6	6

51. Do you trust the state apparatus (bureaucrats)?

	Poland 2004	Poland 2010	Russia 2004	Russia 2010	Ukraine 2005	Ukraine 2010	Ukraine 2012	Ukraine 2015	Russian tax officials 2011
Yes, I trust		30		11		9		4	53
Sometimes I trust, sometimes I don't		37		27		27		20	29
No, I don't trust		29		51		56		70	12
Difficult to answer		4		10		7		5	6

52. Do you trust the courts?

	Poland 2004	Poland 2010	Russia 2004	Russia 2010	Ukraine 2005	Ukraine 2010	Ukraine 2012	Ukraine 2015	Russian tax officials 2011
Yes, I trust		41		25		11		6	58
Sometimes I trust, sometimes I don't		27		31		23		17	27
No, I don't trust		26		32		55		72	9
Difficult to answer		6		13		10		5	6

Appendix I   289

53. Do you trust the regional (oblast, wojewod) state administration?
(Russia 2010 Survey: 'Leader of your oblast (krai, republic).')

	Poland 2004	Poland 2010	Russia 2004	Russia 2010	Ukraine 2005	Ukraine 2010	Ukraine 2012	Ukraine 2015	Russian tax officials 2011
Yes, I trust		29		42				11	60
Sometimes I trust, sometimes I don't		29		33				32	24
No, I don't trust		21		19				45	11
Difficult to answer		21		6				12	5

54. How often do you think the government does the right thing?

	Poland 2004	Poland 2010	Russia 2004	Russia 2010	Ukraine 2005	Ukraine 2010	Ukraine 2012	Ukraine 2015	Russian tax officials 2011
Always, almost always		18		26		10		6	
Sometimes		62		52		49		43	
Almost never, never		15		13		34		34	
Difficult to answer		5		10		8		7	

55. Does your state fulfil its obligations to its citizens?
(Ukraine 2005: Does your government fulfil its obligations to its citizens?)

	Poland 2004	Poland 2010	Russia 2004	Russia 2010	Ukraine 2005	Ukraine 2010	Ukraine 2012	Ukraine 2015	Russian tax officials 2011
Yes		21		24	9	10	12	6	47
Sometimes yes, sometimes no		50		44	35	35	29	29	37
No		26		27	50	52	54	60	14
Difficult to say		4		5	5	3	5	4	2

290 Appendix I

56. Do you think you can trust your state to do what is right?
(Ukraine 2005: Do you think you can trust your government to do what is right?)

	Poland 2004	Poland 2010	Russia 2004	Russia 2010	Ukraine 2005	Ukraine 2010	Ukraine 2012	Ukraine 2015	Russian tax officials 2011
Yes		21		26	9	10	11	6	50
Sometimes yes, sometimes no		50		52	32	49	40	43	31
No		26		13	51	34	43	44	7
Difficult to say		4		10	8	8	7	7	11

57. Does the state relate to all citizens in an equal, fair manner?

	Poland 2004	Poland 2010	Russia 2004	Russia 2010	Ukraine 2005	Ukraine 2010	Ukraine 2012	Ukraine 2015	Russian tax officials 2011
Yes		21		20		15	15	7	51
No		75		73		81	79	87	45
Difficult to say		4		7		5	7	6	4

58. Does the state protect you?

	Poland 2004	Poland 2010	Russia 2004	Russia 2010	Ukraine 2005	Ukraine 2010	Ukraine 2012	Ukraine 2015	Russian tax officials 2011
Yes		43		42		28	28	23	71
No		43		48		64	63	68	21
Difficult to say		13		10		8	10	9	8

59. Does the state fight against corruption well, poorly or not at all?

	Poland 2004	Poland 2010	Russia 2004	Russia 2010	Ukraine 2005	Ukraine 2010	Ukraine 2012	Ukraine 2015	Russian tax officials 2011
Well		27		17		10		5	47
Poorly		46		51		54		56	34
Not at all		15		23		28		34	10
Difficult to say		12		9		8		4	9

Appendix I 291

60. How would you assess the current political system in your country? Give your answer on a scale from '1' to '7,' where '1' means that the political system is very bad, and '7' – very good.

	Poland 2004	Poland 2010	Russia 2004	Russia 2010	Ukraine 2005	Ukraine 2010	Ukraine 2012	Ukraine 2015	Russian tax officials 2011
1		11		8		12		27	
2		10		8		17		20	
3		19		17		24		22	
4		35		33		23		15	
5		16		16		10		6	
6		5		7		6		2	
7		1		3		2		1	
Difficult to answer		4		9		8		8	

61. Generally speaking, do you think the events in your country are developing in the right or wrong direction?

	Poland 2004	Poland 2010	Russia 2004	Russia 2010	Ukraine 2005	Ukraine 2010	Ukraine 2012	Ukraine 2015	Russian tax officials 2011
In the right direction		35		48				16	
In the wrong direction		51		32				68	
Difficult to answer		15		20				17	

Appendix II: Russian Public Officials Survey of Tax and Social Welfare Bureaucrats, 2011

In Russia, the Public Opinion Foundation carried out this survey, designed by this author, from 10 August to 25 October 2011, of 1,015 public officials, of whom 39.5 per cent were tax officials. Also surveyed were those working in the government services responsible for child-care benefits (20.9 per cent of those surveyed), unemployment benefits (19.8 per cent) and registration of property (19.8 per cent.)

With respect to the status of the officials, 20–30 per cent were federal officials, heads of regional offices and their deputies or heads of city departments or their deputies, and 70–80 per cent were officials of middle and lower units.

All survey responses are rounded to the closest per cent.

blank = not asked

1. Has the tax pressure on business over the last two to three years on average increased, decreased or not changed?

	Russian tax officials 2011
Increased	31
Decreased	33
Not Changed	23
Difficult to Say	13

2. If an enterprise were to fulfil all the demands of the tax organs, would it be ruined?

	Russian tax officials 2011
Yes	22
No	71
Difficult to Say	7

Appendix II 293

3. Are inspectors unable to 'catch out' those who fail to comply with the requirements of the tax organs?

	Russian tax officials 2011
Yes, they are unable	32
No, they are able	63
Difficult to say	5

4. Is the job of the tax inspectors to replenish the budget at any cost?

	Russian tax officials 2011
Yes	48
No	48
Difficult to say	3

5. Can anyone easily hide his or her income?

	Russian tax officials 2011
Yes	31
No	63
Difficult to say	6

6. With which enterprises, agencies have you most of all had work over the past year?

	Russian tax officials 2011
Small enterprises	38
State agencies	27
Medium-sized, private enterprises	43
Large, private enterprises	26
State enterprises	18
Other	11
I did not have work with enterprises, agencies	9
Difficult to say	1

294   Appendix II

7. According to which indicators is your work assessed?

	Russian tax officials 2011
Amount of fines, penalties collected	21
Quantity of on-site inspections conducted (considering the size of the enterprise)	20
Effectiveness of on-site inspections conducted	31
Quantity of in-office inspections (desk audits) conducted (considering the size of the enterprise)	20
Effectiveness of in-office inspections (desk audits) conducted	31
Quantity of violations uncovered	30
Quantity of cases opened (prosecutions) regarding administrative violations	14
Amount of taxes collected	44
Another Indicator	29
Difficult to say	11

8. To what extent do these factors reduce the effectiveness of your organization in collecting taxes?

	Russian tax officials 2011
Poor awareness among businesses about the rules and procedures of taxation	
Significantly reduces	28
Insignificantly reduces	44
Does not reduce	18
Difficult to say	9
Dishonesty of business in dealing with your organization	
Significantly reduces	55
Insignificantly reduces	27
Does not reduce	7
Difficult to say	10

Appendix II

9. Generally, according to which standards is your professional activity assessed? (Any number of answers.)

	Russian tax officials 2011	Russian childcare officials 2011	Russian unemployment officials 2011	Russian registry officials 2011	All Russian officials 2011
Number of fulfilled tasks given by superiors	54	45	51	59	52
Number of documents processed	50	48	42	66	51
Number of clients/visitors served	27	44	43	35	35
Quality of administrative services provided	46	60	61	44	51
Positive evaluations by citizens, clients, visitors	42	54	41	44	45
Timeliness of fulfilled tasks	67	61	64	62	64
Other	12	1	6	2	7
Not assessed by any evaluation standard	2	2	1	2	2
Difficult to say	3	4	1	4	3

10. What methods of encouragement used for employees who excel in your organization? (Any number of answers.)

	Russian tax officials 2011	Russian childcare officials 2011	Russian unemployment officials 2011	Russian registry officials 2011	All Russian officials 2011
Financial incentives, bonuses	89	71	80	76	81
Promotion	57	34	39	35	44
Announcement of gratitude	79	67	74	65	73
Other	1	3	4	3	3
No incentives exist	1	5	6	8	4
Difficult to say	1	4	0	4	2

296   Appendix II

11. From the factors listed below, please select no more than five that, in your opinion, restrict your organization from working effectively.

	Russian tax officials 2011	Russian childcare officials 2011	Russian unemployment officials 2011	Russian registry officials 2011	All Russian officials 2011
Insufficient level of staffing	53	31	19	47	41
Lack of competence among personnel	18	12	13	18	16
Lack of financial resources	32	36	25	52	35
Lack of understanding among personnel of their duties and functions	3	3	5	3	4
Low salary	52	46	52	64	53
Bad management in the organization	2	6	4	0	3
Too much dependence on internal, immediately superior supervisory bodies	5	11	20	7	10
Lack of equipment and technical support	33	36	18	33	31
Lack of space	11	32	19	29	21
Contradictory instructions within the organization	5	13	16	5	9
Insufficiently quality of legislation	52	41	40	42	45
Prevalence of corruption	4	1	1	1	2
Too strict regulation of personnel's activity	6	3	9	3	6
Other	2	2	2	3	2
Nothing	10	13	14	5	11
Difficult to say	2	3	1	2	2

Appendix II

12. Has your organization been inspected in the last two years by representatives of any of following authorities? (Any number of answers.)

	Russian tax officials 2011	Russian childcare officials 2011	Russian unemployment officials 2011	Russian registry officials 2011	All Russian officials 2011
Internal, immediately-superior supervisory bodies	88	69	84	62	78
Offices of the Public Prosecutor	58	50	72	82	64
Audit Chamber	12	25	20	9	16
Offices of Rosfinnadzor (Federal Finance Inspectorate)	6	26	43	16	20
Inspectorates or offices of finance and budget oversight of the regional administration	11	34	35	13	21
Independent audit	3	3	1	1	3
Internal audit	12	6	4	5	8
Other	1	4	5	0	3
No one	0	1	0	1	1
Difficult to say	4	9	6	7	6

13. Has anyone in your organization been penalized or sanctioned in the last two years for any of the following? (Any number of answers.)

	Russian tax officials 2011	Russian childcare officials 2011	Russian unemployment officials 2011	Russian registry officials 2011	All Russian officials 2011
Unsuitability for the position being occupied	6	3	2	7	5
Non-fulfilment or violation of duties	47	24	30	46	39
Overstepping one's official authority	2	1	1	3	2
Taking bribes	3	0	0	7	3
Other	2	2	3	2	2
No one has been	29	61	52	30	40
Difficult to say	18	10	13	19	16

298 Appendix II

14. In the organization where I work, all citizens who request services are treated equally.

	Russian tax officials 2011	Russian registry officials 2011	Russian unemployment officials 2011	Russian childcare officials 2011	All Russian officials 2011
Agree	94	89	92	92	92
Disagree	6	8	6	7	7
Difficult to say	0	2	0	0	1

15. The majority of citizens understand how decisions are made in the organization in which I work and in which their requests are reviewed.

	Russian tax officials 2011	Russian registry officials 2011	Russian unemployment officials 2011	Russian childcare officials 2011	All Russian officials 2011
Yes	79	76	88	86	81
No	16	20	9	8	14
Difficult to say	4	4	2	5	4

16. Has the quality of government services provided by your organization increased or decreased over the past five years?

	Russian tax officials 2011	Russian registry officials 2011	Russian unemployment officials 2011	Russian childcare officials 2011	All Russian officials 2011
Increased	90	87	86	83	87
Remained the same	5	7	10	10	8
Decreased	2	2	1	1	2

Appendix II   299

17. How has the level of professionalism of the co-workers of your organization changed over the past five years?

	Russian tax officials 2011	Russian registry officials 2011	Russian unemployment officials 2011	Russian childcare officials 2011	All Russian officials 2011
Increased/more operatively	82	66	83	78	78
Remained the same	8	18	8	12	11
Decreased/less operatively	5	10	4	3	5
Difficult to say	6	5	5	7	6

18. What is your job position?

	Russian tax officials 2011	Russian registry officials 2011	Russian unemployment officials 2011	Russian childcare officials 2011	All Russian officials 2011
Head of the institution (organization, agency)	5	4	13	8	7
Deputy head of the institution (organization, agency)	19	11	15	13	15
Head of department (or other structural government division) of an institution (organization, agency)	18	25	22	25	22
Deputy head of department (or of a structural unit) of an institution (organizations, agency)	10	10	5	3	8
Assistant (advisor, consultant) of the head of the institution (organization, agency)	0	2	0	3	1
Chief specialist-expert	3	12	4	14	7
Leading specialist-expert	4	10	16	12	9
Specialist-expert	3	10	4	8	6
Chief state inspector	10	0	0	0	4
Senior state inspector	9	0	1	0	4
State inspector	8	0	2	2	4
Senior specialist (specialist 1st category)	6	6	4	4	5
Specialist (specialist 2nd or 3rd category)	3	5	2	5	4
Other position	1	2	8	2	3
Difficult to say	0	0	0	0	0

300   Appendix II

19. Do you have official job regulations? And if so, are they clear and understandable?

	Russian tax officials 2011	Russian registry officials 2011	Russian unemployment officials 2011	Russian childcare officials 2011	All Russian officials 2011
Absolutely unclear, unintelligible	2	1	1	1	2
Largely unclear, unintelligible	1	1	1	1	1
Mostly clear, understandable	26	25	32	26	27
Absolutely clear and understandable	70	70	58	67	67
No official job regulations	0	2	6	2	2
Difficult to say	1	0	1	2	1

20. To what extent is your activity regulated?

	Russian tax officials 2011	Russian registry officials 2011	Russian unemployment officials 2011	Russian childcare officials 2011	All Russian officials 2011
Absolutely not regulated	0	0	1	0	0
Largely not regulated	1	2	1	2	2
Mostly regulated	43	50	49	45	46
Absolutely everything is regulated	55	45	44	50	50
Difficult to say	1	2	4	3	2

21. In your opinion, how well developed are the mechanisms for responding to citizen complaints about violations in your office's work?

	Russian tax officials 2011	Russian registry officials 2011	Russian unemployment officials 2011	Russian childcare officials 2011	All Russian officials 2011
Weakly	3	4	5	4	4
Strongly	93	89	90	87	90
Difficult to say	4	6	5	9	6

Appendix II

301

22. Indicate which of the following factors influence your decision to work in the public sector, to be public servants. Choose the most significant factors. (Choose up to five responses.)

	Russian tax officials 2011	Russian registry officials 2011	Russian unemployment officials 2011	Russian childcare officials 2011	All Russian officials 2011
Stable employment	79	78	79	75	78
High level of wages	5	5	8	16	8
Social benefits (health care, availability of pre-school facilities, etc.)	24	17	25	20	22
Flexible working hours	2	3	2	3	3
Balance workload	9	19	17	14	13
Good opportunities for personal development	35	36	27	26	32
High social status and prestige	17	16	7	14	14
Power, wide authorities	1	1	0	1	1
Lack of other employment opportunities	11	14	17	14	13
Personal interest and job satisfaction	36	39	46	44	40
Attractiveness of the goals and objectives of the organization	23	18	24	23	22
Possibility of obtaining additional income	0	1	1	0	1
Good team relations	45	48	49	50	47
Provision of housing and/or service car	1	2	0	0	1
Possibility of taking a high position in business in future	2	4	0	1	2
Possibility of being promoted to the state service (as a career post)	28	27	11	22	23
Acquisition of personal connections	5	6	5	3	5
Continuing family tradition	2	2	2	1	2
Other	2	3	3	1	3
Difficult to say	1	2	0	3	1

302   Appendix II

23. Do you trust the state apparatus (bureaucrats)?

	Russian tax officials 2011	Russian childcare officials 2011	Russian unemployment officials 2011	Russian registry officials 2011	All Russian officials 2011
Yes, I trust	53	57	40	38	48
Sometimes I trust, sometimes I don't trust	29	25	31	38	30
No, I don't trust	12	11	25	15	15
Difficult to say	6	7	4	9	6

Appendix III: Suggested Minimal Tax Compliance Levels for 2010–2015 Surveys

Poland 2010 Taxpayer Compliance Attitudinal Survey

		Would you follow the tax laws even if you do not consider them to be fair?	
		No	Yes
Are the tax laws in your country fair?	No	12% $N = 197$	60% $N = 973$
	Yes	4% $N = 58$	24% $N = 395$

The table suggests that at least 12 per cent of Poles in 2010 do not have intentions to comply with their country's tax laws. *No Mean Replacement*: Not included in this table are 398 respondents who did not provide an answer to either one or both of these two questions.

Russia 2010 Taxpayer Compliance Attitudinal Survey

		Would you follow the tax laws even if you do not consider them to be fair?	
		No	Yes
Are the tax laws in your country fair?	No	21% $N = 423$	36% $N = 717$
	Yes	15% $N = 296$	28% $N = 548$

The table suggests that at least 21 per cent of Russians in 2010 do not have intentions to comply with their country's tax laws. *No Mean Replacement*: Not included in this table are 1,023 respondents who did not provide an answer to either one or both of these two questions.

304 Appendix III

Ukraine 2010 Taxpayer Compliance Attitudinal Survey

		Would you follow the tax laws even if you do not consider them to be fair?	
		No	Yes
Are the tax laws in your country fair?	No	37% $N = 998$	38% $N = 1004$
	Yes	15% $N = 406$	10% $N = 259$

The table suggests that at least 37 per cent of Ukrainians in 2010 do not have intentions to comply with their country's tax laws. *No Mean Replacement*: Not included in this table are 1,348 respondents who did not provide an answer to either one or both of these two questions.

Ukraine 2012 Taxpayer Compliance Attitudinal Survey

		Would you follow the tax laws even if you do not consider them to be fair?	
		No	Yes
Are the tax laws in your country fair?	No	42% $N = 534$	36% $N = 458$
	Yes	7% $N = 94$	14% $N = 177$

The table suggests that at least 42 per cent of Ukrainians in 2012 do not have intentions to comply with their country's tax laws. *No Mean Replacement*: Not included in this table are 745 respondents who did not provide an answer to either one or both of these two questions.

Ukraine 2015 Taxpayer Compliance Attitudinal Survey

		Would you follow the tax laws even if you do not consider them to be fair?	
		No	Yes
Are the tax laws in your country fair?	No	37% $N = 981$	47% $N = 1222$
	Yes	6% $N = 148$	10% $N = 272$

Appendix III

The table suggests that at least 37 per cent of Ukrainians in 2015 do not have intentions to comply with their country's tax laws. *No Mean Replacement*: Not included in this table are 1,402 respondents who did not provide an answer to either one or both of these two questions.

Russia 2011 Tax Officials Survey

		Would you follow the tax laws even if you do not consider them to be fair?	
		No	Yes
Are the tax laws in your country fair?	No	6% $N = 22$	13% $N = 46$
	Yes	16% $N = 56$	65% $N = 226$

The table suggests that at least 6 per cent of Russians tax officials in 2011 do not have intentions to comply with their country's tax laws. *No Mean Replacement*: Not included in this table are 37 tax official respondents who did not provide an answer to either one or both of these two questions.

Appendix IV: Poland Taxpayer Compliance Attitudinal Surveys

Logit Analysis of Tax Compliance Attitudes
(DV = Whether One Would Follow the Tax Laws Even
If Personally Considered To Be Unfair)
Coefficients and (Standard Errors)

	Poland 2004 (1)	Poland 2004 (1) (Sub. Eff.)	Poland 2004 (2)	Poland 2004 (2) (Sub. Eff.)	Poland 2010 (1)	Poland 2010 (1) (Sub. Eff.)
		Deterrence				
Evasion OK If could get away with it	−0.27 (0.32)	−0.01	−0.27 (0.32)	−0.01	−0.38*** (0.14)	−0.05***
		Quasi-voluntary				
Trust in the State scale[1]						
Trusts president	−0.44 (0.44)	−0.03	−0.42 (0.35)	−0.02	0.46** (0.18)	0.06***
Trusts prime minister						
Trusts parliament	−0.32 (0.68)	−0.02	−0.31 (0.68)	−0.02	−0.09 (0.20)	−0.01
Trusts government	1.83** (0.73)	0.08***	1.82** (0.73)	0.08***	0.32 (0.21)	0.04*
Many dishonest tax bureaucrats	0.04 (0.52)	0.002	0.06 (0.52)	0.002	−0.35 (0.24)	−0.05*
Many people evade taxes	0.18 (0.50)	0.01	0.17 (0.50)	0.01	−0.29 (0.26)	−0.04
		Prior contact				
Previous contact with tax bureaucrats	0.30 (0.29)	0.02	0.28 (0.29)	0.02	−0.07 (0.13)	−0.01
		Socio-economic, additional effects				
Income	−0.0005** (0.0002)	−0.02**	−0.0006** (0.0002)	−0.03***	−0.02 (0.036)	0.03
I file my income taxes myself	0.23 (0.30)	0.01	0.20 (0.30)	0.01	−0.10 (0.06)	−0.01*
Occupation[2]			0.70 (0.63)	0.03		
Male	−0.50* (0.27)	−0.03**	−0.53* (0.28)	−0.03**	−0.16** (0.063)	−0.02***
Age	0.001 (0.008)	0.002	0.001 (0.008)	0.003	−0.006 (0.004)	−0.03**
Education	0.73 (0.57)	0.04*	0.53 (0.59)	0.03	−0.42* (0.25)	−0.05*
Constant	2.42*** (0.80)	−	2.48*** (0.79)	−	2.60*** (0.39)	−
N	886	886	886	886	1,861	1,861
Missing observations	Mean replace	Mean replace	Mean replace	Mean replace	Mean replace	Mean replace

*$p \leq 0.10$, **$p \leq 0.05$, ***$p \leq 0.01$ See Footnotes #21 and #22 in Chapter 6 for an explanation of the p-values for the substantive effects.

Notes: The substantive effect measured for "Age" is the change in likelihood for stating that one would obey the tax laws when the "Age" variable is shifted from one standard deviation below the mean to one standard deviation above the mean while holding all other variables even at their mean. All other substantive effects measured are changes in likelihood for stating that one would obey the tax laws when variables were shifted from their minimum to their maximum value and all other variables held even at their mean.

[1] The Trust in the State Scale for the Poland 2010 survey is a composite of trust in the president, the prime minister, the Sejm, the Senate and the government and trust in the state to do what is right and trust in the state to fulfil its obligations to its citizens.

[2] 2004: specialists, managers, self-employed; 2010: white-collar workers, owners.

	Poland 2010 (2)	Poland 2010 (2) (Sub. Eff.)	Poland 2010 (3)	Poland 2010 (3) (Sub. Eff.)	Poland 2010 (4)	Poland 2010 (4) (Sub. Eff.)
			Deterrence			
Evasion OK if could get away with it	−0.39*** (0.14)	−0.05***	−0.38*** (0.14)	−0.05***	−0.38*** (0.14)	−0.05***
			Quasi-voluntary			
Trust in the State scale[1]			0.29*** (0.08)	0.04***	0.29*** (0.08)	0.04***
Trusts president	0.46*** (0.18)	0.06***				
Trusts prime minister						
Trusts parliament	−0.09 (0.20)	−0.02				
Trusts government	0.31 (0.21)	0.04*				
Many dishonest tax bureaucrats	−0.35 (0.24)	−0.05*	−0.33 (0.24)	−0.05*	−0.33 (0.24)	−0.04
Many people evade taxes	−0.29 (0.26)	−0.04	−0.25 (0.26)	−0.03	−0.25 (0.26)	−0.03
			Prior contact			
Previous contact with tax bureaucrats	−0.08 (0.13)	−0.009	−0.05 (0.13)	−0.007	−0.06 (0.13)	−0.007
		Socio-economic, additional effects				
Income	−0.02 (0.04)	0.03	−0.02 (0.04)	0.03	−0.02 (0.04)	0.03
I file my income taxes myself	−0.10 (0.06)	−0.01**	−0.10 (0.06)	−0.01*	−0.10 (0.06)	−0.01*
Occupation[2]	0.19 (0.17)	0.02			0.18 (0.17)	0.02
Male	−0.15** (0.06)	−0.02***	−0.15** (0.06)	−0.02***	−0.15** (0.06)	−0.02**
Age	−0.007 (0.004)	−0.03**	−0.005 (0.004)	−0.02	−0.006 (0.004)	−0.03*
Education	−0.56** (0.28)	−0.08**	−0.38* (0.25)	−0.06*	−0.52* (0.28)	−0.07**
Constant	2.65*** (0.40)	−	2.84*** (0.38)	−	2.89*** (0.38)	−
N	1,861	1,861	1,861	1,861	1,861	1,861
Missing observations	Mean replace	Mean replace	Mean replace	Mean replace	Mean replace	Mean replace

*$p \leq 0.10$, **$p \leq 0.05$, ***$p \leq 0.01$. See Footnotes #21 and #22 in Chapter 6 for an explanation of the p-values for the substantive effects.

Note: The substantive effect measured for "Age" is the change in likelihood for stating that one would obey the tax laws when the "Age" variable was shifted from one standard deviation below the mean to one standard deviation above the mean while holding all other variables even at their mean. All other substantive effects measured are the change in likelihood for stating that one would obey the tax laws when variables were shifted from their minimum to their maximum value and all other variables were held even at their means.

[1] The Trust in the State Scale for the Poland 2010 survey is a composite of trust in the president, the prime minister, the Sejm, the Senate and the government and trust in the state to do what is right and trust in the state to fulfil its obligations to its citizens.

[2] 2004: specialists, managers, self-employed; 2010: white-collar workers, owners.

Appendix V: Russia Taxpayer Compliance Attitudinal Surveys

Logit Analysis of Tax Compliance Attitudes
(DV = Whether One Would Follow the Tax Laws Even If Personally Considered To Be Unfair)
Coefficients and (Standard Errors)

	Russia 2004 (1)	Russia 2004 Sub. Eff. (1)	Russia 2004 (2)	Russia 2004 Sub. Eff. (2)	Russia 2010 (1)	Russia 2010 Sub. Eff. (1)	Russia 2010 (2)	Russia 2010 Sub. Eff. (2)	Russia 2010 (3)	Russia 2010 (3) Sub. E[ff.]
Deterrence										
Evasion OK if could get away with it	-0.97*** (0.12)	-0.22***	-0.97*** (0.12)	-0.22***	-0.30*** (0.09)	-0.07***	-0.30*** (0.09)	-0.07***	-0.31*** (0.09)	-0.07
Quasi-voluntary										
Trust in the State scale[1]										
Trusts president	0.58*** (0.19)	0.13***	0.58*** (0.19)	0.13***					0.11 (0.17)	0.03
Trusts prime minister					0.29* (0.15)	0.07**	0.29* (0.15)	0.07**		
Trusts parliament										
Trusts government										
Many dishonest tax bureaucrats	-0.70*** (0.21)	-0.15***	-0.69*** (0.21)	-0.15***	-0.61*** (0.17)	-0.14***	-0.62*** (0.17)	-0.14***	-0.63*** (0.17)	-0.14
Many people evade taxes	0.22 (0.24)	0.05	0.21 (0.24)	0.05	-0.25 (0.17)	-0.06*	-0.25 (0.17)	-0.06*	-0.26 (0.17)	-0.06
Prior contact										
Previous contact with tax bureaucrats	0.19 (0.13)	0.04*	0.18 (0.13)	0.04*	0.14 (0.12)	0.03	0.13 (0.10)	0.03*	0.14 (0.12)	0.03
Socio-economic, additional effects										
Income	0.00003 (0.00003)	0.05	0.00003 (0.00003)	0.04	0.002 (0.0014)	0.005	-0.003 (0.014)	-0.01	0.003 (0.0015)	0.00
I file my income taxes myself	0.20 (0.16)	0.04*	0.21 (0.16)	0.04*	0.11 (0.12)	0.03	0.11 (0.12)	0.02	0.11 (0.12)	0.02
Occupation (directors, specialists)			0.07 (0.19)	0.01			0.02 (0.21)	0.002		
Male	-0.02 (0.11)	-0.004	-0.02 (0.11)	-0.005	-0.18** (0.09)	-0.04**	-0.18** (0.09)	-0.04**	-0.19** (0.09)	-0.04
Age	0.01*** (0.003)	0.08***	0.01*** (0.003)	0.08***	0.006** (0.003)	0.05**	0.006** (0.003)	0.05***	0.006** (0.003)	0.05
Education	0.38 (0.23)	0.09*	0.36 (0.24)	0.08*	0.22 (0.22)	0.05	0.23 (0.23)	0.05	0.20 (0.22)	0.04
Constant	0.20 (0.36)	–	0.21 (0.36)	–	0.68*** (0.26)	–	0.69*** (0.27)	–	0.82*** (0.27)	–
N	1,637	1,637	1,637	1,637	2,471	2,471	2,471	2,471	2,471	2,471
Missing observations	Mean replace	Mean replace	Mean replace	Mean replace	Mean replace	Mean replace	Mean replace	Mean replace	Mean replace	Mean replac[e]

$^*p \leq 0.10$, $^{**}p \leq 0.05$, $^{***}p \leq 0.01$. See Footnotes #21 and #22 in Chapter 6 for an explanation of the p-values for substantive effects.

Notes: The substantive effect measured for "Age" is the change in likelihood for stating that one would obey the tax la[w] when the "Age" variable was shifted from one standard deviation below the mean to one standard deviation above the me[an] while holding all other variables even at their mean. All other substantive effects measured are the change in likelihood stating that one would obey the tax laws when variables were shifted from their minimum to their maximum value and other variables were held even at their mean.

[1] The Trust in the State Scale for the Russia 2010 survey includes trust in the president, prime minister, parliament (St[ate] Duma) and government and trust in the state to do what is right and to fulfil its obligations to its citizens.

	Russia 2010 (4)	Russia 2010 (4) Sub. Eff	Russia 2010 (5)	Russia 2010 (5) Sub. Eff.	Russia 2010 (6)	Russia 2010 (6) Sub. Eff	Russia 2010 (7)	Russia 2010 (7) Sub. Eff	Russia 2010 (8)	Russia 2010 (8) Sub. Eff
			Deterrence							
Evasion OK if could get away with it	−0.31*** (0.09)	−0.07***	−0.30*** (0.09)	−0.07***	−0.30*** (0.09)	−0.07***	−0.29*** (0.09)	−0.07***	−0.29*** (0.09)	−0.06***
				Quasi-voluntary						
Trust in the State scale[1]							0.16*** (0.06)	0.03***	0.15*** (0.06)	0.03***
Trusts president	0.11 (0.17)	0.03	−0.51* (0.27)	−0.12**	−0.51* (0.27)	−0.11**				
Trusts prime minister			0.41* (0.25)	0.10**	0.41* (0.25)	0.10*				
Trusts parliament			0.54*** (0.19)	0.12***	0.54*** (0.19)	0.12***				
Trusts government										
Many dishonest tax bureaucrats	−0.63*** (0.17)	−0.15***	−0.60*** (0.17)	−0.14***	−0.60*** (0.17)	−0.14***	−0.59*** (0.17)	−0.14***	−0.59*** (0.17)	−0.13***
Many people evade	−0.25 (0.17)	−0.06**	−0.21 (0.17)	−0.05*	−0.21 (0.17)	−0.05	−0.21 (0.17)	−0.04	−0.21 (0.17)	−0.05
				Prior contact						
Previous contact with tax bureaucrats	0.13 (0.10)	0.03	0.15 (0.12)	0.03*	0.14 (0.10)	0.03*	0.13 (0.12)	0.03	0.14 (0.10)	0.03*
			Socio-economic, additional effects							
Income	−0.002 (0.014)	−0.009	0.00007 (0.001)	0.0003	−0.001 (0.01)	−0.003	−0.00007 (0.0015)	−0.0005	−0.002 (0.01)	−0.009
Handle my income taxes myself	0.11 (0.12)	0.02	0.10 (0.12)	0.02	0.09 (0.12)	0.02	0.10 (0.12)	0.02	0.10 (0.12)	0.02
Occupation (directors, specialists)	0.02 (0.21)	0.001			0.002 (0.21)	0.001			0.007 (0.21)	−0.001
Male	−0.18** (0.09)	−0.04**	−0.17** (0.09)	−0.04**	−0.17* (0.09)	−0.04**	−0.17** (0.09)	−0.04**	−0.17** (0.09)	−0.04**
Age	0.006** (0.003)	0.05**	0.007** (0.003)	0.05***	0.007** (0.003)	0.05***	0.006** (0.003)	0.05***	0.006** (0.003)	0.05***
Education	0.21 (0.23)	0.05	0.21 (0.22)	0.05	0.21 (0.23)	0.05	0.23 (0.22)	0.06	0.24 (0.23)	0.06
Constant	0.83*** (0.28)	–	0.65** (0.28)	–	0.65** (0.29)	–	0.81*** (0.24)	–	0.82*** (0.25)	–
	2,471	2,471	2,471	2,471	2,471	2,471	2,471	2,471	2,471	2,471
Missing observations	Mean replace	Mean replace	Mean replace	Mean replace	Mean replace	Mean replace	Mean replace	Mean replace	Mean replace	Mean replace

$^*p \leq 0.10$, $^{**}p \leq 0.05$, $^{***}p \leq 0.01$. See Footnotes #21 and #22 in Chapter 6 for an explanation of the p-values for the substantive effects.

Notes: The substantive effect measured for "Age" is the change in likelihood for stating that one would obey the tax laws when the "Age" variable are shifted from one standard deviation below the mean to one standard deviation above the mean while holding all other variables even at their mean. All other substantive effects measured are the change in likelihood for stating that one would obey the tax laws when variables were shifted from their minimum to their maximum value and all other variables were held even at their means.

[1] The Trust in the State Scale for the Russia 2010 survey includes trust in the president, prime minister, parliament (State Duma) and government and trust in the state to do what is right and to fulfil its obligations to its citizens.

Appendix VI: Ukraine Taxpayer Compliance Attitudinal Surveys

Logit Analysis of Tax Compliance Attitudes
(DV = Whether One Would Follow the Tax Laws Even
If Personally Considered To Be Unfair)
Coefficients and (Standard Errors)

	Ukraine 2005 (1)	Ukraine 2005 (1) Sub. Effects	Ukraine 2005 (2)	Ukraine 2005 (2) Sub. Effects	Ukraine 2005 (3)	Ukraine 2005 (3) Sub. Effects	Ukraine 2005 (4)	Ukraine 2005 (4) Sub. Effects
			Deterrence					
Evasion OK if could get away with it	−0.48*** (0.08)	−0.12***	−0.49*** (0.08)	−0.12***	−0.47*** (0.08)	−0.12***	−0.47*** (0.08)	−0.12***
			Quasi-voluntary					
Trust in the State scale[1]					0.09** (0.04)	0.02**	0.09** (0.04)	0.02**
Trusts president	0.10 (0.19)	0.03	0.14 (0.19)	0.03				
Trusts prime minister								
Trusts parliament	−0.09 (0.21)	−0.02	−0.11 (0.21)	−0.03				
Trusts government	0.16 (0.25)	0.04	0.15 (0.25)	0.04				
Many dishonest tax bureaucrats	−0.43*** (0.16)	−0.11***	−0.44*** (0.16)	−0.11***	−0.39** (0.16)	−0.09***	−0.41*** (0.16)	−0.10***
Many people evade taxes	0.12 (0.16)	0.03	0.13 (0.16)	0.03	0.11 (0.16)	0.03	0.12 (0.16)	0.03
			Prior contact					
Previous contact with tax bureaucrats	−0.06 (0.11)	−0.02	−0.04 (0.11)	−0.01	−0.11 (0.11)	−0.03	−0.08 (0.11)	−0.02
			Socio-economic, additional effects					
Income	0.51** (0.22)	0.05**	0.54** (0.22)	0.05***	0.46** (0.22)	0.04**	0.49** (0.22)	0.05**
I file my income taxes myself	−0.32** (0.15)	−0.08**	−0.26 (0.16)	−0.07**	−0.26* (0.15)	−0.06**	−0.19 (0.16)	−0.05
Occupation (managers, entrepreneurs)			−0.24 (0.18)	−0.06			−0.26 (0.18)	−0.06*
Male	−0.10 (0.08)	−0.03	−0.08 (0.08)	−0.02	−0.06 (0.08)	−0.02	−0.05 (0.08)	−0.01
Age	0.002 (0.002)	0.02	0.002 (0.002)	0.02	0.002 (0.002)	0.02	0.002 (0.002)	0.02
Education	0.34** (0.18)	0.08**	0.37** (0.19)	0.09***	0.42** (0.18)	0.11***	0.46** (0.18)	0.11***
Constant	−0.08 (0.24)	–	−0.11 (0.24)	–	−0.03 (0.23)	–	−0.06 (0.23)	–
N	2,891	2,891	2,873	2,873	2,891	2,891	2,873	2,873
Missing observations	Mean replace	Mean replace	Mean replace	Mean replace	Mean replace	Mean replace	Mean replace	Mean replace

*$p \leq 0.10$, **$p \leq 0.05$, ***$p \leq 0.01$. See Footnotes #21 and #22 in Chapter 6 for an explanation of the p-values for the substantive effects.

Notes: The substantive effect measured for "Age" is the change in likelihood for stating that one would obey the tax laws when the "Age" variable is shifted from one standard deviation below the mean to one standard deviation above the mean while holding all other variables even at their mean. All other substantive effects measured are the change in likelihood for stating that one would obey the tax laws when variables are shifted from their minimum to their maximum value and all other variables are held even at their mean.

[1] The Trust in the State scale for the Ukraine 2005 survey is a composite of trust in the president, parliament and government and of trust in the government to do what is right and to fulfil its obligations to citizens. The Trust in the State scale for the Ukraine 2010 and 2015 surveys includes trust in the president, the parliament and the government and trust in the state to do what is right and to fulfil its obligations to citizens.

	Ukraine 2010 (1)	Ukraine 2010 (1) Sub. Effects	Ukraine 2010 (2)	Ukraine 2010 (2) Sub. Effects	Ukraine 2010 (3)	Ukraine 2010 (3) Sub. Effects	Ukraine 2010 (4)	Ukraine 2010 (4) Sub. Effects
			Deterrence					
Evasion OK if could get away with it	−0.12 (0.08)	−0.03*	−0.12 (0.08)	−0.03*	−0.11 (0.08)	−0.03*	−0.11 (0.08)	−0.03*
			Quasi-voluntary					
Trust in the State scale[1]					0.32*** (0.04)	0.08***	0.33*** (0.04)	0.08***
Trusts president	0.001 (0.21)	−0.0002	0.002 (0.21)	0.001				
Trusts prime minister								
Trusts parliament	0.50** (0.24)	0.13***	0.51** (0.24)	0.13***				
Trusts government	0.39 (0.26)	0.09*	0.39 (0.26)	0.09*				
Many dishonest tax bureaucrats	−0.46*** (0.15)	−0.11***	−0.46*** (0.15)	−0.11***	−0.43*** (0.15)	−0.10***	−0.43*** (0.15)	−0.10***
Many people evade taxes	0.12 (0.15)	0.03	0.11 (0.15)	0.03	0.11 (0.15)	0.03	0.12 (0.15)	0.03
			Prior contact					
Previous contact with tax bureaucrats	−0.15 (0.11)	−0.04*	−0.18 (0.12)	−0.04*	−0.14 (0.11)	−0.04*	−0.17 (0.12)	−0.04*
			Socio-economic, additional effects					
Income	0.21 (0.32)	0.05	0.23 (0.32)	0.05	0.19 (0.32)	0.05	0.21 (0.32)	0.05
I file my income taxes myself	−0.06** (0.024)	−0.01***	−0.06** (0.024)	−0.01***	−0.06** (0.02)	−0.01***	−0.06** (0.02)	−0.01***
Occupation (managers, entrepreneurs)			0.13 (0.17)	0.03			0.12 (0.17)	0.03
Male	−0.03 (0.07)	−0.007	−0.03 (0.07)	−0.008	−0.02 (0.07)	−0.005	−0.03 (0.07)	−0.006
Age	0.0009 (0.002)	0.008	0.0009 (0.002)	0.008	0.0007 (0.002)	0.006	0.0008 (0.002)	0.006
Education	0.16 (0.18)	0.04	0.14 (0.18)	0.04	0.17 (0.18)	0.04	0.15 (0.18)	0.04
Constant	−0.08 (0.22)	−	−0.08 (0.22)	−	0.28 (0.21)	−	0.29 (0.21)	−
N	3,221	3,221	3,212	3,212	3,221	3,221	3,212	3,212
Missing observations	Mean replace	Mean replace	Mean replace	Mean replace	Mean replace	Mean replace	Mean replace	Mean replace

*$p \leq 0.10$, **$p \leq 0.05$, ***$p \leq 0.01$. See Footnote #28 in Chapter 6 for an explanation of the p-values for the substantive effects.

Note: The substantive effect measured for "Age" is the change in likelihood for stating that one would obey the tax laws when the "Age" variable is shifted from one standard deviation below the mean to one standard deviation above the mean while holding all other variables even at their mean. All other substantive effects measured are the change in likelihood for stating that one would obey the tax laws when variables are shifted from their minimum to their maximum value and all other variables are held even at their means.

[1] The Trust in the State scale for the Ukraine 2005 survey is a composite of trust in the president and parliament and in government and trust in the government to do what is right and to fulfil its obligations to citizens. The Trust in the State scale for the Ukraine 2010 and 2015 surveys includes trust in the president, the parliament and the government and trust in the state to do what is right and to fulfil its obligations to citizens.

	Ukraine 2015 (1)	Ukraine 2015 (1) Sub. Effects	Ukraine 2015 (2)	Ukraine 2015 (2) Sub. Effects	Ukraine 2015 (3)	Ukraine 2015 (3) Sub. Effects	Ukraine 2015 (4)	Ukraine 2015 (4) Sub. Effects
			Deterrence					
Evasion OK if could get away with it	−0.40*** (0.08)	−0.10***	−0.39*** (0.08)	−0.09***	−0.40*** (0.08)	−0.10***	−0.39*** (0.08)	−0.10***
			Quasi-voluntary					
Trust in the State scale[1]			0.21*** (0.05)	0.05***			0.21*** (0.05)	0.05***
Trusts president	0.74*** (0.20)	0.18***			0.74*** (0.20)	0.18***		
Trusts prime minister								
Trusts parliament	−0.37 (0.28)	−0.09*			−0.36 (0.28)	−0.09		
Trusts government	0.23 (0.26)	0.05			0.22 (0.26)	0.05		
Many dishonest tax bureaucrats	−0.43*** (0.14)	−0.11***	−0.42*** (0.14)	−0.10***	−0.45*** (0.14)	−0.11***	−0.44*** (0.14)	−0.11***
Many people evade taxes	0.69*** (0.15)	0.17***	0.71*** (0.15)	0.17***	0.68*** (0.15)	0.17***	0.71*** (0.15)	0.17***
			Prior contact					
Previous contact with tax bureaucrats	0.03 (0.10)	0.006	0.03 (0.10)	0.006	0.02 (0.10)	0.004	0.02 (0.10)	0.004
			Socio-economic, additional effects					
Income	0.44* (0.25)	0.10**	0.45* (0.25)	0.11**	0.43* (0.25)	0.10*	0.44* (0.25)	0.10**
I file my income taxes myself	0.08 (0.13)	0.02	0.08 (0.13)	0.02	0.06 (0.14)	0.02	0.06 (0.14)	0.01
Occupation (managers, entrepreneurs)					−0.007 (0.19)	−0.004	0.006 (0.19)	0.002
Male	−0.09 (0.07)	−0.02	−0.08 (0.07)	−0.02	−0.09 (0.07)	−0.02	−0.08 (0.07)	−0.02
Age	0.004* (0.002)	0.04**	0.005** (0.002)	0.04**	0.005** (0.002)	0.04**	0.005** (0.002)	0.04
Education	0.09 (0.18)	0.02	0.09 (0.18)	0.02	0.11 (0.18)	0.03	0.11 (0.18)	0.02
Constant	−0.36 (0.22)	–	−0.18 (0.21)	–	−0.35 (0.22)	–	−0.18 (0.21)	–
N	3,157	3,157	3,157	3,157	3,134	3,134	3,134	3,134
Missing observations	Mean replace	Mean replace	Mean replace	Mean replace	Mean replace	Mean replace	Mean replace	Mean replace

$^{*}p \leq 0.10$, $^{**}p \leq 0.05$, $^{***}p \leq 0.01$. See Footnotes #21 and #22 in Chapter 6 for an explanation of the p-values for the substantive effects.

Notes: The substantive effect measured for "Age" is the change in likelihood for stating that one would obey the tax laws when the "Age" variable is shifted from one standard deviation below the mean to one standard deviation above the mean while holding all other variables even at their mean. All other substantive effects measured are the change in likelihood for stating that one would obey the tax laws when variables are shifted from their minimum to their maximum value and all other variables are held even at their means.

[1] The Trust in the State scale for the Ukraine 2005 survey is a composite of trust in the president, in parliament and in government and trust in the government to do what is right and to fulfil its obligations to citizens. The Trust in the State scale for the Ukraine 2010 and 2015 surveys includes trust in the president, the parliament and the government and trust in the state to do what is right and to fulfil its obligations to citizens.

Appendix VII: Ukraine Taxpayer Compliance Attitudinal Surveys – By Region

Logit Analysis of Tax Compliance Attitudes
(DV = Whether One Would Follow the Tax Laws Even If Personally Considered to Be Unfair)
Coefficients and (Standard Errors)

Appendix VII

	Catholic Ukraine 2005	Catholic Ukraine 2005 Sub. Effects	Non-Catholic Ukraine 2005	Non-Catholic Ukraine 2005 Sub. Effects	West Ukraine 2005	West Ukraine 2005 Sub. Effects	Far West 2005	Far West 2005 Sub. Effects
			Deterrence					
Invasion OK if could get away with it	−0.54* (0.29)	−0.13**	−0.46*** (0.09)	−0.12***	−0.38** (0.18)	−0.10**	−1.02*** (0.25)	−0.25***
			Quasi-voluntary					
Trusts president	−0.84 (0.76)	−0.16	0.05 (0.20)	0.01	−0.12 (0.43)	−0.03	−1.82*** (0.60)	−0.41***
Trusts parliament	2.68*** (0.82)	0.54***	−0.27 (0.22)	−0.07*	1.20** (0.47)	0.29***	1.83*** (0.63)	0.41***
Trusts government	−1.43 (0.99)	−0.30*	0.25 (0.26)	0.06	−0.39 (0.57)	−0.10	−0.11 (0.78)	−0.03
Many dishonest tax bureaucrats	0.17 (0.59)	0.05	−0.52*** (0.17)	−0.13***	−0.38 (0.33)	−0.09	0.29 (0.45)	0.06
Many people evade taxes	−0.57 (0.68)	−0.11	0.16 (0.17)	0.04	0.55 (0.38)	0.13*	0.62 (0.52)	0.15
			Contact					
Previous contact with tax bureaucrats	0.40 (0.50)	0.08	−0.06 (0.11)	−0.01	−0.05 (0.26)	−0.01	0.26 (0.38)	0.06
			Socio-economic, additional effects					
Income	−1.30 (0.80)	−0.11*	0.66*** (0.23)	0.06***	−0.20 (0.47)	−0.02	−0.59 (0.61)	−0.06
I file my income taxes myself	−0.70 (0.57)	−0.16	−0.29* (0.15)	−0.07**	−0.28 (0.32)	−0.07	−0.45 (0.42)	−0.10
Occupation (managers, entrepreneurs)								
Male	−0.27 (0.26)	−0.06	−0.09 (0.08)	−0.02	−0.28* (0.16)	−0.07**	−0.29 (0.21)	−0.07*
Age	−0.01 (0.009)	−0.10*	0.003 (0.002)	0.03*	−0.003 (0.005)	−0.03	−0.004 (0.007)	−0.03
Education	−0.52 (0.68)	−0.11	0.36* (0.19)	0.09***	−0.17 (0.39)	−0.04	−0.69 (0.51)	−0.16*
Constant	2.59** (1.01)	–	−0.18 (0.25)	–	0.14 (0.58)	–	0.95 (0.77)	–
	279	279	2618	2618	643	643	417	417
Missing observations	Mean replace	Mean replace	Mean replace	Mean replace	Mean replace	Mean replace	Mean replace	Mean replace
% would obey	47.37	–	34.57	–	36.43	–	37.18	–

$p \leq 0.10$, $^{**}p \leq 0.05$, $^{***}p \leq 0.01$. See Footnotes #21 and #22 in Chapter 6 for an explanation of the p-values for the substantive effects.

Notes: The substantive effect measured for "Age" is the change in likelihood for stating that one would obey the tax laws when the "Age" variable was shifted from one standard deviation below the mean to one standard deviation above the mean while holding all other variables even at their mean. All other substantive effects measured are the change in likelihood for stating that one would obey the tax laws when variables were shifted from their minimum to their maximum value and all other variables were held even at their means.

318   Appendix VII

	Far West Catholic 2005	Far West Catholic 2005 Sub. Effects	Far West Non-Catholic 2005	Far West Non-Catholic 2005 Sub. Effects	Center 2005	Center 2005 Sub. Effects	Kyiv & Kyiv Oblast 2005	Kyiv & Kyiv Oblast 2005 Sub. Effects
			Deterrence					
Evasion OK if could get away with it	-1.33*** (0.39)	-0.32***	-0.50 (0.36)	-0.11*	-0.63*** (0.14)	-0.16***	-0.42 (0.34)	-0.09
			Quasi-voluntary					
Trusts president	-1.95** (0.98)	-0.39**	-1.89** (0.84)	-0.41***	0.28 (0.32)	0.07	0.14 (0.71)	0.04
Trusts parliament	2.54*** (0.97)	0.53***	0.49 (0.93)	0.12	-0.19 (0.38)	-0.05	-1.69* (0.88)	-0.36**
Trusts government	-0.40 (1.27)	-0.08	0.22 (1.09)	0.03	0.60 (0.43)	0.04	2.66** (1.07)	0.48***
Many dishonest tax bureaucrats	1.03 (0.75)	0.24	-1.14* (0.65)	-0.27**	-0.09** (0.26)	-0.15***	-0.32 (0.63)	-0.07
Many people evade taxes	-0.46 (0.85)	-0.10	2.39*** (0.83)	0.44***	-0.12 (0.26)	-0.02	-1.33** (0.65)	-0.23**
			Prior contact					
Previous contact with tax bureaucrats	0.63 (0.60)	0.13	0.23 (0.57)	0.06	-0.12 (0.18)	-0.03	0.41 (0.49)	0.07
			Socio-economic, additional effects					
Income	-0.61 (0.98)	-0.06	-0.66 (0.88)	-0.05	0.98** (0.38)	0.09***	1.43 (0.96)	0.12*
I file my income taxes myself	-1.27* (0.72)	-0.28**	0.17 (0.58)	0.05	-0.71*** (0.25)	-0.17***	-1.45** (0.69)	-0.32**
Occupation (managers, entrepreneurs)								
Male	-0.31 (0.31)	-0.07	-0.49 (0.32)	-0.11*	-0.008 (0.13)	-0.003	0.16 (0.31)	0.03
Age	-0.02 (0.01)	-0.13*	0.007 (0.009)	0.06	0.002 (0.004)	0.02	0.002 (0.01)	0.02
Education	-1.08 (0.84)	-0.24*	-1.36* (0.75)	-0.30**	0.36 (0.32)	0.09	0.54 (0.72)	0.11
Constant	2.32* (1.31)	–	0.36 (1.07)	–	0.10 (0.44)	–	0.51 (1.12)	–
N	206	206	209	209	993	993	235	235
Missing observations	Mean replace	Mean replace	Mean replace	Mean replace	Mean replace	Mean replace	Mean replace	Mean replace
% would obey	44.57	–	29.60	–	36.39	–	46.87	–

*$p \leq 0.10$, **$p \leq 0.05$, ***$p \leq 0.01$. See Footnotes #21 and #22 in Chapter 6 for an explanation of the p-values for the substantive effects.

Notes: The substantive effect measured for "Age" is the change in likelihood for stating that one would obey the tax laws when the "Age" variable was shifted from one standard deviation below the mean to one standard deviation above the mean while holding all other variables even at their mean. All other substantive effects measured are the change in likelihood for stating that one would obey the tax laws when variables were shifted from their minimum to their maximum value and all other variables were held even at their means.

Appendix VII

	East 2005	East 2005 Sub. Effects	Donbas 2005	Donbas 2005 Sub. Effects	South 2005	South 2005 Sub. Effects	Crimea 2005	Crimea 2005 Sub. Effects
			Deterrence					
Evasion OK if could get away with it	−0.41*** (0.16)	−0.10***	−0.32 (0.26)	−0.08	−0.68*** (0.26)	−0.16***	−0.56 (0.47)	−0.13
			Quasi-voluntary					
Trusts president	0.46 (0.39)	0.11	1.67** (0.72)	0.34**	0.07 (0.65)	0.01	−1.57 (1.24)	−0.31
Trusts parliament	−0.74* (0.40)	−0.18**	1.28 (0.84)	0.28*	−0.86 (0.65)	−0.19*	−1.37 (1.39)	−0.27
Trusts government	−0.41 (0.47)	−0.10	−4.57*** (0.98)	−0.76***	1.83** (0.84)	0.41**	2.53** (1.29)	0.54**
Many dishonest tax bureaucrats	−0.24 (0.31)	−0.06	−0.99** (0.48)	−0.24**	−0.13 (0.51)	−0.03	−1.22 (1.02)	−0.28
Many people evade taxes	0.14 (0.32)	0.04	0.14 (0.48)	0.03	0.20 (0.60)	0.05	−0.19 (0.80)	−0.04
			Prior contact					
Previous contact with tax bureaucrats	−0.34 (0.23)	−0.09*	−0.84** (0.41)	−0.20**	0.47 (0.32)	0.12*	0.16 (0.62)	0.04
			Socio-economic, additional effects					
Income	0.33 (0.41)	0.03	0.48 (0.60)	0.05	0.56 (0.71)	0.05	1.03 (1.42)	0.09
File my income taxes myself	−0.06 (0.29)	−0.01	0.60 (0.54)	0.13	0.16 (0.49)	0.04	−0.11 (0.75)	−0.02
Occupation (managers, entrepreneurs)								
Male	−0.08 (0.15)	−0.02	0.008 (0.22)	0.05	0.18 (0.25)	0.04	−0.41 (0.41)	−0.10
Age	0.004 (0.005)	0.04	0.02** (0.007)	0.13**	0.0006 (0.007)	0.008	0.006 (0.01)	0.05
Education	0.38 (0.36)	0.09	0.85 (0.58)	0.20*	1.18** (0.58)	0.28**	0.41 (1.01)	0.08
Constant	0.11 (0.43)	–	0.11 (0.64)	–	−1.38* (0.78)	–	0.08 (1.23)	–
	803	803	389	389	320	320	132	132
Missing observations	Mean replace	Mean replace	Mean replace	Mean replace	Mean replace	Mean replace	Mean replace	Mean replace
% would obey	37.61	–	42.60	–	32.35	–	26.00	–

$p \leq 0.10$, **$p \leq 0.05$, ***$p \leq 0.01$. See Footnotes #21 and #22 in Chapter 6 for an explanation of the p-values for the substantive effects.

Notes: The substantive effect measured for "Age" is the change in likelihood for stating that one would obey the tax laws when the "Age" variable was shifted from one standard deviation below the mean to one standard deviation above the mean while holding all other variables even at their mean. All other substantive effects measured are the change in likelihood for stating that one would obey the tax laws when variables were shifted from their minimum to their maximum value and all other variables were held even at their means.

320 Appendix VII

	Catholic Ukraine 2010	Catholic Ukraine 2010 Sub. Effects	Non-Catholic Ukraine 2010	Non-Catholic Ukraine 2010 Sub. Effects	West Ukraine 2010	West Ukraine 2010 Sub. Effects	Far West 2010	Far West 2010 Sub. Effects
				Deterrence				
Evasion OK if could get away with it	−0.11 (0.28)	−0.02	−0.12 (0.08)	−0.03*	0.10 (0.17)	0.02	−0.22 (0.22)	−0.05
				Quasi-voluntary				
Trusts president	−1.29 (0.83)	−0.28*	0.15 (0.22)	0.04	−0.47 (0.44)	−0.12	−0.15 (0.58)	−0.04
Trusts parliament	1.33 (0.90)	0.25*	0.40 (0.25)	0.10*	1.27** (0.55)	0.29**	0.61 (0.72)	0.13
Trusts government	−0.51 (0.86)	−0.13	0.48* (0.27)	0.12**	−0.15 (0.53)	−0.04	0.04 (0.69)	0.01
Many dishonest tax bureaucrats	0.64 (0.53)	0.15*	−0.58*** (0.15)	−0.14***	−0.02 (0.33)	−0.005	0.15 (0.42)	0.03
Many people evade taxes	0.17 (0.50)	0.05	0.10 (0.15)	0.03	0.06 (0.32)	0.02	0.39 (0.41)	0.09
				Prior contact				
Previous contact with tax bureaucrats	−0.36 (0.35)	−0.08	−0.16 (0.11)	−0.04*	−0.68*** (0.21)	−0.17***	−0.74*** (0.27)	−0.18***
				Socio-economic, additional effects				
Income	1.49 (1.26)	0.25	0.20 (0.34)	0.05	0.85 (0.78)	0.19	0.92 (0.92)	0.16
I file my income taxes myself	−0.08 (0.08)	−0.02	−0.06** (0.03)	−0.01***	−0.07* (0.04)	−0.02**	−0.04 (0.06)	−0.009
Occupation (managers, entrepreneurs)								
Male	−0.06 (0.25)	−0.01	−0.04 (0.08)	−0.01	0.18 (0.16)	0.05	−0.002 (0.20)	0.0003
Age	−0.004 (0.008)	−0.03	0.001 (0.002)	0.01	0.003 (0.005)	0.03	−0.001 (0.006)	−0.01
Education	−0.08 (0.64)	−0.02	0.12 (0.19)	0.03	−0.03 (0.40)	−0.01	−0.13 (0.50)	−0.03
Constant	0.22 (0.75)	–	−0.11 (0.23)	–	−0.33 (0.47)	–	0.02 (0.59)	–
N	306	306	2924	2924	696	696	453	453
Missing observations	Mean replace	Mean replace	Mean replace	Mean replace	Mean replace	Mean replace	Mean replace	Mean replace
% would obey	48.18	–	43.04	–	42.61	–	47.43	–

*$p \leq 0.10$, **$p \leq 0.05$, ***$p \leq 0.01$. See Footnotes #21 and #22 in Chapter 6 for an explanation of the p-values for the substantive effects.

Notes: The substantive effect measured for "Age" is the change in likelihood for stating that one would obey the tax laws when the "Age" variable was shifted from one standard deviation below the mean to one standard deviation above the mean while holding all other variables even at their mean. All other substantive effects measured are the change in likelihood for stating that one would obey the tax laws when variables were shifted from their minimum to their maximum value and all other variables were held even at their means.

Appendix VII

	Far West Catholic 2010	Far West Catholic 2010 Sub. Effects	Far West Non-Catholic 2010	Far West Non-Catholic 2010 Sub. Effects	Center 2010	Center 2010 Sub. Effects	Kyiv & Kyiv Oblast 2010	Kyiv & Kyiv Oblast 2010 Sub. Effects
			Substantive Effects					
			Deterrence					
Evasion OK if could get away with it	−0.42 (0.35)	−0.09	−0.02 (0.31)	−0.005	0.62*** (0.13)	0.15***	0.50* (0.28)	0.12**
			Quasi-voluntary					
Trusts president	−0.45 (1.24)	−0.09	0.61 (0.69)	0.16	0.59 (0.40)	0.14*	0.16 (0.86)	0.03
Trusts parliament	1.19 (1.14)	0.21	−0.79 (1.01)	−0.19	−1.08** (0.47)	−0.26***	−3.43*** (1.20)	−0.65***
Trusts government	−0.71 (1.23)	−0.18	1.00 (0.91)	0.23	0.84 (0.52)	0.20*	2.90** (1.29)	0.52***
Many dishonest tax bureaucrats	0.59 (0.68)	0.13	−0.39 (0.56)	−0.09	−0.89*** (0.26)	−0.22***	−1.41*** (0.52)	−0.32***
Many people evade taxes	0.21 (0.65)	0.06	0.62 (0.56)	0.14	−0.29 (0.24)	−0.07	−0.44 (0.47)	−0.10
			Prior contact					
Previous contact with tax bureaucrats	−0.61 (0.41)	−0.14*	−0.83** (0.37)	−0.19**	0.05 (0.19)	0.01	−0.17 (0.39)	−0.04
			Socio-economic, additional effects					
Income	1.22 (1.54)	0.17	−0.47 (1.25)	−0.10	1.36** (0.58)	0.30***	1.93* (1.06)	0.38**
file my income taxes myself	0.04 (0.13)	0.009	−0.06 (0.08)	−0.01	−0.12*** (0.05)	−0.03***	−0.96** (0.47)	−0.23**
Occupation (managers, entrepreneurs)								
Male	−0.12 (0.30)	−0.02	0.17 (0.29)	0.04	−0.09 (0.12)	−0.02	−0.45* (0.26)	−0.11**
Age	0.001 (0.01)	0.01	−0.0007 (0.008)	−0.006	0.004 (0.004)	0.04	0.003 (0.008)	0.02
Education	−0.23 (0.78)	−0.05	−0.27 (0.70)	−0.07	0.42 (0.30)	0.10*	−0.05 (0.61)	−0.02
Constant	0.28 (0.93)	–	−0.19 (0.80)	–	−0.28 (0.36)	–	0.90 (0.80)	–
N	224	224	229	229	1137	1137	300	300
Missing observations	Mean replace	Mean replace	Mean replace	Mean replace	Mean replace	Mean replace	Mean replace	Mean replace
% would obey	52.69	–	41.89	–	43.96	–	49.71	–

*$p \leq 0.10$, **$p \leq 0.05$, ***$p \leq 0.01$. See Footnotes #21 and #22 in Chapter 6 for an explanation of the p-values for the substantive effects.

Notes: The substantive effect measured for "Age" is the change in likelihood for stating that one would obey the tax laws when the "Age" variable is shifted from one standard deviation below the mean to one standard deviation above the mean while holding all other variables even at their mean. All other substantive effects measured are the change in likelihood for stating that one would obey the tax laws when variables were shifted from their minimum to their maximum value and all other variables were held even at their means.

322 Appendix VII

	East 2010	East 2010 Sub. Effects	Donbas 2010	Donbas 2010 Sub. Effects	South 2010	South 2010 Sub. Effects	Crimea 2010[1]	Crimea 2010 Sub. Effects
				Deterrence				
Evasion OK if could get away with it	−0.41*** (0.15)	−0.10***	−0.69*** (0.22)	−0.17***	−1.38*** (0.26)	−0.31***	−1.69*** (0.51)	−0.33***
				Quasi-voluntary				
Trusts president	−0.05 (0.40)	−0.01	−0.50 (0.69)	−0.12	−0.33 (0.74)	−0.06	−9.14** (3.95)	−0.66***
Trusts parliament	1.09*** (0.41)	0.26***	2.14*** (0.73)	0.48***	−0.54 (0.82)	−0.11	9.43*** (3.27)	0.94***
Trusts government	0.47 (0.44)	0.12	0.15 (0.85)	0.04	1.85* (0.98)	0.38**	0.79 (3.06)	0.22
Many dishonest tax bureaucrats	−0.57* (0.30)	−0.14**	−0.27 (−0.44)	−0.07	−0.48 (0.45)	−0.11	1.13 (0.87)	0.18
Many people evade taxes	0.24 (0.32)	0.06	0.04 (0.51)	0.01	1.72*** (0.52)	0.40***	0.40 (0.95)	0.08
				Prior contact				
Previous contact with tax bureaucrats	0.22 (0.22)	0.05	−0.28 (0.34)	−0.06	−0.36 (0.38)	−0.09	–	–
			Socio-economic, additional effects					
Income	0.60 (0.61)	0.14	0.44 (0.84)	0.09	−2.38* (1.35)	−0.48**	−2.46 (2.52)	−0.44
I file my income taxes myself	−0.06 (0.06)	−0.02	−0.25* (0.13)	−0.06**	−0.13* (0.07)	−0.03**	0.02 (0.11)	0.004
Occupation (managers, entrepreneurs)								
Male	−0.06 (0.14)	−0.01	−0.02 (0.21)	−0.004	0.05 (0.25)	0.01	−0.59 (0.46)	−0.10
Age	−0.008* (0.004)	−0.07**	−0.003 (0.006)	−0.03	0.008 (0.008)	0.06	0.02 (0.01)	0.09
Education	−0.07 (0.37)	−0.02	−0.26 (0.57)	−0.06	−1.16* (0.62)	−0.25**	2.51** (1.21)	0.39**
Constant	−0.13 (0.45)	–	0.02 (0.73)	–	0.65 (0.77)	–	−0.82 (1.21)	–
N	888	888	428	428	347	347	153	153
Missing observations	Mean replace	Mean replace	Mean replace	Mean replace	Mean replace	Mean replace	Mean replace	Mean replace
% would obey	39.06	–	47.20	–	48.97	–	56.78	–

*$p \leq 0.10$, **$p \leq 0.05$, ***$p \leq 0.01$. See Footnotes #21 and #22 in Chapter 6 for an explanation of the p-values fo the substantive effects.

Notes: The substantive effect measured for "Age" is the change in likelihood for stating that one would obey the ta: laws when the "Age" variable was shifted from one standard deviation below the mean to one standard deviatio above the mean while holding all other variables even at their mean. All other substantive effects measured are th change in likelihood for stating that one would obey the tax laws when variables were shifted from their minimur to their maximum value and all other variables were held even at their means.

[1] In the Crimea 2010 regression, bureau contact dropped out in the original regression, as only 1 of 199 had suc contact.

Appendix VII

	Catholic Ukraine 2015	Catholic Ukraine 2015 Sub. Effects	Non-Catholic Ukraine 2015	Non-Catholic Ukraine 2015 Sub. Effects	West Ukraine 2015	West Ukraine 2015 Sub. Effects	Far West 2015	Far West 2015 Sub. Effects
			Deterrence					
Evasion OK if could get away with it	−0.07 (0.28)	−0.02	−0.42*** (0.08)	−0.10***	−0.32* (0.17)	−0.08**	0.13 (0.21)	0.03
			Quasi-voluntary					
Trusts president	−0.92 (0.65)	−0.23*	0.96*** (0.21)	0.22***	0.43 (0.39)	0.10	−0.93* (0.49)	−0.22**
Trusts parliament	2.13** (0.99)	0.41**	−0.66** (0.30)	−0.16**	−0.41 (0.61)	−0.10	0.41 (0.74)	0.08
Trusts government	−0.27 (0.94)	−0.07	0.27 (0.28)	0.07	0.55 (0.60)	0.13	1.15 (0.71)	0.24*
Many dishonest tax bureaucrats	−0.75 (0.51)	−0.18*	−0.40*** (0.15)	−0.10***	−0.35 (0.33)	−0.08	−0.70* (0.39)	−0.17**
Many people evade taxes	0.07 (0.52)	0.02	0.75*** (0.16)	0.18***	0.37 (0.33)	0.09	0.68* (0.40)	0.16*
			Prior contact					
Previous contact with tax bureaucrats	0.03 (0.33)	0.006	0.05 (0.10)	0.01	0.07 (0.22)	0.01	0.04 (0.27)	0.006
			Socio-economic, additional effects					
Income	0.21 (0.98)	0.05	0.45* (0.26)	0.11**	0.73 (0.60)	0.16	0.17 (0.72)	0.05
File my income taxes myself	0.38 (0.50)	0.08	0.06 (0.13)	0.01	0.25 (0.28)	0.06	0.46 (0.35)	0.10
Occupation (managers, entrepreneurs)								
Male	−0.19 (0.26)	−0.05	−0.08 (0.08)	−0.02	−0.25 (0.16)	−0.06*	−0.26 (0.19)	−0.06*
Age	0.005 (0.008)	0.04	0.005** (0.002)	0.04**	0.002 (0.005)	0.02	0.0004 (0.006)	0.002
Education	0.68 (0.64)	0.16	0.05 (0.19)	0.01	0.21 (0.40)	0.05	0.06 (0.47)	0.01
Constant	−0.03 (0.77)	—	−0.44* (0.23)	—	−0.17 (0.48)	—	0.15 (0.58)	—
N	278	278	2882	2882	687	687	477	477
Missing observations	Mean replace	Mean replace	Mean replace	Mean replace	Mean replace	Mean replace	Mean replace	Mean replace
% would obey	46.33	—	44.46	—	46.27	—	49.82	—

* ≤ 0.10, ** ≤ 0.05, *** ≤ 0.01. See Footnotes #21 and #22 in Chapter 6 for an explanation of the —-values for the substantive effects.

Notes: The substantive effect measured for "Age" is the change in likelihood for stating that one would obey the tax laws when the "Age" variable was shifted from one standard deviation below the mean to one standard deviation above the mean while holding all other variables even at their mean. All other substantive effects measured are the change in likelihood for stating that one would obey the tax laws when variables were shifted from their minimum to their maximum value and all other variables were held even at their means.

324 Appendix VII

	Far West Catholic 2015	Far West Catholic 2015 Sub. Effects	Far West Non-Catholic 2015	Far West Non-Catholic 2015 Sub. Effects	Center 2015	Center 2015 Sub. Effects	Kyiv & Kyiv Oblast 2015	Kyiv & Kyiv Oblast 2015 Sub. Effects
			Deterrence					
Evasion OK if could get away with it	0.14 (0.34)	0.03	0.23 (0.29)	0.05	−0.49*** (0.14)	−0.12***	−0.99*** (0.26)	−0.24***
			Quasi-voluntary					
Trusts president	−1.55** (0.79)	−0.36**	−0.22 (0.68)	−0.06	0.78** (0.33)	0.18**	0.18 (0.66)	0.04
Trusts parliament	2.33* (1.28)	0.43**	−0.97 (1.06)	−0.22	−0.99** (0.44)	−0.24**	−0.12 (0.91)	−0.04
Trusts government	0.02 (1.21)	0.005	1.80* (1.01)	0.33**	0.05 (0.41)	0.01	0.76 (0.79)	0.17
Many dishonest tax bureaucrats	−1.23* (0.65)	−0.28**	−0.25 (0.52)	−0.06	−0.91*** (0.24)	−0.22***	−1.23** (0.51)	−0.28***
Many people evade taxes	0.13 (0.63)	0.03	1.41** (0.57)	0.33***	0.94*** (0.24)	0.23***	0.70 (0.49)	0.17*
			Prior contact					
Previous contact with tax bureaucrats	−0.67 (0.42)	−0.16*	0.70* (0.42)	0.15**	0.16 (0.16)	0.04	0.19 (0.31)	0.05
			Socio-economic, additional effects					
Income	0.64 (1.24)	0.12	−0.65 (0.95)	−0.15	−0.06 (0.44)	−0.02	−0.79 (0.74)	−0.18
I file my income taxes myself	1.67** (0.72)	0.30**	−0.01 (0.44)	−0.006	−0.19 (0.24)	−0.05	−1.05* (0.59)	−0.25**
Occupation (managers, entrepreneurs)								
Male	−0.34 (0.31)	−0.08	−0.22 (0.26)	−0.05	0.008 (0.13)	0.0007	0.39 (0.24)	0.09*
Age	0.002 (0.01)	0.02	0.004 (0.008)	0.03	0.007* (0.004)	0.06**	0.008 (0.008)	0.07
Education	0.36 (0.76)	0.09	−0.15 (0.65)	−0.03	0.16 (0.32)	0.04	−1.14** (0.58)	−0.26**
Constant	0.55 (0.89)	−	−0.61 (0.82)	−	−0.12 (0.38)	−	1.25* (0.73)	−
N	210	210	267	267	1119	1119	335	335
Missing observations	Mean replace	Mean replace	Mean replace	Mean replace	Mean replace	Mean replace	Mean replace	Mean replace
% would obey	48.37	−	50.95	−	45.86	−	44.44	−

*$p \leq 0.10$, **$p \leq 0.05$, ***$p \leq 0.01$. See Footnotes #21 and #22 in Chapter 6 for an explanation of the p-values for the substantive effects.

Notes: The substantive effect measured for "Age" is the change in likelihood for stating that one would obey the tax laws when the "Age" variable was shifted from one standard deviation below the mean to one standard deviation above the mean while holding all other variables even at their mean. All other substantive effects measured are the change in likelihood for stating that one would obey the tax laws when variables were shifted from their minimum to their maximum value and all other variables were held even at their means.

Appendix VII

	East 2015	East 2015 Sub. Effects	Unoccupied Donbas 2015	Unoccupied Donbas 2015 Sub. Effects	South 2015	South 2015 Sub. Effects
			Deterrence			
Evasion OK if could get away with it	−0.38*** (0.14)	−0.09***	0.21 (0.30)	0.05	−0.25 (0.23)	−0.06
			Quasi-voluntary			
Trusts president	0.40 (0.40)	0.09	0.12 (0.80)	0.02	2.42*** (0.70)	0.51***
Trusts parliament	0.27 (0.56)	0.06	2.88** (1.30)	0.47**	0.10 (1.10)	0.02
Trusts government	0.64 (0.51)	0.14	−0.87 (1.06)	−0.20	−1.19 (1.09)	−0.27
Many dishonest tax bureaucrats	0.08 (0.25)	0.02	0.30 (0.57)	0.07	−0.40 (0.47)	−0.10
Many people evade taxes	0.75*** (0.29)	0.17***	1.23** (0.62)	0.29**	−0.38 (0.54)	−0.09
			Prior contact			
Previous contact with tax bureaucrats	−0.18 (0.18)	−0.04	−0.17 (0.38)	−0.04	0.24 (0.28)	0.06
			Socio-economic, additional effects			
Income	1.31*** (0.46)	0.29***	2.19** (0.92)	0.41**	−1.04 (0.69)	−0.25*
I file my income taxes myself	0.04 (0.26)	0.008	−0.79 (0.51)	−0.19*	0.43 (0.29)	0.10*
Occupation (managers, entrepreneurs)						
Male	−0.11 (0.14)	−0.03	−0.36 (0.27)	−0.08*	−0.16 (0.22)	−0.04
Age	0.002 (0.004)	0.02	0.003 (0.009)	0.02	0.01* (0.008)	0.13**
Education	0.14 (0.34)	0.04	0.74 (0.71)	0.17	−0.46 (0.52)	−0.11
Constant	−0.88** (0.42)	–	−2.39** (0.94)	–	0.09 (0.64)	–
N	980	980	279	279	371	371
Missing observations	Mean replace	Mean replace	Mean replace	Mean replace	Mean replace	Mean replace
% would obey	44.21	–	42.50	–	39.13	–

$^*p \leq 0.10$, $^{**}p \leq 0.05$, $^{***}p \leq 0.01$. See Footnotes #21 and #22 in Chapter 6 for an explanation of the *p*-values for the substantive effects.

Notes: The substantive effect measured for "Age" is the change in likelihood for stating that one would obey the tax laws when the "Age" variable was shifted from one standard deviation below the mean to one standard deviation above the mean while holding all other variables even at their mean. All other substantive effects measured are the change in likelihood for stating that one would obey the tax laws when variables were shifted from their minimum to their maximum value and all other variables were held even at their means.

Bibliography

Abdullaev, Nabi. 11 November 2005. 'Civil Servants Called a New Class,' *The Moscow Times*, p. 1.

Accounting Chamber of Ukraine. March 2011. 'Modernizatsiya podatkovoï na gal'makh [Tax Modernization on the Brakes]', March 2011, accessed on 24 August 2015, at <www.ac-rada.gov.ua/control/main/uk/publish/article/16736515>.

Albats, Yevgenia. 15 June 2004. 'Event Summary: Bureaucrats and Russian Transition: The Politics of Accommodation', Kennan Institute, Washington, DC, in *JRL*, No. 8268 (25 June 2004.)

Alexeev, Michael, and Robert F. Conrad. 2013. 'Chapter 10: The Russian Tax System', in Michael Alexeev and Shlomo Weber, eds., *The Oxford Handbook of the Russian Economy* (Oxford, UK: Oxford University Press), pp. 246–264.

Alm, James, Jorge Martinez-Vazquez, and Sally Wallace. January 2001. 'Tax Amnesties and Tax Collections in the Russian Federation', Georgia State University International Studies Program Working Paper Series (Atlanta: Andrew Young School of Policy Studies), No. 01–4.

Alm, James, Pablo Saavedra, and Edward Sennoga. 2007. 'How Should Individuals Be Taxed? Combining "Simplified," Income and Payroll Taxes in Ukraine', Georgia State University International Studies Program Working Paper Series (Atlanta: Andrew Young School of Policy Studies), No. 07–11, pp. 1–31.

Alyakrinskaya, Natalya. 17–23 August 2005. 'Shooting Is Helpless in Fighting Corruption', *Moscow News*, in *JRL*, No. 9226 (18 August 2005.)

Andreyev, Yevgeny. 22–28 October 2003. 'The Shadow Economy', *Moscow News*, cited in JRL, #7382 (24 October 2003.)

Appel, Hilary. October-December 2008. 'Is It Putin or Is It Oil? Explaining Russia's Fiscal Recovery', *Post-Soviet Affairs*, Vol. 24, pp. 301–323.

2011. *Tax Politics in Eastern Europe: Globalization, Regional Integration, and the Democratic Compromise* (Ann Arbor, MI: University of Michigan Press.)

Ash, Timothy Garton. 9 February 2006. 'The Twins' New Poland', *The New York Review of Books*, Vol. 53, No. 2, pp. 22–24.

Åslund, Anders. 1995. *How Russia Became a Market Economy* (Washington: Brookings Institution.)

August 2005. 'Putin's Decline and America's Response', Carnegie Endowment for International Peace Policy Brief, No. 41.

Bibliography 327

20 October 2011. 'Ukraine's Dismal Finances Offer No Simple Way Out', *Kyiv Post*, accessed on 18 September 2016 at <www.kyivpost.com/article/opinion/op-ed/ukraines-dismal-finances-offer-no-simple-way-out-115362.html>.

26 November 2013. 'Basket Case', *Foreign Policy*, accessed on 18 September 2016 at < http://foreignpolicy.com/2013/11/26/the-basket-case/>.

19 December 2013. 'How $10 Billion Gets Embezzled Annually', *Kyiv Post*, accessed on 25 September 2016, at <www.kyivpost.com/article/opinion/op-ed/how-10-billion-gets-embezzled-annually-334016.html>.

2015. *Ukraine: What Went Wrong and How to Fix It* (Washington, DC: Peterson Institute for International Economics.)

9 November 2015. 'Ukraine Needs Responsible Public Finances Now', *Atlantic Council*, accessed on 10 November 2015 at <www.atlanticcouncil.org/blogs/new-atlanticist/ukraine-needs-responsible-public-finances-now>.

Associated Press Newswires. 5 April 2001. 'Russia Boosts Tax Collection', accessed through FACTIVA electronic search engine.

Associated Press. 25 March 2013. 'Russian Officials Raid Amnesty's Moscow Headquarters', *The Guardian*, accessed on 3 August 2015 at <www.theguardian.com/world/2013/mar/25/russian-officials-raid-amnesty-moscow-headquarters>.

Baker & McKenzie, Kyiv Office. 11 February 2016. 'Personal Income Tax and Unified Social Contribution Rates Change', accessed on 18 September 2016 at <www.usubc.org/site/Baker-McKenzie/personal-income-tax-and-unified-social-contribution-rates-change>.

Baranov I.A., and N.N. Fedoseeva. 2009. 'Administrativnaya reforma v sovremennom rossiiskom gosudarstve: konseptsiya realizatsii [Administrative reform in the modern Russian state: The concept of realization]', *Gosudarstvennaya vlast' i mestnoe samoupravlenie [State Power and Local Self-Governance Journal]*, No. 9, pp. 3–5.

BBC Monitoring Former Soviet Union – Economic. 26 November 2001. 'New Year Comes Early for Russia's Successful Tax Men', accessed through the FACTIVA.

BBC Monitoring International Reports. 15 April 2005. 'Polish Audit Body Says Politicians "Impeding" Apolitical Civil Service', accessed through LexisNexis.

BBC Monitoring. 4 April 2012. 'Russia's REN TV Shows Report Slamming Systemic Corruption', in *JRL*, No. 2012–65, 9 April 2012.

BBC News. 22 March 2013. 'Russia Police Raid Rights Group Memorial and Other NGOs', accessed on 3 August 2015 at <www.bbc.com/news/world-europe-21896424>.

27 March 2013. 'Fears for NGOs in Russia as Tax Raids Multiply', accessed on 3 August 2015 at <www.bbc.com/news/world-europe-21952416>.

Bekker, Aleksandr. 24 June 2003. 'There Is Money, But Not Reforms', *Vedomosti*, p. A2.

Berenson, Marc P. 2008a. 'Rationalizing or Empowering Bureaucrats? Tax Administration Reform in Post-communist Poland and Russia', *Journal of*

328   Bibliography

Communist Studies and Transition Politics, Vol. 24, No. 1, pp. 136–155; in Anton Oleinik, ed., *Reforming the State without Changing the Model of Power? On Administrative Reform in Post-socialist Countries* (Oxford, UK: Routledge), pp. 137–156; 'Ratsionalizatsiya ili ukreplenie vlasti chinovnikov? Reforma nalogovykh organov v Pol'she i v Rossii', in Anton Oleinik and Oxana Gaman-Golutvinoj, ed., *Administrativnye reformy v kontekste vlastnykh otnoshenii: opyt postsocialisticheskih transformatsii v sravnitel'noi perspektive.* [Administrative Reform in the Context of Power Relations: Experience of the Post-socialist Transformation in Comparative Perspective] (Moscow: ROSSPEN), pp. 279–301.

2008b. 'Does Political Culture Matter? Deciphering the Whys of Ukrainian Tax Compliance', Max Weber Programme Working Paper (Florence: European University Institute).

2010a. 'Less Fear, Little Trust: Deciphering the Whys of Ukrainian Tax Compliance', in Paul D'Anieri, ed., *Orange Revolution and Aftermath: Mobilization, Apathy, and the State in Ukraine* (Washington, DC: Johns Hopkins University Press), pp. 193–228.

2010b. 'Serving Citizens: How Comparable Are Polish and Russian "Street-Level" Bureaucrats?' *Comparative Political Studies*, Vol. 43, No. 5, pp. 578–605.

Bergman, Marcelo. 2009. *Tax Evasion and the Rule of Law in Latin America: The Political Culture of Cheating and Compliance in Argentina and Chile* (University Park, PA: Pennsylvania State University Press).

Bershidsky, Leonid. 4 June 2015. 'Poroshenko Makes Putin Look Like a Wimp', *BloombergView*.

Bierman, Stephen. 12 June 2012. 'Russia Starts Tax Probe against Anti-Putin Opposition's Sobchak', *Bloomberg Business*, accessed 3 August 2015 at <www.bloomberg.com/news/articles/2012-06-12/russians-protest-against-putin-after-opposition-homes-searched>.

Borkowski, Janusz. 2001. *Jednostka a administracja publiczna po reformie ustrojowej* (Public unit and administration after the structural reform) (Warsaw: Instytut Spraw Publicznych).

Bovt, Georgy. 19 January 2006. *Moscow Times*, cited in E. Morgan Williams, *The Action Ukraine Report*, No. 646 (23 January 2006).

Bowen, Andrew. 16 November 2013. 'The Russian Tax Man: Return to the Bad Old Days?' *The Interpreter*, accessed 25 August 2015 at <www.interpretermag.com/the-russian-tax-man-return-to-the-bad-old-days/>.

Braithwaite, Valerie; and Margaret Levi, eds. 2003. *Trust and Governance* (New York: Russell Sage Foundation).

Bratton, Michael. 1994. 'Peasant–State Relations in Postcolonial Africa: Patterns of Engagement and Disengagement', in Joel S. Migdal, Atul Kohli, and Vivienne Shue, eds., *State Power and Social Forces: Domination and Transformation in the Third World* (Cambridge, UK: Cambridge University Press), pp. 231–254.

Brown, Archie. 1997. *The Gorbachev Factor* (Oxford, UK: Oxford University Press).

Bibliography 329

Brovkin, Vladimir. March/April 1996. 'The Emperor's New Clothes: Continuity of Soviet Political Culture in Contemporary Russia', *Problems of Postcommunism*, pp. 21–28.

Bunce, Valerie. 1999. *Subversive Institutions: The Design and the Destruction of Socialism and the State* (Cambridge, UK: Cambridge University Press).

8 March 2005. 'The United States and Democracy Promotion: Learning from Postcommunist Eurasia', 2004–05 Cyril Black Memorial Lecture, Princeton Institute for International and Regional Studies, Princeton University, Princeton, NJ.

Bureau of Economic Analysis. 2003. 'Glava 2: Nalogovaya politika' [Chapter 2: Tax Policy] in 'Obzor ekonomicheskoĭ politiki v Rossii za 2002 g' [Review of Economic Policy for 2002], manuscript, Moscow.

Bush, Jason. 7 March 2005. 'The Taxman Cometh – Again and Again', *Business Week*, in *JRL*, No. 9079 (6 March 2005).

Butler, Juliet. 6 March 1998. 'Growing Pains: Russians Play Down Harm of Sex, Violence', *Moscow Times*, accessed 15 August 2015, at <www.themoscowtimes.com/news/article/growing-pains-russians-play-down-harm-of-sex-violence/294278.html>.

Bychenko, Andrii, 29 June 2016. 'Transforming Ukrainian Society: Public Opinion on Current Events, International Affairs and the War in Donbas', presentation at Vesalius College, Brussels.

Campos, Nauro F. January 2000. 'Context Is Everything: Measuring Institutional Change in Transition Economies', World Bank Policy Research Paper, No. 2269 (Washington, DC: The World Bank).

Centrum Badania Opinii Społecznej [Public Opinion Research Centre, or CBOS]. July 1999. 'Reforma Podatkowa w Opinii Społecznej: Komunikat z Badań', Warsaw.

CBOS. August 2001. 'Korupcja i Afery Korupcyjne', Warsaw.

January 2002. 'Instytucje Publiczne w Opinii Społecznej', Warsaw.

May 2002. 'Rozliczenia Podatkowe za Rok 2001', Warsaw.

Chmielewski, Zdzisław. 1992. *Pozakancelaryjne Uwarunkowania Procesu Aktotwórczego w Urzędach Administracji 1807–1980* (Extra-chancellery Conditions of the Process of Act-Creation in Public Administration, 1807–1980) (Szczecin, Poland: Wydawnictwo Naukowe Uniwersytetu Szczecińskiego).

Cohen, Josh. 22 December 2015. 'Civil Service Reform May Revolutionize Ukraine', *Atlantic Council*, accessed 6 January 2016, at <www.atlanticcouncil.org/blogs/new-atlanticist/civil-service-reform-may-revolutionize-ukraine>.

5 July 2016. 'Could Ukraine's New Civil Service Law Be Undermined?' *Atlantic Council*, accessed 13 July 2016 at <www.atlanticcouncil.org/blogs/new-atlanticist/could-ukraine-s-new-civil-service-law-be-undermined>.

Cowell, Frank A. 1985. 'The Economic Analysis of Tax Evasion', *Bulletin of Economic Research*, Vol. 37, No. 3, pp. 163–193.

Cowley, Andrew. 7 May 1994. 'Ukraine: The Birth and Possible Death of a Country', in Ukraine Survey Supplement, *The Economist*.

330   Bibliography

Coynash, Halya. 16 July 2016. 'Large Protest in Occupied Horlivka Against Crippling Militant "Taxes,"' *Kharkiv Human Rights Protection Group Website*, accessed 19 July 2016 at <http://khpg.org.index.php?id=1468789216>.

D'Anieri, Paul. 2006. *Understanding Ukrainian Politics: Power, Politics and Institutional Design* (Baltimore: M.E. Sharpe).

February 2011. 'Structural Constraints in Ukrainian Politics', *East European Politics and Societies*, Vol. 25, No. 1, pp. 28–46.

D'Anieri, Paul, Robert Kravchuk, and Taras Kuzio. 1999. *Politics and Society in Ukraine* (Oxford, UK: Westview Press).

Daunton, Martin. 2001. *Trusting Leviathan: The Politics of Taxation in Britain, 1799–1914* (Cambridge, UK: Cambridge University Press).

De Haas, Ralph, Milena Djourelova, and Elena Nikolova. 2016. 'The Great Recession and Social Preferences: Evidence from Ukraine', *Journal of Comparative Economics*, Vol. 44, pp. 92–107.

Deloitte. 2015. *Doing Business in Russia 2015*, accessed 13 January 2016, at <www2.deloitte.com/content/dam/Deloitte/ru/Documents/tax/doing-business-in-Russia-2015.pdf>.

Dempsey, Judy. 9 May 2016. 'Strategic Europe: Poland's Polarizing Politics', *Carnegie Europe*, accessed 13 July 2016, at <http://carnegieeurope.eu/strategiceurope/?fa=63529>.

Djankov, Simeon. September 2015. 'Russia's Economy under Putin: From Crony Capitalism to State Capitalism', Peterson Institute for International Economics Policy Brief, No. PB15–18.

Dranitsyna, Yekaterina. 11 November 2005. 'Tax Reforms Leave Business Unsatisfied', *St. Petersburg Times*, in *JRL*, No. 9293, 13 November 2005.

Dubrovsky, Vladimir. 30 June 2015. 'The Ukrainian Tax System: Why and How It Should Be Reformed, Part I', *Vox Ukraine*, accessed 25 August 2016 at <http://voxukraine.org/2015/06/30/the-ukrainian-tax-system-why-and-how-it-should-be-reformed/>.

Dunlap, John B. 1993. *The Rise of Russia and the Fall of the Soviet Empire* (Princeton, NJ: Princeton University Press).

Easter, Gerald M. December 2002. 'Politics of Revenue Extraction in Postcommunist States: Poland and Russia Compared', *Politics & Society*, Vol. 30, No. 4, pp. 599–627.

September 2009. 'International Leverage vs. Institutional Mimicry: Explaining Tax Reform in Eastern Europe', paper presented at the Annual Meeting of the American Political Science Association, Toronto, Canada.

2012. *Capital, Coercion, and Post-communist States* (Ithaca, NY: Cornell University Press).

December 2013. 'Response to Aaron Schneider's Review of *Capital, Coercion and Postcommunist States*', *Perspectives on Politics*, Vol. 11, No. 4, pp. 1148–1149.

Ebrill, Liam; and Oleh Havrylyshyn. 1999. *Tax Reform in the Baltics, Russia, and Other Countries of the Former Soviet Union* (Washington, DC: International Monetary Fund).

Economist. 1 October 2005. 'Special Report Poland: Can the Eagle Soar?' p. 25.

Bibliography

20 October 2005. 'Blood Money', *Economist*, Print Edition, accessed through <www.economist.com>.

16 April 2016. 'Ukraine's Struggle Against Corruption: Clean-Up Crew', pp. 29–30.

30 April 2016. 'Poland's Rightest Revolution: Red and White Cavalry', pp. 35–36.

Ekiert, Grzegorz. 1996. *The State against Society: Political Crises and Their Aftermath in East Central Europe* (Princeton, NJ: Princeton University Press).

Elsner, Alan. 26 September 1999. 'Gore Blames Communism for Russian Corruption', *Reuters*.

Elster, John, Claus Offe, and Ulrich K. Preuss. 1998. *Institutional Design in Postcommunist Societies: Rebuilding the Ship at Sea* (Cambridge, UK: Cambridge University Press).

Ernst & Young. 2010. 2010 Russia Tax Survey, Moscow.

European Bank for Reconstruction and Development (EBRD). 13 December 2012. Diversifying Russia: Harnessing Regional Diversity, London.

Evans, Peter. 1995. *Embedded Autonomy* (Princeton, NJ: Princeton University Press).

Evans, Peter, and James E. Rauch. October 1999. 'Bureaucracy and Growth: A Cross-National Analysis of the Effects of "Weberian" State Structures on Economic Growth', *American Sociological Review*, Vol. 64, No. 5, pp. 748–765.

Fak, Alex. 5 July 2005. 'Lack of Trust Carries Heavy Toll', *Moscow Times*, p. 1, online edition.

Faulconbridge, Guy. 10 February 2005. 'Kudrin Sets Out His Plans for Tax Service', *Moscow Times*, p. 2.

Fish, M. Steven. 1995. *Democracy from Scratch* (Princeton, NJ: Princeton University Press).

Winter 1999. 'Postcommunist Subversion: Social Science and Democratization in East Europe and Eurasia', *Slavic Review*, Vol. 58, No. 4, pp. 794–823.

2005. *Democracy Derailed in Russia: The Failure of Open Politics* (New York: Cambridge University Press).

Fond Obshchestvennoe Mnenie (Public Opinion Foundation, or FOM). 2011. 'The Practice of Public Service Delivery in Russia' (Moscow).

Fortin, Jessica. August 2010. 'A Tool to Evaluate State Capacity in Postcommunist Countries, 1989–2006', *European Journal of Political Research*, Vol. 49, No. 5, pp. 654–686.

Franklin, Jennifer L. 1997. 'Tax Avoidance by Citizens of the Russian Federation: Will the Draft Tax Code Provide a Solution?' *Duke Journal of Comparative and International Law*, Vol. 8, No. 1, pp. 135–174.

Fritz, Verena. 2007. *State-Building: A Comparative Study of Ukraine, Lithuania, Belarus, and Russia* (Budapest: Central European University Press).

Frunkin, Konstantin. 2 November 2005. 'Government Determined to Pursue Administrative Reform', *Izvestia*, in *JRL*, No. 9286 (3 November 2005).

Fukuyama, Francis. 2011. *The Origins of Political Order: From Prehuman Times to the French Revolution* (London, UK: Profile Books).

332 Bibliography

July 2013. 'Commentary: What is Governance?' in *Governance: An International Journal of Policy, Administration, and Institutions*, Vol. 26, No. 3, pp. 347–368.

Gaddy, Clifford G., and Barry W. Ickes. September/October 1998. 'Russia's Virtual Economy', *Foreign Affairs*, Vol. 77, No. 5, pp. 53–67.

———. 2002. *Russia's Virtual Economy* (Washington, DC: Brookings Institution Press).

Galligan, Denis J., and Daniel M. Smilov. 1999. *Administrative Law in Central and Eastern Europe 1996–1998* (Budapest: Central European University Press).

Gaman-Golutvina, Oxana. 2009. 'The Changing Role of the State and State Bureaucracy in the Context of Public Administration Reforms: Russian and Foreign Experience', in Anton Olenik, ed., *Reforming the State Without Changing the Model of Power? On Administrative Reform in Post-Socialist Countries* (Abingdon, UK: Routledge), pp. 38–54.

Ganev, Venelin I. 2011. 'The Annulled Tax State: Schumpeterian Prolegomena to the Study of Postcommunist Fiscal Sociology', *Communist and Post-communist Studies*, Vol. 44, pp. 245–255.

Gehlbach, Scott. 2008. *Representation through Taxation: Revenue, Politics and Development in Postcommunist States* (New York, NY: Cambridge University Press).

Germanova, Olga. 5 August 2011. 'Re-branding the Image of the Tax Service', *Vestnik*, No. 29, accessed 24 August 2015 at <www.visnuk.com.ua/ru/pubs/fromarchive/1/id/1923>.

Gerth, H.H, and C. Wright Mills. 1958. *From Max Weber: Essays in Sociology* (New York: Oxford University Press).

GfK Ukraine. 25 May 2009. 'STS Modernisation Project KPIS 2008: Presentation of Research Results'.

Ghindar, Angelica. 2009. 'Why Go Democratic? Civil Service Reform in Central and Eastern Europe', Ph.D. Dissertation in Political Science in the Graduate College of the University of Illinois at Urbana–Champaign.

Gimpelson, V.E. 2002. 'Chislennost' i sostav rossiĭskoĭ biurokratii: mezhdu sovetskoĭ nomenklaturoĭ i gossluzhboĭ grazhdanskogo obshchestva' [Number and composition of Russian bureaucracy: Between Soviet Nomenkatura and State Service of Civic Society], Preprint (Moscow: Moscow State University Higher School of Economics). Accessed <www.hse.ru/science/preprint/WP3_2002_05.htm>.

Gintova, M.A. 29 June 2009. Mekhanizmy gosudarstvennogo stimulirovaniya institutsional'nykh reform na regional'nom urovne [Mechanisms of State Incentives Institutional Reforms at the Regional Level], Candidate of Economic Sciences Dissertation, Moscow State University.

Glazunov, Mikhail. 2016. *Corporate Strategy in Post-communist Russia* (Abingdon, UK: Routledge).

Goble, Paul. 25 November 2005. 'Window on Eurasia: Putin's "Power Vertical" Taking Federalism out of the Federation', in *JRL*, No. 9304 (26 November 2005).

Goetz, Klaus H. December 2001. 'Making Sense of Post-communist Central Administration: Modernization, Europeanization or Latinization?' *Journal of European Public Policy*, Vol. 8, No. 6, pp. 1032–1051.

Goetz, Klaus H. and Helmut Wollmann. 2001. 'Governmentalizing Central Executives in Post-communist Europe: A Four-Country Comparison' *Journal of European Public Policy*, Vol. 8, No. 6, pp. 864–887.

Gorchinskaya, Katya. 19 May 2015. 'Ukraine Gets New State Property Chief', *RFE/RL*, accessed 8 January 2016 at <www.rferl.org/content/bilous-named-ukraines-property-chief-despite-poor-report/27025358.html>.

18 July 2015. 'Avoiding Lustration in Ukraine: Senior Prosecutor Evades Sweep of Yanukovych-Era Officials', *RFE/RL*, accessed at <www.rferl.org/content/ukraine-lustration-prosecutor-valendyuk/27135678.html>.

Graham, Thomas. 30 September 1999. Testimony on Corruption in Russia and Future U.S. Policy Before the Senate Committee on Foreign Relations, in *JRL*, No. 3565 (16 October 1999).

Greene, Samuel A. 2014. *Moscow in Movement: Power and Opposition in Putin's Russia* (Stanford, CA: Stanford University Press).

Grigorieva, Ekaterina, and Frumkin, Konstantin. 26 May 2005. 'Government in Instalments: President Putin Delivers His Budget Address', *Izvestiya*, in *JRL*, No. 9160 (26 May 2005).

Grindle, Merilee S. 1996. *Challenging the State: Crisis and Innovation in Latin America and Africa* (Cambridge, UK: Cambridge University Press).

Hale, Henry. July 2010. 'Ukraine: The Uses of Divided Power', *Journal of Democracy*, Vol. 21, No. 3, pp. 84–98.

Hamilton, Christopher. and Wojciech Roszkowski. 1991. 'Bureaucratic Poland: Organized Life inside the Maverick Society', in Jaroslaw Piekalkiewicz and Christopher Hamilton, eds., *Public Bureaucracies Between Reform and Resistance: Legacies, Trends and Effects in China, the USSR, Poland, and Yugoslavia* (New York: St. Martin's Press), pp. 131–178.

Hardin, Russell. 1998. 'Trust in Government', in Valerie Braithwaite and Margaret Levi, eds., *Trust and Governance* (New York: Russell Sage Foundation).

2002. *Trust and Trustworthiness* (New York: Russell Sage Foundation).

Hellman, Joel. January 1998. 'Winners Take All: The Politics of Partial Reform in Postcommunist Transitions', *World Politics*, Vol. 50, No. 2, pp. 203–234.

Herbst, John E. 20 June 2016. 'Why the West Was Wrong about Ukraine's New Government', *Atlantic Council*, accessed 13 July 2016 at <www.atlanticcouncil.org/blogs/new-atlanticist/the-west-was-wrong-about-ukraine-s-new-government>.

Highfield, Richard, and Katherine Baer. 2000. 'Tax Administration for Russia' (Washington, DC: International Monetary Fund, Fiscal Affairs Department).

Hilderbrand, Mary E., and Merilee S. Grindle. 1997. 'Building Sustainable Capacity in the Public Sector: What Can Be Done?' in Merilee S. Grindle, ed., *Getting Good Government: Capacity Building in the Public Sectors of Developing Countries* (Cambridge, MA: Harvard University Press), pp. 31–62.

334   Bibliography

Himes, Susan, and Martine Milliet-Einbinder. January 1999. 'Russia's Tax Reform', in *OECD Observer*, No. 215, pp. 26–29, accessed 1 February 2001 at <www.oecd.org/publications/observer/215/e-himes.htm>.

Hosking, Geoffrey. 2014. *Trust: A History* (Oxford, UK: Oxford University Press).

Huntington, Samuel P. 1968. *Political Order in Changing Societies* (New Haven, CT: Yale University Press).

Huskey, Eugene. 2001. 'Political Leadership and the Centre–Periphery Struggle: Putin's Administrative Reforms', in Archie Brown and Lilia Shevtsova, eds., *Gorbachev, Yeltsin and Putin: Political Leadership in Russia's Transition* (Washington, DC: Carnegie Endowment for International Peace), pp. 113–142.

Huskey, Eugene, and Alexander Obolonsky. July/August 2003. 'The Struggle to Reform Russia's Bureaucracy', *Problems of Post-communism*, pp. 24–33.

Iakovlev, Andrej A. March 2000. 'The Causes of Barter, Nonpayments, and Tax Evasion in the Russian Economy', *Problems of Economic Transition*, Vol. 42, No. 11, pp. 80–96.

Ickes, Barry W., and Joel Slemrod. 1992. 'Tax Implementation Issues in the Transition from a Planned Economy', in Pierre Pestieau, ed., Public Finance in a World of Transition: Proceedings of the 47th Congress of the International Institute of Public Finance/Institut International de Finances Publiques, St. Petersburg 1991, A Supplement to *Public Finance/Finances Publiques*, Vol. 47, pp. 384–399.

INDEM Foundation. 2001. 'Russia Anti-Corruption Diagnostics: Sociological Analysis', Moscow.

Instytut Praw Publicznych (Institute of Public Affairs). 5 March 2012. *National Integrity System Assessment: Poland*, p. 2, accessed 1 January 2016, at <www .transparency.org/whatwedo/nisarticle/poland_2012>.

Interfax (Moscow). 25 July 2006. 'NGO Leaders Says Tax Claims Are Attempt to Pressure Civil Society', in *JRL*, No. 169 (26 July 2006).

Interfax-Ukraine. 21 June 2016. 'Groysman Hopes Tax Reform in Ukraine to Be Drawn Up in September', *Kyiv Post*, accessed 29 August 2016 at <www .kyivpost.com/article/content/ukraine-politics/groysman-hopes-tax-reform-in-ukraine-to-be-drawn-up-in-september-416780.html>.

International Finance Corporation (IFC). 2004. 'Business Environment in Ukraine' (Kyiv and Washington, DC).

2005. 'Business Environment in Ukraine' (Kyiv and Washington, DC).

International Monetary Fund (IMF). May 1999. 'Ukraine: Recent Economic Developments', IMF Staff Country Report No. 99/42.

April 2002. 'Russian Federation: Selected Issues and Statistical Appendix', IMF Country Report No. 02/75.

November 2005. 'Ukraine, Statistical Appendix', IMF Country Report No. 05/417.

January 2016. 'Ukraine: Technical Assistance Report – Reducing Social Security Contributions and Improving the Corporate and Small Business Tax System', IMF Country Report No. 16/25.

Bibliography

1 September 2016. 'Ukraine: Letter of Intent, Memorandum of Economic and Financial Policies, and Technical Memorandum of Understanding', accessed 7 October 2016 at <www.imf.org/External/NP/LOI/2016/UKR/090116.pdf>.

International Tax and Investment Centre (ITIC). 5 January 2005. *ITIC Bulletin*, Special Edition.

IPR Strategic Information Database. 28 November 2002. 'Putin Signs Decree on Reforming the Civil Service', accessed through Factiva.

ITAR-TASS. 19 February 1998. 'Overall Debt to All Budgets in Russia Totals 555 Bln Rbls', accessed through the Dow Jones Interactive Electronic Search Engine.

23 November 2005. '"Under-the-Table" Salaries in Russia Make Up 30% of Total Payroll Fund', in *JRL*, No. 9303 (25 November 2005).

Itrich-Drabarek, Jolanta. 2012. 'Chapter I: The Legal Foundations and the Quality and Ethical Standards of the Polish Civil Service', in Jolanta Itrich-Drabarek, Kamil Mroczka, and Łukasz Świetlikowski, *Civil Service in Poland* (Warsaw: Oficyna Wydawnicza ASPRA-JR), pp. 9–38.

Iuzhanina, Nina. 9 December 2015. 'Ukraine's Tax Reform: The Tax Committee Responds', *Beyond BRICS* Blog, *Financial Times*, accessed 18 September 2016 at <http://blogs.ft.com/beyond-brics/2015/12/09/ukraines-tax-reform-the-tax-committee-responds/>.

Ivanova, Anna, Michael Keen, and Alexander Klemm. July 2005. 'The Russian "Flat Tax" Reform', *Economic Policy*, Vol. 20, No. 43, pp. 397–444.

Ivanova, Svetlana, and Anastasiya Onegina. 28 July 2003. 'NDS ne platyat: po raschetam ėkonomistov, nalog soburaiut na 50–62%' [VAT Isn't Paid: According to Economists, the Tax is Collected at 50 to 62 Percent], *Vedomosti*, p. A3. Translated from the Russian by the author.

Johnson, Chalmers. 1982. *MITI and the Japanese Miracle: The Growth of Industrial Policy, 1925–1975* (Stanford, Calif.: Stanford University Press).

Johnson, David. 1996–present. *Johnson's Russia List (JRL)*, E-mail newsletter. A project of the Institute for European, Russian and Eurasian Studies at George Washington University's Elliott School of International Affairs.

Johnson, Simon, and Daniel Kaufmann. 1997. 'The Unofficial Economy in Transition', *Brookings Papers on Economic Activity*, Vol. 1997, No. 2.

Jones Luong, Pauline, and Erika Weinthal. 2010. *Oil Is Not a Curse: Ownership Structure and Institutions in Soviet Successor States* (Cambridge, UK: Cambridge University Press).

K., L. 16 May 2001. 'Wojciechowski chce pojedynku', *Rzeczpospolita*. Archive section of *Rzeczpospolita* online <www.rzeczpospolita.pl>.

Kamiński, Antoni Z. 1997. 'Corruption under the Post-communist Transformation: The Case of Poland', *Polish Sociological Review*, No. 2, pp. 91–117.

22 March 1999. 'Biurokracja w Polsce (Bureaucracy in Poland)', *Rzeczpospolita*, accessed 6 September 2002 at <www.rzeczpospolita.pl>.

Kaminski, Matthew. 25 August 1995. 'The Taxing Experience of Doing Business in Russia', *Financial Post*.

Karatnycky, Adrian. 11 July 2016. 'EuroMaidan Leaders Launch New Party in Ukraine. Can It Succeed?' *Atlantic Council* on-line, accessed 13 July 2016

336   Bibliography

at   <www.atlanticcouncil.org/blogs/new-atlanticist/EuroMaidan-leaders-launch-new-party-in-ukraine-can-it-succeed>.

Karatnycky, Adrian, Alexander Motyl, and Charles Graybow, eds. 1998. *Nations in Transit 1998: Civil Society, Democracy and Markets in East Central Europe and the Newly Independent States* (Washington, DC: Freedom House).

Katzeff, Paul. 11 April 2002. 'Basket Case Now a Breadbasket: Putin's Crew Transforms Russia', *Investor's Business Daily*, p. A1.

Kaufmann, Daniel, and Aleksander Kaliberda. December 1996. 'Integrating the Unofficial Economy into the Dynamics of Post-socialist Economies: A Framework of Analysis and Evidence', Policy Research Working Paper No. 1691 (Washington, DC: The World Bank).

Kaufmann, Daniel, Aart Kraay, and Massimo Mastruzzi. 2010. 'The Worldwide Governance Indicators: Methodology and Analytical Issues', World Bank Policy Research Working Paper No. 5430.

Kharkhordin, Oleg. 1998. 'First Europe–Asia Lecture: Civil Society and Orthodox Christianity', *Europe-Asia Studies*, Vol. 50, No. 6, pp. 949–968.

Khryshtanovskaya, Olga. 2 July 2003. 'Putin's Dangerous Personnel Preferences', *Moscow Times*.

Khryshtanovskaya, Olga, and Stephen White. October–December 2003. 'Putin's Militocracy', *Post-Soviet Affairs*, Vol. 19, No. 4, pp. 289–306.

King, Gary, Michael Tomz, and Jason Wittenberg. April 2000. 'Making the Most of Statistical Analyses: Improving Interpretation and Presentation', *American Journal of Political Science*, Vol. 44, No, 2, pp. 347–361.

Kitschelt, Herbert, Zdenka Mansfeldova, Radosław Markowski, and Gábor Tóka. 1999. *Post-communist Party Systems: Competition, Representation and Inter-Party Cooperation* (Cambridge, UK: Cambridge University Press).

Kochanowicz, Jacek. 1994. 'Reforming Weak States and Deficient Bureaucracies', in Joan M. Nelson, *Intricate Links: Democratization and Market Reforms in Latin America and Eastern Europe* (Washington, DC: Overseas Development Council), pp. 195–226.

2004. 'Trust, Confidence and Social Capital in Poland: A Historical Perspective', in Ivana Marková, ed., *Trust and Democratic Transition in Post-communist Europe* (Oxford: Oxford University Press), pp. 63–83.

Kochetov, Sergei. 20 May 2000. 'New Minister Intends to Automate Tax Collection', *Moscow Times*. Accessed through the FACTIVA electronic search engine.

Kohli, Atul. 1991. *Democracy and Discontent: India's Growing Crisis of Governability* (Cambridge, UK: Cambridge University Press).

1994. 'Centralization and Powerlessness: India's Democracy in a Comparative Perspective', in Joel S. Migdal, Atul Kohli, and Vivienne Shue, eds., *State Power and Social Forces: Domination and Transformation in the Third World* (Cambridge, UK: Cambridge University Press), pp. 89–107.

Kohli, Atul, and Vivienne Shue. 1994. 'Conclusion', in Joel S. Migdal, Atul Kohli, and Vivienne Shue, eds., *State Power and Social Forces: Domination and Transformation in the Third World* (Cambridge, UK: Cambridge University Press), pp. 293–326.

Kolarska-Bobińska, Lena. 2002. 'The Impact of Corruption on Legitimacy of Authority in New Democracies', in Stephen Kotkin and András Sajó, *Political Corruption in Transition: A Sceptic's Handbook* (Budapest: Central European University Press), pp. 313–325.

Koliushko, Ihor. 2003. 'Administrative Reform as a Precondition for Ukraine's NATO Membership', *National Security & Defence*, No. 7 (43), Ukrainian Centre for Economic & Political Studies Named after Olexander Razumkov, pp. 62–64.

Koliushko, Ihor, and Viktor Tymoshchuk. 2000. 'Administrative Reform in Ukraine: State and Prospects', *National Security & Defence*, No. 5, Ukrainian Centre for Economic & Political Studies Named after Olexander Razumkov, pp. 59–63.

Kosmehl, Miriam, and Andreas Umland. 26 July 2016. 'Established Political Parties Benefit from Ukraine's New Reform', *Atlantic Council*, accessed 7 August 2016, at <www.atlanticcouncil.org/blogs/new-atlanticist/established-political-parties-set-to-benefit-from-ukraine-s-new-reform>.

Kostikov, Vyacheslav. 7 April 2004. 'The New Nomenklatura: Glittering against a Backdrop of Poverty', *Argumenty i Fakty*, in *JRL*, No. 8155 (8 April 2004).

Kotchegura, Alexander. 1999. 'The Russian Civil Service: Legitimacy and Performance', in Tony Verheijen with Alexander Kotchegura, ed., *Civil Service Systems in Central and Eastern Europe* (Cheltenham, UK: Edward Elgar), pp. 15–46.

Kotkin, Stephen. 9 March 2014. 'Fareed Zakaria GPS', CNN Domestic and International. Transcript accessed 3 January 2016 at <http://transcripts.cnn.com/TRANSCRIPTS/1403/09/fzgps.01.html>.

Kotsonis, Yanni. 2014. *States of Obligation: Taxes and Citizenship in the Russian Empire and Early Soviet Republic* (Toronto: University of Toronto Press).

Kovensky, Josh. 2016. 'Corruption in Tax Service Stunts Ukraine's Economic Potential', *Kyiv Post Legal Quarterly*, Vol. 2016, No. 1, p. 24.

Kuchins, Andrew. 8 February 2006. 'Russian Democracy and Civil Society: Back to the Future', Testimony for the U.S. Commission on Security and Cooperation in Europe. Available at <www.carnegieendowment.org>.

Kuzio, Taras. 2008. 'Reviewed Work: *State-Building: A Comparative Study of Ukraine, Lithuania, Belarus, and Russia* by Verena Fritz', *Slavic Review*, Vol. 67, No. 4, pp. 1016–1018.

Kuzmenka, Irina. 16 May 2001. 'Most Russians Still Receive "Black" Incomes', *Gazeta.ru*.

Kyiv Post. 16 September 2015. 'Yatsenyuk Says Ukraine to Investigate State Fiscal Service Heads', accessed 8 January 2016 at <www.kyivpost.com/article/content/ukraine-politics/yatsenyuk-says-ukraine-to-investigate-state-fiscal-service-heads-398010.html>.

    23 March 2015. 'Cabinet Accepts Fiscal Service Head's Resignation', accessed 8 January 2016, at <www.kyivpost.com/article/content/ukraine-politics/cabinet-accepts-fiscal-service-heads-resignation-384248.html>.

    12 July 2016. 'Ukrainian Finance Minister Says IMD Supports Tax Police Liquidation, Relevant Bill Already Prepared', accessed 25 September 2016

338   Bibliography

at   <www.kyivpost.com/article/content/ukraine-politics/ukrainian-finance-minister-says-imf-supports-tax-police-liquidation-relevant-bill-already-prepared-418492.html>.

Lane, David, and Cameron Ross. 1994. 'Limitations of Party Control: The Government Bureaucracy in the USSR', *Communist and Post-communist Studies*, Vol. 27, No. 1, pp. 19–38.

Lazarev, A.M. 2007. 'Some Results of the Russian Administrative Reform in 2006–2007', *Information Analysis Bulletin of the Ural Academy of Public Administration 'Chinovnik'*, No. 5 (51), accessed at <http://chinovnik.uapa.ru/modern/article.php?id=798>.

Ledeneva, Alena. 2004. 'The Genealogy of Krugovaya Poruka: Forced Trust as a Feature of Russian Political Culture', in Ivana Marková, ed., *Trust and Democratic Transition in Post-communist Europe* (Oxford: Oxford University Press), pp. 85–108.

Ledyaev, Valeri. 2009. 'Domination, Power and Authority in Russia: Basic Characteristics and Forms', in Anton Olenik, ed., *Reforming the State Without Changing the Model of Power? On Administrative Reform in Post-Socialist Countries* (Abingdon, UK: Routledge), pp. 18–37.

Levi, Margaret. 1988. *Of Rule and Revenue* (Berkeley, CA: University of California Press).

2003. 'A State of Trust', in Valerie Braithwaite and Margaret Levi, eds., *Trust and Governance* (New York: Russell Sage Foundation), pp. 77–101.

Levi, Margaret, and Richard Sherman. 1997. 'Rational Compliance and Rationalized Bureaucracy', in Christopher Clague, *Institutions and Economic Development: Growth and Governance in Less-Developed and Post-Socialist Countries* (Baltimore, MD: The Johns Hopkins University Press), pp. 316–340.

Levitsky, Steven, and Lucan A. Way. 2010. *Competitive Authoritarianism: Hybrid Regimes After the Cold War* (New York: Cambridge University Press).

Lewin, Moshe. 1991. *The Gorbachev Phenomenon*, expanded ed. (Berkeley, CA: University of California Press).

Lieberman, Evan S. 2002. 'Taxation Data as Indicators of State–Society Relations: Possibilities and Pitfalls in Cross-National Research', *Studies in Comparative International Development*, Vol. 36, No. 4, pp. 89–115.

2003. *Race and Regionalism in the Politics of Taxation in Brazil and South Africa* (Cambridge, UK: Cambridge University Press).

Linz, Juan J., and Alfred Stepan. 1996. *Problems of Democratic Transition and Consolidation: Southern Europe, South America, and Post-communist Europe* (Baltimore, MD: Johns Hopkins University Press).

Logunov, A.B. December 2006. 'Administrativnaya reforma v Rossiĭskiĭ Federatsii: Osnovye etapi realizatsii (Administrative Reform in Russia: The Main Stages of Implementation)', *Analiticheskii Vestnik (Analytical Bulletin)* (Moscow: Analytical Department of the Staff of the Federation Council), No. 22 (310), accessed 7 January 2016 at <www.council.gov.ru/activity/analytics/analytical_bulletins/25774/>.

Lough, John, and Iryna Solonenko. April 2016. 'Can Ukraine Achieve a Reform Breakthrough?' *Chatham House Ukraine Forum Research Paper* (London: Chatham House).

Bibliography

Luzik, Peter C. February 1999. 'International Experience in Tax Reform and Lessons for Ukraine', Centre for Economic Reform and Transformation (CERT) Discussion Paper Series, No. 99/04.

Lyashenko, Galina. 9 January 2003. 'Nalogoviki sorvali plany Kremlya' [Tax Authorities Thwarted the Kremlin's Plans], *Kommersant'*, p. 1.

Malinowska, Elżbieta, Wojciech Misiąg, Adam Niedzielski, and Joanna Pancewicz. 1999. *Zakres Sektora Publicznego w Polsce* (Warsaw: Gdansk Institute for Market Reforms).

Mann, Michael. 1986. 'The Autonomous Power of the State: Its Origins, Mechanisms and Results', in John A. Hall, ed., *States in History* (Oxford, UK: Basil Blackwell), pp. 109–136.

1993. *The Sources of Social Power: Volume II: The Rise of Classes and Nation-States, 1760–1914* (Cambridge, UK: Cambridge University Press).

Manning, Nick, and Neil Parison, eds. February 2003. *International Public Administration Reform: Implications for the Russian Federation: Country Reform Studies* (Washington, DC: World Bank).

Markowski, Radosław, and Joshua A. Tucker. 2005. 'Pocketbooks, Politics and Parties: The 2003 Polish Referendum on EU Membership', *Electoral Studies*, Vol. 24, No. 3, pp. 409–433.

Martin, Isaac William. 2011. 'Review Essay', *Perspectives on Politics*, Vol. 9, No. 3, pp. 731–733.

Martinez-Vazquez, Jorge, and Robert M. McNab. 2000. 'The Tax Reform Experiment in Transitional Countries', in *National Tax Journal*, Vol. 53, No. 2, pp. 273–298.

McAuley, Mary. 2015. *Human Rights in Russia: Citizens and the State from Perestroika to Putin* (London, UK: I.B. Tauris).

McFaul, Michael. 2002. 'Evaluating Yeltsin and His Revolution' in Andrew C. Kuchins, ed., *Russia After the Fall* (Washington, DC: Carnegie Endowment for International Peace), pp. 21–38.

McGregor, Caroline. 2 April 2004. '20% of Civil Servants Face Ax', *Moscow Times*.

Medetsky, Anatoly. 26 November 2013. 'Outcry Prompts Putin Compromise Offer on Tax Investigation Bill', *Moscow Times*, in JRL, 2013, No. 213 (26 November 2013).

Medetsky, Anatoly, and Daan van der Schriek. 12 March 2007. 'Investigators Raid PwC Offices', *Moscow Times*, p. 1.

Michnik, Adam. 14 March 2006. 'A Dictatorship's Past: The Cleansing of Collective Memory', 2005–2006 Cyril Black Memorial Lecture and Princeton Institute for International and Regional Studies Distinguished Lecture, Princeton University, Princeton, NJ.

Migdal, Joel S. 1987. 'Strong Societies, Weak States: Power and Accommodation' in Samuel Huntington and Myron Weiner, eds., *Understanding Political Development* (Boston: Little, Brown), pp. 391–434.

1988. *Strong Societies and Weak States: State–Society Relations and State Capabilities in the Third World* (Princeton, NJ: Princeton University Press).

1994. 'State in Society: An Approach to Struggles for Domination', in Joel S. Migdal, Atul Kohli, and Vivienne Shue, eds., *State Power and Social Forces:*

340   Bibliography

Domination and Transformation in the Third World (Cambridge, UK: Cambridge University Press), pp. 7–36.

1997. 'Studying the State', in Mark Irving Lichbach and Alan S. Zuckerman, eds., *Comparative Politics: Rationality, Culture, and Structure* (Cambridge, UK: Cambridge University Press), pp. 208–236.

Millar, James R. October 1999. 'The De-development of Russia', *Current History*, Vol. 98, No. 630, pp. 322–327.

Ministry of Finance (Poland) (Ministerstwo Finansów). March 2000. 'Informacja w sprawie kształtowania się dochodów i zaległości podatkowych w latach 1995–1999 i prognozy w tym zakresie na rok 2000' [Information on the evolution of income and tax liabilities in 1995–1999 and forecasts for 2000], Warsaw.

September 2000. *Tax Administration and Tax System in Poland*, Warsaw.

2001. 'Informacja w sprawie realizacji zobowiązań podatkowych według stanu na 31 grudnia 2000 r.' [Information on the implementation of tax liabilities as of 31 December 2000], Warsaw.

2002. 'Informacja w sprawie realizacji zobowiązań podatkowych według stanu na 31 grudnia 2001 r.' [Information on the implementation of tax liabilities as of 31 December 2001], Warsaw.

2003. 'Informacja w sprawie realizacji zobowiązań podatkowych według stanu na 31 grudnia 2002 r.' [Information on the implementation of tax liabilities as of 31 December 2002], Warsaw.

May 2004a. 'Informacja w sprawie realizacji zobowiązań podatkowych według stanu na 31 grudnia 2003 r.' [Information on the implementation of tax liabilities as of 31 December 2003], Warsaw.

2004b. *Tax Administration and Tax System in Poland*, Warsaw.

2014. *Tax Administration: Professional, Modern and Customer-Friendly*, Warsaw.

2015. *Tax Administration: Professional, Modern and Customer-Friendly*, Warsaw.

Ministry of Taxes and Dues, Division of RF Ministry of Taxes and Dues for Volgograd Oblast. 2000. 'Tax Administration Modernisation Project of the RF: Volgograd Oblast Report for the Period of 1995 (January)–2000 (June)' (Volgograd, Russia: Ministry of Taxes and Dues).

Mollovan, O.O., O.V. Shevchenko, and O.O. Egorova. 2010. 'Prioriteti reformuvannya podatkovoi politiki Ukraini: yak pereiti vid fiskalizmu do stimulyuvannya dilovoi aktivnosti? Analitichna dopovid" [Priorities of reforming the tax policy of Ukraine. From Fiscal Policy to Stimulation] (Kyiv: Institute of Strategic Research of Ukraine, 2010), accessed 24 August 2014 at <www.niss.gov.ua/content/articles/files/Zalilo_fiskal_politic-69378.pdf>.

Morozov, Alexander. 1996. 'Tax Administration in Russia: Institutional Framework, Performance and Efficiency', Manuscript, Moscow.

Moscow Times. 17 February 2003. 'Tax Police Turn to Lie Detector Tests'.

24 August 2005. "06 Budget Sets Tax Collection Target', p. 6.

17 November 2005. 'FSB Busts Gang Peddling Leaked Tax Data', p. 7.

15 October 2014. 'Fewer Russian Bureaucrats but Salaries Increased 30%, Study Shows', accessed 31 July 2015 at <www.themoscowtimes.com/news/article/fewer-russian-bureaucrats-but-salaries-increased-30-study-shows/509483.html>.

Bibliography

Mularczyk, Chris. 21 October 2002. 'An Uncivil Service', *Warsaw Business Journal*, accessed through LexisNexis on 15 November 2003.

Murrell, Peter. 1993. 'What Is Shock Therapy? What Did It Do in Poland and Russia?' *Post-Soviet Affairs*, Vol. 9, No. 2, pp. 111–140.

Myers, Steven Lee. 18 September 2005. 'Russia Hounds Human Rights Group That Gets U.S. Help', *New York Times*, Section 1, p. 14.

Najwyższa Izba Kontroli (NIK) [Supreme Audit Chamber of Poland]. April 1993. 'Informacja o wynikach kontroli działalności urzędów skarbowych' [Information on the results of the audit of the activity of the tax offices], Warsaw.

June 1993. 'Informacja o wynikach kontroli działalności izb skarbowych w okresie 1990–I pólrocze 1992 r.' [Information on the results of the audit of the activity of tax chambers for the period 1990–First half of 1992], Warsaw.

July 1993. 'Analiza wykonania budżetu państwa w 1992 roku' [Analysis of the implementation of the state budge in 1992], Warsaw.

July 1994. 'Analiza wykonania budżetu państwa w 1993 roku' [Analysis of the implementation of the state budge in 1993], Warsaw.

October 1994. 'Informacja o wynikach kontroli działalności urzędów skarbowych' [Information on the results of the audit of the activity of the tax offices], Warsaw.

December 1994. 'Informacja o wynikach kontroli działalności urzędów kontroli skarbowej w latach 1992–1993' [Information on the results of the audit of the activity of the tax audit offices in 1992–1993], Warsaw.

May 1995. 'Informacja o wynikach kontroli wykonywania uprawnień przez resort finansów w zakresie wydawanych decyzji o zaniechaniu ustalania i poboru podatków' [Information on the results of the audit of the carrying out of entitlements through the finance department in the scope of completed decisions regarding the nonfeasance of arrangement and collection of taxes]', Warsaw.

January 1996. 'Informacja o stanie informatyzacji systemu podatkowego POLTAX' [Information about the state of computerization of the POLTAX tax system], Warsaw.

May 1997. 'Informacja o wynikach kontroli realizacji przez urzędy skarbowe zadań w zakresie egzekucji administracyjnej w latach 1994–1996 (I półrocze)' [Information on the results of the implementation of tasks in the conduct of inspections in the period 1994–first half of 1996], Warsaw.

October 1997. 'Informacja o wynikach kontroli działalności Ministerstwa Finansów i urzędów skarbowych w zakresie poboru podatku od towarów i usług' [Information on the results of the audit of the activity of the Ministry of Finance and the tax offices in the scope of the collection of taxes on goods and services], Warsaw.

June 1998. 'Analiza wykonania budżetu państwa i założeń polityki pieniężnej w 1997 roku: Tom I' [Analysis of the implementation of the state budget and monetary policy guidelines in 1997: Volume I], Warsaw.

May 2000. 'Informacja o wynikach kontroli działalności urzędów kontroli skarbowej' [Information on the results of the audit of the activity of the tax audit offices], Warsaw.

342   Bibliography

June 2000. 'Analiza wykonania budżetu państwa i założeń polityki pieniężnej w 1999 roku: Tom I' [Analysis of the implementation of the state budget and monetary policy guidelines in 1999: Volume I], Warsaw.

April 2001. 'Informacja o wynikach kontroli działaności urzędów skarbowych w zakresie egzekucji i zabezpieczenia zaległości podatkowych' [Information on the results of the audit of activity of the tax offices in the scope of the collection and obtainment of tax arrears], Warsaw.

May 2001. 'Informacja o wynikach kontroli działalności izb skarbowych w latach 1996–1998' [I połrocze) (Information on the results of the audit of the activity of tax chambers for the period 1996–first half of 1998], Warsaw.

June 2001. 'Analiza wykonania budżetu państwa i założeń polityki pieniężnej w 2000 roku: Tom I' [Analysis of the implementation of the state budget and monetary policy guidelines in 2000: Volume I], Warsaw.

June 2002. 'Analiza wykonania budżetu państwa i założeń polityki pieniężnej w 2001 roku' [Analysis of the implementation of the state budget and monetary policy guidelines in 2001], Warsaw.

Naryshkin, S.E., and T.Y. Khabrievoï, ed. 2006. *Administrativnaya reforma v Rossii: Nauchno-prakticheskoe posobie* [Administrative Reform in Russia: Scientific and Practical Handbook] (Moscow: Infra-M).

Nemtsov, Boris, and Vladimir Pribylovsky, 10 February 2005. 'The President, Simple and False: Ten Moments of the State's Lies; The Putin Regime Is Based on Lies, Bureaucracy, and Corruption', *Novaya Gazeta*, No. 10, in *JRL*, No. 9058 (12 February 2005).

Nicholson, Alex. 26 March 2003. '2 Tax Police Officers Caught Red-Handed', *Moscow Times*.

Novecon. 6 March 2003. 'IMF Disagrees with Russian Experts on Income Tax', accessed through FACTIVA electronic search engine.

Nunberg, Barbara. 1999. *The State after Communism: Administrative Transitions in Central and Eastern Europe*, (Washington, DC: World Bank).

Nunberg, Barbara, and Luca Barbone. 1999. 'Breaking Administrative Deadlock in Poland: Internal Obstacles and External Incentives', in Barbara Nunberg, *The State after Communism: Administrative Transitions in Central and Eastern Europe* (Washington, DC: World Bank), pp. 7–52.

Odling-Smee, John. 2006. 'The IMF and Russia in the 1990s', *IMF Staff Papers*, Vol. 53, No. 1, pp. 151–194.

Office of Civil Service (Poland). December 2000. 'Civil Service in Poland: A Brief Introduction', Warsaw.

Office of the Civil Service. 2001. 'Informacja o zatrudnieniu w administracj w latach 1989–1996' [Information on employment in the administration in 1989–1996], Warsaw.

Oleinik, Anton. 2009. 'Introduction: Putting Administrative Reform in a Broader Context of Power', in Anton Olenik, ed., *Reforming the State Without Changing the Model of Power? On Administrative Reform in Post-Socialist Countries* (Abingdon, UK: Routledge), pp. 1–17.

Organisation for Economic Co-operation and Development (OECD). October 2004. *Tax Administration in OECD Countries: Comparative Information Series (2004)* (Paris: OECD Centre for Tax Policy and Administration).

Bibliography

6 December 2012. 'Human Resources Management Country Profiles: Russian Federation', p. 4, accessed 31 July 2015, at <www.oecd.org/gov/pem/OECD%20HRM%20Profile%20-%20Russia.pdf>.

Pan, Philip P. 19 October 2009. 'Investment firm dares to cry corruption in Russia', *Washington* Post, accessed 14 February 2016, at <www.washingtonpost.com/wp-dyn/content/article/2009/10/18/AR2009101802259.html>.

PAP News Agency (Warsaw). 28 July 2003. 'Interior Minister: Corruption in Poland Rule, Not Exception', in *BBC Monitoring International Reports*, 28 July 2003, accessed through LexisNexis.

Papp, Tamás K., and Előd Takáts. 2008. 'Tax Rate Cuts and Tax Compliance – The Laffer Curve Revisited', IMF Working Paper, No. WP/08/7.

Parfitt, Tom. 3 November 2010. 'Alexander Lebedev Accuses Rival of Organizing Police Raid against His Bank', *Guardian* (UK), accessed 3 August 2015 at <www.theguardian.com/world/2010/nov/03/alexander-lebedev-moscow-bank-raid>.

Paton Walsh, Nick. 17 April 2004. 'Putin Hikes His Pay to Fight Corruption', *The Guardian* (UK), in *JRL*, No. 8171 (17 April 2004).

Pavilionis, Peter. 1991. 'A New Constitution for Russia', *The Eurasia Centre: Reports*, Vol. I, No. 2, accessed 7 January 2017 at <https://eurasiacenter.org/archive/1990–1999/1991a_new_constitution_for_russia_by.htm>.

Peleschuk, Dan. 3 August 2015. 'It's Insanely Expensive to Bribe Russian Officials These Days', *USA Today*, accessed 5 August 2015 at <www.usatoday.com/story/news/world/2015/08/03/globalpost-ruble-expensive-bribe-russia/31054829/>.

Petrov, Nikolay. 22 May 2003. 'Ominous Silence on Federal Reform', *Moscow Times*, p. 8.

18 October 2005. 'The Essence of Putin's Managed Democracy', Carnegie Endowment for International Peace meeting, summarized by Matthew Gibson of the Carnegie Endowment in *JRL*, No. 9278 (25 October 2005.)

Petrukhina, Olga. 21 January 2016. '"Neverending Story" of Ukraine's Tax Reforms: UHY Proster Point of View', *Kyiv Post*, accessed 18 September 2016 at <www.kyivpost.com/article/content/business-wire/neverending-story-of-ukraines-tax-reforms-uhy-prostor-point-of-view-406389.html>.

Phippen, J. Weston. 19 September 2016. 'Vladimir Putin's Big Win', accessed 26 September 2016 at <www.theatlantic.com/news/archive/2016/09/russia-election-putin/500555/>.

Polish Information and Foreign Investment Agency S.A. 2011.*Taxes in Poland,* Warsaw.

Polish News Bulletin. 11 December 1997. 'Premier on Civil Service', accessed on Factiva 3 December 2003.

19 December 2001. 'Sejm Passes Controversial Civil Service Bills', accessed on Factiva 3 December 2003.

24 October 2002. 'Civil Service Turnover Stays Party Closed', accessed on Factiva 17 November 2003.

Polomski, Krzysztof. 1999. 'Tax Systems in the Selected Transition Economies: An Overview', *CASE Studies & Analyses*, No. 181 (Warsaw: Centre for Social and Economic Research (CASE)).

344 Bibliography

Popov, Vladimir. 13–14 October 2000. 'Circumstances versus Policy Choices: Why Has Economic Performance of FSU States Been So Poor?' paper presented at the conference 'Ten Years after the Collapse of the Soviet Union: Comparative Lessons and Perspectives', Princeton University, Princeton, NJ.

November 2004.'The State in the New Russia (1992–2004): From Collapse to Gradual Revival?' *PONARS Policy Memo*, No. 342, in *JRL*, No. 9036 (26 January 2005).

Powell, Bill, Yevgenia Albats, Owen Matthews, and Mark Hosenball. 4 October 1999. 'Where Did Russia's Money Go?' *Newsweek International*, in *JRL*, No. 3533 (30 September 1999).

PRIME-TASS News (Russia). 24 April 2002. 'Kasyanov Satisfied with Level of Tax Collection in Russia', accessed through FACTIVA electronic search engine.

21 November 2002. 'Putin Signs Decree, Submits Bill on Civil Service', accessed through Factiva.

23 November 2010. 'Federal Tax Service to Set up Consultative Call Centre for Moscow Taxpayers in 2011', accessed 1 December 2010 at <http://prime-tass.ru/news/0/%7BE34FA6AD-6124–4221-AD96-A6A2730980BD%7D.uif>.

14 March 2011. 'Russia's Federal Tax Service Says Documents Can Be Submitted to Unified Registration Centre Electronically', accessed 22 March 2011, at <www.prime-tass.ru/news/0/%7B07F6C54D-2C12–4DD2-B53C-E704EF1E3CF6%7D.uif>.

Pryadilnikov, Mikhail, and Elena Danilova. 3–6 September 2009. 'Citizens (and Tax Inspectors) against the State: Tracking Changes in Attitudes towards Tax Compliance in Russia, 2001–2008', Paper presented at the American Political Science Association, Toronto, Canada.

Przeworski, Adam. 1991. *Democracy and the Market: Political and Economic Reforms in Eastern Europe and Latin America* (Cambridge, UK: Cambridge University Press).

Putin, Vladimir V. 4 September 2004. 'Terror in Russia: Putin Tells the Russians: "We Shall Be Stronger"' (full transcript of Putin's televised remarks on the evening of 4 September 2004), *New York Times*, September 5, 2004, accessed at <www.nytimes.com>.

Putnam, Robert D. 1993. *Making Democracy Work: Civic Traditions in Modern Italy* (Princeton, NJ: Princeton University Press).

Rachkevych, Mark. 27 December 2015. 'Ukraine's Massive Shadow Economy Robs Treasury and Future of 44 Million Citizens', *Kyiv Post*, accessed 15 August 2016 at <www.kyivpost.com/article/content/business/ukraines-massive-shadow-economy-robs-treasury-and-future-of-44-million-citizens-404982.html>.

Razumkov Ukrainian Centre for Economic and Political Studies (UCEPS). 2000. 'Administrative Reform in Ukraine: Will It Be Possible to Break the Closed Circle?' *National Security & Defence*, Kyiv, No. 5, pp. 2–43.

2005. 'The New Government's Performance in 2005: Section 2: Internal Policy', *National Security & Defence*, Kyiv, No. 12 (72), pp. 31–48.

Bibliography 345

2006. '100 Days of the Coalition Government: A View of Nongovernmental Think Tanks: Home Policy: Inertia of Confrontation, Conservatism of Approaches', *National Security & Defence*, No. 10 (82), pp. 3–25.

2007. '240 Days of Government Activity in the New Format', *National Security & Defence*, Kyiv, No. 3 (87), pp. 2–92.

Remington, Thomas F. 2003. 'Putin, the Duma and Political Parties', in Dale R. Herspring, ed., *Putin's Russia: Past Imperfect, Future Uncertain* (Lanham, MD: Rowman and Littlefield).

Reuters. 17 July 1996. 'Polish Civil Service Law Draws Opposition Attack', accessed on Factiva on 3 December 2003.

Reynolds, Garfield. 19 August 2005. 'Ukraine Revenue Up as Tax Dodging Falls, Premier Says', *Bloomberg News*, in 'The Action Ukraine Report (AUR)' Email Listserv, No. 544, 22 August 2005.

Reynolds, Neil. 27 April 2007. 'Tax Reform, Not Oil, Fuelled Russia's Revival', *The Globe and Mail (Canada)*, in *JRL*, 2007, No. 98 (29 April 2007).

Radio Free Europe/Radio Liberty (RFE/RL). 16 November 2010. 'Thousands Protest Against New Ukrainian Tax Code', accessed 1 December 2010 at <www.rferl.org/content/Thousands_Protest_Against_New_Ukrainian_Code/2221984.html>.

RFE/RL Newsline. 2 March 2004. 'Sociologist Examines Administrative Reforms', Vol. 8, No. 54, Part I.

10 March 2004. 'Putin Cuts 13 Ministries and Almost a Dozen State Agencies', Vol. 8, No. 46, Part I.

19 March 2004. 'Government Reform Reportedly Will Slow Work of Government . . . As Analysts Continue to Mull Changes', Vol. 8, No. 53, Part I.

26 March 2004. 'Putin Reshuffles the Presidential Administration . . . As Titles Change But Portfolios Appear to Remain the Same', Vol. 8, No. 57, Part I.

14 May 2004. 'Bureaucrats' Ranks Swelled by 4 Percent Last Year', Vol. 8, No. 91, Part I.

28 July 2004. 'Civil Servants to Keep In-Kind Benefits Despite Government's Reform Effort', Vol. 8, No. 142, Part I.

15 November 2005. 'Police Probe Leak of Moscow Tax Database', Vol. 9, No. 214, Part I.

26 September 2007. 'Tax Service to Turn Its Attention to the Oligarchs', Vol. 11, No. 179, Part I.

RFE/RL Poland, Belarus and Ukraine Report. 15 October 2002. 'Brussels Recommends Poland for EU Entry in 2004', Vol. 4, No. 39.

RFE/RL Russian Political Weekly. 3 March 2004. Prague: Radio Free Europe/Radio Liberty, Vol. 4, No. 8.

28 July 2004. 'Legislators Give Final Nod to Bill on Civil Service', Vol. 4, No. 27.

RIA Novosti. 4 April 2003. '3 Million Tax Defaulters', *Vedomosti*, p. A1, accessed through LEXIS-NEXIS Electronic Search Engine.

1 April 2004. 'Overhauling the Russian Government', in *JRL*, No. 8148.

7 March 2007. 'Tax Amnesty in Russia: Getting Ready to Tighten Regulations?' in *JRL*, 8 March 2007.

346   Bibliography

9 April 2008. 'Ernst & Young Receives $16 Mln Back Tax Claim in Russia', in *JRL*, 9 April 2008.

RIA Oreanda. 13 February 2003. 'Russia Having Nearly 105 Million Taxpayers', accessed through *LEXIS-NEXIS*.

Roberts, Cynthia, and Thomas Sherlock. 1999. 'Review Article: Bringing the Russian State Back In: Explanations of the Derailed Transition to Market Democracy', *Comparative Politics*, Vol. 31, No. 4, pp. 477–498.

Roeder, Philip G. 1993. *Red Sunset: The Failure of Soviet Politics* (Princeton, NJ: Princeton University Press).

1999. 'Peoples and States after 1989: The Politics Costs of Incomplete National Revolutions', *Slavic Review*, Vol. 58, No. 4, pp. 854–882.

RosBusinessConsulting. 25 January 2005. 'Tax Service Reports on 2004 Collections', in *JRL*, No. 9034 (26 January 2005.)

Rose-Ackerman, Susan. 2004a. 'Introduction', in Janos Kornai and Susan Rose-Ackerman, *Building a Trustworthy State in Post-socialist Transition* (New York: Palgrave Macmillan), pp. 1–5.

2004b. 'Public Participation in Consolidating Democracies: Hungary and Poland', in János Kornai and Susan Rose-Ackerman, *Building a Trustworthy State in Post-socialist Transition* (New York: Palgrave Macmillan), pp. 9–28.

Roth, Jeffrey A.; and John T. Scholz, eds. 1989. *Taxpayer Compliance: Volume II: Social Science Perspectives* (Philadelphia, PA: University of Pennsylvania Press).

Roth, Jeffrey A.; John T. Scholz; and Ann Dryden Witte, eds. 1989. *Taxpayer Compliance: Volume I: An Agenda for Research* (Philadelphia, PA: University of Pennsylvania Press).

Rothstein, Bo. 2004. 'Social Trust and Honesty in Government: A Causal Mechanisms Approach', in János Kornai, Bo Rothstein, and Susan Rose-Ackerman, *Creating Social Trust in Post-socialist Transition* (New York: Palgrave Macmillan), pp. 13–30.

Rudzinski, Aleksandr. 1954. *Polish Public Administration before World War II* (New York: Mid-European Studies Centre).

Russian Federal Service of State Statistics (Rosstat) [formerly State Statistics Committee of Russia, or GosKomStat], *Finansy Rossii: Statisticheskii sbornik (Finances of Russia: Statistical Collection)* (Moscow: GosKomStat, 1998).

Finansy Rossii: Statisticheskii sbornik (Finances of Russia: Statistical Collection) (Moscow: GosKomStat, 2000).

Finansy Rossii: Statisticheskii sbornik (Finances of Russia: Statistical Collection) (Moscow: GosKomStat, 2002).

Finansy Rossii: Statisticheskii sbornik (Finances of Russia: Statistical Collection) (Moscow: GosKomStat, 2004).

Finansy Rossii: Statisticheskii sbornik (Finances of Russia: Statistical Collection) (Moscow: GosKomStat, 2006).

Finansy Rossii: Statisticheskii sbornik (Finances of Russia: Statistical Collection) (Moscow: GosKomStat, 2008).

Finansy Rossii: Statisticheskii sbornik (Finances of Russia: Statistical Collection) (Moscow: GosKomStat, 2010).

Finansy Rossii: Statisticheskii sbornik (Finances of Russia: Statistical Collection) (Moscow: GosKomStat, 2012).

Bibliography 347

Finansy Rossii: Statisticheskii sbornik (Finances of Russia: Statistical Collection) (Moscow: GosKomStat, 2014.)

Russkii Fokus. 24 May 2004. 'Power to the Security and Law Enforcement People', in *JRL*, No. 8231 (31 May 2004).

Rutland, Peter. 18 July 2013. 'The Political Economy of Putin 3.0', *Russian Analytical Digest*, No. 133, pp. 2–5.

Ryavec, Karl W. 2003. *Russian Bureaucracy: Power and Pathology* (Lanham, MD: Rowman and Littlefield).

Rzeczpospolita. 4 February 2014. 'Corruption Is a Widespread Problem', pp. A1 and A5, accessed 30 July 2015 through LexisNexis.

Sachs, Jeffrey D. 1994. *Poland's Jump to the Market Economy* (Cambridge, MA: MIT University Press).

19 September 1999. 'Eastern Europe Reforms: Why the Outcomes Differed so Sharply', *Boston Globe*, p. C7.

Samoylenko, Vladimir. March/April 2004. 'Russia Update', *ITIC Bulletin* (International Tax and Investment Center), pp. 1–2.

June/July 2004. 'Russia Update', *ITIC Bulletin* (International Tax and Investment Centre), pp. 1–2.

September/October 2004. 'Russia Update', *ITIC Bulletin* (International Tax and Investment Centre), p. 2.

November/December 2004. 'Russia Update', *ITIC Bulletin* (International Tax and Investment Centre), p. 2.

Saradzhyan, Simon. 19 June 2003. 'A Plan to Slash Number of Ministries', *Moscow Times*, p. 2.

Schneider, Friedrich, and Colin C. Williams. 2013. *The Shadow Economy* (London: Institute of Economic Affairs).

Sharov, Andrei V. 26 May 2007. 'O resul'tatakh provedeniya konkursnogo otbora programm, planov i proektov federal'nykh organov ispolnitel'noĭ vlasti i vysshikh ispolnitel'nykh organov gosudarstvennoĭ vlasti sub'ektov Rossiĭskoĭ Federatsii po realizatsii administrativnoĭ reformy v 2007 godu' [The Results of Competitive Selection of Programs, Plans and Projects of Federal Executive Bodies and Institutions of Higher Executive Authorities of Subjects of the Russian Federation on the Implementation of Administrative Reform in 2007], presentation, Moscow.

Shavalyuk, Lyubomyr. 19 August 2015. 'Slow out of the Gate: An Overview of Ukraine's New Tax System', *Ukrainian Week*, accessed 13 September 2015 at <http://ukrainianweek.com/economics/143992>.

Sheffrin, Steven M., and Robert K. Triest. 1992. 'Can Brute Deterrence Backfire? Perceptions and Attitudes in Taxpayer Compliance', in Joel Slemrod, ed., *Why People Pay Taxes: Tax Compliance and Enforcement* (Ann Arbor, MI: University of Michigan Press).

Shekhovtsov, Anton. January 2016. 'Is Transition Reversible? The Case of Central Europe' (London: Legatum Institute).

Shelley, Louise I. 1998. 'Organized Crime and Corruption in Ukraine: Impediments to the Development of a Free Market Economy', *Demokratizatsiya: The Journal of Post-Soviet Democratization*, Vol. 6, No. 4, pp. 648–663.

Shlapentokh, Vladimir. 27 June 2005. 'Trust in Public Institutions in Russia: The Lowest in the World', in *JRL*, No. 9186 (28 June 2005.)

348   Bibliography

Shleifer, Andrei, and Daniel Treisman. 2000. *Without a Map: Political Tactics and Economic Reform in Russia* (Cambridge, MA: The MIT Press).

Simankin, Dmitri, and Ekaterina Blinova. 16 August 2005. 'The Army of Arrogant Cynics: Young, Ambitious, Mercenary Pragmatists Will Replace Post-Soviet Bureaucrats; The "Arrogant Caste" of Bureaucrats and Its Ideas', *Nezavisimaya Gazeta*, No. 171, in *JRL*, No. 9226 (17 August 2005.)

Skocpol, Theda. 1979. *States and Social Revolutions: A Comparative Analysis of France, Russia, and China* (Cambridge, UK: Cambridge University Press).

'Bringing the State Back In: Strategies of Analysis in Current Research', in Peter Evans, Dietrich Reuschmeyer, and Theda Skocpol, eds., *Bringing the State Back In* (New York: Cambridge University Press), pp. 3–43.

Slemrod, Joel, ed. 1992. *Why People Pay Taxes: Tax Compliance and Enforcement* (Ann Arbor, MI: University of Michigan Press).

Sluchinsky, Alexi. May 2017. 'Corruption in the System of Audit of the Tax Administration in Ukraine', manuscript, Economics Education & Research Consortium, National University of Kyiv Mohyla Academy.

Solnick, Steven L. November/December 1996. 'The Political Economy of Russian Federalism: A Framework for Analysis', *Problems of Post-communism*, pp. 13–25.

1997. *Stealing the State* (Cambridge, MA: Harvard University Press).

Stanley, Alessandra. 8 March 1998. 'Russia's Tax Police Press Media Message: Pay Up.' *New York Times*, accessed 15 August 2015 at <www.nytimes.com/1998/03/08/world/russia-s-tax-police-press-media-message-pay-up.html>.

Stepanyan, Vahram. September 2003. 'Reforming Tax Systems: Experience of the Baltics, Russia, and Other Countries of the Former Soviet Union', IMF Working Paper No. 03/173.

Stickgold, Emma. 28 March 2007. 'Taxing Questions', *Moscow Times*, p. 11, accessed 28 March 2007 at <www.themoscowtimes.com/stories/2007/03/28/026.html>.

Stoner-Weiss, Kathryn. 1997. *Local Heroes: The Political Economy of Russian Regional Governance* (Princeton, NJ: Princeton University Press).

1999a. 'Central Weakness and Provincial Autonomy: Observations on the Devolution Process in Russia', *Post-Soviet Affairs*, Vol. 15, No. 1, pp. 87–106.

1999b. 'Central Governing Incapacity and the Weakness of Political Parties: Russian Democracy in Disarray', presented at the American Political Science Association Annual Convention, Atlanta, GA.

Suleiman, Ezra. 2003. *Dismantling Democratic States*, (Princeton, NJ: Princeton University Press).

Swedish National Tax Board. 2001. *Tax Statistical Yearbook of Sweden*, Stockholm.

Szczesna, Joanna. 1998. 'Taxpayers vs. Taxes: "Whatever Is Not Prohibited is Permitted"', *East European Constitutional Review*, Vol. 7, No. 1, pp. 76–78.

Szklarski, Bohdan. 1997. *Semi-Public Democracy: Articulation of Interests and Systemic Transformation* (Warsaw: Institute of Political Studies Polish Academy of Sciences).

Bibliography 349

Szołno-Koguc, Jolanta. 2000. *Reforma Polskiego Systemu Podatkowego w Latach 1990–1995 (założenia a realizacja)* [Reform of the Polish Tax System in 1990–1995 (Establishment and Implementation)] (Lublin, Poland: Wydawnictwo UMCS).

Sztompka, Piotr. 1998. 'Trust, Distrust and Two Paradoxes of Democracy', *European Journal of Social Theory*, Vol. 1, No. 1, pp. 19–32.

Talant, Bermet. 30 September 2016. 'OECD: Ukraine's Reforms Great on Paper, Not So Great in Practice', *Kyiv Post*, accessed 30 September 2016 at <www.kyivpost.com/business/oecd-ukraines-reforms-great-paper-not-good-practice.html>.

Tanzi, Vito. 2010. *Russian Bears and Somali Sharks: Transition and Other Passages* (New York: Jorge Pinto Books).

TASS. 9 September 2014. 'Russian Police Search National Reserve Bank over Tax Evasion', accessed 3 August 2015 at <http://tass.ru/en/russia/748765>.

Tétrault-Farber, Gabrielle. 5 February 2015. 'Regional Golos Head's Home, Office Raided', *Moscow Times*, accessed 3 August 2015 at <www.themoscowtimes.com/news/article/regional-golos-heads-home-office-raided/515503.html>.

Tilly, Charles. 1975. 'Reflections on the History of European State Making', in Charles Tilly, ed., *The Formation of National States in Western Europe* (Princeton, NJ: Princeton University Press), pp. 3–83.

Tishinsky, Yaromir, and Nikitia Shmelev. 24 July 2006. 'Let Them Complain: Taxation Authorities Demand 5 Million Rubles from Human Rights Group', *Novye Izvestia*, JRL, 2006, No. 167 (24 July 2006).

Tkachuk, Viktor. 11 September 2012. 'People First: The Latest in the Watch on Ukrainian Democracy', *Kyiv Post*, accessed 5 August 2015 at <www.kyivpost.com/opinion/op-ed/people-first-the-latest-in-the-watch-on-ukrainian-democracy-5-312797.html>.

Torres-Bartyzel, Claudia, and Grazyna Kacprowicz, with Witold Krajewski. 1999. 'The National Civil Service System in Poland', in Tony Verheijen with Alexander Kotchegura, ed., *Civil Service Systems in Central and Eastern Europe* (Cheltenham, UK: Edward Elgar), pp. 159–183.

Trebor, Ilya. 7 April 2016. 'Vzyatki v Ukraine: Daiut bol'she, sadyat men'she' [Bribes in Ukraine: Many Given, Few Jailed], Sevodnya (Kyiv), pp. 1–2.

Tregub, Olena. 2015. 'Do Ukrainians Want Reform?' in Andrew Wilson, ed., *What Does Ukraine Think?* (London: European Council on Foreign Relations), pp. 89–98.

Trenin, Dmitri. October 2005. 'Reading Russia Right', Carnegie Endowment for International Peace Policy Brief, Special Edition No. 42.

Tucker, Joshua A. 2006. *Regional Economic Voting: Russia, Poland, Hungary, Slovakia and Czech Republic, 1990–1999* (New York: Cambridge University Press).

Tucker, Robert C. 1987. *Political Culture and Leadership in Soviet Russia* (New York: Norton).

Tyler, Tom R. 1990. *Why People Obey the Law* (New Haven, CT: Yale University Press).

350   Bibliography

Ukrinform News. 28 May 2012. 'Kyiv Presents Central Office for Servicing Large Taxpayers', accessed 14 January 2016 at <www.ukrinform.net/rubric-economics/1356928-kyiv_presents_central_office_for_servicing_large_taxpayers_283043.html>.

UNIAN News Service. 1 June 2016. 'SFS Head Nasirov Doesn't Want to Disband Tax Police', accessed 29 August 2016 at <www.unian.info/economics/1362163-fiscal-service-head-nasirov-doesnt-want-to-disband-tax-police.html>.

UT Ukraine Today. 10 August 2016. '120 Million U.S. Dollars Stolen by Tax Service During Yanukovych Presidency', accessed 29 August 2016 at <http://uatoday.tv/news/120-million-u-s-dollars-stolen-by-tax-service-during-yanukovych-presidency-713907.html>.

Valencia, Matthew. September 1994. 'The Region's Tax Systems: Unclear and Severe', *Business Central Europe*, p. 69.

Vasil Kisil & Partners. 11 February 2016. 'Amendments to the Tax Legislation of Ukraine', accessed 18 September 2016 at <www.usubc.org/site/recent-news/amendments-to-the-tax-legislation-of-ukraine>.

Vasilyeva, Natalya. 4 February 2010. 'Russian government bureaucracy called "unfriendly"', *Associated Press*, in JRL, 2010, No. 25 (5 February 2010).

Vedomosti. 11 August 2005. 'No More Plans for Taxmen', in *JRL*, No. 9222 (11 August 2005).

Vertsyuk, Ivan. 24 February 2015. Yatsenyuk Suspends Tax Agency Head Amid Corruption Accusations', *Kyiv Post*, accessed 8 January 2016 at <www.kyivpost.com/article/content/business/yatsenyuk-suspends-tax-agency-head-amid-corruption-accusations-381729.html>.

Viktorov, Sergei, and Vadim Bardin. 24 July 2001. 'Bureaucrat Festivities', *Kommersant' Vlast'*, No. 29 (431), p. 11.

Vremya Novostei. 10 October 2005. 'Tax Authorities Find 'Yukos Effect' Beneficial', in *JRL*, No. 9263 (10 October 2005).

Walker, Shaun. 27 March 2013. 'Russia Orders Tax Police to Raid Foreign Charities and Human Rights Watchdogs', *The Independent*, accessed 3 August 2015 at <www.independent.co.uk/news/world/europe/russia-orders-tax-police-to-raid-foreign-charities-and-human-rights-watchdogs-8552270.html>.

Wall Street Journal. 26 November 2002. 'The Putin Curve' (Editorial), p. A24. 11 July 2003. 'Flat Tax Fever' (Editorial), p. A8.

Washington Profile. 10 March 2006. 'Russia's Political Parties: An Interview with Henry Hale', in *JRL*, No. 2006–64 (14 March 2006.)

Webley, Paul, Henry Robben, Henk Elffers, and Dick Hessing. 1991. *Tax Evasion: An Experimental Approach* (Cambridge, UK: Cambridge University Press).

Wenzel, Michał. January 2005. 'Przestrzeganie Praw Pracowniczych i "Szara Strefa" w Zatrudnieniu: Związki Zawodowe w Przedsiębiorstwach', CBOS Report (Warsaw: Centrum Badania Opinii Społecznej).

What the Paper Say (WPS): The Russian Business Monitor. 10 February 2003. 'IMF Mission for Taxation Issues Named Reforming of Russian Tax System 'Impressive'', accessed through FACTIVA electronic search engine.

Bibliography

Whitmore, Brian. 22 September 2016. 'The Morning Vertical' (E-mail newsletter).

Wiatr, Jerzy J. 1995. 'The Dilemmas of Re-organizing the Bureaucracy in Poland during the Democratic Transformation', in *Communist and Post-communist Studies*, Vol. 28, No. 1, pp. 153–160.

Wilson, James Q. 1989. *Bureaucracy: What Government Agencies Do and Why They Do It* (New York: Basic Books).

Wines, Michael. 12 March 2003. 'Streamlining Government, Putin Creates New Anti-Drug Force', *New York Times*, p. A10.

Witt, Daniel A. 5 January 2005. 'Year-End Wrap-Up and Looking Ahead to 2005', *ITIC Bulletin*, p. 2.

Woodruff, David. 1999. *Money Unmade: Barter and the Fate of Russian Capitalism* (Ithaca, NY: Cornell University Press).

World Bank. 1996. *Russian Federation: Toward Medium-Term Viability*, Washington, DC.

19 September 2002. 'Project Appraisal Document on a Proposed Loan in the Amount of US$100 Million to the Russian Federation for a Second Tax Administration Modernization Project', Report No. 23565-RU, Washington, DC.

13 May 2003. 'Project Performance Assessment Report: Russia – Tax Administration Modernization Project (Loan 3853)', Report No. 25915, Washington, DC.

2005a. *Growth, Poverty and Inequality: Eastern Europe and the Former Soviet Union*, Washington, DC.

2005b. *FY05 Report on the Status of Projects in Execution*, Washington, DC.

15 March 2007. *Ukraine: Public Financial Management Performance Report 2006*, Report No. 39015-UA, Washington, DC.

2011. *Ukraine: Public Financial Management Performance Report 2011*, Washington, DC.

18 December 2012. 'Implementation Completion and Results Report on a Loan in the Amount of US $40.0 Million to the Republic of Ukraine for the First State Tax Service Modernization Project', Washington, DC.

Wrobel, Renata. 22 March 1999. 'Tłok za biurkiem' [Pressed behind the Desk], *Rzeczpospolita*.

Yablokova, Oksana. 17 April 2003. 'Duma Votes to Rank Civil Servants', *Moscow Times*.

Yadova, E.V. 7 April 2000. 'O nalogakh i nalogovykh deklaratsiyakh' [On Taxes and Tax Declarations], Public Opinion Foundation, Moscow.

Yatsenyuk, Arseniy. 17 November 2015. 'Yatsenyuk Details Anti-corruption Agenda, Says "None of the Oligarchs Has Any Influence on" Ukraine's Government', *Kyiv Post*, accessed 8 January 2015 at <www.kyivpost .com/article/opinion/op-ed/yatsenyuk-details-anti-corruption-agenda-says-none-of-the-oligarchs-has-any-influence-on-ukraines-government-402271 .html>.

Yekelchyk, Serhy. 2015. *The Conflict in Ukraine: What Everyone Needs to Know* (Oxford, UK: Oxford University Press).

352   Bibliography

Yew, Bee K.., Valentin B. Milanov, and Robert W. McGee. 2015. 'An Analysis of Individual Tax Morale for Russia: Before and after Flat Tax Reform', *International Business Research*, Vol. 8, No. 1, pp. 60–80.

Yurova, Yana. 13 May 2005. 'Tax Reform in Russia: Business Is Happy, unlike Ordinary People', *RIA Novosti*, in *JRL*, No. 9148 (13 May 2005).

Zasuń, Rafał. 7 December 2001. 'Czystka, potem reforma' [Purge, then Reform], *Gazeta Wyborcza*, p. 4.

Zhulin, A.B., T.L. Kuksa, A. Nikolenko, A.V. Chaplinskii, L.Kh. Sinyatillina, A.E. Sarvatdinov, M.A. Gintova and C.B. Datiev. 2010. *Registr polnomochiĭ federal'nikh organov ispolnitel'noĭ vlasti: ėkcpertnaya sistematizatsiya i analiz deyatel'nosti* [Register of Powers of Federal Bodies of Executive Power: Expert Classification and Analysis] (Moscow: Institute of Public Administration, State Higher School of Economics).

Index

1989 revolutions
  aftermath, 25, 26, 46, 229
  and state capacity, 3
  and trust, 45, 253, 259
  importance of, 2, 13
  meaning of, 16
  perceptions, 45
  Poland, 17, 26, 56, 59, 72, 213, 244, 245, 260
  Polish perception, 46, 245
1991 revolutions
  aftermath, 25, 229
  and state capacity, 3
  and trust, 45, 253, 259
  importance of, 13
  Lithuania, 76
  meaning of, 16
  perceptions, 45, 46, 245
  putsch, 87
  Russia, 253
  Russian regret, 29
  Ukraine, 51, 93
Abramovich, Roman, 170
Accounting Chamber (Ukraine), 93, 158, 183, 194
Accounts Chamber (Russia), 182, 183, 194
acquis communautaire, 109
administrative reform, 50–51, 56
  and social networks, 24
  Poland, 37, 51, 57, 60–63, 64–70, 185, 255
    tax administration, 53, 137, 139, 161
  Russia, 51, 73, 76–87
    tax administration, 138, 140, 146
  Ukraine, 39, 51, 87–94
    tax administration, 138, 140, 156
administrative structures, 12, 13, 16, 23–24, 36, 41, 45, 47–48, 56, 58, 259
Albats, Yevgenia, 86
Alexeev, Michael, 101, 111, 133

Amnesty International, 171
Anna, Empress of Russia, 196
Appel, Hilary, 9, 105, 108, 109, 132–134
Arbitrazh Court (Russia), 167
Armenia, 4
Åslund, Anders, 7, 28, 88, 90, 154, 156, 157
attitudes. *See* Taxpayer Compliance Attitudinal Surveys
Australia, 113
Austro-Hungarian Empire, 26, 32, 59–60, 61, 141
Azarov, Mykola, 154–155, 172–174, 176
Azerbaijan, 76

Baer, Katherine, 145, 150, 188
Balcerowicz, Leszek, 46, 64
Baltic states, 3, 4, 65, 91, 107, *See also* Latvia, Lithuania
Baranov, I.A., 80
Bardin, Vadim, 77
barter, 52, 119, 123, 126–127
Bastrykin, Aleksandr, 153
Belousov, Aleksandr, 83
Berenson, Marc P.
  and Freedom House, 176
  and World Bank, 82
  visit to Yakutsk, 84
Berezovsky, Boris, 152
Bergman, Marcelo, 9, 118
Beria, Lavrenty, 155
Bilous, Igor, 157
black market, 119, 123–125
blat, 74
Bosnia-Herzegovina, 4
Bovt, Georgy, 28
Bowen, Andrew, 151
Bratton, Michael, 12
Brazil, 93
Brezhnev, Leonid, 75, 84
Brezvin, Anatoliy, 155
British Know How Fund, 66

353

354 Index

British Petroleum, 170
Brovkin, Vladimir, 30
Browder, Bill, 170, 171
Brown, Archie, 74–76
Bukayev, Gennadiy, 144, 187
Bulgaria, 8, 108
Bunce, Valerie, 8, 35, 36, 46
bureaucracy. *See also* civil service, tax
  administration
  and political parties, 16, 23, 51
  and social networks, 24
  and state capacity, 34–39, 255
  and trust, 44, 47, 55, 265
  capacity of, 49, 50, 53, 55
  historical development of, 56–95
  importance of, 7
  Poland, 37, 51
    fiscal administration personnel, 57
    post-1989, 5, 51, 64–72
    pre-1989, 59–63
    size, 71
  reform of, 2, 33, 254, 257, 259,
    264–269
  relation to society, 53
  Russia, 37–38, 146
    post-1991, 51
    size, 80, 86
    Soviet legacy, 72–76
  Soviet-like, 58, 138
  street-level, 2, 10, 11, 44, 45, 55, 237,
    243, 259, 264, 265
  Ukraine, 39
    post-1991, 51
    size, 94
  Weberian, 10, 36, 39, 49, 56
    importance of, 6
    in new state capacity model, 40, 257
    Poland, 51, 53, 59–62
    tax administration, 137, 155, 162,
      172, 179, 194–195, 264, 266
bureaucratic authoritarian state, 140
bureaucratic autonomy, 34–36, 37, 61, 74,
  139, 141, 174, 179, 194
bureaucratic discretion, 37, 73, 89
  tax administration, 53, 137, 139, 140,
    154, 159–178
bureaucratic rationalism, 41, 47, 53, 56,
  118, 132, 184, 253, 256, 258, 262,
  See also bureaucracy, Weberian
  Poland, 60
    tax administration, 137, 138, 139, 147,
      148, 182, 194–195, 266
Bureaucratic Rationalism
  Poland, 60
Burnt By the Sun (Russia), 58

Business Environment and Enterprise
  Performance Survey (BEEPS), 121,
  148

Cabinet of Ministers (Ukraine), 156, 157
Cadres Administration (Russia), 83
Campos, Nauro F., 7
Canada, 113
cash offsets. *See* tax offsets
Catholicism, 25, 26, 29, 213, 229–231,
  234, 244–250
CBOS Public Opinion Centre (Poland),
  57, 118, 123, 271
Central and East Europe. *See also specific
  countries*
  consolidation of transition in, 16, 24,
    244
  EU assistance, 91
  governance, 2–4, 8, 10, 12, 14, 24, 36
  tax policy, 14, 96, 97, 102, 107, 108,
    109, 132
Centre for Economic and Financial
  Research (CEFIR) (Russia), 148
Centre for Strategic Research (Russia), 78,
  81
Centre for the Promotion of International
  Defence (Russia), 171
Chechnya, 28, 59, 171
Chief Department of Personnel Training
  (Russia). *See* Roskadry
Chmielewski, Zdzisław, 60
Civic Chamber (Russia), 28
Civic Platform (PO) (Poland), 17–18, 68,
  70
civil service, 3, 23, 49, 50, 255–256, *See
  also* bureaucracy, tax administration
  Poland, 37, 51, 57, 59–63, 64–72, 188,
    191
  Russia, 38, 58, 73, 77, 80
  Ukraine, 39, 88–90, 94, 263
Civil Service Act (Poland), 37, 51, 65–67,
  70
Civil Service Council (Poland), 66
Civil Service reform law (Ukraine), 39
civil society, 34, 40, 41, 46, 75, 254
  and religion, 29, 30, 244–250
  Poland, 25, 34, 56–57, 212, 213
  Russia, 18, 27–28, 72, 74, 95, 172
  Soviet, 75
  Ukraine, 23, 31–33, 90, 229, 233, 263
clientelism, 18, 22, 37, 51, 59
coercion, 2, 10–11, 13, 41, 43, 55,
  201–203, 253–259, 270, *See also* tax
  compliance, deterrence theory
  Poland, 207–213, 256

Index

Russia, 19, 49, 53, 55, 166, 168, 172, 195, 196, 213–214, 253–263
Ukraine, 48, 49, 53, 154, 159, 172, 214–220, 231–239, 262
Colombia, 93
command economy, 6, 36
Poland, 100
Russia, 102
taxes, 99
Commission for the Improvement of the Public Administration (Poland), 60
Communist Party (Polish People's Republic), 36, 48, 61, 63, 67, 72, 95
Communist Party (Russia), 19, 58
Communist Party (Ukraine), 21, 22, 39, 93, 104
Communist Party (USSR), 27, 30, 36, 48, 74, 99, 145
computers. *See* tax administration, technological resources
Conrad, Robert F., 101, 111, 133
Constitutional Tribunal (Poland), 63
consumption taxes. *See* added tax (VAT)
corporate income tax (CIT), 52, 110, *See also* Taxpayer Compliance Attitudinal Surveys
arrears in Poland, Russia and Ukraine, 114
collecting
Poland, 141–143, 160–162
Russia, 162–172
Ukraine, 172–178
policy, 96–106
Poland, 96–98, 99–100
Russia, 96–98, 101–103
Ukraine, 16, 103–106
rates, perceptions of, 284
corruption, 4, 15, 253, *See also* tax administration, structures, constraints on corruption
anti-corruption measures, 160, 194, 266
perceptions of, 27, 183, 290, 296
Poland, 5, 37, 212, 256
anti-corruption measures, 139
Russia, 30–31, 38, 86–87, 117, 140, 148, 183
anti-corruption measures, 77, 80, 81, 147
Tsarist Russia, 196
Soviet, 6
Ukraine, 21, 58, 87–88, 93, 94, 117, 155, 157, 175–176, 216, 260

anti-corruption measures, 1, 90, 159, 175, 263
Corruption
Poland, 70–71
Russia
Tsarist Russia, 73
Soviet, 74, 76
Ukraine, 39
Czech Republic, 8, 17, 26, 66, 107

D'Anieri, Paul, 21, 32
Danilova, Elena, 133, 169, 190
Daunton, Martin, 50
De Haas, Ralph, 244
Deloitte & Touche, 165
Democratic Alliance (Ukraine), 23
Democratic Left Alliance (SLD) (Poland), 17, 67–68
direct taxes, 96–97, 110, 130, *See also* corporate income tax (CIT)
personal income tax (PIT)
Dubrovsky, Vladimir, 157, 174
Duda, Andrzej, 18
Duma (Russia), 19, 20, 38, 77, 79, 86, 131, 153, 208, 214, 286
Dunlap, John, 75
Dybula, Michał, 67

Easter, Gerald M., 10, 100, 102, 107–109
Eastern Europe. *See also* Central and Eastern Europe *and specific countries*
governance, 2–4
religion and, 25, 29, 249, 250
study of, 8, 9, 118
Ebrill, Liam, 117
Economic Expert Group (Russia), 116
economic growth
and taxes, 127–131
and taxes collected
Poland, 130
Russia, 130
Ukraine, 130
Ekiert, Grzegorz, 25
Electoral Action Solidarity (AWS) (Poland), 67
Elster, John, 24, 46, 244
Employment Fund (Russia), 84
enterprise profit tax. *See* corporate income tax (CIT)
entrepreneurial tax, 199
Ernst & Young, 93, 165, 166, 170
EuroMaidan Revolution, 22, 23, 32, 94, 104, 105, 109, 157, 159, 174, 199, 204, 218, 233, 236, 260, 261, 262

356 Index

European Bank for Reconstruction and Development (EBRD), 121, 148
European Commission, 68, 71, 109, 158
European Court of Human Rights, 171
European Union, 3, 5, 22, 39, 57, 64, 65, 68, 71, 90, 91, 97, 106–109, 114, 142, 176, 260, 269, *See also* PHARE, TACIS
Evans, Peter, 6, 14, 34
extractive capacity, 110

Fatherland (former Bloc Yulia Tymoshenko) (Ukraine), 22
Federal Committee for Tax Control (Russia), 146
Federal Security Service (FSB) (Russia), 78, 85, 167
Federal Tax Service (Russia), 48, 144, 146, 153, 163, 164, 165, 169, 171, 188
federalism, 84, 253, 257
  fiscal, 9, 38
  Russia, 6, 8, 28, 38, 83, 103, 257
  Soviet, 84
Federation Council (Russia), 19, 38, 77, 286
Fedoseeva, N.N., 80
fiscal sociology, 50, 53
Fish, M. Steven, 8, 19
flat tax. *See also* entrepreneurial tax, personal income tax (PIT)
  Central and East Europe, 107, 132
  IMF, 108
  Russia, 97, 98, 101, 103, 121, 124–125, 132–133, 170, 199
  Ukraine, 97, 98, 103, 105, 121, 132, 199
foreign assistance. *See* tax assistance, international
former Soviet Union. *See also specific countries*
  European Union and, 91
  governance, 2–4, 12, 14, 18, 24, 37, 39
  religion and, 25, 244
  study of, 8, 9, 118
  tax policy, 97, 102, 154
Fortin, Jessica, 4
Fradkov, Mikhail, 79, 80, 145
Franklin, Jennifer L., 117, 163
Freedom House, 20, 32, 37, 38, 176
Freedom Union (UW) (Poland), 67
Friedrich Ebert Foundation (Germany), 171
Fritz, Verena, 21, 91, 105, 176
Fukuyama, Francis, 43, 111

Gaddy, Clifford G., 126
Gaidar, Yegor, 77, 103
Galicia, 60
Gaman-Golutvina, Oxana V., 140
Ganev, Venelin, 50, 53
Gazeta Wyborcza (Poland), 64
Gazprom, 126, 170
Gdańsk Institute for Market Reforms (Poland), 123
Gee, Robert W., 134
Gehlbach, Scott, 9, 102
Georgia, 4, 76
Germany. *See also* Prussian Empire
  Poland's relationship with, 57
GfK market research group, 175
Gimpelson, Vladimir, 84, 85
Gintova, M.A., 82
glasnost, 35, 72, 74, 76, 84, 95
Golos, 171
Gongadze, Georgi, 155, 177
Gorbachev, Mikhail, 31, 35, 63, 72–76, 83–85
Gorodnichenko, Yuriy, 134
governance, 1–10, 12–55, 71–73, 80, 82, 87, 89, 90, 92, 95, 195, 196, 213, 244, 245, 249–252, 253–264
  policy recommendations, 264–269
Graham, Jr., Thomas, 30
Greene, Samuel, 34
grey salaries. *See* black market
Grindle, Merilee, 12
Gusinsky, Vladimir, 152

Hale, Henry, 20, 22
Hardin, Russell, 42, 261
Havrylyshyn, Oleh, 117
Hellman, Joel S., 24, 46
Hermitage Capital Management, 170–171
Higher School of Economics (Russia), 80
Highfield, Richard, 145, 150, 188
Hilderbrand, Mary, 12
historical legacies, 5, 24, 33, 37, 46–47, 50, 52, 56, 58, 59, 94–95, 138, 253, 259
  communist, 259
  Poland, 16, 37, 51, 57, 59–63, 64, 71, 72, 181
  Russia, 30, 56, 72–76, 84, 95
  Ukraine, 56, 58, 90, 229
historical reference points, 56, 57, 139, 194–195, 257, 259, 264, 269
  in new state capacity model, 41, 47–50
  policy recommendations, 265
  Ukraine, 58
Hosking, Geoffrey, 25

Index

Hungary, 8, 17, 25, 65, 66, 107
Huntington, Samuel P., 14, 15, 16
Huskey, Eugene, 84

Ickes, Barry W., 99, 126, 137
InDem Foundation (Russia), 86
indirect taxes, 96–98, 107, *See also*
value-added tax (VAT)
Institute for the Economy in Transition
(Russia), 103
Institute of Public Affairs (Poland), 71
International Monetary Fund (IMF), 33,
99, 106–108, 113–114, 117,
132–133, 134, 144, 145, 147, 150,
159, 263
International Tax and Investment Centre
(ITIC), 146, 150, 152, 166
Investigative Committee of the Russian
Federation, 152–153
Itrich-Drabarek, Jolanta, 69
Iuzhanina, Nina, 106, 125
Ivan III, 74
Ivan IV, 74
Ivanova, Anna, 134
izby skarbowe. See tax chambers
(Poland)

Janik, Krzysztof, 71
Johnson, Chalmers, 14, 34
Jones Luong, Pauline, 102

Kacprowicz, Grazyna, 62
Kaczynski, Lech, 17, 57
Kaliberda, Aleksander, 123
Kamiński, Antoni, 68, 183, 191
Kasyanov, Mikhail, 116
Kaufman, Daniel, 123
Keen, Michael, 134
KGB. *See* Federal Security Service (FSB)
(Russia)
Khabrieva, T.Ya., 78
Kharkhordin, Oleg, 245
Khodorkovsky, Mikhail, 164, 170
Khryshtanovskaya, Olga, 79, 85, 86
Kireev, Oleksandr, 155
Kiriyenko, Sergey, 78
Kitschelt, Herbert, 8, 16–17, 18
Klemm, Alexander, 134
Klitschko, Vitaly, 22
Klymenko, Oleksandr, 157
Kochanowicz, Jacek, 36, 59, 61
Kohli, Atul, 6, 15, 16
Kolarska-Bobińska, Lena, 26
Koliushko, Ihor, 88, 89
Kommersant-Daily, 79

Komorowski, Bronisław, 17, 208
kompromat, 84
Konrad Adenauer Foundation (Germany),
171
Kotkin, Stephen, 21
Kotsonis, Yanni, 9, 196, 268
Krajowa Szkoła Administracji Publicznej
(Poland's State School of Public
Administration), 65, 67–68
Kravchenko, Yuri, 155, 173
Kremlin, 19, 20, 28, 38, 58, 83, 85, 164,
170, 172
Kuchins, Andrew, 20
Kuchma, Leonid, 21, 22, 32, 39, 88,
92–93, 154–156, 174, 176–177,
260
Kuchmagate, 260
Kudrin, Alexei, 168
Kukhta, Pavlo, 159
Kuzio, Taras, 90
Kwaśniewski, Aleksander, 17, 208
Kyiv Post, 260

Lane, David, 74
language and tax compliance, 250–252
Latin America, 45, 118
Latvia, 132
Law and Justice (PiS) (Poland), 17, 18,
37, 57, 70
Law of the Urals Division, the Russian
Academy of Sciences', 83
Lebedev, Alexander, 171
Ledeneva, Alena, 43
Ledyaev, Valeri G., 139, 140
legacies. *See historical legacies*
legitimacy, 13, 40
and trust, 40, 42
measuring, 220
of the transition, 259
Polish People's Republic, 63
Soviet, 35, 76
state's, 27, 44, 220, 227, 259
tax authority's, 43
Lenin, Vladimir, 75
Levi, Margaret, 43–44, 53, 203–205, 218
Levitsky, Steven, 21
Lewin, Moshe, 74, 75
Lieberman, Evan, 97, 98, 110
Linz, Juan, 25, 29, 30, 244, 245
Lithuania, 76, 132
loans for shares (Russia), 27
Logunov, A.B., 81
Lough, John, 226
lustration law (Ukraine), 94
Lutsenko, Yuriy, 158

358   Index

Magnitsky, Sergei, 171
Main Audit Administration of the
 President (Russia), 190
Main Division of Tax Investigations
 (Russia), 149
managed democracy, 28
Mann, Michael, 6, 36, 139
Marcinkiewicz, Kazimierz, 70
Martin, Isaac William, 50
Martinez-Vazquez, Jorge, 117, 134,
 151
Marxism Leninism, 75
McFaul, Michael, 18
McNab, Robert M., 117, 151
Medvedev, Dmitry, 153, 208, 213,
 214
Memorial (Russia), 171
Michnik, Adam, 64
Migdal, Joel, 6, 13, 14, 23, 24
Milanov, Valentin B., 134
Mill, John Stuart, 5
Millar, James R., 29
MIMIC method, 123
mineral extraction tax (MET), 101
Ministry of Economic Development and
 Trade (Russia), 81, 82, 116, 148
Ministry of Economy (Ukraine), 125
Ministry of Finance (Poland), 48, 64, 113,
 130, 141, 144, 161, 162, 180,
 181–182, 185, 186, 190
Ministry of Finance (Russia), 79, 81, 116,
 117, 144, 146, 169
Ministry of Finance (Ukraine), 106, 154,
 155–157
Ministry of Finance (USSR), 99, 144
Ministry of Interior (Russia), 151, 153
Ministry of Interior (Ukraine), 159
Ministry of Revenues and Dues (Ukraine),
 158
Ministry of Taxes and Dues (Russia), 48,
 79, 144, 145, 146, 150, 182, 187
Ministry of the Treasury (Poland), 141
model transference, 10, 32, 38, 54, 56, 72,
 94–95, 139, 259
Monitoring Administration (Russia), 83
Movchan, Andrei, 193
multipurpose centres for state and
 municipal services (MFSCs)
 (Russia), 81, 82
Murrell, Peter, 7
Mylovanov, Tymofei, 33

Naczelny Sąd Administracyjny (Poland's
 Chief Administrative Court, or
 NSA), 61, 63, 143

Najwyższa Izba Kontroli (Poland's
 Supreme Audit Chamber, or NIK),
 48, 63, 68–69, 71, 93, 130,
 142–143, 160, 162, 178–187, 191,
 194, 266
Najwyższy Trybunał Administracyjny
 (Poland's Supreme Administrative
 Tribunal), 61
Nasirov, Roman, 157, 159
National Anti-Corruption Bureau
 (Ukraine), 33
National Bank of Ukraine, 91
National Commission on Fiscal Reform
 (Ukraine), 156
National Patrol Force (Ukraine), 45, 263
National Security & Defence (Ukraine),
 89, 92
nationality and tax compliance, 250–252
natural resource extractment tax (NDPI),
 101
neo-liberal reforms, 7, 8
Netherlands, 158
New Public Management, 81
Nicholas II, 99
Nikolova, Elena, 244
Nozdrachev, A.F., 78
Nunberg, Barbara, 36, 37, 38, 62

Odling-Smee, John, 108
Offe, Claus, 24, 46, 244
Office of Ombudsman (Poland), 63
Office of the Civil Service (Poland), 65
Oleinik, Anton, 137, 139
oligarchs
 Russia, 19, 27, 77, 170, 171
 Ukraine, 21, 23, 31, 32, 39, 58, 88, 104
Olszewski, Jan, 65
Orange Revolution, 22, 32, 89, 91, 92,
 154, 155, 156, 159, 174, 175, 177,
 199, 204, 216, 217, 226, 233, 260,
 262
Organisation for Economic Co-operation
 and Development (OECD), 33, 65,
 73, 107, 110, 113–114, 152, 263,
 See also SIGMA
Our Ukraine Bloc, 22

Paradowska, Janina, 68
Parliamentary Committee on Taxation and
 Customs Policy (Ukraine), 106, 125
Party of Regions (Ukraine), 22
Pastwa, Jan, 69
patrimonialism, 17, 18, 20, 32, 51, 58, 59,
 138
Pavilonis, Peter, 84

Index

PBS DDG Market Research firm
(Poland), 118, 271
perestroika, 35, 74–76
personal income tax (PIT), 52, 96, 108,
110, *See also* Taxpayer Compliance
Attitudinal Surveys
arrears in Poland, Russia and Ukraine,
114
collecting
Poland, 141–143, 160–162, 181,
184
Russia, 167, 170
Ukraine, 125
flat tax in Russia, 124, 132–133
number of taxpayers in Poland, Russia
and Ukraine, 98
policy
Poland, 96–98, 99–100
Russia, 96–98, 101–103
Ukraine, 96–98, 103–106
rates, perceptions of, 135, 282, 284
Peter I, 74, 77, 85
Peter, Klara S., 134
Petrov, Nikolay, 28, 83
Petru, Ryszard Jerzy, 67
PHARE (European Union), 65, 91, 106
plan. See tax collection, target-based
Poland. *See also individual topic, institution
or organization*
Chief Administrative Court. *See
Naczelny Sąd Administracyjny*
choice of Europe, 57
communist state. *See* Polish People's
Republic
elections, 17–18, 37
Germany, relationship with, 57
inter-war period, 51, 56, 59–63, 71, 72,
94–95, 138, 141, 143, 194, *See also*
Second Republic (Poland)
joining the European Union, 64
martial law, 63
parliament. *See Sejm*
partition of, 59, 60
political party system, 17, 18, 66, 72,
212
social security. *See Zakład Ubezpieczeń
Społecznych*
State School of Public Administration.
*See Krajowa Szkoła Administracji
Publicznej*
Supreme Administrative Tribunal. *See
Najwyższy Trybunał Administracyjny*
Supreme Audit Chamber. *See
Najwyższa Izba Kontroli*
Polish Peasant Party (PSL), 66–68

Polish People's Republic (*Polska
Rzeczpospolita Ludowa*, or PRL), 34,
59, 64, 106, 213, 244
Politburo (Soviet Union), 75, 85
political parties
and state capacity, 14–23, 40, 49, 95,
253, 255–257
Poland, 51, 66–68, 70, 91, 95
Russia, 58
Ukraine, 93, 261
political party system, 17, 18, 20, 66, 72,
212
POLTAX information system (Poland),
181, 185, 186
popiwek (Poland), 100
Popov, Vladimir, 7, 130
Poroshenko, Petro, 1, 22, 94, 171, 208,
218, 236, 237, 241–243, 260, 265
post-Soviet states, 5, 6, 8, 19, 30, 57, 76,
87, 88, 118, 259, 265, 270, *See also
specific countries*
power vertical, 38, 83, 140, 257
Preuss, Ulrich K., 24, 46, 244
Price Waterhouse Coopers, 165
privatization, 8, 27, 80, 102, 176
Procuracy (Ukraine), 183
profits tax. *See* corporate income tax (CIT)
Prussian Empire, 26, 59
Pryadilnikov, Mikhail, 133, 169, 190
Przeworski, Adam, 7
Przybyla, Marcin, 67
public administration. *See* bureaucracy,
civil service *and* tax administration
Public Officials' Survey (Russia), 35, 49,
54, 86, 101, 140, 163, 164, 183,
190, 192, 254, 271–291
Public Opinion Foundation (FOM)
(Russia), 119, 271, 292
Putin, Vladimir, 18–20, 27–28, 30–31, 34,
38, 51, 57–58, 72, 73, 78–80, 95,
103, 104, 108, 140, 146, 150, 152,
153, 169, 170, 171, 186, 196, 199,
208, 214, 227, 256, 257
Putnam, Robert, 25, 29, 75

quasi-voluntary compliance, 197–198,
203–205, 207–218, 227

Rauch, James, 6
Razumkov Centre for Economic and
Political Studies (Ukraine), 89, 92,
105, 119, 156, 271
Reanimation Package of Reforms
Coalition (Ukraine), 33, 159
religion and tax compliance, 244–250

360 Index

Remington, Thomas, 19
rent-seeking, 18, 21, 24, 27
Roeder, Philip, 8, 35
Rokita, Jan, 68
Romanov dynasty, 74
Roskadry (Russia's Chief Department of
  Personnel Training), 77
Ross, Cameron, 74
Roth, Jeffrey A., 120
Rothstein, Bo, 42, 44
Russia. *See also individual topic, institution
  or organization*
  elections, 19, 20, 27, 28
  federal districts (*okrugi*), 38, 83, 85,
    145, 149
  parliament. *See Duma* and Federation
    Council
  political party system, 18, 20
  Soviet nostalgia, 58
  State Service Law, 38, 77
  Tsarist Russia, 73
  tax collection, 99, 196, 268
Russian Academy of Sciences, 79, 83, 85,
  124
Russian Academy of State Service
  (RAGS), 48
Russian Empire, 9, 26, 59
Russian Tax Officials' Survey. *See* Public
  Officials' Survey (Russia)
Russian Union of Industrialists and
  Entrepreneurs (RSPP), 116
Russian-Chechen Friendship Society, 171
Ryavec, Karl, 74
Rywingate, 71

Sachs, Jeffrey, 7, 29
Sakha-Yakutia, 84
sales taxes. *See* Value-Added Tax (VAT)
Satarov, Georgy, 86
Schliefer, Andrei, 9
Schnieder, Friedrich, 125
Scholz, John T., 120
Schumpeter, Joseph, 50
Second Republic (Poland), 56, 59, 64, 72,
  141
Sejm (Poland), 63, 65, 66, 68, 71, 131,
  141, 208, 286
Semchenko, Olga, 178
Shatalov, Sergei, 124
Shatrov, Mikhail, 75
Shavalyuk, Lyubomyr, 266
Sherman, Richard, 53
Shevtsova, Tatyana, 163, 165
Shlapentokh, Vladimir, 87
Shleifer, Andrei, 102, 103, 126

shock therapy, 7, 8, 46, 58, 91
Shokhin, Aleksandr, 79
Sibneft, 170
SIGMA (OECD), 66
siloviki (Russia), 85
Skocpol, Theda, 6, 12, 13
Slavic Orthodoxy, 25, 29, 30, 229–231,
  244–250
Slemrod, Joel, 99, 137, 201
Slovakia, 108
Slovenia, 107
Sobchak, Anatoly, 171
Sobchak, Ksenia, 171
social capital, 42, 43, 259
social security contributions
  Poland, 100, 124
  Russia, 133
  Ukraine, 104
Sociology Institute, Russian Academy of
  Sciences, 79, 85, 124
Solidarity, 17, 63, 67, 95, 245
Solnick, Steven, 8, 35, 76
Solonenko, Iryna, 226
Soviet Union, 9, 35, 36, 52, 140
Stalin, Joseph, 58, 75–76, 155
Stanovaya, Tatiana, 153
state capacity, 3–5, 6, 12–55, 56, 97, 98,
  110, 111, 139, 216, 253
  and political parties, 255–257
  and state-society relations, 256
  and structures, 256–257
  and Ukraine, 260–263
  coercion to trust, 258
  new model of, 40, 257–260
  policy recommendations, 264–269
  testing theories of, 255–257
State Customs Service (Ukraine), 156, 157
State Fiscal Service (Ukraine), 94, 113,
  116, 158, 159, 262, 263
State Officials Act, 1982 (Poland), 62
State Property Fund (Ukraine), 91
State Service (Russia), 73, 189, 191, 301
state socialism, 99, 160
State Statistics Service (Russia), 86, 113
State Tax Administration, State Tax
  Service (STA, STS) (Russia), 126,
  133, 144–153, *See also* tax
  administration
State Tax Administration, State Tax
  Service (STA, STS) (Ukraine), 48,
  114, 178, 216, *See also* tax
  administration
state building, 59, 64, 110
state-society relations, 2, 6, 14, 24, 25–34,
  46, 244, 253

Index 361

and religion, 246
and state capacity, 5, 40, 47, 58, 255, 256, 257
Poland, 25–26, 57, 59, 72
Russia, 27–31, 72
Ukraine, 31–33, 229, 236, 246
Stepan, Alfred, 25, 29, 30, 244, 245
Stepanyan, Vahram, 133
Stoner, Kathryn, 8
substantive effects, explained, 209, 210
Suchocka, Hanna, 65
Suleiman, Ezra, 65, 66
Supreme Administrative Tribunal (*Najwyższy Trybunał Administracyjny*), 61
Supreme Audit Chamber. *See Najwyższa Izba Kontroli (NIK) (Poland)*
Sutch, Helen, 67
Sweden, 113
Szczesna, Joanna, 162
Szklarski, Bohdan, 26
Sztompka, Piotr, 42

Table of Ranks, 77, 85
TACIS (European Union), 91
Tanzi, Vito, 99, 106–107
tax administration, 23, 49, 53, 98, 137–196, 264
  bureaucratic rationalism in, 139
  empowerment of, 139–140
  historical references, 138, 159
    policy recommendations, 265
  human resources, 39, 41, 49, 53, 138, 139, 156, 188–195, 256–257, 258, 264, 269
    policy recommendations, 267–268
  Poland, 137–138, 139, 141–143, 160–162, 178–180, 181–182, 184–186, 188–189, 190–191, 193, 194–195
    size, 71
  policy recommendations, 264–269
  Russia, 49, 137–138, 144–153, 162–172, 178, 180, 182–183, 184, 186–187, 188, 189–190, 191, 192, 193, 194–195
  Soviet, 99
  structures, 49, 138, 139, 159, 194, 195, 264, 269
    and state capacity, 256–257
    constraints on corruption, 178–184
    policy recommendations, 266
  technological resources, 41, 49, 53, 138, 184–187, 256–257, 258, 264, 269

  policy recommendations, 267–268
  Ukraine, 105, 137–138, 153–159, 172–178, 180, 183, 184, 187, 188–189, 192–193, 194–195
  USSR, 144
  work philosophy, 47, 49, 53, 138, 149, 178, 194–195, 201, 264, 269
Tax Administration Modernisation Project (TAMP)
  Russia, 107, 146, 147–149
  Ukraine, 107, 158, 177
tax administrative structures, 55
tax amnesties, 86, 117, 133, 170
tax arrears
  Australia, Canada and United States, 113
  Central and Eastern Europe, 108
  measuring, 111
  Poland, 52, 109, 113–116, 125, 127–131, 180, 181, 182
  Russia, 52, 102, 109, 113, 125, 127–131, 148, 180, 256
  Ukraine, 109, 113, 125, 127–131
tax assistance
  international, 106–109
tax audit offices (Poland), 141–143, 150, 162, 181, 185, 189, 194, 255
tax chambers (Poland), 141–143, 161–162, 179, 180, 181–182, 183, 185, 188, 191, 255
Tax Code
  Russia, 107, 108, 133, 164, 167, 181
  Ukraine, 105
tax collection
  and tax rates, 132–135
  as a percent of GDP, 110, 111, 134
  ideal measure of, 111
  Poland, 160–162, 178
  prior experiences, 54, 206, 219–224, 239–243
  Russia, 117, 162–172, 178
    political use of, 170–172
  target-based, 68, 80, 108, 118, 138, 144, 147, 148, 149, 152, 160, 162–165, 169, 170, 172–174, 195, 196, 201, 256, 257, 268–269
  theoretically, 8
  Ukraine, 117, 172–178
    political use of, 176–177
tax compliance, 1, 3, 5, 9, 10, 48, 52–54, 95, 96, 118–121, 137, 197–228, 253, 261, 266
  and language, 250–252
  and religion, 244–250

362 Index

tax compliance (*cont.*)
attitudes, 134, 203, *See also* Taxpayer
Compliance Attitudinal Surveys
individuals vs. businesses, 218
deterrence theory, 197–198, 201–202,
207–228
individual-level data, 118–121
measuring, 109–111, 118–121
Poland, 2, 18
policy recommendations, 264–269
Russia, 2, 114, 134, 147, 149
testing theories of, 135, 207–228,
229–252
control variables, 209, 219–220
Ukraine, 2, 225–226, 229–252
tax effort. *See* tax collection, as a percent
of GDP
tax evasion, 27, 126, 134, 158, 164, 165,
170, 190, 202, 228, 276, 280
tax offices (Poland), 141–143, 160–162,
179, 181, 191, 255
Tax Officials' Survey. *See* Public Officials'
Survey (Russia)
tax offsets
Russia, 116–117
Ukraine, 116–117
tax on goods and services. *See* value-added
tax (VAT)
tax police, 2, 149, 187
Russia, 149–153
Ukraine, 158–159
tax rates. *See* tax regime
and tax collection, 132–135
tax reforms
Ukraine, 106
tax regime
Poland, 99–100
Russia, 101–103
Ukraine, 103–106
tax structure. *See* tax regime
taxes
and economic growth, 127–131
soviet, 14, 96, 99
state socialism, 99
Taxpayer Compliance Attitudinal Surveys,
34, 49, 52, 54, 118–121, 132,
134–135, 197–228, 254, 259, 262,
271–291, 303–305
and language, 250–252
and nationality, 250–252
and religion, 246–250
central Ukraine, 231–233, 235,
236–238, 239–243
Crimea, 231–233, 235, 238–242
Donbas, 231–236, 239–243

eastern Ukraine, 231–236, 239–243
Poland, 71, 118–121, 197–208,
209–213, 218–224, 226–228
Russia, 87, 118–121, 197–208,
213–214, 218–224, 226–228
southern Ukraine, 231–233, 235,
236–238, 239–243
Ukraine, 93, 118–121, 197–208,
214–224, 226–228, 229–252
western Ukraine, 231–236, 239–243,
246–250
Teriokhin, Serhyi, 104
Third Rome Investment Fund, 193
Tikhomirov, Yu.A., 78
Tilly, Charles, 13
Tocqueville, Alexis de, 75
Torres-Bartyzel, Claudia, 62
Transparency International, 31, 39, 71,
86, 93, 171
Treisman, Daniel, 9, 102, 103, 126
Trenin, Dmitri, 27
trust, 2, 10, 34, 54–55, 203–205,
253–269
in bureaucrats, 302
and new model for state capacity, 40–47
and religion, 244–250
definition, 42
in bureaucrats, 288
in government, 287, 289
in the courts, 288
in the parliament, 286
in the police, 288
in the premier, 287
in the president, 286
in the procuracy, 287
in the regional administration, 289
in the state, 42, 289, 290
versus social capital, 42
Poland, 54, 94, 195, 258, 260
policy recommendations, 264–269
post-communist, 25
Public Officials' Survey (Russia), 86
Russia, 54, 78, 87, 94, 137, 172, 195,
256, 258
Soviet Union, 25
testing with the Taxpayer Compliance
Attitudinal Surveys, 197–218,
226–228, 229–252
Ukraine, 2, 51, 53, 54, 88, 94, 137,
156, 174, 178, 195, 226, 258,
260–263
Ukraine regions, 229–252
turnover tax, 97, 144, 161
Tyler, Tom, 220–224, 239–243
Tymoshchuk, Viktor, 88, 89

Index

Tymoshenko, Yulia, 22, 175, 216
Tyumen Oil Company (TNK-BP), 170

Ukraine. *See also individual topic, institution
   or organization*
   and state capacity puzzle, 260–263
   bureaucratic welfare state, 56, 58, 138
   central, 231–233, 235, 236–238,
      239–242, 243
   Crimea, 33, 54, 231–233, 235,
      238–242, 243, 260, 263
   annexation of, 58, 83
   Donbas, 103, 231–236, 238, 239–242,
      243, 260
   eastern, 231–236, 239–242, 243
   elections, 21, 22
   independence of, 90
   language, 250–252
   nationality, 250–252
   parliament. *See Verkhovna Rada*
      (Ukraine)
   police force (new). *See* National Patrol
      Police (Ukraine)
   southern, 231–233, 235, 236–238,
      239–242, 243
   Ukrainian SSR, creation of, 90
   western, 32, 231–236, 239–243,
      246–250
Ukrainian Democratic Allianace for
   Reform (UDAR), 22
Ukrainian Week, 136
United Russia party, 20
United States (USA), 111, 113, 152
unofficial economy. *See* black market
urzędy kontroli skarbowe. See tax audit
   offices (Poland)
urzędy skarbowe. See tax offices (Poland)
US Agency for International
   Development, 7, 33
US Treasury, 145, 147, 149

value-added tax (VAT), 52, 96, 107, 110,
   See also Taxpayer Compliance
   Attitudinal Surveys
   arrears in Poland, Russia and Ukraine,
      114, 130
   collecting
      Poland, 160–162, 181, 191
      Russia, 116, 170, 183
      Ukraine, 155, 157, 158, 175, 176
   policy
      Poland, 96–98, 99–100, 107
      Russia, 96–98, 101–103
      Ukraine, 96–98, 103–106
   rates, perceptions of, 282, 285

Vedomosti (Russia), 79
veksels, 126
Verkhovna Rada (Ukraine), 21, 22, 33, 58,
   90, 92, 104–106, 125, 131, 263,
   286
Viktorov, Sergei, 77
VimpelCom, 171

Way, Lucan A., 21
Weber, Max, 14, 30, 36, 139,
   245
Weberian bureaucracy. *See* bureaucracy,
   Weberian
Weinthal, Erika, 102
West, 'The', 33, 57, 91, 233, 260, 269,
   270
White, Stephen, 85
Whitmore, Brian, 20
Wiatr, Jerzy, 62
Wilson, James Q., 41
Witte, Ann Dryden, 120
Wojciechowicz, Jacek, 67
Woodruff, David, 126, 127
work philosophy, 41, 58, 257, 258, *See also*
   tax administration, work philosophy
   policy recommendations, 268–269
Working Centre for Economic Reforms
   (Russia), 124
World Bank, 3, 4, 5, 7, 33, 73, 81, 88,
   106, 113, 116, 121, 146, 147–149,
   158, *See also* Tax Administration
   Modernisation Project (TAMP)
   government effectiveness indicators,
   3

Yanukovych, Viktor, 22, 33, 39, 93–94,
   105–106, 154–158, 176, 178, 189,
   195, 208, 218, 233–243, 260,
   263
Yatsenyuk, Arseniy, 94
Yekelchyk, Serhy, 32
Yeltsin, Boris, 18–20, 27, 31, 51, 57–58,
   72, 76–77, 83, 84, 95, 101, 257
Yereshenko, Fyodor, 155
Yew, Bee K., 134
Yukos, 164, 165, 170
Yushchenko, Viktor, 22, 32, 39, 88–89, 92,
   93, 155–156, 159, 173, 178, 192,
   208, 233–243

Zakład Ubezpieczeń Społecznych (Poland's
   social security system or ZUS), 100,
   124, 142, 283
Zhurzhiy, Andrei V., 106
Zyuganov, Gennadiy, 19, 58